W9-CDN-506

SEX AND DISABILITY

SEX AND DISABILITY

ROBERT MCRUER AND ANNA MOLLOW, EDITORS

DUKE UNIVERSITY PRESS
DURHAM AND LONDON
2012

© 2012 Duke University Press

All rights reserved

Printed in the United States of America

on acid-free paper ∞

Designed by Nicole Hayward

Typeset in Minion Pro by Tseng

Information Systems, Inc.

Library of Congress Cataloging-in-

Publication Data and republication

acknowledgments appear on the

last printed page of this book.

CONTENTS

....

ACKNOWLEDGMENTS

In December of 2004 we had the honor of participating in a Modern Language Association (MLA) panel, convened by Tobin Siebers, titled "Sex and Disability." As we prepared for our respective talks, querying our colleagues about their favorite writings on the topic, it occurred to Anna: "There should be an anthology on sex and disability." Robert, she immediately realized, would be the ideal collaborator for such a project. Many people aided us in making this idea a reality. From the outset, Lennard Davis enthusiastically supported the book. We are also indebted to Elizabeth Abel and Susan Schweik, who offered encouragement and much valuable advice. The volume benefited immensely from the feedback and critical suggestions of Ellen Samuels and Siobhan Somerville, who each read the entire manuscript, and from Alison Kafer's smart and incisive comments on an earlier version of the introduction.

In 2006 our work on this collection was interrupted by a health crisis in Anna's life, which left her without housing for several months. For their generous friendship and support during this time, she is deeply grateful to Chris Bell, Gretchen Case, Anne Finger, Alison Kafer, Marilee Nelson, Ellen Samuels, and Josh Weiner. She also thanks her parents, Marie Ashe and Ben Mollow, for their love and support. Nada Mills generously provided bodywork that enabled Anna to write; without her help, this book might not have been completed. Warmest thanks to Robert McRuer for sticking with this project, even when disability-related obstacles threatened to derail it, and for his good humor about the considerable effort it took to make our collaboration fully accessible. While a PhD candidate in English at the University of California, Berkeley, Anna was privileged to work with many wonderful teachers; she thanks Catherine Gallagher, D. A. Miller, and Kent Puckett for their support. She is particularly grateful to Susan Schweik, who introduced her to disability studies and whose brilliance, intellectual and political rigor, and generosity continue to inspire her. Most especially, Anna extends her heartfelt thanks to her dear friend Jane Herman: for friendship, love, and a home and for the innumerable kind ways in which she supports her writing and political work.

Robert is grateful for the ongoing love and support of Joseph Choueike and Tom Murray, which sustains him through every project he undertakes. For this project, he feels particularly fortunate to have worked with Anna Mollow, one of the most amazing editors, writers, and thinkers he knows. Her friendship and support have been invaluable, and he appreciates especially her profoundly feminist commitment to pushing him to have difficult conversations about sexuality, gender, disability, and sex that he might otherwise have avoided. His colleagues at the George Washington University have also been incredibly supportive of his individual work, as well as the interdisciplinary work of disability studies more broadly, and Robert particularly wants to acknowledge Jeffrey Jerome Cohen, Holly Dugan, Jonathan Gil Harris, Jennifer James, Tony Lopez, Dan Moshenberg, Rachel Riedner, Gayle Wald, Abby Wilkerson, and Gail Weiss. The members of the Washington, D.C., area queer studies group, DC Queer Studies, which began meeting when this project was just beginning and which continues to thrive, have provided friendship and intellectual support in innumerable ways. Robert also wants to thank Khash Jallaei for bringing so much passion, joy, and laughter to his life during the time this book was being completed.

Monica Bland, Judith Jenna, Elizabeth Thompson, Josh Weiner, and Emily White provided top-notch research and secretarial assistance at various stages of this project. Mandy Earley of Duke University Press was a dedicated and empathetic supporter of *Sex and Disability* for most of its history, and we are grateful that she was our associate editor before going on to continue her graduate studies. Jade Brooks and Rebecca Fowler have continued the fine work begun by Mandy, and we are very thankful for their efforts. We heartily thank Ken Wissoker for his strong commitment to this project from the beginning and for his patience as we have moved it to completion.

To our contributors, for hard work, intellectual risk, and patience through the many stages of revision, you have our utmost gratitude and admiration. Finally, two people to whom we are deeply indebted, both personally and intellectually, and whose influence can be felt throughout this book, did not live to see it completed. The passing of Chris Bell and Paul Longmore is an immeasurable loss to disability studies and to the many disability communities that have been sustained and inspired by their work.

....

ANNA MOLLOW AND ROBERT MCRUER

INTRODUCTION

Sex and Disability: the title of this book unites two terms that are, if not anti-thetical in the popular imagination, then certainly incongruous. The assertion that able-bodiedness is the foundation of sexiness might seem self-evident. After all, the sexiest people are healthy, fit, and active: lanky models, buff athletes, trim gym members brimming with energy. Rarely are disabled people regarded as either desiring subjects or objects of desire. And when sex and disability are linked in contemporary American cultures, the conjunction is most often the occasion for marginalization or marveling: the sexuality of disabled people is typically depicted in terms of either tragic deficiency or freakish excess. Pity or fear, in other words, are the sensations most often associated with disabili-ties; more pleasurable *sexual* sensations are generally dissociated from disabled bodies and lives.

But what if disability were sexy? And what if disabled people were understood to be both subjects and objects of a multiplicity of erotic desires and practices? Moreover, what if examining the ways in which these desires and practices are enabled, articulated, and represented in various contexts—contemporary and historical, local and global, public and private—made possible the reconceptualization of the categories of both "sex" and "disability"? These are among the questions that *Sex and Disability* asks. The chapters in this book—in parts focusing on access, histories, spaces, lives, and desires—develop analyses of the myriad ways in which sex and disability, despite their segregation in dominant cultural representations, do in fact come together.

ACCESS

"Sexuality," Anne Finger wrote in 1992, "is often the source of our deepest oppression; it is also often the source of our deepest pain. It's easier for us to talk about—and formulate strategies for changing—discrimination in employment, education, and housing than to talk about our exclusion from sexuality and reproduction" (9). Reflecting on this observation seventeen years later, Finger suggested to us that sexuality "points to our need for more than rights, for cultural changes—the kind of cultural change we've seen in more recent years in the work (writing, painting, performance, dance) of Eli Clare, Terry Galloway, Riva Lehrer, Sins Invalid, Axis Dance Company, etc."[1]

The cultural change that Finger notes taking place in memoir, performance, visual art, and dance has also been forwarded by some popular and academic texts, which explicitly ponder either the complex meanings of sexual identity for disabled people or, more directly, as in *The Ultimate Guide to Sex and Disability*, the many different ways disabled people might—or do—have sex (Kaufman et al.). The journal *Sexuality and Disability* has been publishing important work by activists, sociologists, anthropologists, and others for many years (including foundational work by Corbett Joan O'Toole, Barbara Faye Waxman-Fiduccia, and Russell Shuttleworth); and in 1996, Tom Shakespeare, Kath Gillespie-Sells, and Dominic Davies published *The Sexual Politics of Disability*, which—as the subtitle to the book suggested—brought to light many of the hitherto "untold desires" of disabled people. A few anthologies particularly focused on the experiences of queer disabled people have appeared over the past two decades, including Raymond Luczak's *Eyes of Desire: A Deaf Gay and Lesbian Reader*, Victoria A. Brownworth and Susan Raffo's *Restricted Access: Lesbians on Disability*, and Bob Guter and John R. Killacky's *Queer Crips: Disabled Gay Men and Their Stories*. And figures such as the "uppity crip scholar-activist and sexologist" Bethany Stevens have begun to use the Internet as a forum for disseminating ideas about sex and disability; according to Stevens, "many of us shy away from" the topics her blog, *Crip Confessions*, centralizes, but we nonetheless crave space for "rants concerning disability, body politics, social movement capacity building, media representation, body modification, sexuality, love, etc."

Still, the major texts in disability studies—those that have become canonical in the field—don't discuss sex in much detail. Lennard Davis's *Enforcing Normalcy: Disability, Deafness, and the Body* talks very briefly about the de-eroticization of disabled people; Rosemarie Garland-Thomson's *Extraordinary Bodies: Figuring Physical Disability in American Culture and Literature* makes a similar point, positing a distinction between the erotic "gaze" and the "stare" that is frequently directed at disabled people's bodies. Important texts such as Simi Linton's *Claiming Disability: Knowledge and Identity* and David T. Mitchell and Sharon L. Snyder's *Narrative Prosthesis: Disability and the Dependencies of Discourse* primarily address questions about disabled cultures, identities, epistemologies, and discourses, not sexual acts and practices. And many of the major anthologies in disability studies—*Disability Studies: Enabling the Humanities*; *The Body and Physical Difference: Discourses of Disability*; *The New Disability History: American Perspectives*—do not include a single scholarly essay on the conjunction of sex and disability; tellingly, if the conjunction is considered at all, it is in a special section including fiction and poetry, as in *The Disability Studies Reader*.

Additionally, the major texts in the much larger field of sexuality studies, including those in queer theory, rarely mention disability. Some of this writing seems to be on the cusp of an engagement with disability studies, and many disability scholars have productively drawn on the work of Judith Butler, Eve Kosofsky Sedgwick, Michael Warner, and others. But disability as a category of analysis, or disability studies as an epistemological field, is only beginning to have an impact upon queer scholarship. The one area in which sexuality studies more broadly has considered the convergence of sex and disability is cultural theory about HIV and AIDS. From the beginning of the epidemic, gay men and their allies knew that theorizing sex, physical impairment, and illness was imperative, as activist interventions such as Michael Callen and Richard Berkowitz's *How to Have Sex in an Epidemic* and scholarly essays such as Douglas Crimp's "How to Have Promiscuity in an Epidemic" illustrated. Yet despite AIDS activists' indebtedness to the disability rights movement, this work currently tends to remain at an uneasy distance from disability scholarship.

Our point here is not that theorists of sex and sexuality should be thinking about disability all the time, or that disability theorists should be thinking about sex all the time (although we don't want to *not* make these points). Rather, we wish to ask: what happens to our models, central arguments, and key claims when we politicize sex and disability together? To address this question, we begin by considering "access," a core political and theoretical concept in disability studies and the disability rights movement. The term "access" is most often invoked in reference to public spaces: movie theaters, restaurants, banks, office buildings. What would it mean to apply the concept to the private sphere? Can disabled people demand "access" to sexual experiences with others? To masturbation? To reproduction? The three chapters in "Access," the first part of this book, address these questions. In the first chapter, "A Sexual Culture for Disabled People," Tobin Siebers—building on work by Waxman-Fiduccia, O'Toole, and others—proposes that people with disabilities be considered members of a sexual minority. Like other sexual minorities, Siebers points out, disabled people are often regarded as "perverted" and are denied access to sexual experiences and control of their own bodies.[2] As Siebers observes, "many people with disabilities are involuntarily confined in institutions," where "medical authorities make decisions about access to erotic literature, masturbation, and sexual partners."

Disabled people's access to sexual partners is further restricted by a pervasive cultural de-eroticization of people with disabilities. In the second chapter of *Sex and Disability*, "Bridging Theory and Experience: A Critical-Interpretive Ethnography of Sexuality and Disability," Russell Shuttleworth, who developed the concept of "sexual access" in his earlier work, shows here that this term, by blurring distinctions between public activities and ostensibly private ones, facilitates politicization of the latter. Explicating the methodology he used in the mid-1990s to interview fourteen men in the San Francisco Bay Area with cerebral palsy, Shuttleworth illuminates the massive, sometimes nearly intractable, barriers they encountered as they attempted to access sexual experiences. As one participant put it, women seemed to be telling him: "You can come in my house, but leave your dick outside!"

Although less tangible than a set of stairs in front of a building or the absence of captioning on a movie screen, barriers such as these, the chapters in this collection suggest, are just as pervasive and equally daunting. Michel Desjardins's chapter, "The Sexualized Body of the Child: Parents and the Politics of 'Voluntary' Sterilization of People Labeled Intellectually Disabled," examines the insidious barriers that confront young adults with developmental disabilities. Even as these men and women have access to sexual intimacy and romantic love, they often undergo "voluntary" sterilization that ensures that "intimacy and love" does not end in pregnancy.

In different ways, each of these three chapters invites us to ask: what does it mean to use the concept of access when speaking of seemingly private issues like sexual activity or parenthood? It is possible, of course, to argue that the term "access" is best applied to only some forms of disability oppression. After all, one can demand certain direct kinds of access to public institutions—a ramp to the front door of a restaurant, an elevator within a hotel—that, obviously, one would not make in regard to the bodies and choices of potential sexual partners. Following this line of thinking, it might seem reasonable to say that a film without captioning is inaccessible to Deaf viewers, whereas one that provides captioning but portrays deaf—or Deaf—characters as asexual or sexually unappealing is not inaccessible but something else instead: controversial, offensive, ableist, or provocative, depending on your point of view. The problem, however, with this reasonable distinction is that it is almost inevitably a hierarchical one: on the basis of their concreteness, their indisputable "reality," we tend to accord more importance to those forms of oppression we label "access barriers" than to the more subtle ones that govern social and sexual encounters. The chapters in this collection ask what it would mean to upend this set of priorities. What if disability scholarship made sex a primary concern, according it all the importance of an access issue to be argued before the Supreme Court?

HISTORIES

In 1988, the disability scholar, historian, and activist Paul Longmore burned his book on George Washington in front of the Social Security Administration offices in Los Angeles. He did this in order to protest the agency's "work disincentives": if Longmore earned royalties from his book, or a salary as a college professor, he would lose Medicaid-funded equipment and services (including a ventilator and personal attendants) upon which he literally depended to survive. His protest signified in ways that reached far beyond what many might have read—and still might misread—as merely his own personal predicament: Longmore demonstrated symbolically that the putatively private matter of disability is in reality deeply political, caught up in long and complex histories of oppression, exploitation, and resistance.

In *Why I Burned My Book and Other Essays on Disability*, Longmore situates this particular instance of disability activism within the history of the disability rights movement. As Longmore interprets it, disability activism since the 1970s has had four key features. First, such activism "redefined the problems faced by people with disabilities. It framed them as mainly social, not medical. It marked as the most serious obstacle pervasive prejudice and discrimination. It presented as the appropriate solution civil rights protection" (109). Second, disability activism shaped coalitions with other new and progressive social movements. Third, it "fashioned ties across disability lines" (109). Finally, and arguably most important, disability activism "produced an unplanned politics of identity," a "positive disability identity" that "showed society—and [activists] themselves—that people with disabilities were not feeble but strong, not incompetent but skillful, not helpless but powerful" (110). According to a historiography that disability studies and the disability rights movement have made familiar, disability identity, forged in the context of other new social movements and emerging from a disability movement explicitly focused on civil rights, led to the passage of the Americans with Disabilities Act (ADA), which was signed into law by President George H. W. Bush in 1990.

And yet a peculiar, and also decidedly "unplanned," politics of identity has shadowed the ADA and similar civil rights legislation. Disabled people and their allies have been dismayed to witness courts' extremely narrow and rigid interpretations of the ADA, which have drastically limited the law's scope and efficacy. In 1999 Ruth Colker analyzed the corpus of ADA cases that had come before the court. Her findings were consistent with those of the American Bar Association less than a year earlier: in 94 percent of federal ADA Title I decisions, employers won (Krieger 6–7). Disabled plaintiffs most often lost their cases not because the accommodations they sought were determined to be "unreasonable," or to impose "undue hardship" on employers, but because the courts decided that the plaintiffs did not qualify as "disabled." For example, in its decision in 2002 in the case of *Toyota Motor Manufacturing v. Williams*, the U.S. Supreme Court ruled that an assembly-line worker with carpal tunnel syndrome and other painful musculoskeletal impairments—which limited her ability to work, shop, do housework, and play with her children—was not a "person with a disability" (Krieger 13; Diller 68). As numerous observers have pointed out, the court's extraordinarily narrow definition of disability has created a double bind for anyone seeking protection under the ADA: a plaintiff who does manage to convince the court that he or she is a "person with a disability" will likely have great difficulty meeting the law's requirement that he or she also be an "otherwise qualified" individual (Hahn, "Accommodations" 47–48; Krieger 10).

Linda Hamilton Krieger observes that "Congress wrote the minority group model of disability into the ADA's preamble" (12). That preamble states that people with disabilities constitute "a discrete and insular minority" historically subjected to "purposeful unequal treatment" (qtd. in Krieger 12). Yet in *Trustees of the University of Alabama v. Garrett*, the Supreme Court ruled that disabled people do *not* constitute a protected class under the Fourteenth Amendment's Equal Protection Clause (Krieger 10–11). Therefore, Krieger concludes, *Garrett* represents a "judicial backlash against the minority group model of the ADA" (12).

Both Krieger's argument and Longmore's historicized analysis of the emergence of disability identity are compelling and important. However, we wish here to complicate the framework for interpreting what Krieger aptly names the "backlash against the ADA." Following Longmore, we do so by attending to the ways in which disability identity is always historical. Disability identity, in other words, is never simply a natural fact; it is, rather, made and remade in historical circumstances and by historical agents. Thus, like Krieger, we locate the Court's pattern of ruling against disabled plaintiffs within an ongoing history of struggles around disability identity. Yet our analysis differs from Krieger's in that we see the backlash against the ADA as arising less from a theoretical rejection of a "minority group model" than from an excessive upholding—an extreme and even punitive application—of constructions of people with disabilities as members of a "discrete, insular" minority group. After all, in *Toyota v. Williams* and many similar cases the courts do, in fact, define people with disabilities as comprising a discrete minority group—to which specific plaintiffs are then determined not to belong. Granted, the courts are not allowing that disabled people are *political* minorities, as the drafters of the ADA had intended. Yet a minority model of disability is nonetheless clearly in operation in ADA case law; it provides the explicit foundation for much of the judicial backlash against the ADA. This point is crucial: it should press us, we believe, to ask difficult questions about the minority group model and about the ways that model moves through history and through authoritative institutions.[3]

In asking such questions—as we will do throughout this introduction—we will be grappling with the often vexed relationship between personal experience and political analysis. Longmore's burning of his book is one of many instances in which disability scholarship and activism, seeming to draw on the second-wave feminist insistence that the personal is political, have demonstrated that the cordoning off of certain categories of experience (such as "sex" and "disability") as "private matters" is itself a profoundly political act, with often insidious effects.

We engage these crucial insights here, at the same time that we also engage political and theoretical approaches that trouble the concept of identity—and thus, perhaps also, of personal experience. In many contexts, the claim that "the personal is political" has had the effect of placing "women's experience" at the center of feminist political analysis; but in others, such as women of color feminism, the construction of "woman" as a primary or foundational identity has persuasively been challenged, long before the moment in 1990 when Butler asserted that "it is no longer clear that feminist theory ought to try to settle the questions of primary identity in order to get on with the task of politics" (*Gender Trouble* xi).

This complex feminist legacy pushed us to wonder, as we began drafting the introduction to this volume in the summer of 2007, whether material from our own "histories" might have a place in it. In an e-mail to Anna regarding this possibility, Robert wrote:

> I understand what you're saying about personal experience, although I also feel somewhat wary of that, given the confessional culture we inhabit and how that culture of confession is linked to truth (especially on the sex side) and authenticity (especially on the disability side). However, I find it intriguing that, as editors, we occupy, in a way, mirrored positions (I will complicate this momentarily, but for now bear with me): in theorizing about sex, it's hard to deny queer theory has a certain pride of place, and hard to deny, despite queer theory's anti-identitarian bent, that "real" lesbians and gay men, with lesbian and gay identities, have done a lot of that labor over the past few decades. In theorizing about disability (or even the body more generally), it's hard to deny, well, disability studies a certain pride of place, and hard to deny, especially with the emphasis on identity and experience in the field, that "real" disabled people, with varied experiences of impairment and disability identities, have done most of that labor over the past few decades.
>
> So, in a crude, reductionist sense that is bigger than both of us, we end up on two competing sides of our title, "Sex and Disability"—each of us could, two-dimensionally, be taken by those who don't know us well as the main representative of one side of the binary. But I'd say, of course, that assessment immediately elicits a "yes, but" from both of us, about both sides of that supposed binary. Given your inner lesbian and given the identity-disintegrating aspects of sex and queerness generally, it's easy to bump me from representativeness on the "Sex" side. But I'm cautious of ceding the

Anna Mollow and Robert McRuer

representative side of "Disability" wholly to you, at the same time that I'm cautious of not ceding it to you, for all sorts of sedimented disability history reasons.

What claim could Robert make that would allow him to dislodge Anna from her apparent position as the main representative of "Disability"? "I'm not disabled," he wrote to Anna, "and would never cavalierly claim that as an identity, in part out of respect for histories of oppression that are not mine." And yet, he continued, "I do want to be clear: I could claim it." Robert went on to "cite some of the evidence (the 'evidence' of 'experience') that would back up the 'I' claim in relation to disability that I'm actually not making." A few entries from Robert's nine-item numbered list:

1. I have at least once had a mental health professional suggest drugs for OCD, in the context of two-year long therapeutic relationship. . . .

3. I have sometimes literally boarded a plane early on "disability" in order to be able to fly comfortably (and I saw this as an accommodation probably because of my disability studies work).

4. Often when I'm on a flight, I can tell you exactly the number of five-minute segments we have left before the plane lands, AS WELL AS what was happening in the same number of five-minute segments, backwards. That probably doesn't even make sense, so to concretize it: at a certain point, I could tell you, "37 five-minute segments to go" and could give you a general sense what had been happening 37 five-minute segments in the past. Of course this is partly contingent on whether we were in a period, during the flight, when I allowed myself to look at my watch (the rules for all of this get very complicated).

Despite the body of evidence Robert cited in support of an identity claim he *could* make, he nonetheless resisted making it, not only because, as he put it, "I really do respect that I'm not disabled and that I have all sorts of able-bodied privilege," but also "because of feeling that [such a claim] is insufficient (perhaps necessary but insufficient) for getting at certain ways of thinking about the body, mind, and behavior. Meaning generally, but also specifically, my body, my mind, my behavior."

In regard to "Sex," Anna occupies a position that mirrors Robert's relationship to "Disability." She wrote:

I'd say I'm somewhere between straight and bisexual, and I don't feel comfortable with either term. To say "I'm bisexual" seems to take something away from LGBT people who are oppressed in ways I'm not. Yet it's not quite accurate to say "I'm straight" — and to do so is to "pass" in ways I also don't feel comfortable with, both because of the heterosexual privilege it confers and because of the ways it risks limiting my own sense of what's possible, what I might desire. (Since this e-mail of 2007, Anna came out as a lesbian.)

Despite her discomfort with making a claim to a minoritized sexual identity that some might regard as tenuous, Anna nonetheless found herself asking, after she read Robert's list of "evidence" in support of a minoritized disability identity claim he did not wish to make: "Robert, why don't you come out?" While the reductiveness of her query was tongue-in-cheek (having been on the receiving end of this question herself, she knew how annoying it was), Anna was serious in asking, why not identify as disabled?

We've begun answering this question here: trepidation about laying false claim to histories of oppression, as well as a reluctance to simplify complex ways of thinking, feeling, and behaving. To this we would add another danger, which begins to point us back toward the authoritative discourses and institutions and the legislative and judicial double binds with which we opened this section: the risk of reifying identity categories that might better be contested. As Robert remarked about the experiences he'd listed in support of a hypothetical identity claim: "Looking back at that list I just gave you: were I desiring to claim any kind of authenticity (and remember, I'm not), the therapist (and even the former lover I told you about who is a doctor) are the ones giving most credence to that claim! Troubling, in some ways, no?" Troubling because, in this instance, an identity claim such as "I'm disabled; I have obsessive-compulsive disorder" would be tied, inescapably, to medical discourses (and diagnoses) both of us perceived as specious. A likely effect of such a statement, in this instance, would be to uphold the power and authority of institutions—modern Western medicine and psychiatry—that have generated and policed the normal/abnormal binary that has been fundamental to disabled people's oppression.

Anna does claim the identity "disabled," and this claiming has been a vexed and complicated process. She has been disabled since 1994 with a set of interrelated impairments—environmental illness (EI), upper and lower back pain, and repetitive strain injury—whose intensities have varied over the years. In March of 2006, after what had seemed to be a six-year disappearance, Anna's

EI recurred, forcing her to leave her graduate studies at the University of California, Berkeley. EI (which is also called multiple chemical sensitivity, or MCS) means that hundreds of substances in everyday life make Anna ill: chemicals in soaps, laundry detergents, perfumes; cigarette smoke; car exhaust; newsprint; magazines; paper; ink; paint; carpet; new clothing; natural gas used in furnaces and stoves; plastics; upholsteries; lawn chemicals; cleaning products. In search of cleaner air and a safe place to live, she moved to Santa Rosa, where she continues to live with her close friend Jane, whom she met through an online list for people with EI. Like many people with EI, Anna is also sensitive to the electromagnetic fields, or EMFS, that electronic appliances emit; she is therefore unable to use a computer. These impairments, combined with a repetitive strain injury, have made continuing her graduate studies impossible.

In her chapter "My Body, My Closet: Invisible Disability and the Limits of Coming-Out Discourse," Ellen Samuels observes that people with invisible disabilities, although often criticized for "passing" or failing to "come out," are in fact required to come out repeatedly; because others assume they are nondisabled, they must regularly identify their unseen impairments and explain their effects. By coming out in the context of this introduction, Anna makes a claim that, she expects, will function differently from the one Robert refrains from making. If to say "I have obsessive-compulsive disorder" might in this instance call up the authority of medical institutions, saying "I have environmental illness" has the potential to contest this authority. This is because, for the most part, mainstream Western medicine does not recognize as legitimate impairments that cannot be diagnosed with conventional medical tests. People who have EI (or similarly "controversial" impairments, such as fibromyalgia, chronic fatigue syndrome, or chronic pain) are therefore often regarded as malingerers or hypochondriacs. The withholding of a legitimate medical diagnosis has consequences that extend far beyond the office of the doctor who says, "All your tests are normal; you're perfectly healthy." For most people with impairments that manifest neither visible bodily differences nor abnormal test results, it is an ongoing struggle to obtain disability benefits, access employment accommodations, or persuade family members and friends that they really are disabled.

In "coming out" here, Anna risks that you, the reader, will, like the health care practitioners, court justices, and others who have the authority to confer or deny disability status, count her as not an authentic "person with a disability." This possibility points to another problem with identity claims: the inevitability, despite the intentions of those forging these identities, of exclusions. Taken together, many influential texts in the field of disability studies can be said to have codified a model identity of a disabled person, who has certain crucial characteristics: his or her body manifests visible difference; physical suffering is not a primary aspect of his or her experience; and he or she is not seeking cure or recovery. In these ways, what might be seen as disability studies' construction of a "paradigmatic" disabled person differs from the self-understandings of many people with chronic pain and illness.[4] Thus, Samuels writes that disability studies' "focus on visuality and the 'gaze' sometimes leads me to question if my extremely limiting and life-changing health condition really qualifies as a disability according to the social model" ("Body" 248).

The discursive marginalization of people with unseen illness may have material effects. For example, while the disability rights movement has succeeded in making requests for wheelchair ramps and American Sign Language (ASL) interpretation seem, at least in some contexts, "reasonable," the accommodations that a person with EI might need to request are most often regarded as wildly unreasonable—in the senses both of "This is too much to ask" and "I don't understand why you would need this." In order for workplaces or other public spaces (including disability organizations) to be made accessible to a person with EI, he or she must make the seemingly impossible request that these environments be free of: toxic cleaning products; new building materials, furnishings, carpet, and paint; air freshener; perfume; dry-cleaned clothing; scented skin lotion, hair products, and deodorant; and many other common chemical substances.

"I have to say, I'm feeling some bitterness about my career," Anna confessed to Robert as they sat in her backyard in 2007, catching up on their personal lives before preparing to outline this introduction.

"You know, that's sex, as well as disability," Robert remarked.

"Why is it sex?"

"Because what you miss is a range of erotic connections. They may not be sexual ones, but there's the sexiness of mingling with minds and bodies at conferences (and I'm not just talking about conference sex!), the thrill of generating energy and knowledge; there's a libidinal investment in all of this."

For Robert, as with Anna, the lines separating the categories of "disability" and "sex" are sometimes blurry. In the course of editing this book, he wrote to Anna about a man he'd recently met: "There are 15 days left before I see him again. I will wake up tomorrow and there will be 14 days left, and on Thursday there will be 13 days left, meaning, that as of Thursday, I'll have only ONE Wednesday to sleep through without him. And then on Friday . . . well, you get the idea." Was this simply a normative case of lovesickness? Or, when read in and through Robert's other mental eccentricities, might it not be interpretable as "disability," a form of sexual obsession or OCD? Rather than choosing one side of a binary division between normality and disability, we instead emphasize here the value of keeping these terms fluid and contestable. Alongside a politics of identity that has successfully shaped minoritized communities and civil rights strategies, a post-identity disability politics—in which what is interpretable as disability need not be tethered to a disabled identity—enables sitings of disability in multiple, often unexpected, locations, rather than solely in the bodies and minds of a few individuals.

Embracing a post-identity politics of disability means conceiving of EI (to take one example) as more than the basis of some North American individuals' disability identities. In her essay "Toxic Animacies, Inanimate Affections," Mel Chen undertakes this work. Chen intersperses personal narrative about her difficult negotiations of public spaces—her attempts to avoid inhaling cigarette smoke and car exhaust as she walks down the street or to "effect a smile" from behind the mask she must sometimes wear when shopping—with an analysis of the ways in which the notion of "toxicity" circulates in global contexts (275). For Chen, telling her own story—in ways, she writes, that consider "toxicity as it has profoundly affected my own health, my own queerness, and my own ability to forge bonds"—is necessary in order to counter readers' likely presumptions that the bodies she writes of enjoy a state of "mythic health," "unadulterated by toxins, and cognitively clear" (273). Yet even as her story of personal disability in part authorizes the questions about global toxicity and "us" that she asks ("how is it that so much of this toxic world . . . laden with injurious chemicals . . . is encountered by so many of us as benign and pleasurable? And how is it that we are doing this, doing all this, to ourselves?"), Chen also immediately notes "such a 'we' is a false unity" (276). Chen is not, she implies, among "those who find themselves on the underside of industrial 'development'—women hand-painting vaporous toys by the hundreds daily without protection; agricultural workers with little access to health care picking fruit in a vapor of pesticides, methane, and fertilizer that is breathable only in a strictly mechanical sense; people living adjacent to spewing factories installed by a distant neocolonial metropolis or downwind of a refinery . . . in the abjected periphery of a gentrified urban 'center'" (276).

Chen's nuanced consideration of the relationship between her own disability and the broader social context in which this disability takes shape has much in common with what Roderick A. Ferguson defines as a "gestural" mode of conceiving of identity (143). A gestural conception of identity, Ferguson argues, animated women of color feminism in the 1970s, in which identity politics was about pointing *away* from the self to the complex array of relations that constituted the social. Identity politics as it evolved over the next few decades became more "emulative"—animated, that is, by a pointing not outward toward the social world in which identities are constantly shaped and reshaped, but instead inward, toward the self or, as we suggested above, toward "representative" identities.

Ferguson's argument about the complexities of the now much-maligned identity politics of the 1970s pushes us to link, rather than oppose, the work of scholars such as Longmore and Chen. Longmore approaches disability identity historically; whether writing or burning his book, he is engaged in an "examination of cultural values regarding 'disability' and their relationship to social arrangements, public policy, and professional practice" (5). Such textured examinations—examinations of the movement of "disability" through history—have been among the primary conditions of possibility for post-identity analyses such as Chen's or our own.

Each of the chapters in "Histories" therefore engages both the making and unmaking of disability, sex, and identity. Michelle Jarman's chapter, "Dismembering the Lynch Mob: Intersecting Narratives of Disability, Race, and Sexual Menace," investigates (as Chen's work does) the ways in which racialized and disabled identifications have intersected and altered each other. Focusing on the southern United States in the late nineteenth and early twentieth centuries, Jarman encourages us to understand the ways in which what she terms "menacing masculinities" were constituted through both racialized lynching narratives and narratives highlighting the eugenic threat of "feebleminded" men. Although these discourses are generally cast as unrelated, Jarman exposes the ways in which the narratives used "to justify and normalize the brutal torture, murder, and bodily destruction that came to define white-on-black lynching" are historically interwoven with eugenicists' construction of cognitively disabled men as "social menaces in a broad sense, but most threatening as sexual predators."

Underscoring that neither "sex" nor "disability" carries static, transhistorical significations, Rachel O'Connell, in "'That Cruel Spectacle': The Extraordinary Body Eroticized in Lucas Malet's *The History of Sir Richard Calmady*," analyzes a Victorian novel vividly detailing the sexual experiences of its visibly disabled protagonist. Investigating divergences between historical and contemporary understandings of sex and disability, O'Connell asks how changing conceptions

Anna Mollow and Robert McRuer

of what Garland-Thomson terms "extraordinary bodies" have contributed to the novel's declining fortunes. Malet's novel, which was published in 1901, was a best-seller in its era; it is all but forgotten today.

Moving thirty-five years forward, Michael Davidson, in "Pregnant Men: Modernism, Disability, and Biofuturity," focuses on another novel, one that is not at all forgotten but that has not hitherto been read through a disability studies lens. Examining Djuna Barnes's *Nightwood*, which was published in 1936, Davidson focuses on the figure of the "pregnant man"—specifically the eccentric figure of Dr. Matthew O'Connor. Davidson reads *Nightwood* "not as a baroque anomaly among stream of consciousness narratives of Woolf, Stein, or Faulkner, but as arguably *the* representative modernist novel insofar as it offers an inside narrative of individuals interpellated within biological and racial science." Figures of male pregnancy have at times been read as simply relocating (or, in the case of male authors, appropriating) gestation. Historicizing the eugenic logics in circulation at the time of *Nightwood*'s publication, Davidson instead crips modernist male pregnancy, reading it as marking for Barnes what he terms "a diaspora of sexual and gendered possibilities among bodies and minds of various abilities and cognitive registers."

As the century continued, sexual identities and orientations, as well as identities connected to disability or "handicap," continued to congeal, but often in contradictory ways. In "Touching Histories: Personality, Disability, and Sex in the 1930s," David Serlin examines an early twentieth-century "personality study," *The Personality and Sexuality of the Physically Handicapped Woman*. Locating this little-known study within two histories that might be understood as opposed, the history of the mid-century obsession to identify and categorize personality "types" and the more anti-identitarian and affective history of touch, Serlin provides rich evidence of disabled women intimately familiar with somatic dimensions of desire and pleasure. The subjectivities discernible in *The Personality and Sexuality of the Physically Handicapped Woman*—"subjectivities consummated through unquantifiable acts of touch"—are, in Serlin's analysis, compellingly "confounding."

SPACES

The chapters in the third part of this book consider the spaces (geographic and discursive) in which disability and sex materialize, the boundaries that demarcate those spaces, and the punishments that ensue when these boundaries are transgressed. The part begins with "Leading with Your Head: On the Borders of Disability, Sexuality, and the Nation," by Nicole Markotić and Robert McRuer, who investigate the uses of nationalist discourses in *Murderball*, a film released in 2005 that documents an ongoing rivalry between American and Canadian quadriplegic rugby teams. Markotić and McRuer examine the ways in which explicit discussion of sex in *Murderball*—sex that is in some ways legible as nonnormative—potentially (but only potentially) disrupts the more direct thrust of the narrative, which moves toward a masculinist incorporation (into the nation) of the proper disabled citizen-subject. Markotić and McRuer contrast the citizen-subject's spectactularized representation in the ludic space of the film (particularly his flexible capacity for crossing national borders) to the lived experiences of nomadic, queer, disabled subjects facing policing and surveillance at and around national borders—in particular, in relation to resources (including health care) perceived as national property.

In "Normate Sex and Its Discontents," Abby L. Wilkerson considers connections among global transgender, intersex, and disability identities and political movements. Developing a notion of what she terms "normate sex," Wilkerson considers transgender, transsexualism, and intersexuality both as departures from normate sex and as sites where a more critical sense of sexual interdependence might be forged. In her analysis of the ways in which Western medical authority travels (often coercively), Wilkerson argues that studies of medicalization in international contexts should recognize and foster the potential for agency in cultural exchange. Considering, for example, gender liminal Polynesians who identify as *fa'afafine* ("like a woman"), Wilkerson attends to the ways in which numerous groups articulate their own experiences and forge alternatives to normate sex. Fa'afafine, she suggests, may "develop their own alternatives to both Western medical and political norms and to their own traditional gender categories." Indeed, as Wilkerson demonstrates, a wide range of interdependent intersex and trans "erotics" actively resist the varied forms of oppression generated by normate sex.

In "I'm Not the Man I Used to Be: Sex, HIV, and Cultural 'Responsibility,'" the late Chris Bell considers the effects that two legal cases in Atlanta had on his self-understanding as an HIV-positive sexual subject. In the first case, in September of 2003, Gary Cox, the deputy assistant to Mayor Shirley Franklin, was convicted of soliciting paid sex acts from a minor (Cox maintained his innocence even as he was sent to prison). Cox was HIV-positive, but his HIV status did not play a major role in the arbitration or representation of this case. In a second legal case discussed by Bell, Gary Wayne Carriker, a medical student at Emory, was convicted in March of 2005 of felony reckless conduct for having sex with another man without disclosing his HIV-positive status. Bell analyzes the reasons that HIV-positive status was central to Carriker's case but insignificant in Cox's. He then carries this consideration of spaces of sexual risk and surveillance in Atlanta to a reflection on his own status as an HIV-positive African American man negotiating similar spaces.

By writing in a scholarly book about intersections of sex and disability in his own life, Bell took considerable risks. For although terms like "libidinal," "erotic," "sex," "sexual," and "desire" circulate widely within academic discourses, these terms usually don't refer directly to any particular academic writer's own experiences. Indeed, personal or explicit discussion of sex—or, to some extent, disability—arguably marks writing about these topics as extra-academic. Bob Flanagan's graphic writings and performances about sadomasochism and cystic fibrosis, for example, make him a popular figure for disability scholars to analyze but preclude interpretation of his work as itself an example of disability scholarship or theory. And while several prominent disability scholars have written (usually in memoirs or other venues not marked as scholarly or academic) about the effects of disability on their marriages or family lives, this personal writing most often makes little mention of sex.

What space could—or should—personal writing about sex have in disability studies? As we ruminated together about this introduction, the question came to preoccupy us: what would it mean to disclose, in this space, personal information about sex and disability? Early in our discussion with each other, we'd begun exchanging e-mails about our own experiences with disability and sex, hoping they would yield insights we could incorporate here. We'd quickly generated a large volume of material that was—to us, at least—provocative and highly stimulating. But most of this writing, we immediately saw, would be inappropriate to include here, or in any scholarly book or essay. "Inappropriate" is precisely the term we want to use: notions of professional propriety were very much at work in our decision to exclude from this introduction most of our personal writing about sex—writing that, frustratingly, we valued in part *because* of its impropriety. This impropriety, we felt, had the potential to disrupt a liberal conception of disability as squeaky-clean and respectable, of a disabled subject eligible for marriage and parenthood—and presumably, therefore, sex, but sex that is discrete, private, proper.

As we considered the status of the personal in scholarly analyses of sex and disability, we divided potential revelations into three heuristic categories or spaces: the proper, the permissible, and the punishable. The personal material we did, in the end, include in this introduction falls (we hope) under the rubric of the permissible. What separates the permissible from the punishable? Certainly, we inhabit a confessional culture; in many spaces and genres (a memoir, performance piece, journal, or therapy session), personal revelations about sex, far from being punishable, instead seem nearly compulsory. Why, then, would the same revelations clearly be "punishable" in an academic context? Part of the answer, as we've said, lies in the bourgeois notions of propriety that infuse all professional spaces, including academia. A related bourgeois value or imperative, that of work, "or marketing the body as an instrument of labor" rather than "an instrument of pleasure," is also relevant (Marcuse 116; qtd. in Floyd 123). That is, while a story about one's own sex life might make perfect sense in, say, a personal essay, it would be hard to identify any function or purpose a similar act of publicizing might serve in a scholarly piece of writing. "What you do in your private life is your business," a reader of an academic essay might say. "Why are you telling us this here?" Indeed, as we argue in the rest of this introduction, the line between which revelations about sex and disability are permissible and which are punishable has much to do with work: what functions they might serve, to what uses they might be put.

LIVES

Each of the three chapters in "Lives" performs or analyzes autobiographical writing about sex and disability. We begin our discussion of disability, sex, and life writing with a pair of stories from our own lives. The first is Robert's; the second is Anna's.

> I go jogging every other day, a quintessentially able-bodied activity, one could say. That is, if one wanted to "picture" able-bodiedness, a snapshot of a runner would serve as well as pretty much anything. But in general my running also comes with elaborate rules about when I turn or reverse course, when I look at my watch, how the scenery gets framed as I do laps, etc. I did have a sexual encounter with a guy who watched me jogging, however. It was a few summers ago, in Malcolm X Park (also known as Meridian Hill Park—the name one uses tends to be connected to one's politics!). His name was Mario or Marco or something like that. And

Anna Mollow and Robert McRuer

he watched me running. And it was very pleasant. And as I did laps, he started to sort of gesture, "Come on, let's go." And I was not in the least averse to the thought. But then I couldn't stop and talk to him until I had ritualistically finished my running in the ways that it ritualistically needed to happen. He was gone by the time I finished, but as I walked back home, he pulled up alongside me, I got in, we went to my house, and had great casual, one-time sex. This is the same park, incidentally, where late one night I got punched out by a group of teenage boys.

The second time I was confronted about parking in a handicapped spot was right after I moved to Berkeley, in the parking lot of Andronico's (a nearby grocery store). This woman had all these pride stickers on her car: disabled, Jewish, queer. And she was yelling at me. "Nobody," she said, looking me up and down, "nobody who looks as good as you can be disabled!" I was twenty-nine years old, wearing a sundress and high-heeled sandals. "You need to educate yourself about invisible disability!" I said. "You need to educate *yourself*!" she shot back. I walked away, shaking and feeling sick to my stomach. I really did need that parking spot; I was in too much pain to walk through even the whole grocery store. But what I hate most about my memory of that moment was that a little part of me sort of liked it: in a way, I liked the idea of looking too good to be disabled, had even been working at looking that way.

To an observer of these scenes, one would seem to be solely about sex; the other, about disability. But Robert's sexual encounter initiated in the park is, as his narrative makes clear, about disability also. In Anna's story, too, both sex and disability are at stake. The confrontation over her right to park in a disabled spot—and by extension, to call herself "disabled"—was played out in reference to sex. If Anna "looked too good" to be disabled, and if she had in fact been cultivating such a look, it was as if her self-presentation had been designed to say, "I'm too sexy to be disabled."

Samuels points out that although "the option of passing as nondisabled" often produces a "profound sense of misrecognition," it also offers "a certain level of privilege" (239). The privilege that comes with not "looking disabled" is exposed and analyzed in Riva Lehrer's "Golem Girl Gets Lucky," which is the first chapter in "Lives." Lehrer writes: "All women know that the sidewalk is a catwalk. From before the first faint ringing of puberty we are judged on the quality of our flesh.

And my entry in the pageant is a body that's more Z-shaped than S-curved." Visibly disabled women's exclusion from the "catwalk," Lehrer perceptively observes, arises from the fear "that our unbalanced shapes hint of unsanctioned desires. On both sides of the bed."

The threat that disabled bodies might experience and elicit unsanctioned desires is mobilized to the advantage of the narrator of "Fingered." Lezlie Frye's story begins with an interpellation, delivered "sly and emboldened and triple-dog-daring style, dripping with eight-year-old arrogance in the bulk bin aisles of the PC market on Franklin Avenue." "Your hand is so freaky, you are a freak!" Frye's speaker takes on this eight-year-old boy, while his mother stands nervously in the background. Responding in kind to his aggressiveness, Frye boldly calls forth the unacknowledged eroticism that animates the common experience, for many people with disabilities, of being put on display, made to answer to the invasive desires of others: "I will them to imagine all the places my hand has been, between which cracks suiting just its shape, into which crevices only it can fit . . . I let my hand hang, taut and heavy before their gaze, erect, bent, unpredictable." Frye's hand is queer: "born to be inside of cunts," she reminds herself as she faces the child and his mother. Thrusting its potentialities into this boy's awareness, Frye refuses to submit to the imperatives of what Lee Edelman calls "the disciplinary imagine of the 'innocent' Child" (*No Future* 19). Indeed, her verbal combat with the boy is evocative of Edelman's contention that "*queerness* names the side of those *not* 'fighting for the children'" (*No Future* 3).

Queerness and disability again come together in "Sex as 'Spock': Autism, Sexuality, and Autobiographical Narrative." In her reading of autobiographical writing by people with autism spectrum disorder, or ASD, Rachael Groner finds many parallels and convergences with queer theory. For example, the authors of ASD autobiographies often emphasize the unstable and fragmentary aspects of subjectivity. "It took me [until age ten] to realize that normal children refer to themselves as 'I,'" writes Donna Williams, one of the autobiographers whose work Groner analyzes. Authors of ASD autobiographies also highlight the performativity of many gendered and heterosexual conventions (for instance, they carefully study and attempt to master the bizarre-seeming "rules" governing dating and sex among "neurotypical" people). Commonalities between ASD autobiographies and queer theory may be linked to interconnected histories of surveillance and disciplining of homosexuality and autism. For example, applied behavior analysis, or ABA, an accepted contemporary practice that uses

    Anna Mollow and Robert McRuer

"aversives" such as slaps, pinches, and electric shocks to compel children with ASD to behave in "normal" ways, was also employed in the UCLA Feminine Boy Project in the 1970s, and the work of its proponents continues to influence the "ex-gay" movement.

A *Washington Post* article from 2007 reminds us that in multiple locations in the United States, adults, too, are compelled to behave in "normal"—that is to say, not queer or disabled—ways. The *Post* story, about locations "similar" to the public toilets in which former Senator Larry Craig was arrested for allegedly soliciting public sex, mentions the same Washington, D.C., park in which Robert picked up Mario (or Marco) and where, "incidentally," he was assaulted the following winter. The "experts" quoted in the article describe "anonymous sex in public places" as a "compulsive behavior" (a form of OCD, perhaps?). The article reports that "U.S. Park police spokesman Robert Lachance," when asked about police activity in and around Malcolm X Park, "would not discuss enforcement activities there" (Duke and Brown).

The stories from our lives that we adduce in this introduction, like each of the pieces in "Lives," address dangers, both physical and psychic. Yet despite the risks they describe and may perform, the narratives of Robert's encounter in the park and of Anna's confrontation in the parking lot nonetheless seemed safe enough for inclusion here. That is, we felt fairly confident that, of the three heuristic categories we sketched out above—the "proper," the "permissible," and the "punishable"—the "permissible" would be the one into which most readers would place our vignettes. The reason, we decided, that our stories would likely not be deemed "punishable" has much to do with a particular kind of work they could be called upon to perform. If we were to distribute either of the stories, without commentary, to the participants of a disability studies seminar or conference, we could envision three broad categories of responses: one would consolidate identity through a process of exclusion (some people are disabled; others aren't, even if they may have impairments); another would seek to expand identity categories in the interests of inclusion (we need to speak about disability oppression in ways that legitimize the experiences of invisibly disabled people and those with cognitive and psychiatric impairments); and a third would desire to move away from identity as the foundation or organizing principle for analyzing disability (we should center our analyses of disability less on individuals' identities than on the social, economic, and discursive contexts in which these identities and experiences materialize).

This broadly schematized spectrum of modes of understanding disability in relation to identity has much in common with the "minoritizing" and "universalizing" conceptions of homosexuality that Eve Kosofsky Sedgwick analyzes in *Epistemology of the Closet*.[5] According to Sedgwick, a minoritizing view sees the issue at hand as of "active importance primarily for a small, distinct, relatively fixed . . . minority," whereas a universalizing view sees an issue "of continuing, determinative importance in the lives of people across the spectrum" (1). While Sedgwick notes that she sympathizes more with universalizing analyses of same-sex desire than with minoritizing ones, her stated aim is not to adjudicate between these two ways of thinking about homosexuality over the past century, but rather to highlight the ways in which the shuttle between the two models invariably results in what she calls "the minoritizing/universalizing impasse" (90). Both homophobic and antihomophobic discourses routinely, and sometimes simultaneously, make use of minoritizing and universalizing claims, Sedgwick notes. Rather than privileging one of these modes of analysis over the other, "the more promising project," for Sedgwick, "would seem to be a study of the incoherent dispensation itself, the indisseverable girdle of incongruities under whose discomfiting span . . . have unfolded both the most generative and the most murderous plots of our culture" (90).

A similar incoherence can be read in contemporary discourses on disability, and we argue that a study of the "incoherent dispensation itself" is similarly a promising project for disability studies. Ableism often takes the form of minoritizing statements: disabled people are fundamentally different from "normal" people and should therefore be segregated from the rest of society in special schools and institutions. But it also frequently invokes universalizing models of disability: everyone's a little disabled, really; we all face physical and mental challenges, but these can and should be overcome with hard work. Similar contradictions are legible in anti-ableist discourses. Minoritizing claims are foundational in disability studies, which, as noted earlier, has often defined people with disabilities as members of a distinct "minority group." Yet universalizing claims also abound in the field, such as the oft-cited observation that "we'll all be disabled if we live long enough." Following Sedgwick, then, we might say that although we too sympathize more with universalizing analyses of disability, we're less interested in aligning ourselves monolithically with any of the three positions on disability identity we've schematized above than in considering the ways in which the two stories we include here, about "sex" and "disability" in our own lives,

Anna Mollow and Robert McRuer

lend themselves to citation in support of any of these seemingly contradictory positions.

Much of the import of Anna's story hinges on the notion of a minoritized disability identity: her insistence that she "really is" disabled and her reactions to having that claim denied. And even as Robert's story undermines the view of disability as the concern of a "distinct, relatively fixed" minority, the legibility of his narrative could still depend on a minoritized sexual identity, if it is connected to the pleasures of being recognized in public as a sexually available gay man (and even if, for both parties, sexual "identities" were not necessarily known — a fact which itself likely intensified the fantasies in circulation — the encounter still took place in a recognizably "gay" Washington, D.C., neighborhood). Thus, although we highlight the porousness and instability of disabled and gay identities, we are unable to displace them completely; indeed, even as we exchanged these stories "privately" with each other, our narratives could not proceed without references to these identities. And so we find ourselves at a "minoritizing/universalizing impasse": while we acknowledge the importance — the necessity, even — of the work of claiming (or abstaining from claiming) identities, and of analyzing the privilege and oppression that such claims and abstentions entail, we also find this work constraining and insufficient. Insufficient partly because the purview of identity-centered analyses is so limited; they tell us primarily about an individual, or a group of representative individuals (gay people, invisibly disabled people). In the remainder of this section, we attempt to read life writing about sex and disability in ways that exceed these identifications.

In both Robert's and Anna's stories above, disability and sex threaten the dissolution of each other. In one, disability makes sex less efficient ("Come on, let's go," the guy in the park gestures, but Robert ritualistically finishes his running) and even threatens its curtailment (he is gone by the time Robert completes his laps). Conversely, sex in this story threatens disability, by rendering it illegible. To a witness of the exchange in the park, disability would be nearly impossible to spot, in part because the image of a sexually attractive jogger serves so easily as the very picture of able-bodiedness.[6]

In other words, a polarization, in the cultural imagination, between sex and disability means that each of these terms potentially disables recognition of the other. If there's disability, according to ableist logic, then there can't be sex (hence, the "tragedy" of a "beautiful woman in a wheelchair"); and conversely, if there's sex (a casual encounter initiated in a park), then presumably there is not disability. This dichotomized construction of sex and disability is also at work in the story of Anna's confrontation in the parking lot, in which conventional markers of sexiness (sun dress, high heels) preclude recognition of disability ("Nobody who looks as good as you can be disabled!").

Disability and sex, then, often threaten to unravel each other. Yet we might also read these two stories as showing, paradoxically, that sex and disability can enable each other. To illustrate this, let us return to the *Washington Post* article that mentions Malcolm X Park and quotes "experts" who describe "anonymous sex in public places" as a "compulsive behavior." Reading Robert's story through the lens of this "expert" diagnosis, we can say that disability ("compulsion") is precisely what makes sex happen. Without disability (compulsion, obsession, addiction), there would be no sex (at least in Malcolm X Park, according to the experts). In Anna's story, too, disability can be read as making sex possible. That is, disability (needing that disabled parking spot) enabled an exchange that, although this would not occur to Anna at the time, was in some ways erotic. After all, an experience that, for many invisibly disabled people, is among the most painful—that of being disbelieved, deemed not "really" disabled—converged in the parking lot incident with one that, for many people (whether disabled or not) is among the most pleasurable: being looked up and down and found to look "good."

We find both pleasure and promise in reading "sex" and "disability" in these expansive ways. An advantage of a fluid understanding of disability is that, by enabling its siting in a multiplicity of unexpected—and often pleasurable—locations, it subverts the popular conception of disability as individual and tragic. And a benefit of thinking of "sex" as more than a set of genital acts—and "sexuality" as more than a set of predefined identities—is the potential for contesting the common cultural assumption that disabled people are not sexual. If we understand sex as more than penetration that occurs in the bedroom, then we can perceive sex and disability coming together in many places we might otherwise have missed them: a heated exchange in a parking lot, a caress on the back of a neck, an online chat mediated by voice-recognition software.

This is precisely the work many of the selections in *Sex and Disability* perform. The authors of these pieces show that sex is at work in a variety of cultural objects and practices not usually regarded as erotic: the use of a "squeeze machine" to calm the anxiety associated with autism or of a blanket to cover and uncover the legs of a visibly disabled protagonist of a nineteenth-century novel;

the insertion or removal of a pair of hearing aids; the display of a hand marked as "freaky"; the orgasmic bliss that might be achieved by sliding down a banister.

DESIRES

Men and women, women and men. It will never work. —Erica Jong

Under the Social Security Act, "disability" means "inability to engage in any substantial gainful activity by reason of any medically determinable physical or mental impairment which can be expected to result in death or has lasted or can be expected to last for a continuous period of not less than 12 months." —Social Security Network

[The ADA] does something important for American business, though, and remember this: you've called for new sources of workers. Well, many of our fellow citizens with disabilities are unemployed; they want to work and can work. And this is a tremendous pool of people.
—President George H. W. Bush, on signing the Americans with Disabilities Act

A man is a worker. If he is not then he is nothing. —Joseph Conrad

In the final section of this introduction, we reflect upon the relationship between sex and disability and work: work in its literal senses of employment and labor and also in some of its more figurative significations of efficacy, productivity, and use value. We argue that thinking about sex and disability in terms of what—and who—does or does not work opens up avenues for continuing dialogue between queer theory and disability studies. Such dialogue, we hope, will make evident the potential queerness of much disability activism, as well as the desirability of valuing illegitimate (perhaps impossible) ways of being disabled; ways, that is, that do not, cannot, or will not work.

Questions about legitimacy and illegitimacy are everywhere in queer theory right now. Indeed, we might even go so far as to diagnose the field as obsessed with what won't work. More specifically, much of the most influential writing in queer theory can be said to analyze, or even impossibly argue for, an illegitimate sex that does not work: on behalf of capitalism, marriage and hetero- or homonormativity, or the production of socially valid gay and lesbian identities. A passage from Butler's *Undoing Gender* is worth quoting at length:

> The stable pair who would marry if only they could are cast as illegitimate but eligible for a future legitimacy, whereas the sexual agents who function outside the purview of the marriage bond and its recognized, if illegiti-

mate, alternative form now constitute sexual possibilities that will never be eligible for a translation into legitimacy. . . . This is an illegitimacy whose temporal condition is foreclosed from any possible future transformation. It is not only *not yet* legitimate, but it is we might say the irrecoverable and irreversible part of legitimacy: *the never will be, the never was.* (106)

Even as some sectors of neoliberal capitalism embrace — or at least "tolerate" — what Butler might call "recognized, if illegitimate alternative" identities such as "gay," "lesbian," and even "bisexual" or "transgendered," queer theorists have argued for other ways of being that refuse or negate that tolerance or embrace, that seem to desire what Butler calls "the irrecoverable and irreversible part of legitimacy: *the never will be, the never was.*"

Suspicious about work as we think we know it and sex as we think it works, materialist critiques in queer theory look critically at the dominant lesbian and gay movement's rush to market, marriage, and the military. Critiquing what she terms a "middle-class logic of reproductive temporality," Judith Halberstam observes that "people who live in rapid bursts (drug addicts, for example) are characterized as immature and even dangerous" (*Queer Time* 4–5). Halberstam suggests that "ravers, club kids, HIV-positive barebackers, rent boys, sex workers, homeless people, drug dealers, and the unemployed . . . could productively be called 'queer subjects'" (10). To us, Halberstam's invocation of addiction and HIV as potentially constitutive of "queer" subjectivities exemplifies a pattern of approach and avoidance that characterizes much of queer theory's relationship to disability analysis. Drug addiction and HIV-positive serostatus are, according to most paradigms, categorizable as "disability." Yet their frequent appearance in queer theory — along with other pathologized conditions, such as "schizophrenia," "psychosis," or "alcoholism," that are seen as foreclosing possibilities of social legitimacy — is seldom accompanied by any sustained engagement with disability studies. To put this slightly differently, we might ask: what is gained — and lost — by referring to "HIV-positive barebackers" and "drug addicts" as "queer subjects" rather than, say, "disabled subjects" — or "crip" or "queercrip" subjects?

Queer theory's frequent references to disability are fitting, since the acts and desires that queer theory invokes to describe lives outside the purview of legitimacy often carry associations with medical terms and paradigms: in contemporary Western cultures one is not merely a "pervert"; one can be diagnosed with sexual compulsivity, gender identity disorder, masochism, sadism, obsessive-compulsive disorder, paraphilia, or addiction — or, in common parlance, one

Anna Mollow and Robert McRuer

is unhealthy, unstable, oversexed, sick. Given that, as Halberstam puts it, we "pathologize" queer lives and desires, it is surprising that queer academic writings about legitimacy almost never explicitly engage with the field of disability studies.

Perhaps this gap in queer theory is partly related to a lacuna within disability studies: a queer theorist turning to disability studies in order to buttress, complicate, or extend her or his discussion of the pathologization of queerness might be disappointed to discover that the illegitimate figures that populate queer academic discourses (addicts, crazies, compulsives, sick people) appear infrequently in disability studies — and are seldom held up as models of proud disabled identities.[7] Susan Schweik, arguing that "a history of disability on the street that ignores the traces of substance abuse is an impoverished one," remarks that "boozefighters are [hard] to claim as disability culture heroes, even of the romantic outlaw sort" (106; 107). Conversely, we might note that in some strands of queer theory it is *especially* the "romantic outlaw sort" of disability that gets marked as queer. If in these contexts addiction or mental illness can be read as queer, then why not those "paradigmatic" impairments disability scholars such as Anita Silvers invoke: "paraplegia, blindness, deafness" (77)?

Relationships among queerness, disability, and illegitimacy are the focus of Anna Mollow's "Is Sex Disability? Queer Theory and the Disability Drive," which is the first chapter in "Desires." Mollow posits that influential arguments by the queer theorists Leo Bersani and Lee Edelman regarding the antisocial and identity-disintegrating aspects of sex have important implications for contemporary theories of disability. Highlighting frequent references to disability in Bersani's and Edelman's discussions of sexuality and the death drive, Mollow introduces the term "disability drive," which describes a structural similarity that she identifies between the concept of "sexuality," as it is elaborated in psychoanalytic theory, and "disability," as it is represented in the cultural imaginary. Responding to Bersani's and Edelman's embrace of the death drive in relation to queerness, Mollow proposes a similar embrace of a "disability drive." Such an embrace would likely have delegitimizing effects for disability theory; it would undercut assertions of proud and positive disabled identities, insisting instead on the ways in which disability and sexuality, as imbricated concepts, entail a rupturing of the self or a disabling of the category of the "human."

In the second chapter in this part, "An Excess of Sex: Sex Addiction as Disability," Lennard Davis analyzes the emergence of the diagnostic category of sex addiction in both popular and medical discourses. In doing so, Davis shows that queer theory's critique of the marriage imperative is an important concern for disability studies as well. Davis illuminates the ways in which heteronormative culture's positing of marriage (or other forms of stable monogamy) as the privileged locus of "healthy" sex functions to pathologize, or disable, sex that occurs, as Butler might put it, "outside the purview of the marriage bond and its recognized, if illegitimate, alternative form" (*Gender Trouble* 106). Constructions of both queerness and disability are thus at work in the creation of the "disease" of sex addiction, even though those who are defined—and define themselves—as sex addicts most often do not claim either disabled or gay identities.

Alison Kafer's "Desire and Disgust: My Ambivalent Adventures in Devoteeism," through an analysis of the phenomenon of "amputee devoteeism," also brings queer theory and disability studies together. Amputee devotees are people who have a strong sexual preference for people with amputations. Devotees portray themselves as members of a sexual minority whose desires have been pathologized. Kafer writes of the conflict she feels between her sympathy with a group whose desires have been cast as illegitimate and her simultaneous discomfort with the many ways in which this group (comprising mostly heterosexual—and, often, heterosexist—men) attempts to legitimize its desires. "Devotee discourses" often authorize exploitation and harassment of disabled women, and although participation in amputee-devotee communities can be affirming and financially rewarding for some women and does seem to counter the pervasive cultural desexualization of disabled women's bodies, devotee discourses nonetheless have the effect of ultimately reinforcing this desexualization. This is because devotees' writing about amputees constructs and depends upon what Kafer calls a "desire/disgust binary," according to which the presence of an amputation makes a woman either desirable (to devotees) or disgusting (to everyone else).

The final chapter of *Sex and Disability*, "Hearing Aid Lovers, Pretenders, and Deaf Wannabes: The Fetishizing of Hearing," by Kristen Harmon, pushes the concept of disability fetishism even further. Beyond a consideration of people who sexually desire disabled bodies, Harmon studies the discourses of a community that finds erotic appeal in the possibility of becoming disabled themselves. The online special interest group whose postings Harmon analyzes includes not only deaf fetishists (who are sexually attracted to deaf or hard-of-hearing people) but also "pretenders" and "wannabes," who derive excitement—often marked as erotic—from the idea or experience of deafness. Some members of the group have deafened themselves and integrated themselves into Deaf signing communities. The volume thus ends, paradoxically, with a group contemplating, or engaging in, the process of claiming disabled identities but doing so in illegitimate ways; ways, that is, that many would necessarily read as (we might as well compulsively repeat ourselves) unhealthy, unstable, oversexed, sick.

Insofar as the four chapters in "Desires" underscore the illegitimacy (or, we might say, the queerness) of the coupling of sex and disability, we read them, taken together, as forwarding an implicit critique of queer theory's frequent elision of the queerness of disability. In most queer theory, it seems, the sex lives and erotic representations (or lack thereof) of amputees, deaf or Deaf people, or people with paralysis have no particular connection to queerness. Conversely, we might also read these four pieces together as containing a challenge to some strands of disability scholarship and activism that seem to us to elide the sexiness of their own projects. According to Tom Shakespeare: "Sexuality, for disabled people, has been an area of distress, and exclusion, and self-doubt for so long that it was sometimes easier not to consider it. . . . Ending poverty and social exclusion comes higher up the list of needs than campaigning for a good fuck" ("Disabled Sexuality" 160). Shakespeare's comments were part of a keynote address he delivered in 2000 at a San Francisco State University conference, "Disability, Sexuality, and Culture." In this talk, Shakespeare reflected on the "low profile" of sex "in the British disability movement, and in the developing field of disability studies," which had struck him, Kath Gillespie-Sells, and Dominic Davies when they wrote *The Sexual Politics of Disability* in the mid-1990s ("Disabled Sexuality" 159).

Interestingly, in Shakespeare's own work, the importance of sex seems to be on the decline. In *Disability Rights and Wrongs*, which was published in 2006, ten years after *The Sexual Politics of Disability*, Shakespeare reevaluates the earlier book: "by making sexuality our primary concern, we failed to understand that intimacy is perhaps a greater priority for disabled people"; indeed, "sex may be comparatively unimportant to a wide section of the population" (168). This section of Shakespeare's argument appears to have been adapted in part from his keynote address in 2000, where he likewise states that "perhaps because we haven't had access to [sex], we've been in danger of overstating" its importance ("Disabled Sexuality" 165).

Shakespeare describes himself as "more than a little queer," and his talk was subsequently published in *Bent*, an online journal for gay disabled men. And yet there's a way in which queerness gets disciplined when he says: "We know about the fascination with gay male culture, which is particularly a fascination about the availability of sex . . . The modern media, the modern fairy tale, is about the possibility of sexual adventure in every public place" ("Disabled Sexuality" 165).

We continue to believe in certain "fairy" tales, and we argue that Shakespeare misses much in his easy dismissal of gay male sexual subcultures. We make two key points about this dismissal, each of which has important ramifications for disability subcultures (which, of course, already overlap, and should overlap more, with gay male subcultures). First, even if the modern media remains fascinated with gay male cultures, for the past two decades neoliberal economic and cultural forces have worked to contain, dilute, and privatize those cultures. This "fascination" must therefore be understood as fascination of a very particular kind; neoliberal capital is fascinated *in general* with the ways that subgroups might be made more profitable and less dangerous or disruptive. Indeed, as Samuel R. Delany and numerous other observers have noted, the gay male sexual subcultures forged over the past half century were about increasing *access* to public space. Consequently, as that access has been sharply circumscribed through "development" and privatization, fewer bodies (including the potential crip outlaws toward which we gestured above) have been able to find each other out in public.

Second, Shakespeare's distancing from these sexual subcultures sits uncomfortably close to a similar, and widely remarked, distancing in the gay and lesbian movement, a distancing that has generated an emphatic privileging of sanitized identities: the "stable pair" and others whom Butler imagines as about to be legitimized. This second point also has implications for disability studies; it should prompt us to think carefully about how an impetus toward legitimacy might function for disability theorists and activists. Like the mainstream gay and lesbian movement, and in contrast to queer theory's impetus toward illegitimacy, many important disability studies texts seem at times to be engaged in the work of establishing the legitimacy, or potential legitimacy, of disabled subjects—in particular, sometimes, as members of the workforce or participants in the marketplace.[8] Garland-Thomson, for instance, cites approvingly (but contradictorily) an advertisement that "markets itself to a disabled, *upscale* audience who are after the look of *affluent* authority and charm" as exemplifying "a rhetoric of *equality*" ("Seeing" 368; emphasis added). Paul Longmore, similarly, famously critiques capitalism—in particular, telethons, as examples of what he calls "conspicuous contribution" ("Conspicuous" 134)—but also insists, in the conclusion to *Why I Burned My Book*: "We, like all Americans, have talents to use, work to

Anna Mollow and Robert McRuer

do, our contributions to make to our communities and country. We want the chance to work and marry without jeopardizing our lives. We want access to opportunity. We want access to work. We want access to the American Dream" (258).

In pointing to these passages that are at times at odds with other parts of a given writer's own work, we do not want to suggest that disability studies as a whole is uninterested in class analysis or uncritical of capitalism. On the contrary, numerous writers in the field (including Longmore and Garland-Thomson) have levied sharp critiques of capitalism, as well as more subtle analyses of the exploitative workings of liberalism and neoliberalism.[9] Nonetheless, disability studies often emphasizes the project of securing places for disabled people within what Deborah A. Stone calls the "work-based system" (21), rather than challenging the structure of that system itself. In these accounts, the story of disability liberation is narrated, or projected forward, as a transition toward what Garland-Thomson calls "an accommodation model of interpreting disability, as opposed to the earlier compensation model" (*Extraordinary Bodies* 18). Although it is easy to read a movement away from social welfare and toward workplace access as a form of progress, the construction of this particular narrative risks rendering less than legitimate the needs of disabled people who cannot work, regardless of what accommodations might be provided—people, for example, with pain or illness that is exacerbated by exertion.

In the United States today, most people whose disabilities prevent them from working depend upon either Supplemental Security Insurance (SSI) or Social Security Disability Insurance (SSDI). SSDI recipients often live near the poverty line; their income is typically less than half of what it was when they were working. Those whose employment histories do not qualify them for SSDI receive SSI, a program that in 2010 pays a California recipient a monthly benefit of $845; in Mississippi, the amount is just over $600. Longmore observes that "nonstigmatizing and adequate welfare" was among the demands of many disability activists throughout the twentieth century (*Burned* 79). Yet most contemporary disability scholarship, while frequently discussing inaccessible workplace environments and other barriers to employment, does not place a high priority on arguments for increasing the amount of disability benefits or access to them.

Emphasizing disabled people's employability and sexual normativity rhetorically confers upon disability the status of what Butler calls the "*not yet* legitimate," as opposed to the "*never will be, never was.*" And although disability studies can by no means be said monolithically to endorse this project of legitimization, there is at present no analogue within the field to what might be called the "legitimacy debate" between queer theory and the mainstream lesbian and gay movement. This debate has at times centered on marriage: advocates for "the stable pair who would marry if only they could" versus those who say "fuck marriage" and what Halberstam calls "reproductive temporality" (*Queer Time* 4). In disability studies, if a comparable debate were to emerge, it might center on the question of work, which is of course not unrelated to marriage, whether in the cultural imagination — sex, talk show hosts and psychologists tell us, may be fun, but marriage is hard work — or in the economic structures of neoliberal capitalism, which uses marriage as a way of privatizing benefits associated with work. In response to the image of the employable disabled person who would work if only reasonable accommodations were granted, others might protest, "Fuck employability: I'm too sick to work; and how am I supposed to live on $845 a month?"

The chapters in *Sex and Disability*, although they do not directly address the above question, might — insofar as they attend to the many ways that sex, as it converges with disability, does and does not work — be described as queering disability studies. Pregnant men, compulsive masturbators, solicitors of public sex in exchange for cash, gender benders, boys who like cunnilingus, and girls who like to be on top are among the more obviously delegitimizing figures who appear in this volume. In perhaps less readily apparent but equally important ways, chapters that analyze conjunctions of sex and disability as sites of violence (such as white-on-black lynching or coerced sterilization) or exclusion (the fear and disgust directed at men with cerebral palsy, female amputees, or women whose bodies are "more Z-shaped than S-curved") are, in their resistance to this violence and exclusion, engaged in imagining disability in ways that exceed or violate norms of propriety and respectability. In ways, that is, that are queer.

Attending to sex and its mergings with disability, this volume engages in the work — and play — of imagining how such joinings might reshape cultural understandings of sex and disability. Disability, the chapters in this collection show, has the potential to transform sex, creating confusions about what and who is sexy and sexualizable, what counts as sex, what desire "is." Conversely, we hope sex might transform and confuse disability, as it is understood in the dominant culture, in disability studies, and in the disability rights movement. We hope not only that you find pleasure in the contacts with sexual "Access," "Histories," "Spaces," "Lives," and "Desires" on the pages that follow, but also that as you read — and, we hope, reread — these chapters, they leave you still wanting more: new positions, further explorations, more demands.

1. Our thanks to Anne Finger for allowing us to quote this personal e-mail of 7 December 2009.

2. Barbara Faye Waxman-Fiduccia, similarly, argued in 1999 that "disabled people, and disabled women in particular, are a sexual minority. Along with gay men, lesbians, bisexuals, transgendered people, fetishists, children and old people, all of these subgroups are considered to exist outside the boundaries of reproduction. Their sexuality is then not only considered to be purposeless, but dangerous, immoral, and perverse" ("Sexual" 280).

3. Arguably, the ADA Amendments Act of 2008 itself poses some of these difficult questions about the minority group model. Recognizing that courts had very narrowly interpreted who counts as having a "disability," the act—while indeed underscoring that the category should have been understood more expansively—attempts to shift courts' focus away from technical questions of who does or does not fit and toward the question of whether discrimination has occurred.

4. Ron Amundson calls "paradigm cases of disability" those that involve "a blind man or a paraplegic woman" (114); Anita Silvers calls "paraplegia, blindness, deafness, and others" "paradigmatic disabilities" (77). Around the question of a model or paradigmatic person with a disability, we find our ideas in generative tension with recent work by Tobin Siebers. Certainly, we are persuaded by Siebers's call for disability studies to "find ways to represent pain and to resist models of the body that blunt the political effectiveness of these representations" (*Disability Theory* 61). Yet it seems to us that Siebers overlooks the ways in which some versions of the disability identity politics he celebrates (he calls identity politics a "political boon" for disabled people [*Disability Theory* 95]) are themselves engaged in constructing models of the body that blunt the political effectiveness of representations of pain. Siebers's *Disability Theory* argues that critics are against identity politics for one of two reasons: they either believe (on the Right) that proponents of identity politics are narcissistic or (on the Left) that they are invested in a politics of victimhood. Our observation that some versions of disability identity politics structurally require deemphasizing pain suggests that critiques of identity politics on the Left are more varied and nuanced than Siebers allows. For critiques of the tendency of the "social model" of disability to exclude representations of suffering or pain, see Wendell, "Unhealthy"; and Crow.

5. Rosemarie Garland-Thomson recognized more than a decade ago the value of Sedgwick's universalizing/minoritizing distinction for disability studies (*Extraordinary* 22). Garland-Thomson's use of Sedgwick, Erving Goffman, Michel Foucault, Mary Douglas, and other theorists in the opening chapters of *Extraordinary Bodies* is explicitly offered to readers as an invitation to further theorizing; hence, we are here expanding upon and reworking Garland-Thomson's application of Sedgwick's rubric.

6. Over the past decade, a few high-profile controversies over runners have con-

firmed both that there is a cultural expectation that the running body serve as a legible sign of a particularly narrow able-bodiedness and that disruption of that cultural expectation is particularly anxiety producing. The South African double amputee Oscar Pistorius, for instance, was initially deemed ineligible to compete in the Summer Olympics of 2008 in Beijing because of his difference from other runners; claims were made that his prosthetic legs gave him an unfair advantage over other runners. The decision to exclude Pistorius was eventually overturned, although he then failed to qualify for the South African Olympic team (he took home gold medals from the Paralympic Games of 2008, also held in Beijing).

7. This is true even of some writing about mental illness in disability studies. For example, Catherine Prendergast argues in "The Unexceptional Schizophrenic" that the words of self-identified "schizophrenics" are often "not rhetorically exceptional in any of the ways postmodern theorists might expect" (293). This view contrasts with Margaret Price's argument, in an important article on "psychosocial disability" and "counter-diagnosis," that mental illness is often "creatively disruptive" of hegemonic forms of identity and identification (11). For a discussion of the relationship between the Mad Pride movement and disability studies, see Lewis. See also Ingram; Laden and Schwartz; Wilson and Beresford.

8. For an example of an exception to this trend, see Taylor.

9. In addition to his foundational work on telethons, see Longmore's writing about the radical labor activist Randoph Bourne and his class-based analysis of the 1930s organization the League of the Physically Handicapped (*Burned* 32–101); see also Garland-Thomson's discussion of the ways that Herman Melville's character Bartleby the Scrivener opts out of the emergent capitalist order ("Cultural Logic").

Anna Mollow and Robert McRuer

I

ACCESS

1

....

TOBIN SIEBERS

A SEXUAL CULTURE FOR DISABLED PEOPLE

Sexuality is not a right which must be earned or a possession that must be purchased, but a state of being accessible to all individuals. Even those who sometimes have to fight for that access. —Lucy Grealy, "In the Realm of the Senses"

The emergence in recent decades of people who define their identities based on sexual preferences and practices is transforming the landscape of minority politics. Sexual minorities are fighting for the rights and privileges accorded to majority populations on many legal and political fronts. The fight over gay marriage is only the most public and contentious of current struggles for full and equal rights by a sexual minority. Proponents of minority sexual identity attack the neat division between the private and public spheres, the relevance of the traditional family and its institutions of marriage and child rearing, and the moral certainty that sexuality is better controlled or repressed than set free. Claims that sexuality is a major part of a person's identity, that sexual liberation is a good in itself, and that sexual expression is a civil right crucial to human happiness have led to new conceptions of civic life linked to sex. Jeffrey Weeks argues that attention to sexual identity gives birth to the "sexual citizen." For him, sexual citizenship remedies "limitations of earlier notions of citizenship" (39), focuses attention on "sexualized identities" (38), and blunts "forces that inhibit" the "free, consensual development" of human relationships "in a democratic polity committed to full and equal citizenship" (38). Kenneth Plummer also represents the new sexual identities as a form of citizenship, defining "intimate citizenship" as "the *control (or not) over* one's body, feelings, relationships: *access (or not) to* representations, relationships, public spaces, etc; and *socially grounded choices (or not) about* identities, gender experiences" (14). Finally, Abby Wilkerson notes that oppressed groups tend to share the experience of sexual repression, explaining that sexual agency is central to political agency and that "sexual democracy should be recognized as a key political struggle" ("Disability" 35).[1]

The emphasis on control over one's body, access to public spaces, and political agency will sound familiar to disability rights activists. Disabled people have long struggled to take control of their bodies from medical authorities and to gain access to built environments and public institutions. Like the sexual minorities described by Weeks, Plummer, and Wilkerson, disabled people experience sexual repression, possess little or no sexual autonomy, and tolerate institutional and legal restrictions on their intimate conduct. Moreover, legal and institutional forces inhibit their ability to express their sexuality freely and to develop consensual relationships with sexual partners.

It would be an exaggeration to define the oppression of disabled people exclusively in the sexual context; not many people with disabilities consider themselves a sexual minority. Nevertheless, I want to argue that disabled people do constitute a significant sexual minority and that recognizing their status as sexual citizens will advance the cause of other sexually oppressed groups. "Sexuality is often," Anne Finger explains about people with disabilities, "the source of our deepest oppression; it is also often the source of our deepest pain. It's easier for us to talk about—and formulate strategies for changing—discrimination in employment, education, and housing than to talk about our exclusion from sexuality and reproduction" (9). The facets of my argument are multiple, but most of them rely on the power of disability as a critical concept to defamiliarize how we think currently about sex. First, thinking about disabled sexuality broadens the definition of sexual behavior. Second, the sexual experiences of disabled people expose with great clarity both the fragile separation between the private and public spheres, as well as the role played by this separation in the history of regulating sex. Third, co-thinking sex and disability reveals unacknowledged assumptions about the ability to have sex and how the ideology of ability determines the value

Tobin Siebers

of some sexual practices and ideas over others. Finally, the sexual history of disabled people makes it possible to theorize patterns of sexual abuse and victimization faced by other sexual minorities.

My argument will hinge on what I call the "sexual culture" of people with disabilities. This phrase is meant to set in motion a process of defamiliarization directed at experiences so intimate and unspoken, so familiar and yet mysterious, that few people will discuss them. These experiences are bundled under what is colloquially called a "sex life"—a term I contrast heuristically to "sexual culture." Sexual culture refers to neither gender assignation nor sexual preference, although obviously they are components of sexual being. Sexual culture references the experience of sex itself. By sexual culture, I mean to suggest two ideas about how disabled sexuality disrupts the notion of a sex life: first, sexuality assumes a larger role in the quotidian life of people with disabilities than the usual phrase "sex life" indicates; second, the idea of a sex life is ableist. Being able-bodied assumes the capacity to partition off sexuality as if it were a sector of private life: that an individual *has* sex or a sex life implies a form of private ownership based on the assumption that sexual activity occupies a particular and limited part of life determined by the measure of ability, control, or assertiveness exercised by that individual. People with disabilities do not always have this kind of sex life. On the one hand, the stigma of disability may interfere with having sex. On the other hand, the sexual activities of disabled people do not necessarily follow normative assumptions about what a sex life is. Neither fact means that people with disabilities do not exist as sexual beings. One of the chief stereotypes oppressing disabled people is the myth that they do not experience sexual feelings or that they do not have or want to have sex—in short, that they do not have a sexual culture.

Two cautions must be remarked before I undertake an extended argument about the sexual culture of disabled people. First, the distinction between sex life and sexual culture does not turn exclusively on the issue of privacy. While disabled people sometimes lack privacy for sex, their situation is not unique. Gay, lesbian, bisexual, queer, and transgendered people also suffer from a lack of sexual privacy, and economic resources may determine whether people have sex in private or public. Crowded housing situations, for example, are as offensive to the conception of private sexual expression as health care facilities. The distinction between sex life and sexual culture relies not on privacy but on access as defined in a disability context: sexual culture increases access for disabled people not only by breaking down the barriers restricting them from sexual locations but also by bringing sexual rights to where they live. Second, the idea of sexual culture strips away what one might call the existential connotations of a sex life. Existentialism posits that identities are constructed by ourselves for ourselves, that all values are subjective, that we are responsible for our choices, and that we are condemned to be free. The notion of sexual culture relies on different presuppositions about identity. I define sexual identities as theory-laden constructions, combining both objective and subjective values, used by individuals to make choices, to test the consequences of their actions, and to explore the possibilities and responsibilities of their sexuality. Sexual culture is designed as a concept to provide a deeper, more sustained idea of how sex and identity interconnect by resisting the partitioning and privatization characteristic of a sex life. It means to liberate sex, allowing it to overflow the boundaries of secured places and to open up greater sexual access for people with disabilities.

NO WALKS ON THE BEACH

I am looking for an intelligent, literate woman for companionship and, perhaps, sexual play. I am, as you see, completely paralyzed, so there will be no walks on the beach. —Personal ad

Sex always happens somewhere. We go to certain places to fall in love or to have sex. A sex life, perhaps to our disappointment, tends to occur in the same places—the bedroom, hotels, automobiles, health clubs, baths, and so on. Sex will not happen if we do not have access to such places or if we cannot return to them once we discover that they permit sexual activity. If sex is walking together on the beach, if it is running across a field of flowers to meet in an embrace, what is the nature of sex apart from the ability to walk or to run? If a person's wheelchair gets stuck in the sand or if low vision makes it uncomfortable to dash across a field, does it mean that this person will have little chance of having sex? Clearly, people who do not do these things or go to these places manage to have sex, but that is not exactly the point. The point is to ask how the ideology of ability determines how we think about sex.

The ideology of ability represents the able body as the baseline of humanness. Absence of ability or lesser ability, according to this ideology, marks a person as less than human. The preference for ability permeates nearly every value in human culture, including the ability to have sex. In fact, sex may be the privileged domain of ability. Sex is the action by which most people believe that ability is

Tobin Siebers

reproduced, by which humanity supposedly asserts its future, and ability remains the category by which sexual reproduction as such is evaluated. As a result, sex and human ability are both ideologically and inextricably linked. Mark O'Brien recounts a story about the belief that the inability to have sex robs the disabled person of human status:

> We watched a movie about disability and sexuality. The movie consisted of four or five able-bodied men joking and laughing about how they once lugged their crippled friend up a flight of stairs to a whorehouse. . . . After the movie, a doctor talked about disability and sexuality. . . . I will always remember his closing line: "You may think you'll never have sex again, but remember . . . some people do become people again." (O'Brien and Kendall 80)

The doctor is speaking loosely about sex and membership in the human community, but he employs a widespread prejudice used against those who have lost human status along with the ability to have sex. What is it about sex that bestows human status? Barbara Waxman-Fiduccia argues that disability assumes the characteristic of a sexual perversion because disabled people are thought unable to produce "quality offspring" ("Current" 168–69). It is reproduction, then, that marks sexuality as a privileged index of human ability. In fact, the ideology of ability underlies the imperative to reproduce at many levels, establishing whether an individual supposedly represents a quality human being. First, sex appeal determines the opportunity to have sex. The greater a person's capacity to attract partners, the more opportunities to have sex. Second, a person must be able physically and mentally to have sex. Third, a person must be able to reproduce, to be either virile or fertile. To fail to be able to reproduce is somehow to fail as a human being. Finally, successful reproduction is thought to pass our essential abilities and qualities to our children. The predominant assumption is that what we are will be visited upon our children. If a person does not measure up to society's ideas about ability, that person's opportunities to have sex will be limited. People with disabilities share with gay men and lesbians the suspicion by majority populations that they cannot, will not, or should not contribute to the future of the human race. They will not reproduce, but if they do, the expectation is that the results will be tainted. Social stigma would have little impact on sexual behavior if it were not for the fact that ability represents the supreme measure of human choices, actions, thoughts, and values.

The concept of a sex life encapsulates many of the ways in which the ideology of ability distorts current attitudes about sexuality. At the most superficial level, a sex life is described almost always in the context of health. A sex life must be, first and foremost, a healthy sex life, and the more healthy a person is, the better the sex life is supposed to be. Whence the imperative in today's culture to "work on" one's sex life, to "improve" or "better" it, to do special exercises or adopt a particular diet for it, "to spice it up" — all for the purpose of discovering "the ultimate pleasure." These and other catchphrases attend the commodification of sex as healthy and satisfying, but the connection between a sex life and ability runs deeper than cliché. When disability is linked to sex, it becomes a clinical matter in which each disability betrays a particular limitation of sexual opportunity, growth, or feeling. The literature on sex and disability recites a litany of limitations for each category of impairment. The blind have trouble with sex because it centers supposedly on a visualization of the body as integral whole, and lacking sight, they cannot visualize what a body is (Hamilton 239). The mobility impaired and paralyzed are apparently cut off from sources of information about sex from peers, and their sexual development remains stunted (Shuttleworth, "Search" 265–66). Because of language delays, deaf people are believed to be emotionally and sexually immature, living without the language tools needed to meet the high standards of communication required for sex (Job 264, 266). Disabled women are said to tolerate sexism and objectification (Fine and Asch 29–30). In general, people with disabilities are thought to suffer from distorted body images, considering themselves ugly, and they do not feel at home with typical gender roles.

Because a sex life depends on ability, any departure from sexual norms reads as a disability, disease, or defect. Moreover, the equation runs in the other direction as well: disability signifies sexual limitation, regardless of whether the physical and mental features of a given impairment affect the ability to have sex. Eugenics and the Human Genome Project design futures for humanity on the basis of the desire to eliminate transmissible traits linked to disability, but the fear of disability also stymies intimate romantic relations, even when reproduction is not an expectation in the relationship. Many people in the disability community are still waiting, as Corbett Joan O'Toole explains, to hear a story in which a man or woman who chooses to be lovers with a disabled person is congratulated by family and friends for making a good choice (217). What sea change in current scientific, medical, political, and romantic attitudes would be necessary to represent disabled sexuality as a positive contribution to the future? To reconceive sexuality apart from ability, it would be necessary to imagine the sexual benefit of a given impairment, to claim and celebrate it as a sexual advantage.

PRIVATE PARTS IN PUBLIC PLACES

I was very shy before my accident. Dealing with lots of nurses doing extremely personal things to you—sometimes in front of other people—knocks off your shyness. —A quadriplegic

If people with disabilities are to develop a sexual culture, they will need to access safe spaces where they may develop new erotic theories and modes of being. A major obstacle to this project is the separation between the private and public spheres and the history of this separation in regulating sexuality in general and disabled sexuality in particular. Feminists identify the private/public split as a source of gender and sexual oppression because it often reifies gender differences and disempowers women. First, men have more power than women to draw the lines between private and public life. Second, men often use this power to maintain or to increase their advantage over women, forcing them into dependency, using privacy to conceal sexual violence, and stifling any attempts by them at political protest. Because the state is reluctant to enter the private sphere, women are imprisoned there, made vulnerable to abuse by domestic partners and given the status of second-class citizens.

Disability studies supports the feminist argument that the private/public split is responsible for political oppression, while deepening the perception that privacy is abandoned at a terrible cost. The experience of disabled people with the medical model has been key to this perception. The medical model thrives by sustaining an essential difference between nondisabled and disabled people, defining disability not as a flourishing of biological diversity but as an individual defect that medical professionals cure or eradicate in order to restore a person to the superior state of health required by the ideology of ability. For twenty-first-century medicine, then, it matters only a little whether you are a man or a woman when a surgeon reaches into your body and puts a hand on an internal organ. Nor does it matter a great deal whether the doctor is male or female. The organ will be removed if the doctor thinks it should, whether the procedure has been discussed or not. Male and female doctors alike have experimented on me, and I never knew that experimentation was happening until later, sometimes years later. Rare is the doctor who explains procedures, let alone allows patients to question them. There seems to be no protected realm, no private sphere, into which the medical establishment cannot reach.

If an urgent task is to protect privacy, while attacking its use in the oppression of women, minorities, and people with disabilities, there is no better place to begin than with the medicalization of the private sphere and, in particular, the impact of medicalization on economic class. Money buys privacy, and many practices, legal and other, follow the money. Clubs using private money need not obey antidiscrimination laws. Customers who pay more win the right to have their own private spaces carved out of the public domain. For example, first-class and business-class passengers on airlines routinely have bathrooms reserved only for their use, into which coach passengers may not go. Property rights based on economic advantage also determine privacy laws. Indeed, laws against trespassing are a primary support to the right to privacy. The spaces that one owns or rents define the places where private things are permitted; if one tries to do private things in public—that is, commonly owned places—police intervention and arrest are more likely to occur. Private dwellings are protected against forced entry and search, unless there is a warrant, while people who live on the street are almost always vulnerable to search and seizure. Public restrooms, rest stops, and community parks have enforced vagrancy and decency laws designed to control economically disadvantaged people and other populations thought marginal. Without the money to buy privacy, there is little protection against public exposure and its invasive extensions.

Yet the presence of disability exposes the fragility of the traditional separation between private and public because economic factors do not obtain for disabled people in expected ways. Medicalization opens privacy to assault, and while economic privilege may make this assault less intrusive, it does not eliminate it. A private room in a hospital, no matter how expensive, is not like a hotel room, although it is leased for a certain period. No "Do Not Disturb" sign, controlled by a patient, will ever hang on the doorknob. Doctors, nurses, aides, and janitorial staff enter and exit at will. Despite the persistent fantasy that doctors, nurses, and nurse assistants provide sexual services, hospital trysts and erotic sponge baths are not part of their job descriptions. In fact, their professionalization hinges on being able to invade privacy while divorcing that invasion from its sexual associations. It may be acceptable, Dominic Davies explains, for a male patient to get an erection when having his penis washed, but "consensual, vigorous washing is seen as forbidden" (183–84). As long as medical staff *act* professionally, they do not consider themselves responsible for sexual side effects, and yet they cross erotic boundaries constantly, with little real regard for the consequences of their actions. Patients in medical institutions do not possess the same rights as non-disabled staff. It is as if sick or disabled individuals surrender the right to privacy in exchange for medical care, even though caregivers work for them. "The difference between those of us who need attendants and those who don't," Cheryl Marie Wade claims, "is the difference between those who know privacy and those who don't" (88).

Group homes and long-term care facilities purposefully destroy opportunities for disabled people to find sexual partners or to express their sexuality. Even though inhabitants in group homes pay rent for their rooms, the money buys no functional privacy or right to use personal space. The staff usually does not allow renters to be alone in their room with anyone of sexual interest. Renters are subjected to intense surveillance, their activities entered in the day log. In many care facilities, staff will not allow two people to sit together alone in the same room. Some facilities segregate men and women. Add to these restrictions the fact that many people with disabilities are involuntarily confined in institutions, with no hope of escape, and the enormity of their oppression becomes palpable. The intimate lives of disabled men and women, as O'Toole phrases it, are "monitored, documented and discussed by others" (220). Medical authorities make decisions about access to erotic literature, masturbation, and sexual partners.

The unequal power relations between staff and patients encourage sexual abuse. We are only beginning to gather data on the sexual abuse of people with disabilities, but initial statistics indicate that the incidence of abuse is high (Ward 1349), perhaps two to ten times more than the experience of the nondisabled population (Kaufman et al. 8; Shakespeare, "Sexual Politics" 63). It is puzzling that paralyzed women are especially vulnerable, given that disabled women are not considered sexually attractive by mainstream society, until a closer look is given to the conditions of abuse. A woman unable to leave her bed is a woman always in bed, and conventionally a bed is a sexual site. Paralysis is also pictured easily as sexual passivity or receptiveness—an invitation to sexual predators, since the erotic imagination thrives on clichéd positions and gestures. No wonder paralyzed women who cannot get out of bed worry about imagining themselves as rape victims, even when engaging in consensual sex (Westgren and Levi 311, 314).[2]

Not surprisingly, the depersonalizing effects of medicalization often wound the psyches of disabled people, inducing feelings of worthlessness and sexual shame. O'Brien recounts how nurses made jokes in front of him about his involuntary erections, saying things like "Looks like someone's having a good time" (O'Brien and Kendall 45). On numerous occasions, therapists engaged in sexual banter and teasing about intimate parts of his body (70–73). Medical staff place patients on bedpans in public, sometimes forgetting about them for long periods of time (O'Brien and Kendall 23; Johnson, "Disability Gulag" 60). Frequently, the abuse is premeditated, representing acts of discipline, payback, or sexual harassment. O'Toole reports that many disabled women experience unacceptable touching by male doctors during medical examinations; they are sometimes publicly stripped and displayed to medical students. These women recount feelings of fear, embarrassment, vulnerability, and shame; they often try to separate themselves from their bodies, pretending that nothing is happening to them (218–19).

Personal choice and autonomy are constitutive features of the private sphere, but once subjected to medicalization, individual preference and self-determination evaporate. When the right to privacy and the medical model come into conflict, a new public sphere, controlled by medical figures and supportive of their authority, appears on the horizon. This medical zone of publicness replaces for people with disabilities everything formerly considered private. It engulfs them in an invasive and discriminatory space where they are viewed exclusively as medical subjects and the most casual stranger feels empowered to touch them, to comment on their disabilities, and to offer medical advice or charity. The medical model too often makes of the world a hospital where the disabled are obliged to be perpetual patients and the nondisabled have the right to play doctor.

THE EROTICS OF DISABILITY

Because I am so sensitive to touch, so acutely aware of a breeze on my neck, a ring on my finger, the rib of a sock pressing into my ankle, when I choose to participate in sexual contact, my unusually heightened physicality works for and not against me.
—Amy Wilensky, "The Skin I'm In"

As a sexual minority, people with disabilities face many limitations on their intimate behavior and erotic feelings. But, aware of their oppression and defiant of its injustice, they have begun to explore an alternative sexual culture based on the artfulness of disability. The progress has been slow because the fight for access has usually targeted the public sphere. For people with disabilities, "the fight to end discrimination in education, employment and other areas of life," Tom Shakespeare explains, "was all about making personal troubles into public issues. But the private lives of disabled women and men were not seen as being equally worthy of concern" ("Disabled Sexuality" 159–60). Furthermore, the social construction model favored by critics of the built environment tends to neglect physical aspects of disability related to sexuality (Shakespeare, "Disabled Sexuality" 162). Consequently, we know much more about the public dimension of disability than about its private dimension; we are at the beginning of a period of sexual investigation for disabled people, where information is scarce and ethnography and sharing of practices need to be pursued.

Nevertheless, there are signs that people with disabilities are claiming a sexual culture based on different conceptions of the erotic body, new sexual temporalities, and a variety of gender and sexed identities. These emerging sexual identities have at least two significant characteristics. First, they represent disability not as a defect that needs to be overcome to have sex but as a complex embodiment that enhances sexual activities and pleasure. Second, they give to sexuality a political dimension that redefines people with disabilities as sexual citizens. It is crucial to understand that sexual citizenship does not translate merely into being able to express sexuality in public—a charge always levied against sexual minorities— but into the right to break free of the unequal treatment of minority sexualities and to create new modes of access for sex. In the case of disabled people, sexual citizenship has particular stakes. Some specific agenda items include access to information about sexuality; freedom of association in institutions and care facilities; demedicalization of disabled sexuality; addressing sexual needs and desires as part of health care; reprofessionalization of caregivers to recognize, not deny, sexuality; and privacy on demand.

While certain aspects of the body are not open to transformation, sexual desire and erotic sensation are remarkably flexible. For example, people with paralysis, who have lost feeling in traditional erogenous zones, have found ways to eroticize other parts of their body. They also develop new ways to please their partners by creating erotic environments adjustable to differently abled bodies. As feminists have made clear, normative sexuality requires a distinctive mapping of the body into limited erogenous zones (Irigaray). A parallel geography exists between the places on the body marked for sex and the places where bodies have sex. Although it is considered kinky to have sex in out of the way places, it does not usually cross one's mind to summon sexual feelings in places on the body not already demarcated by them. Andrew Vahldieck adds a particularly vivid and thoughtful account to the literature on sex after spinal cord injury about the erotics of the disabled body:

> There's a bumper sticker that proclaims, "Quads Make Better Lovers" and perhaps it's true. One positive by-product of adapting to a disability is having to learn to go with the flow of experience, both mentally and physically. After severe spinal injury, one must begin again, and this includes developing alternate sense faculties. My erotic self need not be solely localized at the tip of my cock, where I've lost much sensation; I have learned that other areas of my body can be erotically sensitive and responsive. Sensation is mobile. My passion, desire and heat can be creatively restrained or refocused on more sensitive areas: ears, lips, neck, shoulders. In doing so, I can transfer sensual feeling into areas where sensation is diminished.
>
> Just as important has been learning to free myself from a preoccupation with my own pleasure. To give myself over to my partner. To slow down, not because I'm disabled and have to, but because I want to. This has proved crucial, paradoxically, to building up my own libidinous momentum. By relaxing into a quiet, tender space while stroking and touching my lover, I can engage vicariously in her enjoyment and stimulation so intensely as to share in her—and expand upon my own—felt pleasure. How curious that pleasing women orally has never been held as a form of manly sexual expression. Speaking as a man labeled "severely disabled," this may truly be considered a high and most subtle erotic art.

Disabled sexuality not only changes the erotics of the body, Vahldieck implies, but also transforms the temporality of lovemaking. For example, in the same way that narrative temporality has a beginning, middle, and end, normative sexuality requires beginning, middle, and end points. This is especially true of penetrative sex. Penetration has a preparatory phase, a period of sustainment, and a climax—all designed to prop up the physiognomy of the penis. One gets it up, gets it in, and keeps it up for as long as possible, until one loses it. Penetrative sex figures as a race against fatigue—a performance with a beginning, middle, and end. It also smacks of the assembly or production line, where part after part is added until the product is finished. The dependence of sex on penetration, incidentally, represents one reason why people tend to partition their sex life from everyday existence. Because the temporal phases of penetrative sex are so indel-

Tobin Siebers

ible, its narrative seems relatively autonomous, and it is easy to think of it as an activity apart from all other facets of life.

Because disabled people sometimes require advanced planning to have sex, their sexual activity tends to be embedded in thinking about the day, not partitioned as a separate event. Among disabled people, the so-called sex act does not always qualify as an action or performance possessing distinct phases such as beginning, middle, and end. Moreover, the myth that sex must be spontaneous to be authentic does not always make sense for people who live with little privacy or whose sexual opportunities depend on making arrangements with personal attendants. Rather, disabled sexuality has an ebb and flow that spreads it out among other activities, and its physiognomy does not necessarily mimic conventional responses of arousal, penetration, or orgasm. "I used to get stuck, needing orgasm, needing penetration, etc.," one woman explains. "Now, my sexuality has matured. . . . For example, one of the greatest highs I get (full-body orgasms? or spiritual-like orgasms?) is from having my neck bit" (Kaufman et al. 126). Some people without bodily sensation report experiencing mental orgasms when engaged in kissing, verbal play, or sexual fantasy. Others remark that sexual pleasure grows more intense with the advent of disability, owing either to physical changes or to a greater awareness of their body: "Since I became paralyzed in both legs I have noticed that I have varying kinds of orgasms, depending upon the situation. For example, when I play with myself and rub my clit a certain way my orgasms are much more intense. Sometimes my leg will go into spasm and my crotch feels tingly" (Kaufman et al. 52).

A crucial consideration for people with disabilities is not to judge their sexuality by comparison to normative sexuality but to think expansively and experimentally about what defines sexual experience for them. Sex may have no noticeable physical signs of arousal or may not conclude with an orgasm. When touching is involved, the places being touched may not be recognizable to other people as erogenous zones, which makes sex in public possible and a lot of fun. Sex may extend beyond the limits of endurance for penetrative sex, resembling slow dancing instead of the twist. It may seem kinky by comparison to what other people are doing. According to O'Toole, disabled sex often surprises a person's community, no matter how radical. For example, in Boston in the mid-1990s, Connie Panzarino marched in a gay pride parade with a placard reading, "Trached dykes eat pussy all night without coming up for air" (O'Toole 212). That a woman with little movement below the neck could be the active partner in sex and use her disability to enhance her partner's pleasure stunned and shocked people. "This disabled woman," O'Toole notices, "was using her disability as an advertisement for a sexual partner. She was appealing to partners who like extended oral pleasure. She was turning her apparent severe disability into a distinct sexual advantage" (220–21). O'Toole also mentions an account given by a lesbian amputee about enhancing the pleasure of her partners: "Can I just say that my two leg stumps make fabulous sex toys. I really think my amputated body is tailor-made for lesbian sex: I can crawl on top of my lover and grind my leg into her cunt in ways that I couldn't if I had 'real' legs. Having my little stumps gives me much more freedom of motion and I can get closer, deeper into her that way. Plus, pushing myself into her and away from her and into her again, moving my hips and legs against/on her body is the closest I have come to slow-dancing in years and I love it" (215).

Disabled people may advance a different sexual geography both for the body and for the places where bodies express their sexuality. Just as disabled persons may change places on the body not usually associated with sexual feeling into erogenous zones, they reorganize places inhabited by bodies as locations for sexual culture. Citizenship rights tend to be practiced in certain locations—polling places, town centers, courtrooms, and so forth—and these locations are not always accessible to people with disabilities. Sexual citizenship suffers from the same restrictions, but here the goal is not necessarily to make the built environment more accessible, although it is an important goal, but to bring rights to the places where disabled people want to have sex. Privacy on demand, for example, could transform a hospital room into a safe space for sexual activity, avoiding the difficulties described by this disabled person: "Even though I am often by myself, I never know when someone will walk in on me. I may look back and think, 'I've just had half an hour to myself, I could have masturbated,' but the time wasn't guaranteed. It isn't really my time" (Kaufman et al. 114). Unfortunately, we are still at a stage where there are more negative illustrations of how rights of sexual citizenship fail than positive examples of how they might work. Nevertheless, people intent on having sex find fugitive places to commingle: "Accessible toilets are FAB. . . . One can get pushed in there by a lover and everyone thinks, 'Isn't that sad, someone needs to wipe their bum,' and you can shag away in private and then come out and no one has a clue as to what really went on! It's liberating and definitely one of the few perks of being a wheelchair user!" (Kaufman et al. 130–31). Embracing greater sexual diversity is key to the rights of disabled people, and it might have unanticipated benefits for thinking about sex in general. As one woman explains it, "if you are a sexually active disabled person, and comfortable with the sexual side of your life, it is remarkable how dull and unimaginative non-disabled people's sex lives appear" (Shakespeare, "Disabled Sexuality" 163).

New formations of gender and sexed identity may be the final frontier of sexual citizenship for people with disabilities. Although present currents on the Left and Right wish to abolish identity entirely, especially identities connected with sickness and perceived weakness, gender and sexed identities make sexuality present as a mode of being not easily closeted away or partitioned into isolated temporal and spatial segments. Claiming an identity based on sexual culture thrusts one's minority status into the foreground, politicizes it, and creates the opportunity to clarify sexual needs and desires. It also resists the closeting of gender and sexuality central to Western attitudes about sex. It may be especially valuable for people with disabilities to assert sexed identities, since Western attitudes seem married to the argument that "sex is sick," giving people perceived to be "sick" extra purchase in making counterarguments.

Apart from the urgency of political resistance, it may simply be the case that different identity formations suit people with disabilities better. They often complain that conventional notions of male and female or straight and gay do not apply to them (Shakespeare, "Disabled Sexuality" 163), and it is fairly obvious that their sexual practices depart from many of the founding myths of normative sexuality. Disabled people do not embody gender in "natural" ways because gender stereotypes do not allow it. "It's like I don't have any maleness," one disabled man complains (Shuttleworth, "Search" 272). Certain disabilities appear to offer specific gender limitations. Men with cerebral palsy cannot touch or hug their female partners in the ways to which they are accustomed (Shuttleworth, "Search" 269). Blindness changes sexual flirtation from afar between men. But another person puts a positive spin on flexible gender identity: "Why should men be dominant? Why should sex revolve around penetration? Why should sex only involve two people? Why can't disabled people be assisted to have sex by third parties?" (Shakespeare, "Disabled Sexuality" 163). O'Toole notes that no lesbian equivalent of the missionary position exists, and that partners are not obliged to have orgasms in the same position at the same time (213). Disabled sexuality embraces a similar flexibility. The sexed identities of disabled people are of value to all sexually active people, Shakespeare claims, because they allow for a continuum of sexual practices and encourage a greater willingness to embrace diversity, experimentation, and alternative sexual techniques ("Sexual Politics" 58).

CONCLUSION

If we are to liberate disabled sexuality and give to disabled people a sexual culture of their own, their status as sexual minority requires the protection of citizenship rights similar to those being claimed by other sexual minorities. The challenge of sexual citizenship for people with disabilities is great because they remain one of the largest unrecognized minority populations, little awareness exists about the manner of their oppression, sex is a taboo subject for everyone and for disabled people in particular, and the unquestioned embrace in most societies of ability as an ideology denies participation in the public sphere to those not deemed quality human beings. Integral to sexual citizenship for people with disabilities is the creation of a safe space with different lines of communication about disabled sexuality; they need in effect to invent a new public sphere receptive to political protest, public discussion, erotic association, and the sharing of ideas about intimate practices and taboos, erotic techniques and restrictions, sexual innovation and mythologies.

In the clash of the culture wars, some people have argued for a monoculture where we abandon all identities except nationality, while other people argue for a multiculture where we embrace many identities — racial, ethnic, gendered, national, and sexed. The call for a disability culture in general and a sexual disability culture in particular will arouse, no doubt, the anger of the first group and garner, with luck, the support of the second. But the stakes in the emergence of a sexual culture for disabled people are greater than the dispute between these two political factions. The stakes concern questions about fundamental rights expected by all citizens in a democratic society: freedom of association and intimate companionship, authority over their own body, protection from violence, abuse, and oppression, and the right to pursue a sexual future of their own choosing. Because every citizen will become sooner or later a disabled citizen, the struggle of people with disabilities for sexual rights belongs to everyone.

NOTES

This chapter was previously published as chapter 7, "A Sexual Culture for Disabled People," in *Disability Theory*, by Tobin Siebers (Ann Arbor: University of Michigan Press, 2008), 135–56.

1. A number of other discussions touching minimally on sexual citizenship are worth noting. Sonia K. Katyal proposes the idea of "sexual sovereignty" to address various battles on the fault line between culture, identity, and sexuality, claiming that

the Supreme Court decision in *Lawrence v. Texas* "serves as a starting point with which to build a theoretical model for global sexual autonomy that encompasses many of the anti-essentialist critiques offered by human rights discourse, critical race theory, and queer theory" (1435). Nevertheless, her theory of sexual sovereignty builds on ideas of "independence, personhood, autonomy, and impermeability" (1461), without considering their relation to disabled people as a sexual minority. Lisa Duggan offers an incisive analysis of the use of gay marriage and reproductive rights to advance the reconfiguration of American citizenship rights, arguing that the Right seizes on such cultural issues to conceal its determination to stimulate upward redistribution rather than downward redistribution of economic resources and power (*Twilight*). Finally, Eithne Luibhéid focuses on immigrant sexual minorities, noting that sexuality is an especially dense intersection for power relations bearing on citizenship and noncitizenship.

2. In most cases, however, the women's worries turn out not to be true: "Wherever and whenever the first intercourse took place, all women recollected it as a positive experience: 'I was relieved that my rape-fantasies were wrong'" (Westgren and Levi 312).

2

....

RUSSELL SHUTTLEWORTH

BRIDGING THEORY AND EXPERIENCE

A Critical-Interpretive Ethnography of

Sexuality and Disability

Research on sexuality and disability has historically taken little account of the lived experiences of disabled people. In its formative years (roughly the 1950s through the 1970s), this work focused primarily on sexual functioning, predominantly that of heterosexual men. "Penile Erection Following Complete Spinal Cord Injury in Man" is a typical journal article title from the period (Chapelle et al.). The 1980s through the mid-1990s saw the addition of important issues to the research agenda, such as sexual abuse and the psychological measurement of sexual self-esteem; and gradually women have been included as research participants. A recent review of the research literature from 1997 through 2007 reveals that further diversification is occurring (Shuttleworth and Gore 1–2). Yet researchers continue to resist tackling issues that raise ethical dilemmas, such as facilitated sex; they neglect to include certain groups of disabled people in their research, such as queers; and for the most part, they situate their work within a functional paradigm of sex, although this paradigm has been expanded to include the psychosocial functioning of normative sexual relationships (Shuttleworth and Gore 1–2). Most significantly, disabled people's senses of their sexuality and of their everyday sexual interactions remain under-researched.

Resisting the prevalent objectifying approaches, a recent body of work by disabled writers and artists and their allies prioritizes the diverse voices of disabled people and foregrounds their own reflections on their sexuality. In interviews, memoirs, and personal essays, disabled people have countered the limitations of functional or medical interpretations of their sexuality, creating spaces in which they can talk straightforwardly about sex in their lives. Disabled people's claiming of the authority to describe their own bodies and experiences has been foundational to disability scholarship and activism; it has made possible disability studies' radical reconceptualization of disability as a form of social oppression rather than of individual pathology. Yet many of these first-person accounts of sexuality and disability lack theorization of the complex social, historical, cultural, and political conditions under which the lived experiences they recount take shape. Moreover, despite a growing recognition within academic discourses that both sexuality and disability are socioculturally constructed categories of experience, few politicized scholarly analyses take both sexuality and disability as their topics.

Theorization of sexuality and disability has been especially lacking in terms of discussion of disabled people's sexual access. Sexuality studies has not embraced the sexual access concerns of marginalized groups as a scholarly issue; neither has a recently emerging body of work in disability studies that is beginning to theorize sexuality focused much on this problem.[1] In the latter case, this might seem fitting. After all, the notion of access has historically been tied to a rights-based understanding of equality, pertaining to public spheres rather than private ones. However, what I have in mind is an elaborated sense of access that theorizes the effect that sociopolitical processes and structures and symbolic meanings have on disabled people's sense of desirability, sexual expression and well-being, sexual experiences, and embodied sexual feelings, as well as the resistance they often deploy against sexual restrictions (Shuttleworth, "Disability" 178–80). Much of the new work in disability studies on sexuality tends to focus upon representations and discursive structures, rather than on disabled people's interpretations of experience and of the multiple barriers that can impede their sexual expression. This new work is innovative and theoretically sophisticated; among its important contributions is its attention to the social and discursive structures that make experience articulable as such. Yet indispensable as is the insight that "lived experience" is itself constructed, what often gets lost in poststructuralist analyses of disability is any sense of disabled people's everyday interpersonal interactions or of their own interpretations of these encounters.

In this chapter, I argue for studies of sexuality and disability that take seriously what disabled people themselves actually do and say. Elucidating a critical-interpretive ethnographic approach, I discuss research that I conducted on the sociosexual situation of men with cerebral palsy in the San Francisco Bay Area in the mid- to late 1990s. I also demonstrate the importance of elaborating the concept of access in analyses of disabled people's sexual lives. The fourteen men I interviewed, despite a diversity of ethnic, racial, and sexual identifications, had in common a strong sense of encountering multiple, often intractable, barriers to being perceived as sexual beings and to accessing sexual experiences. Critical-interpretive ethnography, while grounding itself in participants' understandings of their lived experiences, also elucidates the cultural and sociopolitical contexts that give shape and meaning to these experiences. In other words, it neither naively accepts "experience" at face value nor eschews it in favor of "theory." Critical-interpretive ethnography thus brings together the strengths of methodologies that analyze social and discursive structures and those that attend closely to personal experience. For this reason, it is uniquely suited to a study of "sexuality" and "disability," categories of experience that, although they are both highly constructed, are also felt as deeply personal.

ETHNOGRAPHY'S COLLABORATIVE FICTIONS

Lived experience cannot naively be considered a natural process or product. Participants interpret their experience using cultural lenses forged within particular social and familial locations and personal circumstances. The task of the ethnographer is to show the continuity and diversity of interpretations within a community. Indeed, whether practiced by insider, ally, or more traditional outsider ethnographer, ethnography is a research process in which the ethnographer cultivates familiarity and intimacy with research participants in order to observe their everyday interactions and to elicit a diversity of interpretations. These interactions and accounts are progressively contextualized and conceptualized by each participant and the researcher, first within their own terms and then in terms of other participants' accounts. What results is a mutual construction (as many social theorists and human science researchers have observed) and in some sense a negotiated fiction.[2] But as Kirsten Hastrup observes, "Not any fiction will do. . . . We . . . investigate the lived space, which is the experiential counterpart of the implication of cultural space. . . . It will be understood that this is not solely an ideational space, but one which is made up of people and actions" (47).[3]

Consider the collaborative process of interpreting the following quote by Dirk, who has dysarthric speech and uses a wheelchair for mobility; Dirk is one of fourteen men with cerebral palsy whom I interviewed.[4]

DIRK: I used to have trouble breathing. Like if I was laying down with someone, I would get these—well, my disability sort of manifests itself. If I'm upset I have trouble with my diaphragm, maybe it's my throat, anyway, that's how I lose control, I have trouble breathing. . . . It would feel terribly inappropriate. I would feel scared, I would say to myself, why am I feeling scared when I should be feeling anything—I should be feeling the opposite, well, I was excited. I was scared maybe because I was excited. But I think I was scared because—I'm not sure, I guess anticipation of something that I wanted very much. My body, always—well, not always but often betrays me. I feel that undermines me. The one thing that you don't need is less control; you need more control. You don't want to be—it's not very attractive or romantic to have a hard time breathing, to have a hard time laying still, it's just not, and also for me it's very distracting. I mean, forget the other person, it's me too. I can't—it ruins the mood. Like, my body is almost jealous in a funny way. If my body were another person—this is a strange thing to say, but I think it's a jealous woman or a jealous other, not necessarily a woman but a jealous third being. There's me, and then there's the woman, and then there's my body. Usually you and your body are in sync and in agreement with what you're doing, but sometimes it's almost as if my body is behaving as if it didn't want me to do this. I think that what I'm exhibiting are symptoms of fear.

RUSSELL: About what?

DIRK: Well, I don't know. Breathing hard, sweating, it's as if I'm terrified, but I'm not sure why, I'm not sure what it is. If you looked at me, if you did some kind of objective reading of me with some machine, somebody would say, this person's scared. They wouldn't say, this person's sexually aroused. They wouldn't say, I can tell he's in an intimate situation. This person is facing, not a potential sex partner but a lion or a person who is going to assault him. I don't necessarily have those emotions; I'm not afraid emotionally, but my body seems to be behaving like it's afraid. But I don't really have access to what the root of that fear is; I think it's afraid like an animal is afraid. I don't know—you know when you first get an animal and it isn't tamed? You have to be very gentle, and you can't always pet it; I need to be tamed very slowly. I needed to be tamed and the animal, I don't know what—I guess it's afraid of being harmed, but of course it isn't aware of it. And my body—I'm not aware of it, but my body seems to be.

Dirk had been repeatedly rejected whenever he attempted to move a friendship to a more sexual place. In one interview he characterized what he believed women meant by this limitation: "You can come in my house, but leave your dick outside!" Harlan Hahn put it well almost thirty years ago, when he wrote: "In a society dominated by physical standards and conventions which visibly disabled persons seldom can hope to approximate, they are frequently compelled to assume a role that denies the sexual aspects of their being" ("Social" 226). This was substantiated by many of the men whom I interviewed.

For Dirk even when he was finally on the verge of being sexually intimate with a woman, his difficulties were not over. Although Dirk knew the conditions that would trigger his bodily betrayal, he could not cohere all aspects of his sociosexual situation into a satisfying theory of his fear. My contribution relied on situating the story of this particular fear in the context of his entire narrative, drawing from his discussion of his theories about his hypersensitivity and of the judgment that he felt often came between him and nondisabled others in social situations more generally. For example, we were discussing the issue of "putting yourself out there socially." Dirk had just told me a story about a recent everyday social encounter in which he "fell apart" because he felt he was being judged. I asked him to expand on what he thought was going on in such situations:

I respond a lot to what I think the other person's putting out . . . people who I think are a little iffy, I kind of fall apart with. I lose control physically because I lose control emotionally, unfortunately. So even though I had just finished tutoring people all day without even thinking about my speech, all of the sudden I found that—I could talk, but I was having more trouble [inaudible] . . . that was because I was feeling—my best answer is that I was responding to his doubts about me. I mean that's a kind of small example, we were talking about people who try and who are out there. But I think the reason that you're out there or not is made up of many . . . individual encounters, the sum total of which either they leave you confident or . . . they undermine you. As I get older I'm better at it, but it's still hard for me. . . . I think that people will look at me and think I'm a fool or an idiot.

Like I look funny, so therefore I must be less [inaudible] . . . I'm a little too empathetic. Empathy is a double-edged sword [inaudible]. When I want to torture myself, I often imagine how I would be under torture.

As William Wilkerson notes, "experiences have meaning only in relation to the broader context in which they are experienced" (260). From Dirk's discussion of not only other sexual encounters but also, importantly, of nonsexual interactions in which he experiences what he describes as "empathy" with another's evaluative gaze, he and I constructed a coherent interpretation of his fear in sexual situations. My part was to provide some of the theoretical glue to bind together his various insights into both his sexual and nonsexual interpersonal encounters and to help crystallize a plausible explanation. Given the background of his hypersensitivity to the evaluative gaze, it appeared that Dirk had become habituated to staying on the platonic side of the line between friendship and sexual intimacy and that crossing that line had severe bodily consequences. His embodied fear of being rejected as a lover results not only from his social dys-appearance (his failure, that is, to conform to nondisabled carnal contexts of meaning)—although this does underlie his sense of bodily difference—but also from his empathetic incorporation of others' evaluative gazes in everyday habitual interactions. During a sexual encounter, although Dirk intellectually understands that he is finally being allowed to cross a boundary, his body responds out of habit, as if he were still being judged.

Ethnographic interpretations are collaborative fictions whose stories resonate in meaningful ways with the diversity of research participants' interpretations of their lived experience. Collaboration also exists in situating these individual accounts in relation to one another, as patterns of similarities and differences are noted and then interjected by the ethnographer into conversations and interviews to elicit participants' sense of what they mean. In addition, ethnographic interpretations must be analyzed and situated within a heuristic schema of the relevant personal, sociocultural, and political contexts.

A CRITICAL-INTERPRETIVE ETHNOGRAPHY
OF SEXUALITY AND DISABILITY

In the late 1980s Nancy Scheper-Hughes and Margaret Lock developed a critical-interpretive heuristic schema that has been extremely influential in medical anthropology. This schema consists of three bodies: the individual or lived body;

the social body; and the body politic. Each of these bodies corresponds to a particular level of analysis: phenomenological, social-symbolic, and political-structural. Scheper-Hughes and Lock's goal was to reveal the interactions among these three bodies in "the production and expression of health and illness" and to show in particular how emotions often functioned to mediate among them ("Mindful" 31). More broadly, Scheper-Hughes and Lock's approach participated in anthropology's renewal of cultural critique in the 1970s and 1980s, drawing especially from the critical theory of the Frankfurt School, whose work had moved beyond a strict Marxian approach to incorporate criticism of science and culture.[5] Their approach also reflects interpretive anthropology's focus on reflexivity and hermeneutics, stresses the negotiation of meanings in specific localities, and explores the symbolism that pervades human social life (Lock and Scheper-Hughes, "Critical" 48–50).[6] Scheper-Hughes and Lock's approach thus explicitly incorporates a critique of symbolic meanings and their social import and the structuring of contexts in terms of their political import; but it also attempts to show how participants contend with and resist these meanings and structures in their daily practices, embodied experiences, and emotional lives. Their tripartite schema was proposed as a heuristic device; in discourse and experience, all three bodies overlap.

Critical-interpretive ethnography, minus the focus on health and illness favored by Scheper-Hughes and Lock, is well suited for interrogating the sexual access issues of disabled people in which sociocultural meanings, political structures, and disabled people's interpersonal interactions converge in particular sociosexual situations. A social-symbolic analysis can ascertain how cultural meanings of disability and sexuality imbue disabled people's sociosexual situations; a political-structural analysis can reveal how particular hierarchies and relations of power are embedded in these meanings of disability and sexuality and disabled people's sociosexual situations; and an analysis of disabled peoples' interpretations of their lived experiences can impart how their felt sense incorporates and resists these meanings and hierarchical relations in everyday life.[7]

THE INCORPORATION OF SEXUAL OPPRESSION

The ethnographic research I conducted focused on the sociosexual situation of fourteen men with cerebral palsy who lived independently in the San Francisco Bay Area. I recorded their personal life histories; their sexual narratives, including stories of sexual rejection and successes; their theories on why they experi-

Russell Shuttleworth

enced sexual prejudice and oppression in interpersonal relations and from the larger society; my participant observations of their daily life and any sexually relevant encounters and interactions that occurred. While more than half of these men had been involved in sexual relationships at one time or another, and in fact several men were in relationships when I was interviewing them, most of them conveyed to me a powerful sense of their contention with what they perceived as negative prejudices toward their sexuality. They offered many insights about the sources of these negative views, providing theories that ranged from a Darwinian account of survival of the fittest to a sensitively drawn psychodynamic model; I included many of their ideas in the final ethnographic text. Their diverse perspectives had in common a concern with what, retrospectively, I have defined as sexual access.

The disability rights movement and disability studies often use the notion of access to evaluate the effects of a disabling society. But while barriers to disabled people's sexual expression and experiences have certainly been noted in prior work (Shakespeare, Gillespie-Sells, and Davies 16–43), disability studies scholars have balked at taking the extra step of theorizing this state of affairs as an access issue.[8] Perhaps this reluctance occurs in part because putting sexuality on par with such topics as education, work, and the built environment shatters the cultural fantasy that sex and love are somehow separate from the mundanity of everyday life. Making sexuality an access issue, however, politicizes disabled people's sexual lives and, in doing so, demands a critique of the concept's prior restriction to rights-based discourse. A quote from one of the participants in this research clearly illustrates this point: "I don't give a flying fuck about the ADA because that's not gonna get me laid!" (qtd. in Shuttleworth, "Search" 264).[9] Indeed, there are clearly many aspects of sexuality and desire in contemporary cultural contexts that can benefit from critique, especially in conjunction with a political analysis of disability. For example, preferences for certain physical and social characteristics in a sexual partner vary across cultures, and access to typical avenues of sexual expression and sexual negotiation are highly influenced by how well one embodies the cultural norms and expectations of personhood and desirability in a society. In present-day U.S. society, for instance, expectations of masculine dispositions and practices, efficient bodily functioning, self-sufficiency, and so on, set up an adverse context with which disabled men must contend. In one way or another, all barriers encountered by the men with whom I conducted fieldwork can be traced to these men's perceived failure to adequately embody these social norms and expectations.

Carl, a disabled college student, analyzes the ways in which normative meanings and expectations act upon his sexual sense of self and constrain him in his sexual negotiations with desired others:

> I don't even envision myself as a sexual individual. I pretty much see myself as asexual. Not that I don't have sexual feelings, but like me in a relationship seems too foreign and so impossible . . . because I can't see myself doing it. Part of me doesn't feel worthy. . . . I think *the biggest barrier for me is me*. I don't feel adequate and it's sort of like, a circular reason sort of thing. . . . The reason that I don't feel adequate is because of other things out of my control, like social constructions of the body, of masculinity, of my ability to do the proper kind of courtship and stuff. . . . So when I say *the biggest barrier is me*, yeah me but "it's me" consists of a lot of external factors that are not within my control.

Brent, a thirty-two-year-old gay man, refers specifically to how his body image is affected: "I was not good at meeting people and I didn't have a very good image of myself, especially in regards to feeling attractive and feeling sexy. . . . You're not going to fit the look that many people are looking for if they have a pretty narrow physical type. . . . Very rarely am I going to fit that real well because I walk with crutches and I don't sit up straight and my body is relatively undeveloped." One analytical tool that was particularly useful in apprehending these men's sense of contention within their sociosexual situation was analysis of the lived metaphors they used.[10] Lived metaphors are ontological metaphors that disclose "the interdependency of body and mind, self and world" (Jackson 9). "Falling," for example, is similarly felt ontologically as disorienting, whether it is a physical fall or a social fall that is the actual referent. The most striking metaphors these men employed to describe their sociosexual situations were of barriers such as walls and other kinds of blockages. These metaphors enabled the participants to describe complex convergences of cultural, sociopolitical, and interpersonal layers of exclusion in ways that indicated an embodied sensitivity to their sociosexual situation. Several men predominantly employed metaphors locating these barriers in society's normative expectations or in the explicit and implicit rejections of those with whom they desired sexual intimacy. For example, Jim, a man with both a mobility and a speech impairment told me: "after I get to know them better and they know me, I will try to make certain advancements, and *a wall will come*; and that's when I get very mad and angry because I don't understand the purpose of *that wall*, and I don't believe that I'm moving too fast or anything, but I'm often surprised at how fast *that wall comes up.*"

Some men's metaphors, however — even though the men rationally know it is the other's evaluative gaze that fixes them as lacking sexuality and masculinity — tended to focus on themselves. They spoke of themselves as having constructed protective barriers ("I've *blocked off* that sexual part of me"), or they focused on an aspect of the self that seemed to stifle their intentions ("the dark or weak side of me rises up"). A few men used metaphors that spoke simultaneously of others' resistances to their sexual overtures and to their own sexual self-doubts. Josh, for example, who uses a wheelchair and communication board, in describing his experience of wanting but not being able to express romantic interest to a particular woman, would tell me, "Russell, I feel *blocked.*" Such metaphors were the most striking indication of what is often termed internalized oppression, but what I think would better be described as an embodied incorporation of adverse cultural meanings and habituation to sociosexual rejection.

In Josh's particular case, we explored the contexts surrounding the use of his metaphors, and I brought into play my long-term observations and participation in his everyday life.[11] I interpreted his sense of blockage as expressing simultaneously his implicit self-comparison to hegemonic ideals of attractiveness and desirability, an embodied (felt) sense of others' resistance to seeing him in a sexual light, and the grip that these had on his self-agency. Josh, it seemed to me, felt this barrier ontologically, as a culturally derived hierarchical structuring of desirability and body-self values that effected sociosexual force and that negatively gripped his sexual agency (Shuttleworth, "Symbolic" 76). This interpretation shows how social-symbolic and political-structural aspects imbue Josh's felt sense within his particular sociosexual situation. I presented this interpretation to him, albeit in less conceptual terms, and Josh conveyed to me that it indeed made sense.

RESISTING THE IMPOSITION OF ASEXUALITY

Most of the men I interviewed intermittently resisted the cultural imposition of an asexual status upon them. Some were particularly adept at what I term "defusing the adverse context of disability and desirability"; that is, they were able to psychically, emotionally, and socially render virtually impotent the cultural meanings and interpersonal relations that worked to deny their sexuality. In a sense, defusing is the transformation of these men's everyday contentions with barriers to sexual intimacy into a mode of resistance in which they refuse to resign themselves to the ways that they are negatively perceived in the cultural imaginary. This move has previously been interpreted as inverting or reversing dominant cultural perceptions of asexuality, transforming them into the basis of a positive sense of sexuality (Guldin, "Self" 236). For example, David, who uses a wheelchair and has dysarthric speech, describes the process of reframing his despair by turning upside down the sexual hierarchy in which, he perceived, he was positioned at the bottom: "it became increasingly like I was reaching into society's sleeve and turning it completely inside out. And from the moment of very, very deep despair, I was able to completely turn the situation around. And I chose the most comfortable situation, which was, I would say, 'I was sane living in an insane world'" (qtd. in Shuttleworth, "Pursuit" 207). An active resistance enabled some of these men to take advantage of the nonconventional contexts that they inhabited, such as rehabilitation hospitals, summer camps for disabled adolescents, 1970s communes, and the interpersonal situation of being provided with personal assistance. In these spaces sexual interactions might occur and relationships bloom. Then, too, resistance could lead to employing nonnormative bodily functioning as sexual catalysts. For example, one man gave sensual massages with his feet, and another incorporated his spasticity into his lovemaking. Countering the normative view of desire and desirability by the deployment of sexuality with their own sexualized bodily difference, several of these men further developed an alternative sexual ethics through certain self-practices (Shuttleworth, "Pursuit" 216–21). For example, Fred, who uses a wheelchair and an alphabet board and is in a group marriage with several women and men, was able to cultivate a shift in his own life and in the lives of many of those with whom he comes into contact by facilitating nude performances involving communal intimacy: a shift from genitally focused sex to intimate erotic play in which emotional communication is prized.[12]

Resistance can also take collective form, as in the movement for disabled people to be included on the sexual rights agenda (Shakespeare, "Sexual Politics" 159; Shuttleworth, "Disability" 192–94). What Anne Guldin refers to as disabled people's current "claiming of sexuality" counters the cultural myth of asexuality and undesirability and marks a collective bid for sexual subjectivity ("Self" 232). For example, the Sins Invalid performance in 2006 in San Francisco showcased a diversity of artists whose bodily configurations transgress normative models. These artists expressed themselves on sundry sexual issues with the intent of challenging the dominant cultural understanding of disabled sexuality and what constitutes a desirable body. As the advertisement for the show boldly proclaimed:

> Sins Invalid: An Unashamed Claim to Beauty in the Face of Invisibility. Sins Invalid invites a re/view of embodiment, with performers and video artists speaking their minds and stripping taboos off of sexuality and disability. A performance event to reveal poetic bodies and hot activism, it is a healing for all who challenge themselves honestly when unearthing sexual expression. Expect to hear an unabashed claim of desirability in a world of embodied and enforced norms.

Is this particular collective claiming of sexuality in the face of a hierarchy of social personhood and bodily desirability, however, simply a bid for normative sexual subjectivity? Or does it indicate something more? In short, do images such as "poetic bodies" and "hot activism," both in the show's advertisement and also performed on stage that night, reveal an aspiring impetus to search out new terms of erotic understanding beyond those circumscribed by desire (Foucault, *History* 157)?

TRANSFORMATIONS?

Several years ago, buoyed from talks with several research participants on their erotic cultivation of particular bodily and functional differences and their impetus toward creative sexuality, I concluded: *Disabled sex* could assist in transforming our vision of sexuality from one of function, hierarchy, idealized relationships to one of creative communication. Certainly, disabled sex as more creative than non-disabled sex was an interpretive move by participants to invert ability and disability (Guldin, "Self" 236). Yet to limit this move to inversion would be to ignore the heightened awareness of communication that can sometimes be obtained through creative endeavor and would thus strip it of an implicit transformative potential" ("Pursuit" 293).[13] From a different but no less culturally suggestive perspective, Margrit Shildrick's recent work theorizes disabled people in their everyday lives as assuming a performative interconnectivity (for example, through the use of personal assistants or prosthetic devices) that "break[s] with the putative emergence of a coherent sexual subject from practices of embodiment" and allows for transformative possibilities ("Queering" par. 17). In a larger sense that also moves beyond the focus on disabled people's sexuality, Shildrick further suggests that the restrictive "performativity of (sexual) subjectivity could be radically transformed" for everyone if the Western notion of the autonomous individual and integrated identity were opened up to allow for more flexibility ("Queering" par. 20). While Shildrick acknowledges that "it is not that disability is a unique case, but only that its forms of embodiment seem to overdetermine the fragility and instability of corporeality in general," the implication is clear that disabled bodies can serve as a window onto the construction and transformation (and thus transformative potential) that all bodies undergo ("Queering" par. 20).

Yet while I would not want to dampen a visionary aspiration, in disability studies and the larger culture, toward the transformation of desire and sexual subjectivity into terms based less on hierarchy and more on interconnectivity and intimate communication, perhaps my inclination for ethnographic grounding requires that I raise a note of caution. Indeed, speculations about cultural transformation are far removed from most disabled people's immediate concerns. In fact, despite the erotic cultivation of bodily difference by some of the men I interviewed, the immediate aspiration for the majority was to bring into and maintain in their own lives sexually intimate relations with others, without necessarily transforming cultural understandings. Only later in several of the men's description of their development is there an overt understanding of the cultural stakes involved (Shuttleworth, "Disability" 192). And while notions of impairment or disability, shorn of their employment as markers of identity, as paradigmatic models of subjectivity, or as suggestive of potentiality, are seductively invoked in disability theory in the past decade, in retrospect such analyses may appear to have participated in a degree of romanticism.[14] Human science researchers are continually reminded of the significance of cultural context and social location for the particularities of a group's pragmatic situation in the world and their identification with, and interpretive perspectives on, that situation. It might therefore be prudent to exert a certain cautious skepticism in our aspirations to transpose positively construed local outcomes to a more general cultural sense, even though the notion of sex as creative communication and perception of the fragility and instability of corporeality may be open to all. Any such attempts will inevitably entail arduous conceptual and pragmatic challenges.

Russell Shuttleworth

NOTES

The research in this chapter was assisted by a fellowship from the Sexuality Research Fellowship Program of the Social Science Research Council with funds provided by the Ford Foundation. I want to thank Anna Mollow for important critical feedback.

My use of the term "sexuality" in this chapter does not strictly accord with certain uses of the term, influenced by Michel Foucault, that are common in the humanities today. A Foucauldian understanding of sexuality certainly lends itself to analysis of the deployment of this historical formation and its manifold effects on subjects. Nevertheless, participants in the research I report on in this chapter interpret their sexuality as a multilayered, dynamic, and expressive aspect of their sense of self. While on one level this reaffirms Foucault's analysis, and I sometimes employ the term in his sense, I also want to respect participants' understanding of the complexity of this notion as they believe it plays out in their lived experience, especially when using the concept of sexual access. I have used the term "sex" sparingly in this chapter, because I do not want sexual access to be misconstrued as simply about physically intimate encounters and relationships (even when that is the overt meaning in a particular case).

1. In 2002 Linda Mona and I referred to some of the many issues that disabled people confront in their sexual lives as sexual access issues (Shuttleworth and Mona 2–5).

2. See, for example, Holstein and Gubrium 141–42; Clifford 6–7; Lock and Scheper-Hughes 48–49.

3. Depending on their theoretical proclivities, different researchers working with the same participants would construct different ethnographies, although many participant concerns would likely remain similar. In the spirit of critical theory, however, an emancipatory principle remains central to my research, according to which social responsibility to participants is a mandatory component. See Meekosha and Shuttleworth 51–56; and Shuttleworth, "Disability" 181–84.

4. All names are pseudonyms. I chose to study men in order to facilitate participant and researcher rapport during interviews on what I considered a very sensitive topic. However, I also interviewed a few women for a gender contrast. In retrospect, my fears that women would not open up to a male interviewer appear to have been unfounded. My snowball sample turned up eleven men who were solely attracted to women; one gay man; one man who, although identifying as heterosexual and in a relationship with a woman when I interviewed him, had experienced several brief "one nighters" with men and following the completion of the study came out as gay; and another man who was in a group relationship with several men and women. The latter man refused to categorize his sexual orientation, although in many hours of interviewing him and in the fourteen years I have known him, he appears more sexually attracted to women.

5. For a consideration of anthropology's renewal of cultural critique, see Marcus and Fischer.

6. It bears repeating that Clifford Geertz, the acknowledged guru of interpretive anthropology, was significantly influenced by Paul Ricoeur's hermeneutics and his textual approach to human interaction (Geertz 3–30).

7. I don't want to give the impression that the critical-interpretive ethnography that participants and I fashioned was strictly oriented by Scheper-Hughes and Lock's approach. Theirs was simply one perspective among many that formed the background to the conceptual framework that I employed. However, in retrospect their heuristic device of the three bodies encapsulates neatly the aspects that were important for me to elucidate. In an important paper that predates my own write-up, Anne Guldin explicitly refers to Scheper-Hughes and Lock's notion of the lived body in her own ethnography of the sexuality of seven mobility-impaired persons in the United States ("Claiming" 45–48). To my mind, though, Guldin fails to adequately flesh out this idea in the texture of her participants' lived experience.

8. Tom Shakespeare's work on sexuality and disability references the British social model, discusses some of the social and cultural barriers that disabled people encounter in their sexual lives, and also suggests the relevance of other disciplinary and conceptual perspectives (for example, sexual citizenship, feminism, and queer theory) in tantalizing ways but does not rigorously theorize sexual access. I am nevertheless deeply indebted to Shakespeare's groundbreaking work.

9. As I have argued in my other work, the concept of access resonates with an existential-phenomenological sense of being obstructed—or not—in our everyday experiences of the world. The existential resistance and felt obstruction toward an intention can be (but, of course, is not always) the cue to our restricted access or exclusion from a sociocultural context within a society that may or may not be amenable to rights-based strategies. See Shuttleworth, "Disability" 179.

10. See Shuttleworth, "Pursuit" 166–89; and "Symbolic" 79–89.

11. I have been a friend of Josh's for many years and first started working for him as a personal assistant in 1984. In the mid- to late 1990s, I also resided with him as a live-in personal assistant, at which time he became the main participant in the study.

12. This is not to say that genitals and orgasms are banned from Fred's eroticism, just that they are not accorded dominant status. See Shuttleworth, "Pursuit" 209–16.

13. I am indebted to Linda Mitteness for helping me clarify that an aspect of what these men were trying to convey was a change in the meaning of sex from instrumental self-gratification to emotionally charged erotic communication. Although this is most clearly seen in Fred's story, it is also implied in some of the other men's accounts.

14. See, for example, Davis, *Bending* 9–32.

3

....

MICHEL DESJARDINS

THE SEXUALIZED BODY OF THE CHILD

Parents and the Politics of "Voluntary" Sterilization

of People Labeled Intellectually Disabled

According to social sciences literature of the past few decades, the sexuality of people labeled intellectually disabled has been systematically repressed within Western societies since the rise of the Industrial Revolution and the bourgeois moral order (Gateaux-Mennecier 81). During the past two hundred years, this literature posits, two rival images have been used to legitimize the containment of the sexuality of these people: the seraphic idiot and the Mephistophelic idiot (Block 250).[1] The seraphic idiot is a person labeled intellectually disabled who is believed to be an eternal child: pure and asexual, guileless and fragile, and unable to face the dangers of sexuality (Dupras, "Désexualisation" 47; Edgerton 97). In contrast, the Mephistophelic idiot is a wild and diabolical being, half-beast and half-demon, dominated by instincts, without morals or law, concupiscent and libidinous, whose hyper-sexuality jeopardizes the security of the social order (Block 245; Gateaux-Mennecier 32; Ryan and Thomas 102). Even if these two figures had been part of the Christian imaginary since its beginning (Stiker, "Symbolisations" 37), they acquired a new profile at the turn of the industrial age, when asexuality (for the seraphic idiot) and depraved sexuality (for the Mephistophelic idiot) suddenly became their dominant traits.

Medicine and social work had the mission of identifying and controlling those among the pauperized, the outcast, and the "defective" who were not sexually disciplined before they spoiled the whole of society; it did so by way of therapies or eugenic measures (Stiker, "Franchir" 237). In the case of people labeled "idiots," "morons," or "feebleminded," according to the authors of that time, unbridled sexuality could take two opposite forms, one passive, the other active. Some of the "feebleminded" were held to be too vulnerable to resist the advances of the unruly; by contrast, others were held to be insatiable sexual predators. In response to these opposing representations, some factions of society felt an urgent need to protect the angelic idiot from the dangers of sexuality, while other factions wanted to protect society from the lasciviousness and the vices of the demonic idiot. Between 1800 and 1960, three measures were adopted in order to attain both of these goals: institutionalization, eugenic sterilization, and special education (Stiker, "Symbolisations" 40; Gateaux-Mennecier 115). These three measures and the two rival figures of the idiot (seraphim and Mephistopheles) began to be criticized by the beginning of the 1960s, coinciding with the emergence of civil rights movements. Scientists, health professionals, educators, workers in community-based organizations, and parents of intellectually disabled people began to criticize the pitiful life conditions within asylums and the involuntary sterilization of many residents. This movement of reforms rapidly extended beyond the asylum to contest other forms of discrimination toward people labeled intellectually disabled (Rodier 7).

Today in Quebec, where I conducted the research I will discuss in this chapter, most people labeled "intellectually disabled" live within the community, and their rights are highly respected by public institutions and services. Involuntary sterilization became illegal two decades ago, and the majority of service institutions have adopted charters that protect the sexual rights of mentally disabled individuals. From a legal, governmental, and institutional perspective, during the past forty years individuals labeled intellectually disabled have been progressively stripped of their imagined sacred attributes (seraphic or Mephistophelic), as their full humanity and right to be regular members of society have been affirmed. Nevertheless, Pamela Block and others note, the figure of the Mephistophelic idiot is still invoked today, both in the defense of those accused of sexual abuse against intellectually disabled women and in the prosecution of intellectually disabled men accused of sexual crimes (245).[2] In contrast, she and other researchers note, some contemporary parents see their intellectually disabled children as asexual and chaste seraphim, juvenile and lacking in any erotic desire, and unable to face the many dangers of sexuality (such as abuse, prostitution, illness, and unwanted pregnancies).[3] In conformity with this representation, Block and others claim, parents systematically constrain the sexuality of their disabled children, monitoring all of their social activities and movements in order to prevent exposure to potential dangers.

Contemporary authors agree that people labeled intellectually disabled must be liberated from their parents' confining, overprotective shield. Intellectually disabled individuals must leave the family sanctuary and start to live within the world of adults. However, these authors specify that this passage from the family to the world beyond, from infancy to adulthood, cannot be achieved without the parents' contribution. Therefore, the parents' conceptions of their children must change through education, in order to emancipate them from the archetypal figures of the seraphic idiot or the eternal child. In particular, these researchers argue, the parents must be freed from their superstitions, the phantasms and the taboos that regulate their attitudes toward their children's sexuality and keep them apart from modernity, reason, and human rights.

This research makes important observations and arguments. Yet it is not clear that such a severe and disqualifying judgment does justice to the richness of the parents' ways of life, the complexities of their knowledge systems, or the nuances of their representations of their children. Indeed, none of the authors mentioned above has listened to the stories of the parents in their totality. These authors do not look beyond the references to the angelicism of the child and the worries related to sexuality. They do not attempt to understand from the inside, that is, from the perspective of the cultural meaning systems that structure the parents' lifeworlds, the parents' representations, attitudes, and conduct.

In response to what I regard as an unjustifiable disqualification of the parents of intellectually disabled people, the research I present in this chapter explores parents' representations and attitudes toward the sexuality of their disabled children. Specifically, I aim to reconstruct the cultural meaning systems that structure parents' behaviors, attitudes, and the representations of their intellectually disabled children's sexuality. By means of open-ended and semistructured interviews, fifteen parents were invited to share their visions of their children's status as people; they were asked to share thoughts on their children's social status, body, intelligence, emotions, romantic life, sexuality, desire for children, reproduction, capacity to marry, school education, leisure activities, place in the family, place within society, and future prospects. The sample, which was recruited from twelve families, included twelve mothers and three fathers, whose ages ranged from forty to seventy years. The parents were interviewed three times, with one open-ended life history interview and two semistructured interviews (nine parents individually and six as couples), between January 2000 and May 2000, usually in their homes. The parents resided in various areas of greater Montreal. All were French speakers, and only one was an immigrant to Canada (the seventy-year-old father, who, at the time of the interviews, had lived in Quebec for almost forty years). To recruit participants, I sent letters to the parents of clients of a rehabilitation center and to the members of two relevant community-based associations.

The children of the participants (seven males and five females) were labeled intellectually disabled and were aged between fifteen and twenty-five years (the mean age was eighteen), which means that they were born between 1975 and 1985. This particular era was a period of rapid and significant cultural changes in Quebec regarding the status and the rights of disabled people. By the midseventies, the ideology of normalization and integration had become the dominant trend within service establishments and community-based organizations. Some of the largest institutions in Quebec closed during this time and were replaced by services integrated into the community (Rodier 5). Following the publication of the ministerial document *L'Intégration des Personnes Présentant une Déficience Intellectuelle: Un Impératif Humain et Social* in 1988, the late 1980s were marked by the universalization of programs of reintegration and normalization within the service establishments of the province. During the same period as well, the sexuality of intellectually disabled people began to be normalized and accepted, at least in official discourses and politics. As stated above, involuntary sterilization became illegal, and service establishments and community-based organizations alike began to adopt charters to protect the sexual rights of their clients or members. These included the rights to sex education, sexual rehabilitation (of sexual offenders), protection against sexual abuse, expression of sexuality, reproduction, and parenting. In short, the fifteen participants in this research raised their children during a period of major innovations and changes, filled with optimism for the future of intellectually disabled people, and with the support of governmental agencies and community-based organizations that promoted mainstreaming and normalization in all domains, including sexuality.

In this chapter I explore the attitudes of the parents toward the sexuality of their intellectually disabled children, the parents' visions of their children as people and sexual beings, the parents' strategies for controlling their children's fertility, and the dynamics between the parents' practices and the global social context of which the children are a part. Among other things, I will describe the means by which, despite the recent openness of the parents in regard to the expression of their children's sexuality, the prohibition against reproduction is nonetheless implemented. Further, I will demonstrate that the parents, through the use of the bioethics procedure, succeed at transforming the law banning imposed sterilization into a fiction, a mystification; this transformation, I show, symbolically turns the child's subjugation into assertiveness. Finally, I will consider the ambiguous nature of this mystification, which reflects simultaneously the parents' skillful resistance to the normative power of the state and their submission to this very state, as it confirms that they endorse the extraordinary world that the state—in contradiction of its own laws and politics—actually imposes on their children, namely the "scale model world" of intellectual disability.

THE NEW "EXTRAORDINARY SEXUALITY"

As I was conducting the interviews, I observed with surprise that, contrary to what is claimed in the literature, the parents did not "angelicize" their child, did not "asexualize" him or her, did not transmit to him or her a negative attitude toward sexuality, and did not block the expression of his or her sexuality (Desjardins, "Tabou" 59). Indeed, according to the parents, eight (four males and four females) of twelve adolescents and young adults regularly (involving eleven of the fifteen parents) express nongenital sexuality, and they do so with the approval of their parents, who consider that these exchanges contribute to their child's sexual development. As far as genital sexuality is concerned, eleven young people (the exception is a nineteen-year-old female) practice (or have practiced) autoeroticism, once again with the support of their parents (thirteen parents of fifteen), who consider that masturbation is a normal step of sexual growth. Only one young adult (a twenty-five-year-old female) has access to heterosexual intercourse, with the approval of her mother. Three other young adults (eighteen, nineteen, and twenty-one years old; two females and one male) enjoy parentally supervised access to caressing and mutual masturbation, with parents (four of fifteen) favoring a step-by-step progression toward heterosexual intercourse. Four other parents affirm that, even if their child (seventeen, eighteen, and nineteen years old; three males and one female) has never experienced genital exchanges, he or she will likely eventually do so; the parents not only approve but also encourage this by registering their sons and daughters in sex education courses and by talking about sexuality with them on a regular basis. Five other parents said that because of their children's (fifteen, eighteen, and nineteen years old; three males) mental health problems, severe language disorders, or major cognitive impairments, they are uncertain if they will eventually have intercourse, but they want their children to have this experience because they believe that it will enhance their physical and emotional well-being. In brief, only two parents do not wish such an outcome for their adult child, a nineteen-year-old female. The parents of this young adult believe that genital sexuality is not part of her desires and interests, which the parents equate to those of a five-year-old. By contrast, all the other parents acknowledge that their adolescent or adult children are sexual beings; that masturbation, genital exchanges, and intercourse are, or will be, part of their sexuality; and that they must be taught how to appropriately express sexuality.

Yet despite this new recognition of the importance of genital sexuality in the lives of people labeled intellectually disabled, the sexuality of this group can still be considered abnormal—separated, that is, from the sexuality of the majority, and subjected to a series of extraordinary rules and controls. The adolescents and young adults labeled intellectually disabled are permitted to express nongenital sexuality only within particular spaces, where they can be seen and/or are subject to others' rules (e.g., in supervised ballrooms or in the family house). The child's participation in genital sexual exchanges with others is orchestrated by the parents. Further, the young adult's access to intercourse is subject to three conditions imposed by their parents: use of contraception, precautions against venereal disease, and monogamy with a loved partner. While Malthusian measures, antivenereal prophylaxis, and love are valued in modern societies, they are not usually imposed by a third party. Furthermore, the prohibition against reproduction is one of the dominant features of the social control of the sexuality of mentally disabled people; the ostensible necessity of this prohibition serves to justify the extreme surveillance these individuals are subjected to in every context. It seems that some parents have participated in the creation of a new "extraordinary sexuality" for their adult or adolescent children. This is neither the sexuality of the angel, or the eternal child, nor that of the majority of the population (who are not prohibited from reproducing). As a first step toward investigating the meaning, function, and moral value of this new "extraordinary sexuality," I carefully examine the conceptions and representations that the parents have of their adult and adolescent children, as people and as sexual beings.

In their discourses and stories, the parents represent their children through three images: the "perpetual child," the "normal adolescent or young adult," and the "special adolescent or young adult." In accordance with these three figures, they say that their child is not one but three persons, three entities, each evolving in a distinct world: the world of childhood, the world of mainstream life, and the adapted world of intellectual disability. According to this model, the intellectually disabled person's development is not homogeneous and linear but is instead divided among three parallel times and life cycles, one for each of his or her entities and worlds. The first of these life cycles includes the multiple aspects of the intellectually disabled individual's lifestyle and being that remain youthful despite his or her adolescence or young adulthood. Examples include passion for "children's" toys, movies, and games; reduced competency in some spheres of intellect, such as mathematics, literacy, and temporality; extreme vulnerability; exceptional need for support and protection; unbridled spontaneity; exuberant kindness; unbounded generosity; and remarkably acute emotional intelligence. The second life cycle comprises the diverse aspects of the individual's lifestyle and being that the parents associate with "normal" adolescence or young adulthood. Examples of these include cherished music and clothing, a passion for love, attraction toward sexuality, posters hung in the individual's bedroom, insistent requests for more autonomy, and the miscellaneous daily life competencies that are mastered to proficiency by other people of similar ages. The third life cycle refers to the numerous aspects of the individual's lifestyle and being that take place within adapted contexts or environments: for example, the special pedagogic program within the ordinary class, the special class within the ordinary school, the special high school, the adapted workshop or job, the special dance or adapted holiday camp, the special bowling league, the Special Olympics, the supervised apartment or group home, and so forth. In each of these scenes, the intellectually disabled individual behaves neither as a child nor as a nondisabled adolescent or young adult, but instead as a "special" adolescent or young adult. The individual's life within these enclaves is both like and radically different from that of nondisabled adolescents or young adults. Even if the young person studies, works, practices sports, dances, kisses, goes camping, travels, resides in an apartment, and so on, each of these activities is accomplished at a reduced scale. That is, these "special" activities are designed according to norms, principles, rules, criteria, obligations, privileges, and rights that have been adapted to the intellectually disabled individual's capacities and particular needs (Desjardins, "Jardin" 182).

The parents are convinced that their children will forever remain divided into three persons. Thus, when the individual attains maturity as an adult, he or she will still remain a trinity: a "perpetual child," a "normal adult," and a "special adult." One part of the child will still be puerile, another part will have fully grown into adulthood, and a third part will have blossomed into an exceptional form of adulthood, a miniature version of typical adulthood. The parents infer from this triple identity that their children will never be either completely integrated into society or completely excluded from it. Rather, throughout his or her life, the intellectually disabled person will have to move constantly, as circumstances dictate, between the center and the fringes of collective life. The parents emphasized that they had resisted this sporadic model of social integration for a long time. They had seen this model as contradictory to their initial efforts to integrate their children into the whole of society. But the parents realized, as their children grew up, that total inclusion could not respond to all of their needs, and especially two: the need to succeed in life and the need to belong to a "star group."[4] In other words, the parents have come to think that *sometimes* their adult or adolescent child has a better chance of getting a sense of well-being, and of real satisfaction, from activities and social relationships pursued within the confines of the adapted world of intellectual disability (among peers) than within mainstream society.

THE TRIPLE SEXUALITY OF THE INTELLECTUALLY DISABLED PERSON

Consistent with the model discussed earlier, the parents view the sexuality of their adult and adolescent children in three ways: certain aspects of sexuality are "normal," others are childlike, and some others are adapted to a scale model version of "normal sexuality."[5] Most of the parents (thirteen of fifteen) believe that their children (eleven of twelve) have erotic drives that are similar to anybody else's and that they must be allowed to explore their own bodies, masturbate, exchange kisses, share caresses, engage in foreplay, and, when ready, experience sexual intercourse. These parents are convinced that if their adult or adolescent children are supported adequately, they will eventually be able to enjoy fulfilling erotic bonds. Further, these parents are dedicated to providing their children with appropriate guidance. For the majority of parents (thirteen of fifteen), this attitude toward the intellectually disabled person's rights to express his or her sexuality (eleven of twelve) is not tied to any specific sexual orientation. Twelve parents said that they were convinced that their children were heterosexual, since they had always been strongly attracted to individuals of the other sex. Among this group, ten parents (ten of fifteen) declared that they would not restrain their children's sexual expression (nine of twelve) if they realized that their children were not heterosexual, while two parents (two of fifteen) said that in such a case they would not approve their child's sexual activity (one of twelve, a female). The three other parents (three of fifteen) said that they were not sure about their child's sexual orientation (two of twelve, two males) since they thought that they were still too shy or too young to have clarified this issue. However, they specified that the clarification of this issue would not affect their willingness to respect their sons' need to express their sexuality.

The majority of parents (thirteen of fifteen) also believe that their children have the same capacity to reproduce, and the same likelihood of conceiving non-disabled children, as anybody else. Only two parents, whose children have Down syndrome and Williams syndrome, respectively, believe that there is a high probability that their children would give birth to a disabled newborn. Nevertheless, their adult children's capacity to reproduce worries all the parents, as they do not believe that these intellectually disabled adolescents and young adults will ever be capable of carrying out the role of parent. When the parents speak about this aspect of their child's sexuality, they often stop using the child's first name or the pronouns "he" or "she," favoring instead the plural and category-specific "they." These pronominal substitutions indicate quite clearly the particular moments in which the intellectually disabled person ceases to be viewed by his or her parents as one of "us" and becomes one of "them."

According to almost all the parents (fourteen of fifteen), the combination of their children's desires and capacities to have heterosexual intercourse and their ability to reproduce imperils any children who might be born to them (who would not be looked after appropriately), as well as the intellectually disabled individuals themselves (who would feel both incompetent and alienated when their children were placed for adoption by public services) and the parents of intellectually disabled adults (who would feel forced to be responsible for their grandchildren, taking on a position that they abhor, that of perpetual parent). In order to avoid such disruptive outcomes, these fourteen parents have sought a solution that would take into account their children's capacity to express their sexuality, as well as their unfitness for parenthood. All these parents arrived at the same conclusion: the need to liberate their children from the threatening ability to reproduce in order that they might express genital sexuality in safety. To achieve this goal, the parents required that their child adopt permanent contraceptive devices. Thus, a new sexuality is created for the disabled adolescent or young adult: a "special sexuality" — or, if you prefer, "an adapted sexuality," conceived at the scale of the individual's unfitness — that includes sexual intercourse but prohibits reproduction. This "special sexuality" is the child's "third" sexuality and accords with his or her status as a "special person," as well as with the adapted world of intellectual disability generated by the step-by-step approach of the ideology of normalization (Desjardins, "Jardin" 206; Stiker, "Débat" 33). Indeed, this last sexuality is a miniature, a scaled model — or, if you prefer, a simulacrum — of the sexuality of the majority (Lévi-Strauss 150; Deleuze 297; Goodman 14). The "normal sexual behaviors" that this last sexuality comprises have been stripped of one of their most essential elements, as these are commonly understood in modern liberal democracies — the capacity to procreate — and have been subjected to a series of extraordinary rules, controls, and prohibitions (Becker 111; Durham; 145; Park 39).

THE SEARCH FOR AN APPROPRIATE BIRTH CONTROL DEVICE

Although it was clear to the majority of these parents, from the beginning of their children's puberty, that they had to be liberated from a disruptive ability to procreate, the parents were initially undecided about the best way to achieve this end. At first, they convinced their children to try some form of chemical or mechanical contraceptive device, such as contraceptive pills, condoms, or Depo-Provera injections. However, the parents changed their minds when they realized that their children could not easily use these devices or that they caused side effects or posed long-term health risks. Thus, the parents turned to what they regarded as a safer, less disruptive, more convenient, and more effective solution. Sterilization, they noted, offered the additional advantage of being definitive, thereby liberating the intellectually disabled person forever from the dangers of procreation. Rather than insisting that their children be sterilized right away, the parents took time to think about it, either alone or in conversation with other parents and with the counsel of several rehabilitation and health professionals. At the moment of data gathering, only one adult had been sterilized (a twenty-five-year-old woman). However, almost all the others (ten of eleven) were on their way to being sterilized: in one or two years for those individuals over twenty, in three to five years for those between eighteen and twenty, and in six to eight years for those under seventeen. Sterilization is the result of a long process, which starts when the intellectually disabled person is approximately sixteen to eighteen years old and is usually completed by the time he or she is twenty-one to twenty-three years old.

This decision-making process regarding sterilization can be divided into three steps: the parents' evaluation of the morality and legitimacy of sterilization, the conversion of the intellectually disabled person's desire for offspring into a desire for infertility, and the application for sterilization to a bioethics committee and its eventual fulfillment. In this chapter, I consider the first two steps of this process, as only one adult had reached the third. Once the parents realized that chemical or mechanical contraceptives were not satisfactory solutions for their adult children, they embarked on deliberations between themselves, with other parents, and with various professionals regarding the morality and legitimacy of sterilization. All the parents came to the same conclusion: in this specific case, sterilization is morally ambiguous. On the one hand, it reinforces the intellectually disabled person's otherness and exclusion; on the other hand, it fosters social inclusion by giving him or her access to sexual intercourse. In regard to the intellectually disabled person's otherness and exclusion, the parents considered three specific factors. First, their adolescent or adult child is subjected to an exceptional prohibition. Second, this prohibition deprives him or her of what, for the parents, was a key index of normality and adulthood. And third, the intellectually disabled person loses a part of his or her body. Clearly, it is not easy for these parents to participate in taking away their children's right to procreate and parent; they have fought relentlessly, since their children's births, for normalization and inclusion within most social contexts. At the same time, the parents also feel that the *non*sterilization of the intellectually disabled young adult is also morally ambiguous; by respecting their children's bodily integrity, the parents would endanger both their well-being and their sense of normality. The intellectually disabled person would either be forbidden to engage in sexual intercourse or subject to the seizure of any offspring by child welfare services. Either way, the parents conclude, their children will lose something crucial: if sterilized, fertility and parenthood; if not, sexual intercourse or offspring. Reluctantly, they chose sterilization, as the lesser of two evils.

Since involuntary sterilization is banned nowadays, the parents must convince their child that procreation and parenthood are not desirable and that sterilization is the only suitable means of contraception. Only then can any medical procedures commence. However, parents initially react with ambivalence to these various options. On the one hand, they consider that the law focuses too much on the individual's choice and does not sufficiently take into account their child's •
difficulty in evaluating the consequences of childbirth, as well as his or her inability to become a parent. Further, the parents are annoyed that their voice is almost totally silenced from the deliberations of the bioethics committee, even though the outcome of these deliberations will affect their lives and futures as much as those of their child. In the end, after all, the parents of the intellectually disabled individual will become the de facto parents of their child's newborn. On the other hand, the parents condemn the massive involuntary sterilization drive that marked the first half of the twentieth century, notably within asylums, because of its brutality and lack of concern for the sterilized person's dignity, sensibility, and self-esteem. Of these two options — being at the child's mercy or exposing him or her to brutal treatments — the parents prefer the first. They believe in their chances to make their child see "reason" so that he or she will ask, on his or her own initiative, to be sterilized. In addition, they feel that from this procedure their child will gain a sense of "empowerment," instead of subjugation, since sterilization will appear to everyone as if it were the fruit of his or her own initiative.

The conversion of the child's desire for offspring into a desire for infertility is dispersed, as circumstances dictate, over a period of two to five years, while the child or young adult is between sixteen and twenty-two years of age. This is achieved mainly by means of four persuasion devices: syllogistic method, role-playing, catastrophic rituals, and apocalyptic narratives. Specifically, the parents explain rationally to the child the dangers of reproduction and the necessity of using safe contraceptive device, namely sterilization. They also engage the child or young adult in role-playing that simulates, with the help of dolls or raw eggs, the burden of parenting a newborn. In addition, the parents create babysitting rituals that are designed to demonstrate to their child that without the saving intervention of a "normal adult," a situation could have disastrous consequences for the individual's offspring. Finally, the parents tell the child various apocalyptic narratives that announce the horrors and sufferings that will afflict them all if the mentally disabled individual reproduces. According to the parents, these tactics usually prove fruitful: the young adult not only agrees to sacrifice fertility but claims it as a right and demands to be sterilized. The young adult is then ready to set in motion the final step of the sterilization process, which is to submit an application for sterilization to a bioethics committee and to undergo the surgery. At the moment of data gathering, only one young adult had progressed to this step, but three were just about to submit their applications for sterilization, seven others were involved in the conversion of their desire for offspring into a desire for infertility, and the mother of the last individual was just starting to debate the morality of sterilization.

These persuasion devices, and the anticipated success of the young adult's applications, illuminate the reality that the law banning imposed sterilization is more often than not a fiction, a subterfuge, which mystifies everyone, including the parents. Indeed, once the bioethics application is approved, the hold that the parents had on their child during the second step of the sterilization process is pushed into the background; it appears to have been erased by their child's voice. It is, above all else, the young adult's own will and understanding of sterilization that the bioethics committee evaluates, rather than the process that has led him or her to apply for sterilization. In so doing, the bioethics procedure seemingly turns a fundamentally collective process of subjugation into an assertion of an individual's desire. This semantic reversal makes it a lot easier for everyone to deal with the child's forced sterilization. First, as stated above, the parents antici-pate that their child will not feel alienated by the sacrifice of his or her fertility since he or she will be the one to claim it in order to avoid the torments of invol-untary reproduction. Second, the parents consider that the weight given to their child's voice during the bioethics procedure releases them from the oppressive responsibility of imposing a nonstandard sexual destiny on him or her. In the end, the parents say that sterilization has become their child's personal choice instead of theirs. Finally, the parents underscore that the respect of their child's free will is crucial for global society, since it enables the collectivity to reconcile the moral foundation of modern democratic societies (particularly the notion of equality as defined by human rights) with the sterilization of mentally disabled people.

In addition to the aforesaid advantages, the parents are delighted with the beneficial effects of sterilization on their child's general growth and sexual ful-fillment. In the parents' discourse, the nonsterilized child is considered to be "prenubile"; that is, he or she is sexually unfinished, immature, split into two in-compatible poles (one childish, the other adult) and thus unfit for sexual intercourse. In contrast, the sterilized child is said to be "nubile," or sexually complete: mature, liberated from inner conflicts, and ready to engage in genital exchanges, sexual intercourse, loving ties, and marriage. In other words, the parents conceptualize sterilization as not only a prophylactic device and a manifestation of their child's self-assertion but also as a rite of passage into eroticism, conjugal love, and adulthood.

Before moving on to focusing on the simultaneous resistance and subjugation of the families to the state's order, I would like to underscore the relative homogeneity of these parents' attitudes toward their child's sexuality and reproduction. Indeed, the majority of the parents (thirteen of fifteen) do not angelicize or desexualize their child (eleven of twelve), do not block their child's access to sexual intercourse, and do associate the child's development and well-being with the expression of his or her sexuality. The majority of them (fourteen of fifteen) do also think that their child (eleven of twelve) will never be able to be a parent, that they would be the actual parents of their child's offspring, and that sterilization is a prerequisite for their child's well-being and sexual blossoming. Overall, the few variations among the parents that were observed were related not to their child's gender but to his or her age, his or her assumed impairment, or to the parents' ideological affiliations.

"ADAPTED SEXUALITY" AND "SCALE MODEL WORLD"

The access to genital sexuality and coitus represents a major breakthrough in the sexual life of individuals labeled intellectually disabled. Nevertheless, as outlined above, the sexuality of these twelve adolescents and young adults is still abnormal (i.e., distinct from the sexuality of the majority of the population) because it is subjected to a series of extraordinary requirements, sterility among the most important. This raises a series of questions that the data presented in this chapter do not answer. In the first instance, we do not yet know the reach of this "new extraordinary sexuality" and of this new form of cloaked "imposed sterilization." Are they specific to the greater Montreal area, or are they spread across all of the province of Quebec? Within the population of Montreal, are only a few families, or the majority of them, affected? Are they specific to the French-speaking families, or are they in vogue among all the linguistic, religious, and cultural communities? More broadly, are they spread across Canada, the United States, or even the rest of the Western world, or are they specific to Quebec? For instance, Alain Giami observes the rising popularity of sterilization in France as a pathway to sexual intercourse for people with intellectual disabilities (283). However, Giami does not mention if the symbolic reversal that we have observed in Quebec is also present in France. In the same vein, is the gender uniformity found in this research specific to this sample of parents, or can it be generalized on a broader scale? On another level, we also do not know how the people labeled intellectually disabled actually react to this new exceptional sexuality—or, in line with the normalization vocabulary, to this "adapted sexuality." Do they enjoy it and cherish it, or do they feel alienated from parenthood? Are males and females affected in the same way by the sacrifice of their fertility? And how will they experience their infertility ten or fifteen years from now, when they will be thirty or thirty-five years old? To address these numerous questions, new research should be initiated in forthcoming years that will look, on the one hand, at the dissemination of this "new extraordinary sexuality" across societies, regions, social classes, religions, languages, and cultural belongings, and, on the other hand, at intellectually disabled adults' experiences of sterilization over time. This information won't be sufficient, however, to determine what we should think of this veiled form of "forced sterilization," of this disguised "new extraordinary sexuality," of this "theater of free choice," which facilitates the family's control of their child's fertility and partially dehumanizes him or her by constructing him or her as Other. Nor will it tell us what we should do about these family practices: we should tolerate them or eradicate them? Once again, more research will be needed if we hope to provide answers to these questions. These future research endeavors will first need to establish whether the parents' imposed prohibition on their children's reproduction is detrimental or beneficial to these young adults.

In this respect, the results of some of my previous research suggest that the parents' practices cannot be judged without regard to the global social context (Desjardins, "Jardin" 222). This research observed, for a period of twenty-four months, the world of seventeen adults labeled intellectually disabled who were engaged in rehabilitation programs based on the principles of normalization, designed to initiate them to normal life and to integrate them within global society. The world of these individuals presented four main characteristics: despite their integration into the urban fabric, they were still living in a parallel community made up of the users of the rehabilitation center; the adapted places within which they lived were small-scale replicas of common places; within these enclaves they mimicked, as best they could, the ways and customs of the majority of the population; and their transition from otherness to normality, within the confines of these veiled margins, will never end. Taken in their entirety, these simulacra and mimicries form a "palace of signs" that hides the otherness of these individuals and their exclusion from society behind the signifiers of normality. In other words, these individuals are enclosed in margins where they are taught not to become regular members of society, as declared in the official discourse, but rather "shadows" or "doubles," that is, stylized images of "ordinary people." The "new extraordinary sexuality" that the present chapter describes fits perfectly with that world of images, pretence, simulacra, and "shadows," which is also the world within which these young adults will live once they will leave the family home. Like this "scale model world," this "imposed sterile sexuality" is a miniature, too, that is, a scale model, an adapted version or a simulacrum of the sexuality of "ordinary people," as it is nowadays socially constructed. The body, the self, and the world of people labeled intellectually disabled are thus not isolated units, independent of one another, but parts of a unified whole produced by a series of institutions that are—as suggested notably by Michel Foucault in his theory of power (*Volonté* 132)—partly autonomous and partly interdependent, as well as partly contradictory and partly complementary. Indeed, as soon as we shift our attention from the ideologies, the values, the laws, and the policies of modern society to its actual practices, the contradiction between family and society, between individual parents and the state, vanishes, giving way to concordance, symmetry, and continuity. It is as if the parents resisted society's official discourse—notice, as stated above, that they do it not by creating a counterdiscourse but by twisting, through underground tactical moves, the official discourse from its initial purpose (de Certeau 37)—only in order, ironically and paradoxically, to better adapt to its actual discriminatory practices.[6] Therefore, if we want to eradicate the forced sterilization of people labeled intellectually disabled, we will have to change not only the family's practices, attitudes, or beliefs but also the actual world that modern society has developed for them, namely the world of "shadows" (Desjardins, "Jardin" 187). This involves ultimately changing these aspects of our social, economic, and symbolic order that make this "scale model world"—or, if you prefer, this "veiled margin"—necessary in present-day society. These aspects include notably our obsession for academic success, individual autonomy, competitiveness, and profitability, as well as our intolerance toward unproductive or dependent beings. These factors all continue to justify the confinement of people labeled intellectually disabled into veiled parallel worlds within contemporary society.

NOTES

This research project has been funded by the Conseil québécois de la recherche sociale, the Centre de Recherche CIRADE and the research group Girafe-CRIR. In addition, I would like to thank Shannon Ellis, James Waldram, Raissa Graumans, and Robert Mc-Ruer for linguistic revision and critical advice. Translations of French-language texts and interviews used in the text are mine.

1. I have decided to group under the figures of seraphim and Mephistopheles the representations of people labeled intellectually disabled. These refer respectively to individuals' putative lack of sexuality and vulnerability or to their supposed excess of sexuality and ominous libido. Many different images are used in the literature to evoke these two traits: for seraphim, angel, saint, shamanic healer, perpetual child, heroic Cinderella, and others (Block 241; Giami, Humbert-Viveret, and Laval 103); for Mephistopheles, beast, demonic succubae, libidinous savage, concupiscent primitive, and others (Block 245; Dupras, "Sexualité" 187; Edgerton 97; Kempton and Kahn 107).

2. See also Giami, Humbert-Viveret, and Laval 187; Dupras, "Sexualité" 189; Nuss v.

3. See Giami, Humbert-Viveret, and Laval 47; Block 247; Dupras "Désexualisation" 47 and "Stérilisation" 909.

4. "A star group is the one with which a person identifies most deeply and in which he finds fulfillment of his major social and personal strivings or desires . . . It is in one's star group that one looks most for love, recognition, prestige, office, and other tangible and intangible benefits and rewards" (Turner 69).

5. Three parents also add a fourth sexuality to the three previous ones: the sexuality of Mephistopheles, which is associated with illicit or invasive sexual behaviors. However, they connect these not to their children's intellectual disabilities but rather to serious mental health problems or to major communication disorders. They hope that their children will learn to control disruptive aspects of their sexuality and appropriately express genital sexuality in the future.

6. This skillful and cunning use of the law and bioethics procedure, by the parents, presents the typical features of tactics, as defined by de Certeau: "A *tactic* is a calculated action determined by the absence of a proper locus. . . . The space of a tactic is the space of the other. Thus it must play on and with a terrain imposed on it and organized by the law of a foreign power. It does not have the means to *keep to itself*, at a distance, in a position of withdrawal, foresight, and self-collection: it is a maneuver 'within the enemy's field of vision,' as von Bülow put it, and within enemy territory. . . . It is a guileful ruse. In short, a tactic is an art of the weak" (36–37). In other words, de Certeau calls "tactic" the invisible and silent micro-resistances people use to adapt the cultural forms imposed by a dominant order to their own ends, which is precisely what the parents do with the law and the bioethics committee.

II

HISTORIES

4

....

MICHELLE JARMAN

DISMEMBERING THE LYNCH MOB

Intersecting Narratives of Disability, Race,

and Sexual Menace

Late in September 2003, in the small town of Linden, Texas, four young white men assaulted Billy Ray Johnson, a cognitively impaired African American man who had lived within the community for over forty years. As a result of the attack, Johnson sustained a brain hemorrhage that left him in a coma for a week, and his injuries ultimately led to his confinement in a nursing home. Even presented with such stark and undeniable facts, jurors recommended suspended sentences and probation for his assailants in lieu of jail time. Unsatisfied with the jury's decisions, the judge imposed additional penalties, but ultimately none of the men spent more than sixty days in jail. Johnson's beating and ensuing court case generated national attention and was rightly condemned by family spokespersons, the NAACP, and the media as a bleak reminder of enduring racial injustice in the region.[1] Shifting the focus slightly from the undeniable racism involved, I invoke this story to open a discussion of the complications inherent in interpreting race *with* disability—complications that, I argue in this chapter, are inextricable from the deeply enmeshed histories of racist and ableist violence in the United States. Focusing on the early twentieth century, this chapter closely examines discourses surrounding white-on-black lynching and the eugenic cas-

tration of cognitively disabled men. I argue that these seemingly distinct historical practices are in actuality profoundly interconnected; in illuminating their
relationship to each other, I seek to demonstrate how reading race and disability
as interrelated, dynamic processes can inform our understanding of both past
and present violence.

Witnesses' statements make it clear that the assault on Johnson was motivated by racism *and* ableism. On September 27, John Owens, Dallas Stone, James
Hicks, and Christopher Amox picked Johnson up as he was walking along a road,
brought him to a rural party, plied him with liquor, and then taunted him to
dance and perform for their amusement. Witnesses said Johnson was subjected
to myriad "racial slurs" and harassed by threats that the KKK might come for
him. Johnson's cognitive impairment was also exploited for the crowd's pleasure.
He was encouraged to reach into the fire to retrieve a burning log, apparently to
flaunt his difficulty in discerning between safe and dangerous acts. By the end
of the night, the abuse escalated; Amox hit Johnson so hard he was immediately
knocked out. The men then loaded him into their truck, drove him a few miles,
and threw Johnson's unconscious body on the ground next to a public dump, on
top of a nest of stinging fire ants. He was left there for hours, until Hicks called
the police to report seeing a man who had "passed out on the ground" (Witt,
"Old South" 18).

Local authorities used Johnson's disability to downplay the racial nature of
the attack against him. For example, Malcolm Bales, from the Cass County U.S.
attorney's office, stated: "This was a bunch of guys who were mean-spirited and
cruel, and they abused a black man who was retarded." While admitting that
the offense was "terrible," Bales didn't think it should "give rise to a federal civil
rights case" (Witt, "Old South" 18). Bales draws upon the widespread cultural
understanding of disability as personal misfortune in order to position the act
as a juvenile schoolyard taunting rather than a hate crime. That is, he attempts
to defuse what he sees as the more volatile, divisive, and political issue of race
by invoking the seemingly medical and individual issue of impairment. In this
rhetorical maneuver, he relies upon a shared, cross-racial tolerance of disability
prejudice to deflect accusations of racism.

Perhaps because this strategy has been effective, the media coverage and the
NAACP's responses were couched primarily in racial terms. Johnson's disability
was portrayed as accentuating the cruelty of a racially motivated crime but was
not treated as itself affording a crucial lens of analysis. Lennard Davis makes a
similar observation about the brutal murder of James Byrd Jr., which occurred

a few years earlier in Jasper, Texas. The conviction of two white supremacist co-conspirators in 1999 marked the case as a racial hate crime, comparable to lynchings in the early part of the twentieth century.[2] Davis points out that while Byrd's racial identity was highly publicized, the fact that he was disabled—arthritic and prone to seizures—was hardly mentioned in the press (*Bending* 145–46). Davis reads this as evidence of widespread ableism in U.S. society and of an unwillingness to seriously consider disability discrimination as embedded within or connected to racially motivated attacks: "Whenever race and disability come together . . . ethnicity tends to be considered so much the 'stronger' category that disability disappears altogether" (*Bending* 147). Davis's point about media inattention to disability oppression is important. Yet his assertion—which entails a hierarchical rather than an intersectional analysis of race and disability—is complicated by the media coverage of the attack against Johnson, whose cognitive impairment, rather than "disappearing," has been repeatedly invoked. This invoking, however, has not referenced questions about how his disability contributed to his being targeted, or how the assault against him connects to a long history of violence against people with disabilities. As a result, the public discourse around these events has been truncated and one-dimensional.

In an effort to contribute to a more multidimensional approach, I argue for the importance of reading disability and race together—not as equal or competing, but as dynamic social and discursive processes that inform each other. In doing so, I propose that both the nature of the attack on Johnson and the interpretations surrounding it gesture back to historical narratives interweaving race, disability, and masculinity. Investigating these nodes of cultural meaning, I turn to the early decades of the twentieth century to look at two specific, racially charged, and disability-saturated cultural narratives: those surrounding racialized lynching and eugenic sterilization. To illuminate these rhetorical relationships, I read historic practices against literary figurations, paying particular attention to representations, in William Faulkner's *The Sound and the Fury* and Zora Neale Hurston's *Seraph on the Suwanee*, of the presumed sexual threat of cognitively disabled men during this time period. These representations, I argue, support and are supported by the era's racist discourses around lynching.

HISTORICAL NARRATIVES OF DISABILITY, RACE, AND MENACING MASCULINITIES

In the early decades of the twentieth century, white apologists for racial violence invoked the sexual threat of a mythic black rapist to justify and normalize the brutal torture, murder, and bodily destruction that came to define white-on-black lynching.[3] During this same period, eugenicists constructed cognitively disabled men as social menaces and sexual predators. Increased media attention to this putatively growing sexual threat (assumed to be directed against the sanctity of white womanhood) worked to promote public acceptance of institutionalization, surgical castration, and sterilization. Although the ritualized violence of lynching differed in form and overt purpose from the institutionalized violence of surgical sterilization, the intertwining narratives of rape and the extreme corporeal punishments enacted upon black and disabled bodies share important similarities. I suggest that even as racist mob violence and surgical sterilization followed distinct historical trajectories, the ubiquitous presence of lynching in the public imagination during the period from 1890 to 1940 may have informed and helped naturalize the rationale used to support medical castration and asexualization. Conversely, eugenic narratives of pervasive and uncontrollable sexual deviance among "feebleminded" classes likely bolstered the culture's conflation of sexual "perversion" with the highly racialized category of cognitive inferiority, providing scientific language to describe the sexual "deviance" and purported aggression of African American males.

In her compelling study connecting the histories of sexuality and race, Siobhan Somerville argues that the rhetorical formations of "whiteness" and "blackness" in the early twentieth century were deeply intertwined with emerging conceptualizations of homosexuality. Her work resists making simple analogies between sexual orientation and racial identity, instead focusing on how these "discourses had varying degrees of power to shape cultural understandings of bodies" during this period (9). While Somerville is cautious about equating these discursive practices, her analysis demonstrates that the emerging field of sexology was deeply underwritten by racist discourse and in turn illustrates the ways in which nonnormative sexualities were racialized. In a similar vein, I suggest that although the discourses of race and disability were distinct, they functioned fluidly and were often employed to undergird one another. Eugenics, of course, has been widely recognized and critiqued as a racialized and racist discourse, as well as an ableist one. Examining the racism and ableism of eugenics together

Michelle Jarman

makes it possible to glimpse some of the ways in which the discourse of race was intensified by a growing intolerance toward disability during this era.

While the manifestations of disability and race oppression differed significantly during the era I am discussing, they are governed by a shared political logic. In her book *Sapphic Slashers: Sex, Violence, and American Modernity*, Lisa Duggan's juxtaposition of lynching narratives at the turn of the twentieth century with a highly publicized lesbian love murder in Memphis provides an interesting methodological frame for the link I am developing between eugenic narratives of abnormal sexuality and the rape stories used to mobilize racist mob violence. Duggan suggests that the melodramatic public discourse around the black rapist and the homicidal lesbian positioned these nonnormative subjects as particular threats to white masculinity and the sanctity of the white middle-class home. Duggan's intent is not to imply equivalence between the (rare) lesbian love murder and (all-too-common) racialized lynching as social practices, but rather to explore how the historical linking of interracial and homosexual sexuality with violence effectively controlled public discourse. As Duggan states, "narrative technologies of sex and violence have been deployed to privatize and marginalize populations, political projects, and cultural concerns in the United States, promoting the substitution of moral pedagogy for public debate" (3). She points out that both narratives constructed an erotic triangle of power in which either the black rapist or lesbian lover disrupted both white patriarchy and the normative white heterosexual union. Like Duggan's lesbian murderess, the "black rapist" and the sexually aggressive "moron" represented tangible threats to the sanctity of white domesticity. White men, through their control of new media, the legal system, and cultural justifications of lynching, cast themselves as chivalrous heroes who rescued "their" women and families by eliminating these menaces.[4]

The schema of the love triangle, which Duggan utilizes in her analysis, is also useful in developing the connections between eugenic and lynching narratives. The importance of the black rapist as the villain of the lynching story, while widely acknowledged as a white cultural fantasy, cannot be overstated. As the historian Jonathan Markovitz states, "Rape was such an integral part of white southerners' common sense understanding of lynching narratives . . . that it hardly needed to be stated explicitly" (10). In other words, the enactment of lynching implied an interracial rape, and the rape of a white woman by a black man was considered so heinous a crime that anything less than lynching would have been too mild. This imagined violation of white women also provided justification for white men to blatantly exceed their own laws. In a widely quoted defense of lynching, the governor of South Carolina, Ben Tillman, explained that preserving white femininity made violence a moral imperative:

> The white women of the South are in a state of siege . . . some lurking demon who has watched for the opportunity seizes her; she is choked or beaten into insensibility and ravished, her body prostituted, her purity destroyed. . . . Shall men . . . demand for [the demon] the right to have a fair trial and be punished in the regular course of justice? So far as I am concerned he has put himself outside the pale of the law. . . . Civilization peels off us . . . and we revert to the original savage type whose impulse . . . has always been to kill! Kill! Kill! (qtd. in Markovitz 182)

The cultural power of this narrative to incite violence was clearly demonstrated by the staggering number of lynchings carried out during this period. From 1882 to 1930, the years when historians agree the best records were kept, at least 3,220 African American men, women, and children were murdered by lynch mobs.[5] Although less than one fourth of the lynchings of African American men were in response to official charges of sexual assault (most of which were false accusations), the connection of lynching with sexual transgression was assumed. Already labeled as "demon" rapists, black male victims of lynch mobs became public spectacles through the mutilation rites of lynching. These protracted horrors often included being beaten or shot as well as all forms of torture, including castration and the cutting and parceling out of body parts to members of the crowd as souvenirs. This was followed by hanging or burning— or both. Historically, lynching has been mainly thought of as a regional terror, a phenomenon largely isolated within the racial animosity of the South. Recent scholarship, however, suggests that lynching and its supporting narratives were integral to modern American cultural formation more generally.[6] Examining the ways these murders often became mass cultural events, Grace Elizabeth Hale argues that "spectacle lynchings" were products of modernization (206). In the years around the turn of the century, as white witnesses and participants began to disseminate lynching stories, share photograph postcards and pamphlets, and publicize upcoming mob executions in newspapers, the events themselves became more ritualized, and their narratives took on standardized forms. As much as the mob executions themselves, the proliferation of accounts and expansive public participation functioned to normalize lynching as an expected, and even justifiable, response to racial and sexual transgressions. In this way, each mob

Michelle Jarman

killing demonstrated and further secured the expansive regulatory reach and oppressive power of the white majority.

Jacqueline Goldsby extends this idea by suggesting that lynching actually contained a "cultural logic" very much aligned with broader national assertions of primacy and strength in the modern era. She points out, however, that the extreme violence of lynching has complicated the nation's willingness to remember "because lynching's violence was so unspeakably brutal—and crucially, since the lives and bodies of African American people were negligible concerns for the country for so long a time.... [We] have disavowed lynching's normative relation to modernism's history." "Lynching's 'secrecy,'" Goldsby insists, is "an historical event" (6). The unspeakable brutality made lynching both highly visible and impossible to claim. Even as white people witnessed lynching's viciousness, they also rejected it as unbelievable, unreal, and, in Goldsby's terms, "spectacular." This concurrent cultural normalization and disavowal of lynching has blurred its historical significance.

Goldsby's framing of lynching as a spectacular cultural secret enables an important historical reclamation. In addition to the extreme violence of lynching, I would suggest that the racialized sexual threat—the myth of the demon rapist— has also been crucial to the collective forgetfulness about these murders. While these staged executions were dramatically public events, the supposed sexual attack precipitating the mob's response allowed each murder to maintain an element of the private and individual. The rape narrative provided an essentially unique crime to "fit" the violent response of the lynch mob. In addition, the sexualization of the murder itself—especially in the form of castration—reinscribed the victim as sexual predator, regardless of the actual reasons behind his capture.

Robyn Wiegman suggests that the violent, ritualized castration enacted in most lynchings underscored black men's "threat to white masculine power" (14). As a disciplinary tool, castration was central to defining the power and powerlessness among the participants in this cultural drama: "that of the mythically endowed rapist, the flower of civilization (the white woman) he intended to violently pluck, and the heroic interceptor (the white male) who would restore order by thwarting the black phallic insurgence" (93). Wiegman pays particular attention to the homoerotic dynamics among members of the white mob. Paradoxically, though, despite the charged physical intimacy inherent in ritualized castration, its more potent force seems to have been its reassertion of the primacy of white heterosexuality. Moreover, the intimacy with the victim's sexual organs functioned in two additional but opposing directions: at once inscribing and objectifying the presumed excessive sexuality of the black male on a public scale, castration also rendered the rite personal and private. This public and private function of castration mirrors what Goldsby refers to as lynching's secrecy and adds to the complicated nature of this violent history.

Against this public and private dynamic of the sexual violence of lynching and its adherent cultural narrative, I want to consider the contemporaneous emergence of surgical castration as a eugenic strategy to control and sexually punish cognitively impaired men. I focus primarily upon the public rhetoric constructing previously unmarked white male bodies as sexually "deviant." While African American men were sterilized during this period, they were often caught up in different systems of control. In the South, for example, institutions devoted to the care and training of "feebleminded" individuals were strictly segregated, so African Americans with cognitive disabilities were housed in mental institutions, imprisoned, or left with families (Noll 98–103). The segregated nature of institutions was mirrored by racially distinct discursive practices. Institutional directors spent little time justifying treatment of African American inmates (which was invariably inferior to that of whites), but they did feel compelled to rationalize surgical castration and sterilization of white boys and men in their care.

Preoccupied with preserving the sanctity and strength of the white race, leading eugenicists stressed the importance of controlling the reproduction and sexuality of "feebleminded" people. They defined broad categories of inadequate classes—in addition to designations based upon physical impairments and disease—in terms of sexual promiscuity, excessive appetites, and prodigious reproduction. Walter Fernald, a leading eugenicist, argued that controlling the sexual impulses of such people should be of the highest priority: "Perhaps the chief function of these classes in America has been to demonstrate that the community is not the place for an adult imbecile . . . an adult human being, with the mind of a child and the body and passion of an adult, is a foreign body in any community" (416). Nonconforming sexuality functioned as a foundational indicator of otherness and was deployed by eugenicists to secure the public's approval of medical regulation and confinement.

In the United States, the first law permitting sterilization went into effect in Indiana in 1907; by 1921 fifteen states had laws on their books. Even before the turn of the century, arguments favoring eugenic and punitive castration were common. In 1894 a large public debate was instigated when Dr. Hoyt Pilcher, superintendent of the Asylum for Idiots and Feebleminded Youths in Winfield,

Kansas, admitted to castrating forty-four boys in his institution. While Pilcher was publicly rebuked and removed from his position, many doctors and leading eugenicists came to his defense, and he was ultimately reinstated (Reilly 29). During this period, even though castration and sterilization were not legal, many institutional leaders took it upon themselves to pioneer such eugenic controls. Much as white lynch mobs asserted their racial privilege against African Americans, some administrators used their institutional power to move fluidly outside legal confines to enact what they perceived as correct and *correctional* measures upon the bodies entrusted to their care.

As states began enacting eugenic laws during the first decades of the twentieth century, much of the support for surgical sterilization continued to come directly from superintendents, many of whom were doctors. Martin Barr, the chief physician at the Pennsylvania Training School for Feeble-minded Children in the 1920s, was one such vocal enthusiast of sterilization. "Personally I prefer castration for the male . . . as insuring security beyond a peradventure," he stated plainly. Making a small concession to those who might consider castration to be extreme, he went on to add, "if for sentimental reasons the removal of the organs are objected to, vasectomy . . . may be substituted" (234). Medical professionals' cavalier attitudes toward massive surgical procedures did much to normalize the idea of medically regulating disabled bodies. In addition, continued public support was elicited through the promulgation of the idea that adult men with disabilities were unpredictable, foreign, and sexually dangerous.

FAULKNER'S EUGENIC VILLAIN (AND VICTIM)

To look more closely at the potency of this eugenically constructed predator, my analysis turns to literary representations of disability. Specifically, I consider how the characterizations of disabled white men seem informed not only by deterministic assumptions of sexual deviance but also by the racially inflected hypersexuality attributed to the purported villains (and inevitable victims) of lynching narratives. In order to better imagine the social mindset behind eugenic sterilization, I discuss Benjamin Compson's castration in *The Sound and the Fury*. Through Benjy's "gelding" in response to his supposed attack of a neighbor girl (263), Faulkner depicts social acceptance of eugenic thinking among the residents of Jefferson, Mississippi. After his beloved sister Caddy is exiled from the family compound, Benjy continues his daily ritual of lingering at the gate to watch the girls returning from school—in a timeless anticipation of her return. One fateful day, the gate is left open, allowing Benjy to venture from the confines of the yard and (presumably) to sexually attack a neighbor girl. Witnessing the event (or in response to the girl's cries), her father, Mr. Burgess, assails Benjy. The ultimate punishment for this transgression is Benjy's rapid removal to a hospital to be surgically castrated.

Faulkner provides the details of this event from two differing points of view, that of Benjy and that of his brother Jason. Benjy's stream-of-consciousness narrative portrays a series of miscommunications rather than a directed attack. His memories suggest nonthreatening motivations: "I opened the gate and they stopped, turning. I was trying to say, and I caught her, trying to say, and she screamed and I was trying to say" (53). From this point of view, Faulkner's novel suggests that Benjy's attack was an attempt to reach out to people beyond the parameters of his yard. On the other side, Jason might be seen as the narrative embodiment of the eugenic mindset that supports stigmatizing interpretations of cognitive impairment and compels the family to pursue castration in response to Benjy's transgression. Jason admits that Benjy didn't know "what he had been trying to do" (263), but he also reads the incident deterministically—as the inevitable outcome of Benjy's disability: "This family is bad enough, God knows. I could have told you, all the time" (52). The Compsons understand that Benjy crossed a moral line that must be restored; something drastic must be done to reestablish Benjy's docility within the neighborhood. Internalizing a eugenic perspective, Jason believes that if they don't institutionalize Benjy, which his parents refuse to do, they must do something decisive—something permanent—to assure their neighbors that such an attack will never happen again.

These contrasting perspectives within *The Sound and the Fury* demonstrate how vulnerable a nonlingual, cognitively impaired man is to the interpretations of others. The "truth" of Benjy's intentions and actions are determined externally and inscribed upon his body, in this case surgically. His script is written by those observing him, judging him from a standard by which he has already been coded "deviant," sexual, and dangerous. When Benjy's family and neighbors witness an eighteen-year-old "idiot" (the scientific term used during this period) approach and touch a schoolgirl outside of his fence, one interpretation, that he is a sexual menace, presents itself as the natural, and only, conclusion. As Fernald's assertion that "the community is not the place for an adult imbecile" makes clear, there was no socially acceptable place for a person like Benjy.

Michelle Jarman

Within Faulkner's framework, Benjy's castration takes place when he is eighteen years old, in 1913. During this era, men with cognitive impairments similar to those embodied by Benjy were highly vulnerable to surgical asexualization. In his historical research on "feeblemindedness," James Trent points out that "most sterilizations were castrations, and the majority were done on idiots and low-grade imbeciles whose 'obscene habits' were most bothersome to superintendents and their staff" (195). Within this social and historical context, a fictional figure such as Benjy already signaled to readers the potential danger of transgressive sexuality. The eugenic rationale of surgery functions to guarantee Benjy's sexual complacency and at the same time to ensure his limited freedom within the confines of his yard.

THE SOCIAL MENACE OF THE "MORON"

In the early part of the twentieth century, eugenicists pursued sterilization and castration primarily to control the behavior and reproduction of people diagnosed as "idiots" or "imbeciles"—the scientific terms for those not expected to advance beyond a mental age of seven years, many of whom were already confined in institutions or sequestered in family homes. By the 1920s and 1930s, however, as eugenicists became more concerned with "morons"—borderline "feebleminded" individuals who could pass for normal—they began sounding an alarm against the imminent sexual threat posed by these purported predators. Again, untarnished white women were invoked as the targeted prey of "deviant" and feebleminded men. Echoing the familiar rhetoric of the racialized mythic rapist to underscore the sexual threat of "morons," the female physician Isadore Dyer stated, "we ourselves . . . should try to establish or have enacted a law protecting our sisters and our descendants from the possibilities to which they have been exposed" (22).

In Chicago and other cities in the United States, numerous news articles reported on the sexual crimes of "morons," and new laws to confine and unsex these supposed criminals were widely discussed. In his court testimony, the psychologist David Rotman stressed the danger of letting such borderline individuals remain free and unsupervised: "Often they seem innocent enough, but they are responsible for a large percentage of our sex crimes. We will have no real solution of the moron problem until our legislators recognize the potential peril of these individuals" ("Urge" 3). In stories supporting the push for tougher laws, sexual crimes were graphically reported. In some cases, the perpetrators had been diagnosed with cognitive impairments, but in many instances the nature of the crimes themselves—specifically sexual crimes against children—were used by the media as conclusive evidence of the perpetrators' intellectual incapacity. Increasingly, sexual criminality was seen as synonymous with cognitive impairment. For example, when the Illinois state representative Peter Granata introduced a bill in the 1930s that would castrate *anyone* who committed a sexual offense against a boy or girl under the age of sixteen, media coverage consistently referred to the proposed legislation as the "bill to unsex morons" ("Bill" 1).

Returning to the intersections between narratives surrounding white-on-black lynching and those authorizing eugenic castration, I suggest that the excesses of lynching—the spectacularization of murders as cultural events, the barbaric mutilation, and communal participation—served a contrastive function to eugenic methods, rendering their purportedly scientific rhetoric and medicalized violence seemingly more benign. In addition, lynching and surgical castration had in common an ambiguous legal status. Although mob lynchings were conducted arrogantly outside the law, the repetition, public acceptance, and widespread participation in white-on-black violence allowed lynching to function as a sanctioned cultural practice. In fact, the extralegal nature of lynching demonstrated to its victims that the boundaries of the law were quite permeable along the racial divide, as the practice persisted, usually with full participation or complicity of judges, sheriffs, and local officials.[7] Sterilization and medical castration, by contrast, because they were most often enacted by white doctors upon white inmates (and often rhetorically situated as an intraracial problem) during this period, needed to be integrated into the rationality of law. Thus, while untold numbers of sterilizations were carried out behind institution walls, medical professionals used these illegal operations as evidence to build public acceptance and provide arguments for changing policy. At first officially outside the law, but ultimately either incorporated within it (surgical castration) or supported by legal authorities (lynching), each of these two modes of sexualized violence—the spectacularized, ritual castration and murder of African American men, and the more quietly conducted, scientifically rationalized castration and sterilization of cognitively disabled men—likely had the effect of normalizing and legitimizing the other. Certainly, each responded to what can be interpreted as the same culturally produced fear: that of a threat, animalistic and sexual, to the sanctity of normative white heterosexuality—a threat whose extremity necessitated drastic and violent responses.

Michelle Jarman

HURSTON'S RESCRIPTING OF THE LYNCHING NARRATIVE

In the 1930s and 1940s, the public proliferation of accounts featuring the threat of "morons" appears to have seemed more credible to some than the equally frequent invocations of the mythic racialized rapist. Zora Neale Hurston's final novel, *Seraph on the Suwanee*, replaces the latter of these figures with the former, rewriting the familiar lynching narrative so as to feature a white disabled villain. Published in 1948 but set in the early decades of the 1900s, *Seraph* traces nearly twenty-five years of marriage between Jim and Arvay Meserve, a hardworking white couple living on the edges of the Florida swamplands. Until recently, many critics had dismissed *Seraph* as an abandonment of Hurston's rich black folk tradition,[8] but over the last decade, several scholars have demonstrated that although the plot revolves around an insecure white woman and her domineering husband, Hurston's novel nonetheless develops complex social, racial, and gendered critiques.[9] Yet although disability looms large within the novel, driving much of the marital conflict, critics have, in keeping with *Seraph*'s own governing assumptions, tended to treat disability as a problem to be solved or, more specifically, as a domestic disruption the family must extirpate in order to achieve normative harmony. In closely examining representations of disability in Hurston's novel, I seek to underscore the tacit eugenic narrative at play in the text.

Situated centrally in the novel is Earl, the eldest son of Arvay and Jim, who is born with an unspecified cognitive impairment and minor physical disabilities. Earl seems to possess a violent and uncontrollable nature. As a baby, he demonstrates an "unnatural" appetite, "ferociously" attacking his mother's breast (68). As a toddler, he becomes unrecognizable to Arvay when he emits "animal howls" in response to losing a piece of fruit (100). His atavistic nature—a loose designation common in eugenic and racist rhetoric—portends his ultimate crime. Years later, Earl sexually assaults the teenage daughter of their neighbor, an act for which he is spectacularly hunted down and killed. In ways that exceed those of Benjy Compson's castration, Earl's murder becomes reminiscent of a lynching narrative. This parallel is troubling, given *Seraph*'s apparent endorsement of Earl's death. The novel depicts the murder as unavoidable and as a necessary sacrifice that solidifies the survival and growth of his parents' marriage. Thus, Hurston's novel can be read as strategically deploying the sexual threat of a disabled figure in order to displace the figure of the mythic black rapist as the villain of the lynching story. More important, although the novel calls attention to the lynching narrative, its deployment of the eugenic threat as the basis of an alternative script obscures the ways in which these cultural narratives bolster each other.

Hurston's representation of Earl reiterates eugenically inflected stereotypes tying cognitive and physical impairment to immorality, animalistic impulses, violence, and criminality. It is therefore not surprising that Earl's sexual awakening takes the form of an animalistic frenzy. When he is nearly sixteen, one of his father's friends, Alfredo Corregio, moves his family into the cabin behind the Meserve home. The Corregios have two daughters, the eldest of whom—the teenage Lucy Ann—immediately becomes an obsession to Earl. Recognizing the danger Earl suddenly represents, Jim and Arvay attempt to confine him to the house. Predictably, these efforts fail, and within weeks Earl executes his escape. Pretending to go to sleep after dinner, he cuts a hole in his screened window and slips out. Sitting at her sewing after dinner, Arvay is startled by shrieks mixed in with "howl[s]" and "yelps" coming from the grove (142). She immediately recognizes Earl's animal-like cries and runs toward the cottage to join a group crowded around Lucy Ann, who lies unconscious on the ground. "Blood was running down from a mangly spot on the side of her neck," Arvay observes. "The fingers of the white hand that lay limply across her body were chewed and bloody." The girl's skirt was torn and pulled up to reveal "a bleeding wound on one thigh" (143). Judging from her wounds, which seem more animalistic than sexual, Lucy Ann looks as if she had been attacked by a wild creature, not a young man.

The novel's representation of disability as animalistic reinstates deterministic rhetoric established by eugenicists in the early part of the century. Barr, the influential physician supporter of surgical sterilization quoted earlier, expressed the common eugenicist belief: "What is not fully recognized is the fact that mental defectives suffer not only from exaggerated sexual impulses, but from mental and moral debility . . . leaving them greater slaves to the impulse of the moment" (232). *Seraph* reifies these cultural assumptions in its depiction of Earl, who is portrayed as incapable of reigning in his destructive impulses. This is underscored when Earl turns upon his mother, who has been his lone defender. When Arvay discovers Earl hiding in the house, he attacks her: "The weak fingers feeling for her throat . . . the intent was here, only the strength was lacking" (148). Even this threat upon her own life fails to fracture Arvay's motherly devotion, which the novel depicts as misguided: Arvay urges Earl to run from the posse of men forming outside.

Michelle Jarman

By establishing Earl as an undisputed sexual "deviant," Hurston's novel displaces the mythic black rapist as the villain of the lynching narrative. Instead, it seems to suggest that some disabled white men should rightly be understood as very *real* threats to women of all races. The efficacy of this reversal depends upon the very similar ways in which these two figures have been narrativized. In other words, the novel's counternarrative calls attention to the parallel ways African American and cognitively impaired men were discursively produced as sexual predators in the early twentieth century. However, in its exposure of the racialized rape narrative as false, the novel has the effect of reinscribing the imagined sexual threat attributed to cognitively disabled men. This is a key and troubling point for two reasons: first, in order to challenge a racist cultural narrative, *Seraph* constructs cognitively disabled men as dangerous; second, even as the novel relies upon the similarity of these narratives, its textual displacement opposes and disconnects these two deeply imbricated figures.[10]

My intention is not to detract from *Seraph*'s critique of white-on-black lynching but rather to investigate the ramifications of deploying ableist narrative strategies as a means of counteracting racist practices. Such deployments, in foreclosing possibilities of reading racist and ableist narratives in conversation, obscure the ways in which eugenic discourses and rationales for racialized lynching may historically have lent support to each other. The interconnectedness of racist and ableist cultural assumptions is evident in the scene in which Earl leads his trackers into the depths of the swamp. Seemingly to trope upon the historic racism in evolutionary science, *Seraph*'s representation of Earl's retreat to the swamp, a murky home to earlier forms of life, marks him as atavistic. After hunting for Earl all night, the posse goes to Joe Kelsey's house to see if he has taken refuge there; it is Joe, Jim's African American overseer, who suggests they look "in the Big Swamp somewhere" (149). Joe assures the men that he has seen Earl "ducking and dodging down in there . . . too many times" (149). By using an African American character to point the white men in the right direction, Hurston's novel hints at a connectedness between the marginalization of blackness and disability.

This is not, however, to suggest that racism and ableism function in identical ways. For one thing, the posse hunting for Earl seems civilized in comparison to lynch mobs. By the 1940s, the extraordinary brutality and violence of lynching were well known, and so the contrast between a lynching and the tracking of Earl would have been striking to Hurston's readers. It is also worth noting that this manhunt is led by Earl's father—a detail that brings to the surface another crucial difference between race and disability. In contrast to racial violence, which functioned to control whole communities of African Americans, regulation of people with disabilities often involved the active participation of family members. In an effort to keep the group of men from hurting Earl, Jim leads the search into the swamp, knowing "if it wasn't for [his] presence, they would have killed Earl a long time ago" (153). For hours, Jim begs him from a distance to relinquish his rifle and give himself up. Earl not only ignores his pleas but threatens his father's life: "seeing his father where he had no chance of escape, [Earl] advanced to get Jim exactly under his gun-sight again" (153). Witnessing Jim helpless in front of his son, the men fire on Earl, killing him instantly.

While the events leading up to Earl's killing echo the rape narratives associated with lynching, Earl is not tortured or mutilated as lynching victims were. His death thus stands in contrast to the barbaric violence of lynching. This seeming restraint of violence in the novel, like the scientific rationalization of surgical castration, may have been instrumental in procuring the familial acceptance of such measures that was crucial to their success. As Jim says to Arvay: "You ought to be able to see how they wouldn't want nobody like Earl loose on the community" (148). In participating in Earl's removal, Jim validates the eugenic solution to disability: death or incarceration.

CONCLUSION

In considering the eugenic constructions of the sexually menacing male in relation to the rape story that fueled white-on-black lynching, I have traced the ways both discourses functioned within turn-of-the-century public discourses to support a reconsolidation of power in the white, heterosexual, nondisabled domestic structure. These discourses, and the social practices they supported, demonstrate some of the ways in which the promises of a more inclusive democracy initiated in the post–Civil War period were dramatically shut down and contained in the early decades of the twentieth century. One of the reasons these sensationalized stories proved to be so culturally salient is that they potently stigmatized non-white, disabled, and sexualized bodies in ways that compelled a public response. At the same time, however, because the victim was successfully positioned by those in authority as the perpetrator or criminal, his or her—if we remember Duggan's lesbian love murder—personal fate (the violence enacted upon him or her by the lynch mob, the court, or the surgeon) was strategically removed from the political to the personal sphere. In other words, much as the spectacu-

Michelle Jarman

lar violence and sexualized backstory of lynching subverted the public nature of the events, the deterministic—and also sexualized—diagnostics around disabled men during this period tended to privatize the social, surgical, and institutional controls enacted upon them.

Returning to contemporary manifestations of violence against African American and disabled people, it is important to remember the historical narratives informing such acts. The turn-of-the-century period is particularly relevant because in many ways, in the early decades of a new century, we find ourselves in a somewhat analogous political milieu—one in which the promises of feminism, civil rights, gay liberation, and disability rights continue to be curtailed and contained in various ways. However, these libratory social movements have succeeded in engendering widespread intolerance to violence that was commonplace in an earlier era. The jurors in Johnson's civil case against his attackers, for example, sent a clear message that such targeted violence would not be tolerated, awarding Johnson nine million dollars in damages (Witt, "$9 Million" 3). At the same time, however, apologists for Johnson's white assailants cited the brutality of lynchings as evidence of the comparative innocuousness of Johnson's attack. These arguments are disingenuous, of course. Moreover, the men who attacked Johnson were motivated by both racism and ableism. Not only did his cognitive disability contribute to his being targeted for abuse but the attack produced more impairments, resulting in his permanent incarceration in a nursing home. This makes evident the continued inextricability in contemporary U.S. culture of racially motivated and ableist violence. The violence enacted against Johnson should be understood as the legacy of intersecting discourses that underwrote both lynch mob violence and surgical castration in the early twentieth century: while the brutality of his attackers' actions echoes and perpetuates a history of spectacularized public violence against African American people, Johnson's incarceration in an institution is also a form of violence—one that shares much with the privatizing discourses of eugenic science that rationalized and promoted the castration of cognitively disabled men. Indeed, much as early twentieth-century doctors represented castration, sterilization, or permanent confinement of disabled people as compassionate treatments, some contemporary commentators have interpreted Johnson's confinement as beneficial to him. As one supporter of the defendants stated, "[Johnson] is better off today than he's ever been in his life" (Witt, "Old South" 18). Locking Billy Ray Johnson up in a nursing home outside of town may allow the locals the luxury of forgetting his story, but as the legacies of lynching, surgical sterilization, and cultural violence remind us, distorting memories of these oppressive and intersecting rhetorical strategies prevents us from condemning ableism and racism as interacting processes, and this is certainly a "luxury" we cannot afford.

NOTES

Many thanks to Lennard Davis, David Mitchell, and Sharon Snyder for helping me begin to think through these issues during my dissertation research. I am especially grateful to Robert McRuer and Anna Mollow for their invaluable insights during the many stages of revision of this chapter. I would also like to express my gratitude to the anonymous reviewers for their helpful comments. Finally, I want to acknowledge and remember my dear friend, Chris Bell, whose legacy continues to encourage and inform my work on race and disability.

1. As reported by Howard Witt, Johnson's family members, with the legal and financial support of the NAACP, are pursuing the case as a racial hate crime. The FBI has been brought in to determine whether Johnson's attack should be classified as such; their investigation is ongoing.

2. James Byrd Jr. was kidnapped and brutally murdered by white supremacists John William King and Lawrence Russell Brewer. These men chained Byrd to a truck, dragged him for over two miles, and dismembered his body.

3. I use the term "black rapist" purposefully to call attention to the way this figure was deployed historically to objectify, dehumanize, and stereotype African American males.

4. The term "moron" was coined by eugenicists to refer to individuals who were cognitively disabled but who could "pass" as nondisabled. As I discuss further, this ability to pass became more and more troubling to eugenic reformers, and socially unacceptable sexual behavior—among women and men—was increasingly seen as evidence of cognitive disability.

5. For more detailed information on lynching statistics, see "Appendix C" in Tolnay and Beck 271–72. These figures summarize lynching from the Deep South and do not include antiblack violence in other regions of the country. For limitations of these numbers, see "Appendix A" in Tolnay and Beck 259–63.

6. In addition to the invaluable records kept by the NAACP and other antilynching groups to document lynching in the United States, recent photographic collections and publications have ushered in a renewed interest in this important history. The shocking and powerful photographic collection compiled by James Allen and exhibited across the country was also published in book form in 2000 under the same title, *Without Sanctuary: Lynching Photography in America*. Anne Rice's *Witnessing Lynching*, published in 2003, is a careful selection of literary works, essays, and journal articles by leading figures in the antilynching movement. Most recently, Christopher Waldrep's

Lynching in America constructs a fascinating history of lynching out of primary source documents from the early 1800s through 1945.

7. Although lynching was never considered legal, the federal government's resistance to actually criminalizing these acts as murder effectively provided amnesty to lynch mobs. As Jacqueline Goldsby points out, each time antilynching legislation was introduced—in 1901, 1921, 1922, and 1934—Congress rejected the bills, ostensibly to protect states' rights (18–20).

8. Mary Helen Washington, for example, suggests that the novel fails because Hurston abandons the wellspring of "her unique esthetic—the black cultural tradition" (12). Alice Walker, who pioneered a revival of public interest in Hurston's work, flatly rejects *Seraph*: "[Hurston's] work, too, became reactionary, static, shockingly misguided and timid. This is especially true of her last novel, *Seraph on the Suwanee*, which is not even about black people, which is no crime, but *is* about white people who are bores, which is" (xvi).

9. Claudia Tate, for one, argues that *Seraph on the Suwanee* engages in a persistent joke on white culture's fetishization of passive female desire (371). Janet St. Clair also suggests that feminist dismissals of Hurston's protagonist too easily accept a superficial reading of Arvay as a passive, self-abnegating, and dependent wife, while failing to acknowledge the "subversive undertow" at work in the "feminist substory . . . [that rejects] both oppression and, more important, the mental submission to oppression" (38). Although *Seraph*'s resolution to the marital battles waged between Jim and Arvay Meserve doesn't represent a straightforward feminist victory, it is true that, as Ann DuCille points out, the novel does expose the sexual violence and oppression endemic to heterosexual marriage.

10. For a provocative consideration of the ways in which historically situated counternarratives are constructed to contest and rescript melodramatic dominant discourses, often using but resignifying the same discursive material from the dominant narrative, see Duggan's discussion of the counternarratives to the lynching narrative constructed in the journalism of Ida B. Wells (*Sapphic* 20–22).

5

....

RACHEL O'CONNELL

"THAT CRUEL SPECTACLE"

The Extraordinary Body Eroticized in Lucas Malet's

The History of Sir Richard Calmady

SIR RICHARD CALMADY'S EXTRAORDINARY BODY

The History of Sir Richard Calmady (1901) is a book about the extraordinary body of its eponymous protagonist.[1] Sir Richard Calmady is afflicted by a curse, cast on his family in the distant past by a mistreated peasant woman. The curse decrees that all Calmady men will die young, until one is born, "half angel, half monster," who will atone for the wrongs of his philandering forefathers (Malet 40). Soon after the premature death of his own father, Richard is born with no lower legs, his feet attached to his thighs just above where his knees would have been.

The novel focuses on Richard's progress into adulthood, narrating his various romances and his anxieties about his sexual and reproductive future. His principal and most enduring romance is with his protective, passionate, and compelling mother, Katherine, who refuses to acknowledge his bodily difference openly. As a young man just out of university, however, he enters into an engagement with his innocent and unimaginative neighbor, Lady Constance Quayle. It is eventually revealed that Constance has been forced into the engagement by her family, who are after Richard's money, and that in fact she is, and has always been, horrified by Richard's body. She finally breaks off the engagement to marry the athletic soldier Mr. Decies. Humiliated and embittered, Richard flees to the continent to live the life of a libertine, embarking on a period of debauchery that culminates in a steamy affair with his cousin, Helen, who has since childhood been infatuated by his extraordinary physique. After one night of passion with Helen, a chastened Richard returns to England, wracked by remorse and illness, to live a life of temperance devoted to good works. At this point he enters into a seemingly celibate marriage with his other cousin, Honoria, a protolesbian, protofeminist character who wishes to contribute to Richard's charitable endeavors. Richard and Honoria adopt the child of a near relative, rather than having their own children, and settle down to live happily ever after with Katherine, who in fact appears to be the primary erotic object for both Richard and Honoria.

The novel's sustained and explicit account of Richard's sexual experiences and desires renders it exceptional in the era of eugenics, during which the sexuality of disabled people was a taboo subject. The book, therefore, like its protagonist, is a fascinating anomaly. It was a bestseller in 1901, outsold only by Rudyard Kipling's *Kim*. Its author, Lucas Malet, was a respected if controversial avant-garde writer, the daughter of the Victorian cultural leader Charles Kingsley (her given name was Mary St. Leger Kingsley). Both *Kim* and Malet's novel dwell with covetous fascination on boys on the brink of manhood, but while *Kim* has become a classic, *The History of Sir Richard Calmady*, despite its initial notoriety, drifted into utter obscurity during the first half of the twentieth century. It was recovered only recently, due to a renewed interest in the works of noncanonical Victorian and Edwardian women writers. The contrasting fates of *Kim* and *The History of Sir Richard Calmady* invite reflection on the ways in which the politics of canonicity intertwines with the politics not only of gender but also of disability.

The book's rediscovery coincides opportunely with the continuing growth of the academic field of disability studies, for which it offers thought-provoking material. This novel deserves to be part of our developing disability studies canon; yet it is hard to know what to do with it, for it manages to combine very intimately the radical and the deeply offensive. It thematizes and draws on the conventions of the freak show, describing Richard's body in visual terms and posing him in tableaux dripping with emotive significance, so that the novel as a whole becomes a kind of textual stage upon which Richard is displayed as a freak. Yet the novel dwells on Richard's body with fascination, desire, and perhaps even love. Richard's body is its central object, the fine point upon which all its characters, histories, and themes coalesce; at the same time the fantasies his body arouses diffuse through the text like the fog that so often surrounds its characters, infusing the imaginative world of the novel with an affect of melancholy, yearning passion. This novel's commitment to, its caress of, the disabled body is a rarity in the field of representations of disability, at least until recent years.

The excessive presence and hypervisibility with which Richard's body is invested in this novel evokes Rosemarie Garland-Thomson's work on disability and visual culture, as presented in her discussions of freak shows and photography. In her essay, "The Politics of Staring: Visual Rhetorics of Disability in Popular Photography," Garland-Thomson observes that the "history of disabled people in the Western world is in part the history of being on display, of being visually conspicuous while politically and socially erased" (56). In *Extraordinary Bodies*, her seminal book on freak shows and other cultural representations of visible disability, she argues that "the exhibited body became a text written in bold face to be deciphered according to the needs and desires of onlookers" (60). This transformation of body into text deprives the freak of subjectivity and power: "the body envelops and obliterates the freak's potential humanity" (59). Meanwhile, the audience, in the position of interpreter, is empowered to make use of the freak as "a generalized icon of corporeal and cultural otherness" on which all kinds of fantasies and disavowals can be imposed (80). In "The Politics of Staring," Garland-Thomson analyzes the ways in which photography of disabled people draws on and develops from the freak show, offering opportunities to stare at the extraordinary body in an era in which the freak show has become distasteful. Producing a powerful frame through which to approach visual images of disabled bodies, she creates a set of four categories, or "rhetorics," of images: the wondrous, the sentimental, the exotic, and the realistic. She argues that while the first three rhetorics evoke the distanced, privileged responses of amazement (the wondrous), pity (the sentimental), and desire (the exotic), realistic representations "banish the strange and cultivate the ordinary, radically reimagining disability by installing people with disabilities in the realm of human commonality" (74).

Garland-Thomson's work is a force for the cultural emancipation of disabled people, who have for generations been assaulted and objectified by the able-bodied gaze, and an important aspect of her project appears to be a search for potentially empowering modes of representation, such as the realistic mode in photography. At the same time, Garland-Thomson's writing leaves hanging some intriguing loose ends and evocative asides, which open up the possibility of exploring in detail the diverse and particular relationships that objectifying modes of representation foster between onlooker and spectacle. For example, although

Rachel O'Connell

Garland-Thomson argues that the able-bodied gaze subjects and objectifies the disabled body, her description of the "visual relation" as "an awkward partnership that estranges and discomforts both viewer and viewed" destabilizes this paradigm, suggesting a connection in which both parties are vulnerable ("Politics" 57). In addition, she offers a thought-provoking conception of the freak show: "At the freak show, cultural self and cultural other hover silently for an historical instant, face to face in dim acknowledgement of their unspoken symbiosis" (*Extraordinary* 65). This striking image emphasizes not only hierarchy but also interdependence, and the moment of confrontation between the onlooker and the extraordinary body becomes a tense encounter that is both surreal and revelatory.

The History of Sir Richard Calmady, with its intertwining of caress and contempt, describes and embodies a relationship between onlooker and extraordinary body that is characterized by an edgy breathlessness, encompassing both desire and hurt, both solicitation and retreat. The novel represents, in fact, the kind of "awkward partnership" that, according to Garland-Thomson, may be invoked by the "visual relation" ("Politics" 57). The novel thus extends an invitation to follow up some of the tantalizing loose ends that emerge in Garland-Thomson's writings. *The History of Sir Richard Calmady* demands a reading that is attentive to the fluidity and interdependence of viewer and spectacle; it thereby asks the reader to inhabit and reflect upon the strange intimacy between onlooker and extraordinary body.[2]

VISUAL RHETORICS IN *THE HISTORY OF SIR RICHARD CALMADY*

Throughout *The History of Sir Richard Calmady* connections are drawn between Richard's body and practices of display. Richard's story is bookended by paradigmatic encounters with two practices of spectacle and display, the freak show and the opera; both of these encounters serve to suggest that Richard himself is at risk of being made an object of display. Indeed, the two encounters frame Richard's story much as conventions of display frame (imprison, interpret, and present) the extraordinary body.

Early in the novel, Richard encounters a freak show when as a youth he goes out riding. The show is part of a country fair, which also displays captive animals, including a lion grown "weary of the rows of stolid English faces staring daily, hourly, between the bars of his foul and narrow cage, heart-sick with longing for sight of the open, starlit heaven and the white-domed, Moslem tombs amid the prickly, desert thickets and plains of clean, hot sand" (Malet 105). Riding past the fairground listening to the desolate roar of the lion, Richard sees the sign for the freak show. This has a strong effect on Richard, leaving him with "a blind terror of insecurity, which, coursing through the boy's mind, filled him with agonised and angry pity towards all disgraced fellow-beings, all enslaved and captive beasts. Dimly he recognised his kinship to all such" (Malet 106). At several points later in the novel, when he is experiencing moments of suffering, Richard is again compared to the lion; at one point he is described as "a creature, captive, maimed, imprisoned, perpetually striving, perpetually frustrated in the effort to escape" (Malet 347). This repeated comparison draws the reader back to the first sight of the freak show, implying insistently that it is social responses to Richard's physical difference that entrap him, imprisoning him in the gaze of the rows of stolid faces, like a fly congealed in amber.

Toward the end of the novel, Richard experiences a rehabilitative moment of revelation that drives him to return to England and embark on a life of temperance and good works. Delirious with fever in his box at the opera in Naples, Richard imagines that the audience stares, not at the figures on the stage, but at him. He believes himself to be surrounded by "velvet-like, expressionless eyes. And all those eyes were fixed upon him, and him alone. He was the centre towards which, in thought and action, all turned" (Malet 329). This self-referential passage perfectly describes the way in which Malet has chosen to locate the extraordinary body in her novel. While Richard is represented as a character with a subjectivity, an approach that encourages the reader to identify with him and sympathize with his situation, the novel also participates in the forceful conventions of display that assault its hero. That is, it presents Richard's body as a spectacle. Of course, this is a somewhat paradoxical statement, since the novel's mode is language, not vision. But through its cornucopia of descriptive passages (one of the features that make it as a whole so very lengthy), Malet's novel seems to incorporate the dynamic developments in visual culture that were occurring at the turn of the nineteenth century. The novel repeatedly offers showpiece scenes that have an almost cinematic quality, and early cinema was at this time producing footage of disabled subjects, capitalizing on the tradition of display associated with them.

Consider, for example, the scene in which Honoria first sees Richard. Honoria is collecting Constance from Richard's home after Constance has broken off her engagement with him:

Rachel O'Connell

Suddenly the sharp peal of the bell, the opening of the door, the dragging of silken skirts, and hurrying of footsteps. — Honoria gathered up
her somewhat scattered courage and swung out into the hall. Lady Constance Quayle came towards her, groping, staggering, breathless, her face
convulsed with weeping. But to this, for the moment, Miss St Quentin
[Honoria] paid small heed. For, at the far end of the hall, a bright light
streamed out from the open doorway. And in the full glare of it stood a
young man — his head, with its cap of close-cropped curls, proudly distinguished as that of some classic hero, his features the beautiful features of
Katherine Calmady, his height but two-thirds the height a man of his make
should be, his face drawn and livid as that of a corpse, his arms hanging
down straight at his sides, his hands only just not touching the marble
quarries of the floor on either side of him.

Honoria uttered an exclamation of uncontrollable pity and horror,
caught Constance Quayle by the arm, and hurried out into the moonlit
square to the waiting carriage. (Malet 235)

The flurried, rapid action of the scene — the women making their escape — is
halted by the sudden, contrasting, short sentence — "But to this, for the moment,
Miss St Quentin paid small heed." Action makes way for the stasis of portraiture,
as Richard is described. The narrative pauses to make way for a moment of visual
contemplation of Richard's body, dwelling on aspects of his appearance that emphasize his physical difference: his shortness of stature, and the way his hands
almost reach the floor. Honoria is turned from actor into spectator, gazing on
Richard's revealed bodily difference, and the reader is drawn into her emotions of
"pity and horror." After offering the reader this emotive snapshot of Richard, the
scene transforms itself again with Honoria's sudden cry, which breaks the silence
and stillness of the moment. The characters abruptly return to their roles, and
the narrative resumes. The image of Richard's body has momentarily conveyed
the reader into a different place and time, outside the flow of the narrative, to experience the pregnant, ominous stillness of spectacle. The extraordinary body is
constructed as inherently spectacular, wordless, antithetical to the developmental and discursive nature of narrative.

In the example above, the representation of Richard's body participates in
the "sentimental" visual rhetoric Garland-Thomson has identified, soliciting pity
toward Richard by modeling sympathy through Honoria. Yet, at the same time,
the descriptive focus in this passage on the beauty of Richard's hair and face,

and the long reach of his phallic arms, betrays Honoria's pity as alloyed with a more "uncontrollable" attraction, complicating the response demanded from the reader. The construction, in this novel, of the extraordinary body as an object of desire is particularly evident in passages in which Helen is the agent of the gaze—the gaze to which Richard is subjected and into which the reader is initiated. In these passages the text adopts a rhetoric that might be categorized, again following Garland-Thomson, as "exotic": a mode that "presents disabled figures as alien, distant, often sensationalized, eroticized, or entertaining in their difference," making "the disabled figure large, strange, and unlike the viewer" ("Politics" 65–66).

The following exoticizing passage, for example, occurs during a scene in which Richard and Helen are lunching together in his garden at Naples:

> Silently he slipped down from his chair, stood a moment, supporting himself with one hand on the edge of the table, and then moved forward to that side of the pavilion which gave upon the garden. Here the sunshine was hot upon the pavement, and upon the outer half of each pale, slender column. Richard leant his shoulder against one of these, grateful for the genial heat.
>
> Since her first and somewhat inauspicious meeting with him in childhood, Helen had never, close at hand, seen Richard Calmady walk thus far. She stared, fascinated by that cruel spectacle. For the instant transformation of the apparently tall, and conspicuously well-favoured, courtly gentleman, just now sitting at table with her, into this shuffling, long-armed, crippled dwarf was, at first utterly incredible, then portentous, then, by virtue of its very monstrosity, absorbing and, to her, adorable, whetting appetite as a veritable famine might. (Malet 297)

In this passage, as in the one with Honoria above, the action of the scene (which in this case is the dialogue between Richard and Helen) is suspended when Richard silently takes his pose—a choreographed, static pose that distances him from the onlooker, placing him in the remote, unreachable space of the spectacle. His shortness of stature is exaggerated through the contrast between his body and the tall slenderness of the column against which he leans, much as, in freak shows, dwarves were often paired with giants to emphasize, through contrast, their respective heights. The passage then is focalized through Helen; the reader is invited to participate in her absorption in and fascination with the sight of Richard's body. In Helen's visual field, Richard's figure is further enlarged and exaggerated, as he becomes "this shuffling, long-armed, crippled dwarf," and Helen revels in the visual pleasure that the experience of staring at Richard offers, acknowledging him as an object of desire.

Helen's exoticizing vision creates, to use Garland-Thomson's words, "a sensationalized, embellished alien" ("Politics" 66). Garland-Thomson argues that the exotic "reproduces an ethnographic model of viewing characterized by curiosity or uninvolved objectification," and yet this passage suggests that desire carries a cost for its agent as well as its object ("Politics" 65). Even as Helen asserts her own power and privilege by objectifying Richard, the chaotic flurry of emotions that she experiences at the sight of him (fascination, absorption, starvation) suggests a loss of agency, indicating that in her desire to possess Richard, Helen risks losing possession of herself. It is in this current, the play of desire, that the novel invites the reader to understand and experience the relationship between onlooker and extraordinary body as radically unstable and ambivalent.

PASSIONATE PRURIENCE

The complexity of the relationship between onlooker and extraordinary body in *The History of Sir Richard Calmady* is best illustrated through contrast with a strikingly stable model of a hierarchical visual relationship. In *Extraordinary Bodies*, Garland-Thomson, while discussing how the freak's body can be "fixed" by the gaze of the observer, refers to John Tagg's account of Victorian photographs of social deviants used in medical and social case studies: "the body isolated; the narrow space; the subjugation to an unreturnable gaze; the scrutiny of gestures, faces, and features; the clarity of illumination and sharpness of focus" (62). Tagg's description starkly indicates the disempowerment of the deviant in the context of a specific visual practice, and Garland-Thomson analogizes medical photography to the freak show in order to indicate the disempowerment of the freak. Yet the very starkness of the images described by Tagg, their lack of adornment in terms of costume and spiels, their insistence, indeed, on naked "truth" over myth, narrative, and fantasy, differentiates them from the freak show, which depended on story and visual embellishment.

Malet's novel, if read as a solicitation to, or embodiment of, one kind of gaze that might have been turned upon the extraordinary body, suggests that while the medical specimen is naked and exposed, the extraordinary body may in particular instances constitute a more mysterious object, continuously receding from a yearning gaze. Even as the novel constructs Richard's body as an object of display, it simultaneously maintains a level of secretiveness and coyness, which leaves both its characters and the reader with a sense of mystery. Richard is described approvingly as having a "wholesome pride," which is manifested in his "carefulness to avoid all exposure of his deformity" (Malet 194). His desire to avoid exposure of his legs and feet leads him to cover them all the time with rugs and blankets, which are tantalizingly inadequate to their task: "He leaned sideways, stretching out to a neighbouring chair with his right hand, keeping the light, silk-woven, red blanket up across his thighs with his left" (Malet 217); "He turned on his elbow restlessly, and the movement altered the lie of the bed-clothes, thereby disclosing the unsightly disproportion of his person through the light blanket and sheet" (Malet 199); and so on. In a novel that emphasizes the visual, and presents the reader with visual tableaux of Richard, it is striking that there is very little in the way of detailed visual description specifically of Richard's legs and feet. This visual reticence is supported by numerous narrative choices. For example, when a doctor visits Richard's home to try various prostheses on him, the narrative focuses not on Richard and the doctor, but rather on Richard's mother as she waits outside Richard's room. Thus the text refuses to allow the reader to witness certain passages in Richard's history that would reveal his body at too-close quarters. What is offered in this novel is not the money shot, but the burlesque dancer's play with fans and feathers—only in this perpetually repeated striptease act the props are rugs and blankets.

Richard's body comes to represent not the painfully, contemptibly knowable and known (the object of the medical photograph in Tagg's account), but rather the realm of the unknown and perhaps unknowable: the unthinkable experience and bewildering flesh of a unique and extraordinary being. For the amorous Helen, in this situation of visual dearth, even the outline of Richard's body, tantalizingly glimpsed through its various coverings, offers a drop of water in the desert: "her eyes, following down the lines of the fur rug, received renewed assurance of the fact of his deformity—hidden as far as might be, with decent pride, yet there, permanent and unalterable" (Malet 159). Helen is a self-conscious aesthete, who not only desires and seduces Richard but also, throughout the novel, offers a metatextual commentary on her own activities. Her interior monologue delineates in very suggestive terms the kind of desire that Richard's body arouses. She observes that "the man before her, by his very abnormality and a certain secretness inevitable in that, heightened her passion. He was to her of all living men most desirable, so that she must win him and hold him, must see and know" (Malet 298). The "secretness" of Richard's body produces a desire to "see and

Rachel O'Connell

know," but this desire is not the intellectual curiosity of the dispassionate scientist or medical photographer; it is passionate, urgent, and physical. It seeks not principles but experience, not objectivity but intimacy: it requires not only to see and know its object but also to approach it, to caress it, to hold it. Far from accepting the distinction between privileged self and subjugated other, Helen longs to break the barrier between freak and audience—to climb up onto the stage with Richard.

We could describe Helen's desire as a kind of passionate prurience, and we will do well to bear in mind the interdependency of the experiences of desire and curiosity to which the word "prurience" alerts us, as we seek to understand the gazes that pursue the disabled body, and the relation between disability and sexuality. In the seventeenth and eighteenth centuries, the word referred to the experience of "having an itching or longing." This older meaning seems to haunt Helen's prurience, which stems from the sense of longing that Richard's ever-receding body produces in her. The repeated loss of the sight of his body, as it is wrapped in blankets and concealed under rugs, creates a lack that incites her curious desire. Her interior monologue renders in text the gaze that Richard attracts. This gaze encompasses not the orgy of visual explicitness offered by the well-lit medical photograph, but rather a failing struggle to capture moving shadows, to bring blurred images into focus, to grasp at objects receding into the darkness.

Helen openly expresses her desire to Richard, telling him: "I do not say it would affect all women alike. . . . But there remain the elect, Richard, among whom I dare count myself. And over them, never doubt it, just that which you hate and which appears at first sight to separate you so cruelly from other men, gives you a strange empire. You stimulate, you arrest, you satisfy one's imagination, as does the spectacle of some great drama. . . . I saw you, and so doing I saw mysteries of joy in myself unimagined by me before" (Malet 306–7). The act of imagining is referred to twice in this passage and is repeatedly mentioned, particularly by Helen, throughout the novel. The mystery, the loss of Richard's body as it recedes from view, acts upon the imagination, stimulating it as though it were a sexual organ. The imagination attempts to fill in narrative gaps that the half-hidden body leaves empty. Desire must complete the body: not to make it "whole" again, but to make it reveal itself, to make it speak. Thus, when Helen gazes on Richard's partly covered body, in her imagination she (re-)creates Richard's "deformity" for herself from the imprecise form outlined by the rug that covers him.

The entire novel could be read as an expression of the affect of loss, and the resulting compulsion to embellish, that characterizes this gaze. By its very existence this unfashionably (for its time) prolix novel bears witness to a compulsion to plug up gaps in experience, to substitute unattainable intimacies with great wads of imaginative work, of narrative. In its insistence on "the honest depiction of aspects of life heretofore considered too repulsive for the novel," *The History of Richard Calmady* draws on the naturalism of Zola and Gissing (Schaffer xvi). Yet that naturalism takes on an unexpected edge if its explicitness is understood as the expression not of social conscience but of desire, the obsessive constructing of narrative prostheses to fill out the image of a cherished but mysterious body.[3] The novel's naturalism is inflected by the opium-soaked, entranced logic of aestheticism, whose style it adopts; it dwells with a kind of acquisitive wonder on Richard's body, much as Dorian Gray gazes, mesmerized, at his precious gems and embroidered cloths. This Peeping Tom of a novel looks upon the extraordinary body with a yearning gaze and caresses it with a trembling, covetous, nervously aggressive hand. In so doing, it invites us to retheorize the gaze of the freak show spectator and, more broadly, to reconsider the relationship among disability, desire, and visual culture.

The small example of Helen's imaginative recreation of Richard's blanketed body encapsulates the impulse behind Helen's much grander and more complex flights of fantasy about Richard, the "spectacle of some great drama" that he evokes in her mind. And yet the content of Helen's grandiose fantasies is left vague and nebulous. It is not clear what is at stake for Helen in the matter of Richard's body. Rather, the "great drama" of Helen's imagination exists in the novel as a floating placeholder, marking off a space of ludic fantasy. Helen's response to her imaginings, however, is more explicitly depicted. Helen is "Fired by . . . thoughts" of Richard. They "filled her with a certain intoxication, a voluptuous self-love. . . . She caressed her own neck, her own lips, with lingering finger-tips. She bent her bright head and kissed the swell of her cuplike breasts" (Malet 260).

The explicit association made between imagination and masturbation through Helen's character raises a self-referential question about the purpose of the novel, itself a work of imagination, about its genre, we might say. Helen is no stranger to stimulating fictions. She thinks mischievously of scandalizing lady tourists in Italy by suggesting that they "increase their knowledge of the Italian character and language by study of the Novelle of Bandello," a sixteenth-century collection of bawdy tales (Malet 259). Her maid reads a "yellow-paper-covered novel" while waiting for Helen on the steps of a church; in the 1890s the yellow cover would have suggested sexually explicit French fiction (Malet 288). Helen is also familiar with the corrupting literature of her lover, the debauched poet Destournelles, whose "technique is as amazingly clever as his thought is amazingly rotten" (Malet 296). Helen, the figure in the novel who represents the practice of generating narrative, produces not high art but masturbatory fantasies, and her favorite works of imaginative writing occupy a place not in the lofty canon of literature but in the soiled boudoir of trash, profanity, and smut.

Helen's presence as a proxy author figure facilitates a tacit admission that the novel itself has the potential to be ensconced within the curtains of that tawdry boudoir. *The History of Sir Richard Calmady* engages in narrative practices that border on the pornographic, as the novel makes use of certain qualities specifically associated with the extraordinary body for the purpose of titillation.[4] The ever-receding extraordinary body produces desires stemming from experiences of loss and lack; the secrecy surrounding the extraordinary body leaves it eminently textualizable, open to interpretation, inviting the elaboration and embellishment that take on the impossible task of filling the gap of desire. Thus, the extraordinary body opens up the expansive space of pleasure-oriented fantasy, the space of Helen's "great drama."

One night, sitting indoors in a lighted room, Helen gazes upon Richard standing on the dark balcony of his house in Naples: "slowly she raised her downcast eyes and looked after Richard Calmady, his figure a blackness, as of vacancy, against the elaborate wrought-ironwork of the balcony. And so doing, an adorable sensation moved her, at once of hungry tenderness and of fear—fear of something unknown, in a way fundamental, incalculable, the like of which she had never experienced before" (Malet 305). This image encapsulates the way in which Richard's body comes to operate as a placeholder, a chalk outline, a blank space or page on which the wildest narratives of perverse fantasy can be written and rewritten without end. Like a prairie or a tundra, the "strange empire" that Richard's body represents for Helen is a vast, empty, and unknown space, eerie and at the same time redolent with a sense of possibility, enticing to a colonizing imagination.[5] Or we might imagine the "strange empire" of the extraordinary body as a keyhole: that dark shape outlined against the door, that tiny, innocent aperture that, for the voyeur, coyly implies unlimited salacious possibilities. *The History of Sir Richard Calmady* is just one fantasy, one "great drama," emanating from this productive space.

Through its investment in the desire incited by the extraordinary body, the novel throws light on the potentially pornographic pleasures offered by the freak show and, more broadly, the powerful and perhaps transgressive sexual resonance of the extraordinary body. The location of Richard's body not only outside of but also in opposition to normative sexuality is indicated by the way in which the presence of his body disrupts the flow of the narrative in the novel. I have already observed that the novel contains spaces outside the narrative in which the text moves into a descriptive mode, conveying striking, theatrical tableaux of Richard's body that recall the freak show. These interludes represent the space of the spectacle, which introduces a moment of stillness and absorption. These ecstatic moments are contrasted with the conventional narratives that interweave with them: the stories of minor characters who obey the dictates of the marriage plot, bear (able-bodied) children, and generally participate in the dynamic, forward-moving time of progress, maturation, production, reproduction, and linear narrative development.

The History of Sir Richard Calmady repeatedly claims that the tragedy of Richard's life is that his physical difference debars him from participating in this (re)productive time of linear narrative. Yet in another sense Richard's location outside of this time indicates the potential that attaches to his physical difference. Moments in the novel that step outside the narrative of normativity offer a respite from its forceful flow, an escape from its narrow bounds. These spectacular moments make it possible to draw connections between the pleasures offered in this novel and queer theory's critiques of what Judith Halberstam calls "reproductive temporality" (*Queer Time* 4). The novel's temporal disruptions seem to anticipate and momentarily engage something like Halberstam's notion of "queer time," within whose "alternative temporalities . . . futures can be imagined according to logics that lie outside of conventional culture's paradigmatic markers of life experience—namely, birth, marriage, reproduction, and death" (2). *The History of Sir Richard Calmady* invites its readers to explore the "strange empire" of the extraordinary body: the territory of the spectacle, a location outside of progressive time and linear narrative in which the extraordinary body incites the desire and destabilizes the identity of the spectator and initiates countercultural ways of seeing social and sexual worlds.

By way of ending we might return to Garland-Thomson's observation, quoted at the start of this chapter, that the "history of disabled people in the Western world is in part the history of being on display" ("Politics" 56). Another way of describing this inheritance would be to say that conventional modes of representing the disabled body often overlap with the pornographic. Garland-Thomson argues that the situation of being on display is that of "being visually conspicuous

Rachel O'Connell

while politically and socially erased" ("Politics" 56). Malet's novel, however, asks us to reevaluate our expectations of the prurient, the smutty, and the obscene: to consider the possibility that pornography might have the capacity to give voice to a social critique.

NOTES

An earlier version of this chapter was published as "Cripsploitation: Desire, the Gaze, and the Extraordinary Body in *The History of Sir Richard Calmady*," in *Nineteenth Century Gender Studies* 4.2 (Summer 2008).

I have been lucky, in writing this chapter, to have had the support of several generous and supportive editors and interlocutors, all of whom have provided invaluable and transformative insights. I thank Robert McRuer and Anna Mollow for working with me so patiently and helpfully to prepare this chapter for publication in this collection. My thanks also go out to Mark Mossman and Martha Stoddard-Holmes, who helped me to prepare an earlier version of this chapter for publication in *Nineteenth Century Gender Studies*, a special issue on disability and the body in nineteenth-century Britain, of which they were the editors. I also thank Talia Schaffer, who first introduced me to *The History of Sir Richard Calmady*, who first instigated me to write about it, and who generously offered her insights on several drafts of this article. Finally, I offer my thanks to my colleagues and friends in the Disability Studies Reading Group, Alicia Blegen, Lezlie Frye, and Akemi Nishida, who did not work with me on this article but have supported me as I have learned about disability studies and about working with a disability.

1. The useful phrase "extraordinary body," coined by Rosemarie Garland-Thomson, refers to bodies that are now commonly described as "disabled" and that have in the past been called "disfigured": bodies that transgress or exceed culturally constructed definitions of the norm.

2. Robert McRuer argues that all of the four photographic rhetorics proposed by Garland-Thomson have "counterhegemonic" potential (*Crip Theory* 193). The argument I offer in this chapter is similar to McRuer's claim that, in the writing and performance art of Bob Flanagan, the exotic mode is rendered transgressive.

3. I take this useful phrase from David T. Mitchell and Sharon L. Snyder's *Narrative Prosthesis: Disability and the Dependencies of Discourse*.

4. We might deploy here the word "cripsploitation," a term of unclear provenance that in recent years has begun to be used sporadically in the fields of disability studies and disability performance.

5. I use the word "colonizing" to draw attention to the colonial resonance of Helen's phrase, "a strange empire." Race, nation, and empire constitute significant themes throughout the novel. The comparison of Richard to a lion, discussed earlier in this

essay, is another moment in which disability is connected to national and racial "otherness." In contrast, Richard's father is associated with a profoundly nostalgic and idealized version of Englishness. Perhaps the novel's strangest and most complex image, in terms of race, emerges during Richard's dream vision at the opera. Richard gazes upon Helen, who, sitting in a box at the opera, looks like "a woman fashioned . . . of ivory and gold" (Malet 324). As he watches her, a black creature, exquisite and lascivious, emerges from Helen's mouth and sits in her lap, beckoning to Richard (Malet 325). The way in which blackness, sexual lasciviousness, femininity, and freakishness coalesce in this creature brings to mind representations of Saartjie Baartman, a woman from what is now South Africa who was displayed as a freak in Europe in the early nineteenth century. In the novel's extraordinary image, then, the "Hottentot Venus" appears to emerge from the mouth, and sit in the lap, of a European woman of idealized beauty—a European woman, moreover, who is attending that bastion of high European culture, the opera. The interplay among race, nation, empire, and the extraordinary body in this novel is a topic that needs further research and analysis.

Rachel O'Connell

6

···························

MICHAEL DAVIDSON

PREGNANT MEN

Modernism, Disability, and Biofuturity

What you get married for if you don't want children?
—T. S. Eliot, *The Waste Land*

God, I never asked better than to boil some good man's potatoes and toss up a child for him every nine months by the calendar. Is it my fault that my only fireside is the outhouse? —Dr. Matthew O'Connor in Djuna Barnes, *Nightwood*

QUEER FUTURES AND THE REPRODUCTIVE HORIZON

During the last years of his governorship of California, in the aftermath of the presidential election of 2008—in which it was debated whether the candidates, including Senator Hillary Clinton, were *man* enough for the job— Arnold Schwarzenegger found his gendered authority under scrutiny. He had lately rocked the Republican cradle by supporting stem cell research, domestic partner legislation, and—depending on the month—abortion rights. Over the course of his career, he has morphed from body builder to Terminator to Governator. Perhaps as foreplay to his run for the nomination for the California governorship, Schwarzenegger's movie *Junior*, released in 1994, shows him morphing from Terminator into progenitor. He and Danny DeVito play genetic scientists who experiment with in vitro fertilization by implanting a fertilized egg in Arnold's hunky body. The plan is to bring the fetus into the first trimester, market a hormone that facilitates growth, and then terminate the pregnancy while cashing in on the new patent. The experiment works, and soon the Terminator is coming to terms with the inconveniences of morning sickness, hormone imbalance, and having to buy a full-figure wardrobe. Despite these discomforts, the formerly dour Arnold likes the kinder, gentler person he becomes through pregnancy and refuses to follow through on the plan to abort. The joke involves seeing Mr. Olympia become Mrs. Olympia, and although Arnold becomes a mom, cross-dressing at one point as a steroid-enhanced ex–East German female athlete at a maternity hospital, the film makes sure to reinforce the idea that he is not a girlie man by introducing a love interest between him and Emma Thompson, a fellow genetic scientist. Their relationship is complicated by the fact that the "anonymous donor" egg Arnold has fertilized (unbeknownst to her) is one of her own that she is using in her research. Thus in the end, Arnold has the baby that the two of them would have had anyway, and in the last scene, a visibly pregnant Emma shows that the Governator still has the right stuff.

Junior poses a question that may become more common in the genomic future: if a pregnant woman is the most natural thing in the world, what is a pregnant man? The movie's answer is that he's simply a more sensitive male, but perhaps another answer is that he is disabled. As DeVito tells Arnold, "if this gets out, you're a freak!" It turns out that the proximity of nonheterosexual reproduction and "freakish" disability is a common concern in a number of recent films and novels beginning with *Blade Runner* and continuing through *Coma*, *Never Let Me Go*, *Oryx and Crake*, *The Island*, *Gattaca*, the *X-Men* trilogy, and *The Children of Men*. In these texts, which raise bioethical questions about genetic research, surrogacy, and transplant surgery gone awry, the fantastic—or comic—narrative of a pregnant man becomes one among multiple futuristic scenarios for the biologically modified natural order. Such works are usually classified as speculative or science fiction, but one could also see them as disability narratives insofar as they defamiliarize the presumed normality of embodied life and display the nightmares of genetic futurity as the lived realities of disabled and dependent people.

If the scenario of a pregnant male has provided a freakish lens for the representation of disability, it has offered a normalizing lens on queer identity in an age of same-sex marriages, gay domesticity, and transgender parenting. Nowhere

Michael Davidson

is this phenomenon more evident than in the case of Thomas Beatie, a transgender, legally male individual who is married to a biological female, Nancy. The couple had wanted a child, but when Nancy had to undergo a hysterectomy, due to endometriosis, they decided that Beatie would stop taking the testosterone injections that had prevented his menstrual cycles and attempt, with the aid of a sperm donor, to become pregnant. After a first unsuccessful pregnancy, Beatie became pregnant again and delivered a baby girl in 2008. In an article in the *Advocate*, Beatie remarked on his then pregnant state: "How does it feel to be a pregnant man? Incredible. Despite the fact that my belly is growing with a new life inside me, I am stable and confident being the man that I am. In a technical sense I see myself as my own surrogate, though my gender identity as male is constant" (Beatie p. 3, par. 3). Beatie's pregnancy and his interviews with Barbara Walters, Oprah Winfrey, and others sparked an outcry in tabloids and on late-night television, many commentators echoing DeVito's concern about the freakish nature of the condition of male pregnancy. Yet in all of his interviews, Beatie stresses the ordinariness of his desire to give birth and his confidence in his masculine identity.

Although he does not address Beatie's pregnancy, Lee Edelman sees such events as a symptom of a new pronatalist scenario of compulsory reproduction that challenges queer identity's historically subversive character. Edelman argues that futurity is increasingly being written around the Child, capital "C," which remains "the perpetual horizon of every acknowledged politics, the fantasmatic beneficiary of every political intervention" (*No Future* 3). This family values scenario has, of course, been operative within the religious Right for some time, but it now applies to activism on behalf of gay marriage, domestic partner legislation, and child-raising that threatens to transform queer politics into something a good deal more mainstream. Edelman notes the peculiar logic of this syndrome that says if the Child represents the positive future for gays and lesbians, then queer must mean negative futurity: "*queerness* names the side of those *not* 'fighting for the children,' the side outside the consensus . . . outside and beyond its political symptoms, the place of the social order's death drive" (*No Future* 3). Why death drive? Because within the all-consuming logic of biological futurity, not accepting the telos of the child involves naming "what the queer, in the order of the social, is called forth to figure: the negativity opposed to every form of social viability" (*No Future* 9). It is here that queer and crip identities merge insofar as "social viability" usually means "compulsory able-bodiedness" as well as heteronormativity.[1] In the legal rhetoric of euthanasia proponents, to be "invalid" as a subject means having a life "not worth living." Hence, by a similar logic, crip futurity might be seen as the negation of those forms of embodiment and reproduction that medicine, psychoanalysis, and genetics must reinforce and affirm. As the Theresa Schiavo case in 2005 and the controversy over the film *Million Dollar Baby* in 2004 demonstrate, the nonproductive body that medical science would consign to the dustbin is always, potentially, the body we wouldn't want our daughter to bear, the body we wouldn't want to keep on life support, the body that, could it speak, would want not to be born. Edelman's argument is not about disability, but it does raise the question of what embodied futures can be envisioned when reproduction is no longer the province of the heteronormative family, when the Child no longer authorizes the narrative of biofuturity. Debates about surrogacy and in vitro fertilization invariably circle around whether such biotechnologies simply update eugenic practices that historically isolated and in some cases euthanized the deviant, disabled, or "feebleminded." If social reproduction mirrors biological reproduction, the Child, as Edelman says, performs important cultural labor in securing the Holy Family against contamination (*No Future* 19). When reproduction occurs outside of the female womb, the child that results—like Dionysus, born from the thigh of Zeus—may lead to social chaos and bacchic excess. As I will argue with respect to Djuna Barnes's *Nightwood*, the figure of the pregnant male is the site of such uncanny futurity—a figure feminized in his ability to bear children, queer in challenging traditional gender roles, disabled because freakish and often subjected to medical and therapeutic care.

As my example of Dionysus indicates, the theme of male pregnancy is hardly new. It is the foundation of many Western narratives—from Greek myth (the birth of Athena from the head of Zeus) to the Old Testament (Eve born from Adam's rib) to rituals of male couvade and sympathetic birthing to early modern literature. Plato in *Thaeatetus* speaks of "philosophical pregnancy," in which the corporeal pregnancy of women is contrasted to the philosophical travail enabled by Socrates.[2] Eighteenth-century molly houses, or gay taverns, included yearly "Festival Nights" in which men participated in acts of cross-dressing, birthing, and lying-in as forms of gay parturition camp.[3] As Sherry M. Velasco points out, the image of male pregnancy appears in numerous medieval and early modern works by Cervantes, Boccaccio, Shakespeare, and Dryden. In such early narratives the trope of male pregnancy posits epistemological or aesthetic creativity against female conception, gestation, and birth (in his prologue to *Don Quixote*, Cervantes describes his book as "the child of my brain").[4] In the modernist era, however, what had been a metaphor for aesthetic fecundity—the male author's ability to transmit his literary legacy parthenogenetically—became a biofuturist potentiality. At a moment in which racial science and eugenics presented brave new worlds purged of defective, degenerate bodies, and in which sexological discourse made visible (and pathological) a new set of practices and subjects, the spectacle of male pregnancy was enlisted to imagine futures written in biopolitical terms.

Modernist cultural representations of the pregnant male foreground the spectacle of reproduction loosed from its putative organic site in the female body and displace it elsewhere: the test tube, the surrogate womb, the male body, and—not insignificantly—the novel. This displacement effects both a queering and a cripping of normative attitudes toward reproductive health and the futures that such embodiment implies. The displacement of pregnancy away from female bodies warps traditional *narrative* attitudes toward biological futurity when the family romance no longer reproduces the heterosexual family. It is in this context that I read Djuna Barnes's novel *Nightwood*: not as a baroque anomaly among stream-of-consciousness narratives of Woolf, Stein, or Faulkner, but as arguably *the* representative modernist novel insofar as it offers an inside narrative of individuals interpellated within biological and racial science.[5] Rather than seeing the cultural logic of male pregnancy as a simple displacement of gestation from female to male body, I see it as a figuring diaspora of sexual and gendered possibilities among bodies and minds of various abilities and cognitive registers.

Throughout the Progressive Era, practical versions of eugenic theories were applied in asylums, hospitals, and prisons, in which "inverts" and mental "defectives" were sterilized, incarcerated, or euthanized in the name of racial and psychological purity and national consolidation. If eugenics imagined a future of better babies and healthy families, it also constructed a past to which those deformed and disabled bodies could now be consigned. Thus the "Old World" could be used to describe both the backwardness of immigrants who refused to relinquish their cultural traditions and those deemed lower (and earlier) on a social Darwinian evolutionary scale. Prompted by the writings of Francis Galton, Magnus Hirschfield, Otto Weininger, and Richard von Krafft-Ebing, modernist writers often annexed their futurisms—including their linguistic innovations— to such biopolitical reforms. These fatal alignments have made it impossible to dissever Ezra Pound's historical poetics, Gertrude Stein's theories of the bottom nature, F. T. Marinetti's posthuman futurism, or T. S. Eliot's anthropological interests from their intellectual pursuits of racial science and eugenics. Nor were their investments strictly theoretical. Here, for instance, is D. H. Lawrence: "If I had my way, I would build a lethal chamber as big as the Crystal Palace, with a military band playing softly, and a Cinematograph working brightly. Then I'd go out in the back streets and main streets and bring them in, all the sick, the halt, and the maimed; I would lead them gently, and they would smile me a weary thanks" (qtd. in D. Childs 10). Lawrence's fusion of commercial exhibition site and gas chamber suggests that within the cultural advance guard two futures were envisioned, one for racial others, persons with disabilities, and sexual "inverts," and another for Northern European, heterosexual, able-bodied persons. The latter were provided with utopian solutions, socialist and fascist, for a future free of what was politely called "amalgamation." For the former, however, there was to be no future. They represented the past, the ill-formed, the animal, that needed to be expunged for the "right" future to be possible. As we will see with respect to *Nightwood*, this negative future also produced a carnivalesque modernism that contests Lawrence's draconian version.

In this context, male maternity becomes a metaphor that enables modernism to figure negative futures in relation to the threat posed by nontraditional forms of reproduction. The figure of the pregnant male could be seen as a camera obscura on modernity's anxieties over violated biology and traduced nature. Dr. Schreber is the exemplar. In Freud's case study of 1911, Schreber's paranoid psychosis, as Schreber describes it in his *Memoirs of a Neurotic*, takes the form of a messianic feeling that he must redeem the world by producing a superior race of men. In order to fulfill his destiny, he must first be transformed into a woman and then become impregnated by God. Reading this fantasy as a diversion of Schreber's conflicting homosexual desires onto a transgendered scenario, Freud does not confront the maternity that is at the heart of the fantasy. In order to diagnose the *vehicle* of Schreber's fantasy—homosexuality as pathology—Freud must avoid the fantasy of parthenogenesis—his "womb envy"—that is the troubling *tenor*.[6] This form of desire (and Freud's attempt to contain it within a diagnosis of "perverse" sexuality) becomes particularly salient at a historical moment in which medical science is intervening in reproduction; that is, as eugenic social policies and practices attempt to stabilize gender and racial differences and monitor reproductive processes and potential sexual partners. Within eugenic futurity, such engineering would force women to cede control of reproduction to males and thus become ancillary to the biological order. As Freud's diagnosis illustrates, Schreber's desire to redeem the world through pregnancy is the "outburst of homosexual libido" that must be returned to heterosexual conformity (*Three* 145). The specter of male maternity is among those forms of reproduction

Michael Davidson

that cannot be figured either as part of the Progressive Era's narratives of health and improvement or in terms of modernist aesthetics' formalism of the spatial or organic text.

Dr. Schreber is one among a small but significant modernist gallery of male characters who in various ways assume feminine reproductive roles. Another candidate for this category is Ralph Touchett in Henry James's *Portrait of a Lady*. Ralph's mysterious, lingering illness serves as a period of gestation during which—since he cannot produce a child with Isabel Archer—he may produce a surrogate by assigning his inheritance to her. Isabel is then free to choose a future for herself, unencumbered by financial concerns, a freedom she sacrifices by marrying the Machiavellian Gilbert Osmond. As Eve Kosofsky Sedgwick points out with reference to James's bachelors, Ralph's illness represents his inability to imagine heterosexual futurity, not because he is homosexual—the category had barely emerged discursively—but because his lack of heterosexual desire renders him invalid within the terms of social viability.[7] He is an "invalid," not only in the medical sense but also according to the proprieties of late-Victorian sexual mores, which can imagine a procreative future only within the family. To fail to imagine such a future is to enact a form of invalidism or perpetual bachelorhood. By transferring his paternal inheritance to Isabel, Ralph may produce a family in absentia, leaving Isabel—as it turns out—to suffer the grim consequences of confusing Ralph's bequest with freedom of choice.

A second and more obvious example of male maternity is Leopold Bloom in Joyce's Nighttown chapter of *Ulysses*. Bloom relives his daytime cultural and racial ostracism at night through a sadomasochistic nightmare of abjection in Bella Cohen's brothel. Wearing a corset and forced onto his knees by the "whoremistresses" Bella, he endures the slings and arrows of female domination and authority (402). Stately plump Buck Mulligan, in his capacity as medical student, appears on this phantasmagoric scene to pronounce Bloom, who is about to have a baby, "bisexually abnormal" (429). "O I so want to be a mother," Bloom declares, whereupon he promptly produces "eight male yellow and white children . . . wellmade, respectably dressed and wellconducted, speaking five modern languages fluently and interested in various arts and sciences" (Joyce 403). During his peregrinations throughout Dublin, Bloom has mourned the loss of his son, Rudy, and repressed his sexual alienation from his wife, Molly. Now, in his nightmare confrontation with his own femininity, he becomes, as Mulligan says, "a finished example of the new womanly man" (Joyce 403). Sandra Gilbert and Susan Gubar read such fantasies of "sexual inversion" as signs of "the excesses of female misrule associated with women's liberation during the war years" that Bloom casts off in the novel's final scenes by taking control of his domestic situation (334). But as with Freud's analysis of Dr. Schreber, critics like Gilbert and Gubar tend to read such scenes of feminized masculinity as signs of historical gender trouble that patriarchy strives to monitor. They do not account for the "womb envy" and erotic pleasure identified with female sexuality that Bloom has experienced throughout the day and that appear in their more carnivalized forms in Joyce's "Circe" chapter of *Ulysses*.

My third example of male pregnancy appears in Ezra Pound's "Canto XII," in which the speaker repeats a story that the lawyer and arts patron John Quinn has told a group of bankers about a sailor who, while in hospital following a bout of drinking, appears to have delivered a child. When the sailor wakes up from his ordeal, the hospital staff presents him with a child just delivered by a poor prostitute and then declare: "Here! this is what we took out of you" (Pound 56). The sailor recovers, saves, and invests his money, and having prospered, sends his child to college. On his deathbed, the honest sailor responds to his son's solicitude:

> "Don't, don't talk about me, I'm all right,
>   "It's you, father."
>   "That's it, boy, you said it.
>   "You called me your father, and I ain't.
>   "I ain't your dad, no,
>   "I am not your fader but your moder," quod he,
>   "Your fader was a rich merchant in Stambouli" (Pound 56–57)

Pound draws upon the Dantean condemnation of usurers and sodomites as those who pervert nature through economic and sexual practices that prevent natural increase. Quinn's story mocks the bankers he addresses ("*Alias* usurers in excelsis") by suggesting that the sailor's belief that he has produced a child due to a homosexual encounter is a bawdy version of what the bankers themselves practice by charging interest. Like Eliot's Mr. Eugenides in *The Waste Land*, who solicits a homosexual tryst with the poem's speaker, the honest sailor of "Canto XII" is identified with the merchant class, whose mobility and cosmopolitanism are a threat to both heterosexual and national stability. Male pregnancy, in each of the examples I have described, is linked to the conflation of material wealth and biological dystopia, whether through Ralph Touchett's diversion of his paternal inheritance to facilitate a loveless marriage, Bloom's absorption of anti-Semitic slurs about thrift and money lending, or the honest sailor's merging of childbirth with the increase of wealth. And although it may seem a stretch to link these scenes of male pregnancy with disability, they lay bare the artifice of bodily normality by imagining biological reproduction as an unnatural act performed through an unnatural body.

"IMPERMISSIBLE BLOOD":
NIGHTWOOD AND THE GENEALOGICAL IMPERATIVE

A more complex instance of this intertwinement of sexuality, disability, and reproduction is the representation of Dr. Matthew O'Connor in Djuna Barnes's *Nightwood* (1936). Although his qualifications as a pregnant male are not quite as overt as in my previous examples, O'Connor's queerness is organized around his feminized reproductive desires: "for no matter what I may be doing, in my heart is the wish for children and knitting. God, I never asked better than to boil some good man's potatoes and toss up a child for him every nine months by the calendar" (Barnes 91). As a sham gynecologist-cum-psychoanalyst, O'Connor is the carnivalesque version of those late nineteenth-century professionals who monitored the minds and bodies of women, disabled people, and homosexuals.[8] O'Connor violates the terms of clinical practice, with his filthy room and brimming "swill pail," his decaying obstetric equipment ("a rusty pair of forceps, a broken scalpel"), and his reversal of the psychoanalytic protocols (he *asks* rather than *answers* the questions; he lies on the couch while the patient occupies the analyst's position in the chair).[9] But as self-acknowledged outsider, "the old woman in the closet," O'Connor is uniquely positioned to advise one of the main characters, Nora Flood, about the vagaries of interstitial identity. In the novel's central scene, Nora encounters him late at night at home, crossdressed in a woman's nightgown and wig, heavily made-up, and surrounded by cosmetics ("perfume bottles, almost empty, pomades, creams, rouges, powder boxes and puffs" [Barnes 79]). She has sought his counsel on the matter of her abortive lesbian relationship with Robin Vote, but his elliptical answers are informed as much by his own abject status as by his psychoanalytic understanding. As someone whose "only fireside is the outhouse" and who haunts the "pissoirs as naturally as Highland Mary her cows," he domesticates the underworld of Paris and regards his circulation within the queer demimonde as a bucolic dérive that, if it includes casual sex in public, may as easily include a stop at the Catholic Church—not, as it turns out, to hear Mass, but to masturbate. In short, his queerness occupies narratives of both sexual abjection and domestic or institutional normality.[10]

As a cross-dressing male with maternal desires, as the doctor who "brought [Nora] into the world," Dr. O'Connor combines the roles of father and mother, obstetrician and pregnant woman, analyst and analysand, which medical science segregates. By blending these roles he functions much as Tiresias does in *The Waste Land*, as a prophet of dystopic futurity, albeit in a more Rabelaisian version. If he is *un*-reproductive as mother or doctor, he is *pro*-ductive as raconteur and storyteller, his bawdy anecdotes and salacious gossip providing much of the "matter" of the novel. O'Connor's rambling speeches refuse any linear narrative that would end with familial resolution and restoration of order. The novel's non sequiturs, baroque rhetoric, and elaborate hyperbole force attention onto the surface of language, rather than elucidating some interior psychological state. Barnes's novel is the antithesis of the modernist interior monologue, which attempts to render some subterranean, unchanging bottom nature or core personality. O'Connor's monologues shatter stable identities, merging scatological and theological rhetoric, vernacular and dynastic culture, ornate metaphors and performative denunciations. Such linguistic mixing is a textual version of that racial and sexual ambiguity that threatened the interwar European bourgeoisie. And as I will show with respect to Barnes's portrayal of disabled characters, O'Connor's verbal grotesquerie is a textual equivalent of the nontraditional body, the circus freak or mentally ill patient who cannot be assimilated into normative models of health, growth, and the statistical average. In this respect Dr. O'Connor's "child" is the text his logorrhea continually produces.

O'Connor's reproductive desires are expressed within a novel with a child at its center, but the child, rather than redeeming history, often serves as a reminder of its loss. The novel's opening lines suggest that in *Nightwood* childbirth is a matter not of biology but of discourses about race and the body:

> Early in 1880, in spite of a well-founded suspicion as to the advisability of perpetuating that race which has the sanction of the Lord and the disapproval of the people, Hedvig Volkbein—a Viennese woman of great strength and military beauty, lying upon a canopied bed of a rich spectacular crimson, the valance stamped with the bifurcated wings of the House of Hapsburg, the feathered coverlet an envelope of satin on which, in mas-

Michael Davidson

sive and tarnished gold threads, stood the Volkbein arms—gave birth, at
the age of forty-five, to an only child, a son, seven days after her physician
predicted that she would be taken. (1)

As Joseph Boone has observed, this opening passage establishes a theme of "es-
trangement and permanent wandering" that characterizes this marginal society
and that finds its primal form in the birth trauma (238). The child, Felix Volkbein,
is born not into the *heimlich* family but into perpetual alienation and dislocation;
he is a product of his parents' aspirations for national and cultural authority. To
some extent he is the prototype for all the novel's other characters, in their deterritorialized relationships to family, nation, and heteronormativity. Barnes's
baroque prose, with its multiple subordinate elements and qualifiers, imitates the
ornate features of the Volkbein coat of arms, a design whose elegance contains
both the schematic memory of Habsburg greatness and the anti-Semitism at its
secret heart. It turns out that the heraldic design is utterly fabricated, a pastiche
invented by the father, Guido Volkbein, in an attempt to fashion a noble lineage
as a bulwark against racial memory.[11] Like so much else in the novel, surface design belies uncertain origins. Hedvig Volkbein's dedication to Austro-Christian
militarism is qualified by her fear that the son she is about to bear contains the
"impermissible blood" of the Jew. Her husband, although steeped in Christian
and aristocratic trappings, is Jewish and lives with the memory of his historic
racial oppression. For early critics of the novel like Philip Rahv, who felt that
Barnes simply "exploited perversion to create an atmosphere of general mystification and psychic disorder," such passages suggest that the "psychic disorder"
has a historical referent in the anti-Semitism that haunted fin-de-siècle Europe
and would lead, ultimately, to the death camps (qtd. in Parsons 60).

As the child with whom the novel opens, Felix Volkbein embodies the dying
embers of empiric Europe, epitomized by his mother's Habsburg origins and
father's diasporic (Italian and Jewish) lineage. His father, Guido, wears a hand-
kerchief commemorating a fifteenth-century Roman ordinance that forced Jews
to race in the public square with a rope about their necks "for the amusement of
the Christian populace" (Barnes 2). Through this bit of sartorial display, Guido
Volkbein signals a tragic awareness of his racial otherness yet at the same time
distances himself from the "impermissible blood" that is his heritage. Felix in-
herits his father's "remorseless homage to nobility" and his Viennese mother's
militarism; he hopes to pass both on to his own son (Barnes 2). Lacking any contact with his biological parents and obsessed with history, Felix creates a mythi-

cal past based on "Old Europe," old masters' paintings, excellent manners, royal titles, and the Catholic Church. Because he has no authentic link to royalty, he creates a soi-disant aristocracy out of the circus and the theater, "sham salons in which he aped his heart" (Barnes 11). Caught between fake aristocrat and wandering Jew, Felix is the epitome of the "rootless cosmopolitan" despised equally by Hitler and Stalin, whose home is the café, the salon, and the hotel foyer and whose origins lie in the racially assimilated culture of Habsburg middle Europe.

If Felix expresses a nostalgia for the blood of aristocratic privilege and the hierarchical authority of the sovereign, his own son, also named Guido, is a stereotype of eugenicist degeneration theory through inbreeding:[12] "as time passed it became increasingly evident that his child, if born to anything, had been born to holy decay. Mentally deficient and emotionally excessive, an addict to death; at ten, barely as tall as a child of six, wearing spectacles, stumbling when he tried to run, with cold hands and anxious face, he followed his father, trembling with an excitement that was a precocious ecstasy" (Barnes 107). The fact that the son of Felix Volkbein and Robin Vote, a Jewish man and a lesbian, is mentally ill is no small feature of the novel's representation of the ostracized other; it is a fact as important to its modernist diagnosis of decay as Benjy Compson's cognitive disability is to *The Sound and the Fury* or the hemophilia of the czar's son, Alexis Romanov, is to the narrative of the Bolshevik Revolution. The disabled child becomes the specter of tainted blood that eugenics sought to control.[13]

The child's historically overdetermined existence—mentally retarded, Jewish, motherless, physically stunted—marks the novel's thematic treatment of the child as the site of dystopic futures. Unlike the romantic Bildungsroman, which must return the orphaned child to his or her familial legacy, Barnes's children—real and imagined—are perpetual isolatoes who upset the domestic ideal of the stable, heterosexual family and the continuity of biologically reproductive futurity that is the centerpiece of much narrative fiction. Young Guido is not the only child in the novel. The discrete object of desire in the novel, Robin, is often called a child—her bisexuality, sexual adventurousness, and somnambulism suggesting Freud's preconscious, infant state, which exists outside of or prior to socialization. If O'Connor is logorrheic, Robin is virtually mute, uttering only a few phrases in the novel as a sign, perhaps, of her preoedipal, prelinguistic status. The lesbian relationship she shares with Nora is defined as one between an overly protective mother (Nora) and a wayward child (Robin). Although Robin is figured as a child, she is also a mother of a child, Guido. Yet her maternal abilities are nonexistent; she leaves the child-raising aspects of her married life

Michael Davidson

to her husband, Felix. Childlike in her passiveness and blankness, Robin bears some similarity to a doll. The doll becomes an important metonym for the lesbian relationship itself and an object toward which charged emotional energies are focused. Nora and Robin share a doll that they call their "child," and when she becomes angered at Nora's possessiveness, Robin smashes the doll on the floor. Later, when Robin leaves Nora for a new lover, Jenny Petherbridge, the latter gives her a doll as a sign of their new relationship (Barnes 147). O'Connor, ever wise in the meaning of partial objects, links dolls specifically to queer identity: "The last doll, given to age, is the girl who should have been a boy, and the boy who should have been a girl! The love of that last doll was foreshadowed in the love of the first. The doll and the immature have something right about them, the doll because it resembles but does not contain life, and the third sex because it contains life but resembles the doll" (Barnes 148). This comparison of the queer and the doll summarizes the period's sexological characterizations of homosexuality as a stage of arrested (bisexual) development, but it hints at the performative character of queer identity in which the doll becomes a theatrical surface upon which "normal" sexual relations are embossed. Where Krafft-Ebing or Havelock Ellis pathologized the "third sex," for Barnes it seems to be a form of innocence that escapes both Felix's genealogical imperative and Nora's parental restrictions. O'Connor, in his late night analytic session with Nora, encourages her to "bow down" to that innocence, for which the doll is a partial object, and accept difference as a mode of being.

Nightwood was written at a transition point in eugenicist and sexological discourses. Although the date of its origin is in dispute—it was possibly begun as early as 1927 and was published, with the help of T. S. Eliot, in 1936—it clearly chronicles Barnes's passionate love affair with Thelma Wood, which began in 1921 and ended in 1929.[14] Despite the fact that many of her contemporaries and friends (Mina Loy, Natalie Barney, Gertrude Stein, and T. S. Eliot) had absorbed eugenic theories, Barnes is not known to have been interested in movements for racial purity. However, her novel's cast of queers, cross-dressers, disabled persons, and racialized outsiders seems drawn from one of Bertillon's or Lambroso's catalogues of "defectives." The period during which *Nightwood* was composed saw a shift from theoretical to more material applications of eugenics through the increased use of incarceration, euthanasia, and sterilization, which would lead to the Nazi Final Solution.[15] Felix Volkbein's sham aristocracy and nobility ape the racialized and sexualized characters' perverse relationship to eugenic taxonomies. Against the imperative to categorize and monitor bodies, Barnes creates a

world, as Jane Marcus writes, of "merging, dissolution, and above all, hybridiza-
tion–mixed metaphors, mixed genres, mixed levels of discourse from the lofty to
the low" (223). Barnes's characters, far from being a sideshow to the main event,
are the primary agents of the novel; they accept their outsider status and form
what Joseph Boone characterizes as "demimonde of the 'inappropriate'" (234).

The centerpiece of this demimonde is the circus. Most of the characters are,
in some way, connected to carnival and theater as a sign of their marginal relationship to the dominant society. Significant events occur in dressing rooms
and backstage areas, where the divisions between reality and fantasy, body and
costume, human and animal become confused. The false Baron, Felix Volkbein,
frequents the circus because its denizens defy his acquisitive temperament: "The
circus was a loved thing that he could never touch, therefore never know. . . . The
people of the theatre and the ring were for him as dramatic and as monstrous as
a consignment on which he could never bid" (Barnes 12). Through Dr. O'Connor,
we meet Nikka, the black, tattooed bear wrestler; the trapeze artist Frau Mann;
"the Duchess of Broadback"; and others, "gaudy, cheap cuts from the beast life,
immensely capable of that great disquiet called entertainment" (Barnes 11). In
a world in which characters are already marked racially or sexually, the circus
provides a richly embroidered backdrop for that inversion of roles that Bakh-
tin characterizes as the carnivalesque. Felix's obsession with royal titles is mimicked in the circus performers' adoption of titles: Princess Nadja, Principessa
Stasera y Stasero, and King Buffo. Nora is a publicist for the Denckeman Circus in New York; she meets Robin in front of the lion cage. Robin meets Jenny,
for whom she leaves Nora, at a performance of *Rigoletto*, an opera with a court
jester and hunchback in its title role. Robin meets Nora at an evening at Count
Altamonte's in which the attendees are described as "living statues." O'Connor's
speeches themselves always seem to be dramatic monologues, full of quotations
from plays (in his preface Eliot compared the novel to Elizabethan tragedy).
Felix provides the best gloss on the value of carnival performativity when he
says, "[one's] life is peculiarly one's own when one has invented it" (Barnes 118).
Readers may hear vestiges of Wildean aestheticism in this remark — and, indeed,
Felix does seem to be a kind of deterritorialized dandy — but it achieves particular historical valence in the context of Weimar era disruptions.

Perhaps most important in reinforcing the carnivalesque are the many references to animals. Robin is described as a "beast becoming human"; elsewhere,
Dr. O'Connor describes her as "an eland coming down an aisle of trees . . . a
hoof raised in the economy of fear" (37). Like the animal trainers and sideshow

Michael Davidson

characters in Tod Browning's movie *Freaks*, released in 1932, circus performers often resemble the animals they tend ("the men smelling weaker and the women stronger than their beasts" [Barnes 11]). In the novel's last scene, Robin, in order to demonstrate her abject status to Nora, gets down on all fours in front of Nora's dog, barking and crawling after him in a "fit of laughter, obscene and touching" (Barnes 170). The inversion of the word "God" in "dog," coupled with Robin's performance of this act in a chapel, suggests the ultimate reversal of theological and sexual values implied in the eugenicist term "degeneration." With respect to this chapter's concern with biological futurity, such moments call into question species identity and blur the boundaries between human and animal, animate and inanimate, sacred and profane. Robin's much analyzed imitation of a dog seems less a sign of her lesbian abjection, as critics have said, than a fulfillment of O'Connor's injunction to Nora to "bow down" to the animal nature her rational human subjectivity repudiates.

"THERE IS MORE IN SICKNESS THAN THE NAME OF THAT SICKNESS"

Critics have devoted extensive attention to *Nightwood*'s feminist, lesbian, and antiracist features, but they have not attended to its representations of disability, either as embodied in the novel's characters or as a diagnostic tool for testing attitudes about bodily normality. On the one hand, Barnes trades in stereotypes of impairment as character flaw, Guido's mental illness and his father's monocular vision being the most obvious examples.[16] On the other hand, disability underlies many of the characterizations of marginality in the novel, making it a kind of *ur*-identity for the stigmatized body—from Nikka's tattooed body to Robin's dementia. Despite (or because of) his fake credentials as a doctor, O'Connor offers an excellent diagnosis of the social model of disability. Speaking of Guido's mental illness, he notes that

> His sanity is an unknown room: a known room is always smaller than an unknown. If I were you, the doctor continued, I would carry that boy's mind like a bowl picked up in the dark: you do not know what's in it. He feeds on odd remnants that we have not priced. He eats a sleep that is not our sleep. There is more in sickness than the name of that sickness. In the average person is the peculiar that has been scuttled, and in the peculiar the ordinary that has been sunk; people always fear what requires watching. (Barnes 120)

Instead of regarding Guido as a "defect" or "retarded child," O'Connor treats him as a field of potential, a reminder of the "peculiar" that the rational mind must repress. O'Connor anticipates current theoretical accounts that regard disability not as the name that medicine gives to impairment but as those limits that the so-called average person imposes on nonnormative bodies and processes of cognition. O'Connor's remarks recognize the anxiety—what Ato Quayson calls "aesthetic nervousness"—over bodily contingency that disability occasions among able-bodied persons. As O'Connor concludes, in a remark that could apply to many of the marginal figures in *Nightwood*, "people always fear what requires watching."[17] Since all the characters in the novel are objects of a scopic regime, whether as theatrical actors or as cross-dressing freaks, they "require watching." O'Connor's play of words on "require" suggests that persons with disabilities "require" policing and monitoring, yet their difference fascinates and amazes.

A second modality of disability in the novel is as a metaphor for excessive or liminal existence. Barnes compares Nora's desire for Robin, during the latter's late night perambulations, to the aftereffects of an amputation: "As an amputated hand cannot be disowned because it is experiencing a futurity, of which the victim is its forebear, so Robin was an amputation that Nora could not renounce. As the wrist longs, so her heart longed, and dressing she would go out into the night that she might be 'beside herself'" (Barnes 59). Robin has begun to "wander," both literally into the city and sexually into other relationships, and Nora stays awake at night like an anxious parent, experiencing her lover's absence as a phantom limb. In Barnes's complicated figure, disability is a marker of absence, but it is also a marker of lesbian desire insofar as the body from which Nora feels alienated is like her own. Nora acknowledges that "Robin has been both my lover and my child. For Robin is incest, too; that is one of her powers" (Barnes 156). Hence, when she goes out at night, Nora is "beside herself" with anxiety for the beloved but also one with the beloved as an aspect of herself. Freud regarded homosexuality as an arrested stage in the evolution of normal sexuality out of its bisexual childhood nature. Barnes repudiates this logic, writing in a letter to Emily Coleman, "[well] of course those two women would never have been in love with each other if they had been *normal*, if any man had slept with them, if they had been well f—and had born a child." To the heterosexist logic that equates fulfillment with male intervention, Barnes responds that this is "ignorance and utterly false. I married Robin to prove this point, she had married, had a child yet was still 'incurable'" (qtd. in Plumb xviii). Barnes's mocking use of queerness as disease ("incurable"), heterosexuality and ableism as cure, undercuts the way that biologistic theories of normative sexuality and embodiment reinforce a heteronormative ideal whose default is reproduction. As one of Eliot's cockney pub denizens asks Lil in *The Waste Land*, "What you get married for if you don't want children?" (42).

Eliot's speaker's question states in demotic terms the poet's elegiac theme of unproductive nature, but whereas the author of *The Waste Land* bemoans the aridity of sexual relationships, Barnes sees pronatalism's compulsory character as a ruse to isolate and marginalize. Despite these differences in evaluation, Eliot's admiration of *Nightwood* stems from the way Barnes figures the crisis of post-Habsburg Europe through images of debased, abjected bodies that bear the full weight of historical loss. In one crucial passage, Dr. O'Connor tries to describe Felix Volkbein: "There's something missing and whole about the Baron Felix—damned from the waist up, which reminds me of Mademoiselle Basquette, who was damned from the waist down, a girl without legs, built like a medieval abuse. She used to wheel herself through the Pyrenees on a board" (Barnes 26). O'Connor sees Felix (whose false baronial title mimics the doctor's own fake medical credentials) as the inverted reflection of Mademoiselle Basquette, whose missing legs damn her from the waist down, the more so because they render her vulnerable to abuse: "a sailor saw her one day and fell in love with her. . . . So he snatched her up, board and all, and took her away and had his will; when he got good and tired of her, just for gallantry, he put her down on her board about five miles out of town, so she had to roll herself back again, weeping something fearful to see, because one is accustomed to see tears falling down to the feet" (Barnes 26). Mademoiselle Basquette's vulnerability as a disabled woman is the other side of Felix's disability as a Jew in pre-Nazi Austria. O'Connor's response to this story is to see her pathos in terms of the way that disability unsettles the usual image of suffering: "Ah, truly, a pin board may come up to the chin of a woman and still she will find reason to weep. I tell you, Madame, if one gave birth to a heart on a plate, it would say 'Love' and twitch like the lopped leg of a frog" (Barnes 27). In his elaborate metaphor O'Connor reduces love to an involuntary muscle, one that, like Nora's phantom limb relationship to Robin, is both separate from the body yet able to live an independent life. On the one hand, it is a figure of the endurance of affect—the idea that even in the most reduced circumstance, the heart has its reasons of which reason is unaware. On the other hand, it is a figure of abjection that we see everywhere in the novel—the body without organs, the body violated, and most importantly, the disabled body subject to the able-bodied sailor.

By reading *Nightwood* against the backdrop of Fascism, Marcus and others have usefully shown how the novel's carnivalesque treatment of an alternate society of Jews, queers, and disabled persons must be read within the context of Hitler and Mussolini's rise to power in Europe, as well as through the period's use of medical science in the name of racial purity. Cognitive impairment becomes, in the public mind, the logical outgrowth of aristocratic inbreeding and women's independence. In *Nightwood* there is no redemptive, atavistic survival or folkloric tradition waiting to redeem the shards of fragmented culture. The modernism of *Nightwood* rests in its exposure of the cultural logic whereby bodies and affective states are marshaled into categories of able-ness and heteronormativity. Barnes strikes at the heart of how those categories are normalized within the family by queering the family unit: her novel presents us with a transgender obstetrician who wants to become pregnant, a lesbian mother who is more a child than her own child, and a heterosexual Jewish male who wants his mentally retarded son to be the next czar. If these scenarios sound like variations on Freud's case studies of sexual delusion, they also constitute the family values ethos of Barnes's Rabelaisian fiction and pose a different (and more sympathetic) assessment of those "hooded hoards" and neurasthenic women that populate modernist texts.

LEGAL FICTIONS

In her book *Pregnant Men*, the feminist legal theorist Ruth Colker argues that restrictions on reproductive freedom for women are hampered by the fact that the Supreme Court refuses to regard that freedom as gender based: "Put simply, there are no pregnant men to which we could compare women to show gender-based treatment. All pregnant *people* are treated alike; it is irrelevant (to the Supreme Court) that all pregnant people are women" (128). In the early 1990s, when Colker's book was written, this formulation may have seemed unremarkable. Today, with the increased use of genetic engineering, surrogacy, and in vitro fertilization, the question of pregnant personhood is a good deal more complex.[18] In order to deal with gender discrimination around pregnancy and reproductive health, Colker observes, "We need a way to talk about pregnant men" (128). If we could, she observes, we would see that many of the legal claims for equal rights do not take female biology into account, nor do they take into account the misogynist nature of groups that oppose abortion and support violence against women and doctors at abortion clinics. Colker uses a legal fiction —

a pregnant male—to situate a legal reality that ultimately disempowers women by ceding reproduction to males.

In reading male pregnancy through the lens of disability theory, I am positing a way of talking about repro-futurity outside of its heteronormative frame. Doing so illustrates what happens when reproduction is removed from female biology and shifted discursively onto other bodies. I am not saying that we should seriously consider male parenting as equivalent to childbearing (as popular self-help books seem to be doing lately). Rather, I am suggesting that to speak about male pregnancy is implicitly to describe a close relationship between disability and sexuality. We might say, adapting Stuart Hall, that disability is a modality through which sex is lived.[19] The castration complex, to take one example, involves aligning a missing limb with an attitude about male sexual potency—and, by extension, the lack of that potency in women. The fear of losing that limb, in Freudian thought, translates into the fear of becoming a woman. Or as Dr. O'Connor says of Nora, "[she is] one of those deviations by which man thinks to reconstruct himself" (Barnes 53). Historically, the merging of disability and sexuality has occurred through the pathologizing of the "invert" as mentally defective and by sexualizing the cognitively disabled person as a threat to the gene pool or as sexual predator. The castrating of mental patients during the eugenic 1920s, during which *Nightwood* was written, is only one version of a more pervasive form of violent eugenics based around the control and monitoring of disability.

What Colker diagnoses as a problem with legal equality theory applied to women's health also applies to contemporary LGBT politics, insofar as it is invested in reproductive futurism. The new queer family values ethos, which Edelman critiques in *No Future*, utilizes the seemingly egalitarian claims for male pregnancy and the integrity of the child to remove control of female biology from women while reinscribing heteronormativity onto queer culture. As I have indicated, cultural producers have been talking about pregnant men for some time, albeit from rather different metaphoric vantages. The figure of the reproductive male in modernism, as Dr. Schreber and Dr. O'Connor illustrate, is a sign of the ways that negative futures were being written around homosexual men. But we need to distinguish between the two doctors by considering how their two authors—Freud and Barnes—figured that futurity. For Freud, Schreber's paranoid delusion that he must become a woman and become impregnated by God is a form of homosexual panic, the result of Oedipal anxieties regarding Schreber's father, who was a doctor, and his own doctor, Flechsig (this staging of homosexual panic as "doctor panic" is one of Freud's less acknowledged contributions to disability studies). According to Freud, Schreber's gender-bending fantasies of impregnation and pregnancy are pathological, signs of mental illness that necessitate institutionalization and analysis. For Barnes, on the contrary, Dr. O'Connor is comfortable as "the old woman in the closet," whose "wish for children and knitting" stand in stark contrast to Felix's rigid code of masculine filial piety or to Nora's rather bourgeois notion of lesbian monogamy. O'Connor's acceptance of his oxymoronic position as female-male gives him a queer perspective on Nora's bourgeois normativity—her desire to create Robin as a faithful spouse—and on her need to "bow down" to her own sexuality. Where Freud sees disability, Barnes sees an alternate ability; where Freud sees deviant homosexuality, Barnes sees a spectrum of sexual identities in a world facing a fascist and eugenically controlled future.

In the beginning of this chapter I posed a question that pertains to the new biopolitical order: if childbirth in women is nature, what is childbirth in men? Is it, for example, disability? By framing the question this way, I want to complicate the usual binaries of nature/culture, reproduction/production, that have dominated sex roles for centuries and ask whether in a world in which reproduction is being increasingly divorced from gender the default of nature is not culture but, rather, disability, read as the defamiliarizing condition for the spectacle of bodily normality. We could complicate this chiasmic ratio further by asking if the birth of the male child into self-consciousness is the ground of the Bildungsroman, what happens when that birth is literalized in and through the male body? Does this alter the ideological course of narrative as a recuperative vehicle for family values and pronatalist futurity? What eugenics attempted to secure within the heteronormative family, novels like *Nightwood* explode into the biofuturistic scenarios of William Burroughs, Octavia Butler, Samuel Delaney, and Margaret Atwood—and ultimately pop culture films like *Junior.*

NOTES

1. On "compulsory able-bodiedness," see Robert McRuer, *Crip Theory* 1–32. The use of the term "crip" has become, in disability rights discourse, somewhat equivalent to "queer" in gay and lesbian discourse. Like "queer," the term "crip" rearticulates a term of opprobrium to expose ableist assumptions about bodily normalcy. The term also implicitly repudiates more technical or patronizing terms such as "handicapped," "wheelchair bound," or "differently abled."

2. Socrates says to Theaetetus, "My art of midwifery is in general like [that of female

Michael Davidson

midwives]; the only difference is that my patients are men, not women, and my concern is not with the body but with the soul that is in travail of birth. And the highest point of my art is the power to prove by every test whether the offspring of a young man's thought is a false phantom or instinct with life and truth" (Plato 150b). I am grateful to Page DuBois for pointing out this reference to me.

3. As Ned Ward, an eighteenth-century journalist, wrote, on Festival Nights men would "cusheon up the Belly of one of the *Sodomitical* Brethren, or rather Sisters as they commonly call'd themselves, disguising him in a Womans Night-gown, Sarsnet-Hod, and Nightrale, who, when the Company were met, was to mimick the wry Faces of a groaning Woman, to be deliver'd of a joynted Babie they had provided for that Purpose, and to undergo all the Formalities of a Lying in" (qtd. in Norton, "Of the Mollies Club").

4. For a thorough catalogue of male pregnancy figures, see Sherry M. Velasco, *Male Delivery* 1–27.

5. I am echoing Jane Marcus, who argues that "*Nightwood* is the representative modernist text, a prose poem of abjection, tracing the political unconscious of the rise of fascism, as lesbians, blacks, circus people, Jews, and transvestites—outsiders all—*bow down* before Hitler's truly perverted Levitical prescriptions for racial purity" (231).

6. Velasco uses the phrase "womb envy" to refer to the various ways that males have performed pregnancy, either through couvade, in which the male participates in a symbolic childbirth with the mother, to more recent popular literature surrounding male parenting. Jane Marcus uses the phrase to speak specifically of Dr. O'Connor in Djuna Barnes's *Nightwood*.

7. See Eve Kosofsky Sedgwick's chapter on James's "Beast in the Jungle" in *The Epistemology of the Closet* (182–212).

8. Although he is described as a gynecologist whose primary work is the delivery of babies, there is every indication that he is also an abortionist.

9. Jane Marcus provides a lucid summary of the ways that O'Connor inverts the Freudian analytic session (231–50).

10. On *Nightwood* as a tale of urban slumming, see Scott Herring, *Queering the Underworld* 150–92.

11. Everything about Guido and Hedvig's life is fragmentary or fake. Guido found the family portraits that he displays on his walls "in some forgotten and dusty corner and had purchased them when he had been sure that he would need an alibi for the blood" (Barnes 7). The originals for the portraits turn out not to be a royal couple at all but a couple of actors.

12. Michel Foucault speaks of modernity as marking a shift from a culture based on power expressed through "blood" and the sovereign's power over bodies, to a "society of sex," in which "mechanisms of power are addressed to the body, to life, to what causes it to proliferate, to what reinforces the species" (*History* 147). Although he does

not discuss *Nightwood*, the novel is a brilliant, condensed version of Foucault's formulation.

13. I have discussed the threat of infected blood with regard to hemophilia and AIDS in *Concerto for the Left Hand: Disability and the Defamiliar Body* 35–57.

14. The precise date that Barnes began to write *Nightwood* is unclear. According to Cheryl Plumb and based on entries in Emily Coleman's diary, the origins of the novel could have begun as early as 1927, the date of Barnes's breakup with Thelma Wood. It is clear that she was well under way in 1932 when she was living at Peggy Guggenheim's summer residence in England, Hayford Hall.

15. Robert McAlmon reports that Barnes and Thelma Wood, the prototypes for Nora Flood and Robin Vote, spent time in Berlin along with Berenice Abbott, Marsden Hartley, and McAlmon and lived near Magnus Hirschfeld's Institute for the Study of Sexual Sciences. According to McAlmon, they encountered a number of transgender individuals in the streets of Berlin, but Barnes did not accompany the group on its late-night forays into what Deborah Parsons calls "the fluid space of an itinerant and liminal subculture" (70).

16. Felix not only wears a monocle but also has sight only in one eye (Barnes 9).

17. Ato Quayson calls this anxiety "aesthetic nervousness" to refer to moments when "the dominant protocols of representation within the literary text are short-circuited in relation to disability" (15). The primary form that this takes is the interaction between disabled and able-bodied characters, but this nervousness may extend to "tensions refracted across other levels of the text such as the disposition of symbols and motifs, the overall narrative or dramatic perspective, the constitution and reversals of plot structure, and so on" (15). I find Quayson's phrase useful for speaking of how Barnes's baroque prose style, while not specifically engaged with the depiction of a disabled character, nevertheless annexes through verbal excess those qualities of the uncertainty that attend nontraditional bodies.

18. Velasco notes that adding to the de-gendering of pregnancy is the return of various forms of couvade in popular parenting literature with titles like *Birthing Fathers: The Transformation of Men in American Rites of Birth* or *Pregnant Fathers: Becoming the Father You Want to Be* (8).

19. Hall's remark, paraphrased by Paul Gilroy, is that "[race] is the modality in which [class] is lived" (qtd. in Gilroy 85). Gilroy, speaking of 2 Live Crew, adapts Hall's comment to say "gender is the modality in which race is lived" (85).

7

....

DAVID SERLIN

TOUCHING HISTORIES

Personality, Disability, and Sex in the 1930s

In May 2009, a reporter for the *New York Times* surveyed numerous incidents of consensual hugging among adolescents at middle schools and high schools around the United States. Framed by some parents, teachers, and psychologists as a reaction to a lack of shared intimacy by an overscheduled, overmedicated generation alienated from physical affection, hugging, according to one sixth-grade teacher, "gets to that core that every person wants to feel cared for, regardless of your age or how cool you are or how cool you think you are" (Kershaw p. 2, par. 8). By contrast, some school administrators interviewed for the article stigmatized hugging as a threatening breach of social protocol; according to one junior high school principal, "[t]ouching . . . is very dangerous territory" (Kershaw p. 1, par. 13).

While the article ponders how and why certain forms of touching, such as hugging, are perceived to be both harmless and dangerous, it remains silent on the ontology of touch as a medium of interpersonal communication. Neither the adolescents nor the teachers nor the parents interviewed for the *New York Times*, for instance, were explicitly identified as members of populations for which touch, including hugging, might sometimes carry a different set of meanings—

those on the autism spectrum, for example, or the chronically ill, the elderly, or people with mobility or other physical impairments—than it does for the average teen. Although unfortunate, this omission is by no means surprising, given the virtual invisibility in mass culture of differently abled people of any age, outside of representations of heroic supercrips or intentionally oddball figures. Nonnormative children and adults are routinely exempted or excluded from being shown engaged in voluntary physical intimacies with people other than family members or caregivers and are almost never understood as possessing sexual subjectivities in which they are agents of sexual pleasure. Why should one expect it to be otherwise with disabled adolescents?

How might we think about touch as both a medium of communication and a system of meaning making that engages with the erotic potential that inheres in the experience of disability? In the early twenty-first century, the idea of touch is often imbued with fear: touch as a permeable boundary of sexual danger or inappropriate conduct or as an epidemiological vector of contagion. The forms touch takes—or does not take—often function as markers of economic status or the privileges that accrue to social hierarchies, such as those who are deemed "untouchable" by their putative superiors. Yet these dominant modes of understanding touch render illegible the significance of tactility as a medium of communication for disabled people, as well as for those who desire touch outside of models of physical and sexual interaction normalized within modern culture. The tactile, scholars such as the late Eve Kosofsky Sedgwick have argued, is infused with complexities of performance, affect, and desire that confound categories of sexual orientation and gender (*Touching Feeling*).

Yet tempting as it may be to make universalizing claims for the inherent queerness of touch, such an understanding of tactility's instability must also be understood as historically contingent and culturally specific. The architectural theorist Juhani Pallasmaa, for example, has argued that vision and hearing in late modernity "are now the privileged sociable senses, whereas [senses like touch are] considered as archaic sensory remnants with a merely private function, and . . . are usually suppressed by the code of culture" (16). Historically, however, tactility has served a public function; indeed, touch as a contested medium of communication in the public sphere has had a profoundly political nature. At eugenics conferences during the 1930s, for instance, some exhibits featured displays of animal pelts, which patrons were invited to touch.

As Barbara Kirshenblatt-Gimblett has pointed out, these exhibits were created with the intention of demonstrating that the ability to distinguish "quality"

"Specialized Tests for Sense of Elegance: Quality in Fur," an exhibit featured at the Third International Eugenics Conference (1932) and held at the American Museum of Natural History, New York City. Reprinted with permission of the Harry H. Laughlin Papers, Truman State University. Image reproduced courtesy of the Image Archive of the American Eugenics Movement, Dolan DNA Learning Center, Cold Spring Harbor Laboratory.

fur through tactile means was an inherited trait passed down through superior genes (26–27). Here, touch was not only a socially sanctioned activity that valorized good breeding but also one that was meant to convey its political distinction from the other senses. Like hugging in contemporary high schools, the evidence of touch, in this example, was far from "suppressed by the code of culture." Rather, it was a highly regarded component *of* the code of culture, especially as mediated by the putatively neutral truth claims of science. In this chapter, I ask how we might think through the complexities of touch as a medium of communication by examining another case study, also drawn from the early twentieth century, in which tactility was deployed as a category of scientific and sexual knowledge that measured an individual's libidinal urges as well as his or her ability to curb those urges in order to manage norms of social evolution.

In the second half of the 1930s, Carney Landis, an associate professor of psychology at Columbia University, undertook a research project with his colleague, M. Marjorie Bolles, a researcher at the Psychiatric Institute of New York, in which they conducted interviews with and analyzed the sex lives of one hundred women between the ages of eighteen and twenty-five.[1] These women had been institutionalized prior to Landis and Bolles's investigations and were identified as handicapped, in the parlance of the day, with a range of conditions classified under the broad rubrics "orthopedic," "spastic," "cardiac," and "epileptic." Over the course of four years, Landis and Bolles interviewed the women about their sex lives, sexual identities, and relationships to their bodies, and they published the results of their study in 1942 under the title *The Personality and Sexuality of the Physically Handicapped Woman*.

Of Landis's and Bolles's reputations, and the impact of their study on either sexology or research on the sexuality of disabled people, virtually nothing has been written. In Landis's obituary for the *American Journal of Psychiatry* in 1962, William A. Hunt observed that "the influence of Landis's work probably is likely to have been more widely felt among his generation than will be noted for history" (509). Landis and Bolles's work has not fared much better even under late-twentieth-century scholarship; according to one prominent historian of sexology, their work on disabled women's sexuality "should be noted more for its intent than for its results" (Bullough 164). My goal in examining Landis and Bolles's work, particularly their research project on the sex lives of disabled women, is not intended to serve as a recovery project in the classic academic sense: it is not, in other words, a campaign to recover a marginal or obscure figure in order to resurrect his or her importance and thus reshuffle the hierarchies of value that constitute historical knowledge. Instead, an examination of *The Personality and Sexuality of the Physically Handicapped Woman* enables us to grasp anew the ways in which touch and tactility functioned in the early decades of the twentieth century, both for the researchers and research subjects. By paying attention to the role of touch in the women's narratives and its corresponding significance (or lack thereof) in Landis and Bolles's observations, we gain insight into forms of self-expression and subjectivity that, in addition to struggling against clinical prejudices or hierarchies of meaning, are ones that we tend not to associate with histories of either disability or sexuality.

While the topic of disabled women's sexuality was unique among studies conducted by U.S. psychologists and sex researchers in the 1930s, *The Personality and Sexuality of the Physically Handicapped Woman* is a rather familiar quantitative study that reflects the predominant models used to conduct sex research during the era. Landis and Bolles were contributing to a cottage industry that had been

David Serlin

TABLE 1

SOURCE OF REFERRAL OF SUBJECTS

	No. of Cases
Institute for the Crippled and Disabled...........................	28
New York State Education Department, Bureau of Rehabilitation......	2
Columbia-Presbyterian Medical Center...........................	20
Hospital for the Ruptured and Crippled.........................	4
New York Orthopaedic Dispensary Hospital......................	2
Bellevue Hospital...	12
Brooklyn Hospital...	6
Craig Colony for Epileptics.....................................	14
Mt. Sinai Hospital of the City of New York......................	2
Hartford Dispensary...	2
Hartford Municipal Hospital.....................................	3
(Referred by another subject)...................................	5
Total...	100

TABLE 2

INTELLIGENCE RATING

	Orthopedic	Spastic	Cardiac	Epileptic	Total
Subnormal.............	1	1	0	1	3
Dull..................	9	4	3	12	28
Low average...........	2	3	10	10	25
High average..........	8	12	10	2	32
Superior..............	5	5	2	0	12
Total..........	25	25	25	25	100

TABLE 3

AGE AT ONSET OF HANDICAP

	Orthopedic	Spastic	Cardiac	Epileptic	Total
Birth...................	9	22	0	2	33
1–3 years.............	10	0	1	5	16
4–6 years.............	2	0	5	1	8
7–9 years.............	3	1	9	3	16
10–12 years...........	1	2	9	5	17
13 years..............	0	0	1	9	10
Total..........	25	25	25	25	100

"Tables of Vital Statistics." These tables distill important background information for the disabled women involved in the study: the institutions where Landis and Bolles located their subjects, how their subjects' intelligence was rated, and the age at which their subjects' "handicap" developed. From Landis and Bolles, *The Personality and Sexuality of the Physically Handicapped Woman* (New York: Paul B. Hoeber, Inc., 1942), 147. Reprinted with permission of Lippincott Williams & Wilkins.

in full production mode for nearly two decades. In the furtive and well-funded research period following World War I, American psychiatric and sexological researchers collected and analyzed voluminous quantities of sexual data on both "normal" and "abnormal" American women, including studies such as "Sexual Behavior and Secondary Sexual Hair in Female Patients with Manic Depressive Psychoses" (published by C. E. Gibbs in 1924) and *Factors in the Sex Life of 700 Psychopathic Women* (published by Francis M. Strakosch in 1934). Katherine Bement Davis's study, *Factors in the Sex Life of Twenty-Two Hundred Women*, published in 1929, was a landmark volume in which Davis asked women to talk about not only their sexual practices but also about their sexual relationships to themselves. The degree to which Davis's study focused on female masturbation (and, sadly, its apparently precipitous decline among women over thirty) is a minor miracle of interwar American ethnography, cataloguing the ingenuity with which girls and young women in the early twentieth century found ways to turn everyday experiences into opportunities for autoerotic gratification.

Significantly, Davis's study is distinguished from the work of other American sexological researchers of the era in that she collected her information through oral histories, which permitted her research subjects to identify their sexual subjectivities without necessarily defining themselves according to clinical or conventional categories of sexual identity. This was a radical break from the seemingly rational strategies used by contemporary researchers to define desire and deviance. As Michael A. Rembis has shown, for instance, in his study of teenage girls institutionalized as juvenile delinquents in Illinois in the early twentieth century, putatively "objective" methods of measuring gender or sexual deviance were regularly deployed to generate evidence that seemed to corroborate supposed "truths" about questionable or nonnormative bodies. As Heather Lee Miller has argued, sexologists, psychiatrists, and medical professionals during the early twentieth century were committed to quantifying the social behaviors and sexual characteristics of women, such as prostitutes and lesbians, who fit into recognizable categories of sexual and gendered deviance. Taxonomies were created through the use of physical examinations that involved measuring, comparing, and cataloging varieties of breasts, clitorises, labia, nipples, and pubic hair—those body parts thought to be morphologically correlated with deviance. "As women's sexual desire and behavior became a site of anxiety for society at large," Miller writes, "and as women served to participate in such gender transgressive behaviors as feminism, professional work, prostitution, and same-sex behavior, [sexologists] . . . began to 'read' female bodies for 'anatomical evidence' of sexual desire and behavior" (79). "Whether she chose under examination to recall her 'sin' or not," Miller observes, "a woman's genitalia revealed her confession to the sexologist, her confessor" (80), thus revealing the tensions surrounding tactility in a professional setting where touch exists both as an extension of the clinical gaze and a facilitator of social discipline.

Such examinations also suggest that, long before the era of medicalizing the sexually aberrant or the physically nonnormative body, tactility played a central role in producing hierarchies of social distinction. The French historian Alain Corbin, for example, has argued that the ascent of modernity helped to accelerate the process by which those who routinely experienced bodies on a tactile basis were distinguished from those who were able to distance themselves experientially from the bodies of others through economic privilege, social mobility, or political stature. Before this rupture, Corbin argues, village dwellers and their urban counterparts alike experienced physical difference, illness, and death as part of a shared continuum of living and working together. With the rise of industrial capitalism, professionalization, and forms of expert knowledge, economic and social distinctions increasingly emerged between those who engaged with the full range of somatic experiences and those who employed manual laborers, appointed policemen, hired doctors, and dispatched missionaries and church representatives to do work for them. To touch or not to touch, to be touched or not to be touched: for Corbin, these experiential categories reflect powerful hierarchical structures that increasingly identified seeing and hearing and even tasting as intellectual, superior, and refined, while touching and smelling remained connected to the physical with its potential association with the dirty and stigmatized. Disabled bodies belonged to the latter category; their relationship to touch not only exposed their physical vulnerability and therefore their dependence but also challenged post-Enlightenment moral and political philosophies that privileged bodily autonomy and self-control as markers of civilization.

Katherine Bement Davis's decision to foreground self-narration among her informants marked a significant break from the diagnostic techniques that presumptively linked physical differences with sexual differences that could be visually verified. It also provided the framework within which Landis and Bolles began to conceptualize their work. *The Personality and Sexuality of the Physically Handicapped Woman* might be regarded therefore as a missing link that completes a genealogical arc that emerges in Davis's work in the 1920s and is fulfilled in Alfred Kinsey's work in the 1940s and 1950s. But it is important to recognize that Landis and Bolles did not undertake their study to contribute to an understanding of disabled women's sexuality per se. They positioned themselves neither as explicit advocates for disabled people nor as harsh critics of the individuals or institutions that cared for them. Disabled women weren't recognized as belonging to that group of self-possessed young women who, like the nondisabled women interviewed by Davis, could narrate their own sexual subjectivities. Disabled women were understood to constitute a subset of women whose frustrated sexual subjectivity, if they could even own such a thing, was evidence of the absence of what Freud called the "sexual moment," an originary or primary insight into one's sexual self that allows one to narrate ostensibly normative heterosexual desires. For Landis and Bolles, disabled women were useful to the fields of psychology and sexology because they were perceived to be voiceless, sexual *tabulae rasae* whose social alienation confirmed psychological theories of psychosexual development and sexological theories that correlated sexuality with the "truth" of the self. Which population, after all, would be better suited to demonstrate the effects of social ills on psychosexual development than the disabled and disabled women in particular?

Landis and Bolles, like other researchers in this era, were fundamentally influenced by the presumption that there was an *a priori* linkage between evidence of physical disability and expressions of neurotic behavior. They argued emphatically for a correlation between hyposexuality (that is, a subnormal diminished sex drive or the absence of one altogether) and psychosexual immaturity, attributing some of it to the young woman's lack of social engagement but much of it to the perception that disabled women were socially maladjusted and neurotically inclined. Throughout their text, Landis and Bolles make explicit links between their research subjects' personalities and their respective sexual histories (or lack thereof), the inner mechanisms of which they believed were fundamental to understanding disabled women's sexuality in relation to existing categories of psychopathology that were applied, with equal vigor, to nondisabled women, who were regarded for all intents and purposes as physically normal if also psychologically neurotic. The category of the "neurotic," charged with late nineteenth-century conceptions of the assault on the body by the pace of modern life, was typically gendered female since it played directly into the period's understanding of women's hysteria as rooted in their essentially vulnerable constitutions. This is a legacy that continued, as Jonathan Metzl has argued in his book *Prozac on the Couch*, well into the 1990s with the feminization of depression and mood disorders in both clinical and popular discourses.

David Serlin

Clearly, Landis and Bolles's study was building upon and responding to conventions of early twentieth-century sexology research on disabled women and their neurotic nondisabled counterparts that had been firmly in place for some time. But one could argue that contemporary forces also shaped their study. Building upon the reformist zeal of the New Deal during the second half of the 1930s, Landis and Bolles imagined this marginalized and stigmatized group of women as potential beneficiaries of a social and economic system in which they might eventually be included. They believed that, like many who underwent physical rehabilitation to become productive workers and citizens, their disabled interviewees might thrive if the researchers could, by recalibrating what they perceived as self-absorbed, narcissistic dimensions of their subjects' psyches, transform these women into dynamic, extroverted, altruistic personalities. For Landis and Bolles, the key to this transformation, which promised to produce economically and socially productive individuals, was the role of personality in neutralizing the stigma of disability.

Personality studies — that is, theories of personality in relation to psychological development, as well as individual studies of enigmatic or complicated personality types — held a special aura in scientific circles in the United States during the early decades of the twentieth century. These studies came on the heels of the first published translations of Freud into English during the early twentieth century and the first formal studies of propaganda, advertising, and the cult of personality by communication researchers such as Paul Lazarsfeld and Walter Lippmann. Among psychological researchers, the 1920s and 1930s galvanized enormous support for what were called "personality inventories," large-scale quantitative analyses of personality traits, typically conducted through questionnaires in which individuals were asked to self-report on their own cognitive experiences and behavior patterns. Initially developed to screen out so-called mental defectives from society at large, these studies were later adopted by public relations firms, political pollsters, advertising agencies, and even the armed forces during World War II to identify those with so-called antisocial tendencies. These categories speak volumes about the period's compulsive commitment to civic training as a rational instrument of social control.

Such personality inventories were not merely the terrain of psychological or sexuality researchers. As Joel Pfister has argued, during the 1920s and 1930s the diagnosis of certain forms of neurosis — particularly self-absorption and narcissism — was routinely decoupled from diagnoses of insanity or the eugenic category of feeblemindedness. Indeed, as Pfister points out, during the 1920s the label of "neurotic" held tremendous cultural capital. Through the mass media allure of popular films, Broadway plays, serial radio dramas, celebrity magazines, and romantic novels, Pfister argues, the neurotic personality "type" captured the imagination of the public and became intertwined with a glamorous upwardly mobile profile, a vision of leisurely self-aggrandizement that long predates the contemporary era of celebrity rehab. For researchers like Landis and Bolles, personality studies were an easy interface with sexological studies, since the sources of both neurosis and sexual deviance could be definitively located in the psyche through the act of gathering and interpreting self-narrations. As Davis's work had demonstrated, sexual subjectivities of various kinds could be classified and systematically deployed in order to make generalizations, which could then be applied to individuals or groups.

Landis and Bolles built upon these conventions of personality studies through the use of controlled interviews, Rorschach inkblots, and medical history intakes. These diagnostic tools, which still had an aura of novelty in the 1930s, dovetailed nicely with a topic that attracted numerous social psychologists as well as industrial psychologists: the rehabilitation of the disabled for the purposes of social integration and social productivity. After World War I, civic training in its various iterations had included the rehabilitation and reformation of the personality, often in accordance with expectations of economic productivity and social civility. In 1940, for example, psychological researcher Theodora M. Abel observed that "subnormal girls may make a successful industrial adjustment provided they obtain job satisfaction, a desirable first job, and stable hours" (qtd. in Dorcus and Case 486). Writing in 1941, Rudolph Pintner asserted that "in the education and training of physically handicapped persons a personality concept must be built up which will make it possible for them to interact freely with physically normal people. While the physically handicapped must view the limitations imposed by their handicaps objectively and realistically, there must be no injury to their *self-esteem*. This will only be possible if the physically normal persons in the environment of the handicapped react to them understandingly but without maudlin sentiment or morbid curiosity" (Pintner, Eisenson, and Stanton 16; emphasis added).

Yet labor historians tell us that in the predominantly industrial economy of the 1930s, personality was not necessarily a factor, minor or otherwise, in employment decisions, let alone opportunities for performing acts of civic duty. According to Pintner himself, even those "crippled" laborers who were able to find work during the Depression typically performed jobs in which having an extroverted personality, or a discernable personality type of any kind, was a negligible component of one's work identity. In a study conducted at the nadir of the Depression in 1932, 70 percent of jobs held by disabled workers were unskilled, and only 6 percent were skilled. This suggests that the emphasis on personality—its capacity to win friends, influence people, and earn cash, as conceived by Dale Carnegie in 1936—was to some degree a fabricated criterion. Despite this, Pintner's exploration of the psychological profiles of disabled men and women provides insight into the period's construction of those with disabilities, which ranged from physical disabilities produced by illness or accident to chronic conditions including epilepsy, diabetes, encephalitis, and tuberculosis, the etiologies of which Pintner believed to be responsible for producing particular social types whose personalities were "bound up in the very nature of the disease." Pintner characterized the epileptic, for example, as "self-centered, constantly demanding his own way and violently resenting interference. He is subject to outbursts of temper and is often moody and peevish" (Pintner, Eisenson, and Stanton 303–4).

Such conclusions about the relationship between physical disability and defects in personality and the possibilities of rehabilitation were reinforced in much of the prevailing psychological literature of the period. Writing in 1937 about "neurotic tendencies in crippled girls," Betty Rosenbaum argued that "as [disabled] girls grow older and mature emotionally and physically, [they] are deterred in making normal social adjustments because of their handicaps [and] tend to become more and more introverted and neurotic" (428). Rosenbaum's study relied heavily upon the Thurstone Personality Schedule, one of the most widely used diagnostic tools among social psychologists in the United States during the 1930s, which enabled Rosenbaum to compare the personalities of the "crippled girls" with those of college-age "normal girls."

That Rosenbaum as well as Landis and Bolles used young women from the New York metropolitan region as a research population suggests how important the urban setting was to psychology researchers' understanding of geographical difference as an adjunct to social and physical difference. In the interwar period, when the city was studied as the primary locus of modern social organization (and, for scholars like Robert Park and the urban sociologists at the University of Chicago, the genesis of modern social ills), urban environments and the neuroses they were believed to generate were central concerns for psychologists as well as industrial managers and economic theorists. Urban subjectivities enabled researchers to investigate the ways in which modernity and neurosis were dialectically constituted, with vice, crime, sociopathic behavior, and sexual deviance

MASCULINE PROTEST

Objective Scale

1. No evidence.

2. Desire to be a boy before puberty; marked preference for boys' games, activities, etc.; dislike of girls' games, dress, and lack of freedom.

3. Resentment of being a woman because of social handicap; men have more privileges, more freedom, do more things than girls, have more fun in life; men more likely to succeed, have more determination, will power, etc.; men can be more unconventional.

4. Choice of passive, effeminate type of man (as husband, dream lover, or man attracted to).

5. Resentment of being a woman because of physical handicap; menstruation a bother, nuisance; envies boys' health and strength; feared childbirth; wished she were a boy so she couldn't give birth to a child.

6. Extreme aggressiveness keynote of her activity, more interested in having own career than in marrying—marriage interferes with career; holds tenaciously to aggressive political views—subordinates everything else to them; general character trait of mannishness (i.e., clothes, hair-comb, walk, noted either by what friends have said about her or examiner's notation).

7. Derives pleasure from putting boys at a disadvantage; satisfaction in playing dominant role by leading boys on, without emotional response on girl's part; sexual teasing a method of getting revenge on men; this is the basis of the relationship with all boys.

Importance to Individual

	ORTHOPEDIC	SPASTIC	CARDIAC	EPILEPTIC
1. No evidence of masculine protest: no evidence checked on the objective scale.....	7	8	12	16
2. Indication of slight masculine protest....................................	11	9	9	6
(a) Single item checked on objective scale				
(b) Two items out of Nos. 2, 3, and 4				
3. Evidence of definite masculine protest.......................	5	7	3	2
(a) Nos. 2, 3, and 4				
(b) One item from Nos. 5, 6, and 7, plus one item from Nos. 2, 3, and 4				
4. Evidence of very marked masculine protest.......................	2	1	1	1
(a) Two items out of Nos. 5, 6, and 7				
(b) Any three items including Nos. 5, 6, or 7				
(c) Four or more items				
Total..	25	25	25	25

"Masculine Protest: Objective Scale." Scales such as these were typical of psychosexual profiles of mid-twentieth-century psychologists, emerging from the fear that modern neuroses might upend conventional (and deeply heteronormative) understandings of gender roles. Here it is used to indicate that some proportion of the subjects in the study showed signs of nonnormative gender behavior, thus underscoring the significance of the concept of "masculine protest." From Landis and Bolles, *The Personality and Sexuality of the Physically Handicapped Woman* (New York: Paul B. Hoeber, Inc., 1942), 137. Reprinted with permission of Lippincott Williams & Wilkins.

serving as somatic manifestations of the ill effects of the urban environment on the fragile bodies of the most vulnerable populations.

Historians such as Pamela Haag have argued that during the 1920s and early 1930s the lauded goal of making socially and economically productive adults depended on teaching a generation of young men and women how to be extroverted, how to avoid isolation, and how to connect and interact with others for the purposes of social solidarity (and, one might cynically imagine, for the purposes of consumer identification). Normative understandings of personality,

Haag asserts, were mediated through advice literature and popular self-help oriented texts that traveled in circuits of amateur and semiprofessional knowledge
production. These goals depended upon developing one's capacity to tell one's
own story, presuming that one had a story to tell about one's self: a story that
included a physical history, an account of social obstacles one had overcome, a
projection of self-esteem, and a sense of social belonging. Furthermore, as Haag
observes, during the 1920s self-narration became the predominant form for expressing not only one's personality but one's sexual history: "the unnatural and
class-specific artifices of narration and self-stylization emerged as tools by which
a woman might invent or earn her sexual subjectivity, by distinguishing it both
from the commodified sexuality of the prostitute or the gold digger and from the
'unconscious' sexuality increasingly ascribed to the 'vulgar' classes" (165). Haag's
insight suggests that a younger generation of women built personality profiles
to distinguish their desires from those "uncouth" women who expressed their
sexuality through primitive sexual urges.

Landis and Bolles's interviews, by contrast, were not designed explicitly to endorse the promotion of disabled women's personality profiles or to champion the
centrality of their sexual histories to psychological growth. Their interviews were
anchored in the objective pursuit of pure research; they implied that there was
something valuable to be gained from studying women whose social experiences
were perceived to be so thoroughly excluded from the typical currents of social
life. But within the often state-sponsored physical rehabilitation schemes that
these women inhabited, the prospect of social rehabilitation, clarified through
the techniques of self-possession and self-narration, was part of the missionary
zeal with which sexologists and psychiatrists plied their trade in the 1930s.

Sometime after World War II, Landis deposited his and Bolles's complete data
sets for *The Personality and Sexuality of the Physically Handicapped Woman* in the
archives of what is now the Kinsey Institute for Research in Sex, Gender, and Reproduction at Indiana University. Alfred Kinsey, its director, would soon become
famous for publishing the results of his own research, using interview techniques
similar to those of Landis and Bolles, which he had developed during the 1940s
with his own subjects. Landis and Bolles's raw data, when compared with the
published versions of their study, make it evident that the researchers omitted a
large number of individual narratives from their final conclusions. Landis and
Bolles's study seems, on the surface, rather unflinching in its characterization
of disabled women who are far more intimately familiar with their bodies than
one might have imagined at midcentury point. For example, in one of the tables

AUTOEROTIC PRACTICES
(Masturbation)

	ORTHOPEDIC	SPASTIC	CARDIAC	EPILEPTIC
Occurrence				
1. Never...	20	20	20	14
2. Rare (once a year)..	2	2	1	2
3. Occasional (once or twice per month).................	1	3	2	3
4. Frequent (once per week)................................	2	0	2	5
5. Excessive (once per day or more).......................	0	0	0	1
Total..	25	25	25	25
Affective Response				
1. No masturbation reported (not applicable).............	20	20	20	14
2. No expressed guilt of any kind; pleasant experience; no hesitation in discussing; greater pleasure than intercourse; only masturbated as small child; no recollection of affective response.......................................	1	3	1	1
3. Moderate guilt feeling; felt guilt earlier but now tends to consider it natural; felt wrong, but no undue reaction to it; regrets practice, but feels it necessary; feels not right but does not believe any mental or physical harm has resulted.............	1	2	2	8
4. Marked guilt; much ashamed but could not help it; marked resistance to discussing subject; unable to stop the practice although feels it is physically and mentally harmful; worried about practice, feared others would know about it; blocks completely on report of affective value although positive evidence of occurrence................	3	0	2	2
5. Extreme guilt feeling; great confusion and embarrassment in discussion; subject revolting and vulgar; considers masturbation to be at bottom of feeling of sex inferiority; thinks some connection between masturbation and nervousness; considers it a sin, or a degenerate, abnormal practice........................	0	0	0	0
Total..	25	25	25	25

"Autoerotic Practices (Masturbation)." One would have to infer from such research that the vast majority of disabled women in the New York City metropolitan area during the late 1930s constituted a masturbation-free population. From Landis and Bolles, *The Personality and Sexuality of the Physically Handicapped Woman* (New York: Paul B. Hoeber, Inc., 1942), 134. Reprinted with permission of Lippincott Williams & Wilkins.

appending their text presenting data on autoeroticism, Landis and Bolles give the impression that the vast majority of their informants either rejected masturbation outright or practiced it so infrequently that it was, generally speaking, a negligible component of their sexual subjectivities. From such a table, one might be tempted to extrapolate that disabled women in the New York metropolitan area constituted a mostly masturbation-free population.

If one examines Landis and Bolles's original notes, however, the provocative character of the qualitative data that produced these quantitative conclusions tell a different, more richly nuanced story. For example, when one informant was asked whether she experienced physical pleasure, she stated that of her earliest sexual memories "the only thing I remember is sliding down the banister. I still like it, and started again about five years ago." She also reported: "I have had experiences where I had my legs crossed, someone plumped themselves into my lap and I had a very nice sensation. [I was] about 15 or 16." Landis and Bolles rated this informant, a young adult when she was interviewed in the late 1930s, as someone who "never" masturbated, and the details she herself provided were omitted from the final version of their book. Another interview subject, diagnosed with cardiac arrhythmia and living in an institutional setting, described sex play with a female neighbor who "often stayed with me because she loved my home. We were very intimate and she purposely missed trains to be with me. [She] [d]isplayed quite a bit of physical affection. . . . I remember we were so free, I'd take a shower and then I bathed her." Landis and Bolles rated this subject also as someone who did not masturbate, proving that quantitative analysis makes little or no room for cohabitations of the bathtub or shower. In a slightly more guarded and hesitant interview by a different research subject, another young woman recalled that, as a young girl, "I enjoyed remaining in the bathroom for long periods of time, feeling the warmth comfort me. I found great pleasure in being nude," she remembered, "but then I never looked at myself in the mirror." The hesitation coming from this particular research subject is painful to contemplate, as it suggests a measure of emotional repression and psychic control enforced not by visual or tactile pleasure but by external standards of visual and tactile disidentification generated by others and applied against one's self. As yet another informant told Landis and Bolles, "There was a time when I did not like anyone to touch me. I could not stand it. The nurses used to do it a great deal when I first came here. I shrank from it. Now this [has] completely changed . . . since coming to the hospital here."

In noting that Landis and Bolles excluded these insights from their subjects' self-narrations, I am not suggesting that the researchers were deliberately stripping their informants of complex sexual subjectivities by removing their messy or rough edges to fit conventional ontologies of sexuality. Instead, one could argue that these young women had sexual narratives that were far more confounding than anything Landis and Bolles understood how to grapple with, especially given the Freudian narratives that so structured sex research for the first half of the twentieth century. The narratives gathered by Landis and Bolles conveyed subjectivities consummated not through quantifiable acts of conventional (and/ or heterosexual) penetrative sex or through recognizable patterns of oral-genital or digital-genital contact. Instead, they were subjectivities consummated through unquantifiable acts of touch: self-touch, being touched through one's clothes, or touching one's erogenous zones by rubbing against an object. In the 1930s, such practices of touch may well have been viewed as provocative Freudian peccadilloes of polymorphous perversity. But they also may have been regarded as terra incognita for researchers like Landis and Bolles, who were trained in the field of psychiatry rather than that of sex research. That sexological studies conducted in the early twentieth century would be, with few exceptions, entirely and hopelessly complicit with heteronormative social scripts is wholly unremarkable. What seems remarkable, however, is the degree to which forms of sexual subjectivity are being constructed in these self-narrations, which—especially when they are mediated primarily through acts of touch—remain largely irretrievable as recognizable social practices with definable features. Indeed, they seem to be confounding alike to the early twentieth-century researcher and to the early-twenty-first-century historian trying to grapple with a contemporary analysis of such practices.

In an essay on the queer dimensions of love and affect, Lauren Berlant has argued that many of the tropes or conventions of heterosexual romance are more normalizing, in terms of the "truths" about the self that they produce, than the tropes or conventions of heterosexual desire. As Berlant writes: "To the degree that gay and lesbian thoughts and desires threaten to impair the comfort people have learned to find in the formal inevitability of their intimate leanings, the resistance to what's *queer* about them can be read not just as a symptom of normativity in general, or as a sexual defense, but also as a fear of what will happen when those forms are separated from loving" (448; emphasis in original). To this end, touch could be regarded as an intersubjective form of communication that has the capacity to challenge the "formal inevitability" typically ascribed to patterns of heterosexual norms and sexual orientation in general. Touch disrupts these patterns by introducing forms of interaction and physical presence that may be shaped by normative sexual scripts but that, in their multivalence and unpredictability, exist to a large degree outside of conventions of the normative. Indeed, the public presentation or performance of certain perceived forms of romantic tactility (such as holding hands, grasping hands, touching hands, and so forth) are forged not necessarily in terms of sexual orientation but in terms of the complexities of social relations. One could make the same argument about the ways in which characteristic and identifiable forms of touch—stroking, petting, rubbing, holding, massaging, fingering, tracing, fisting, inserting, encircling, slapping, grasping, poking, and exploring with the fingertips—are physi-

David Serlin

cally performed more within the complex interactive dimensions of tactility than they are within established conventions of sexual orientation.

Among early sexologists, touch was perhaps regarded as a window into the mechanisms of compulsory heterosexuality, mechanisms that must be institutionalized in ways that make them appear enduring and natural. As Patrick White has described, well through the late twentieth century sex education manuals directed at blind adolescents were modeled on heterosexual scripts that policed the potentially queer boundaries of the tactile. Yet the affects and gestures that we use in our engagements with the world are routinely channeled by cognitive forces that exceed the explanatory power attributed to the institution of heterosexuality. As Sara Ahmed has argued, this is not simply about compulsory heterosexuality or compulsory forms of heteronormativity; rather, it is about compulsory forms of phenomenological normativity that orient the body into predictable channels of communication that can be directed, shaped, and controlled. In this way, certain possibilities of subjectivity are foreclosed in deference to others. Orientation here is more akin to the notion of what urbanists call an "orientation device": a semiotic signifier, such as a building or statue, which registers both individual and collective subjective impressions. As a high school freshman observed in the *New York Times* article with which I began this chapter, "If somebody were not to hug someone, to never hug anybody, people might be just a little wary of them and think they are weird or peculiar" (Kershaw p. 1, par. 12). Here hugging is regarded as a compulsory form of social interaction, weighed down with all the expectations of normativity exerted by other institutionalized forms of social engagement. Perhaps this is why tactility is perceived as inherently dangerous for both the person who touches and the recipient of that person's touch. Even if we acknowledge the dual nature of touch, as a message simultaneously sent and received, the power relationships involved are nonetheless unclear and messy. This is perhaps one reason why, in the *New York Times* article on hugging, young people are sometimes cast as vulnerable objects of touch rather than empowered agents in control of their own touching.

The critical examination of the evidence of touch (and its inadvertent disavowal) in Landis and Bolles's study helps to reconstruct the power relations that inhere in histories of disability and sexuality, as well as the sensuous and experiential dimensions of history more broadly. It provides multiple conceptual bases for thinking about how to historicize certain subjective dimensions of phenomenological experience—such as tasting, touching, smelling, feeling, hygiene, and affect—that do not entirely depend on able-bodied status. And it poses a challenge to conventional methodological approaches to the sensorium that either privilege the visual or subordinate smell, taste, and touch, the so-called lower senses, to the rigors of the rational mind. As Ahmed writes, "history cannot simply be perceived on the surface of the object, even if how objects surface or take shape is an effect of such histories. In other words, history cannot simply be turned into something that is given in its sensuous certainty, as if it could be a property of an object" (41). For the young women who served as research subjects for *The Personality and Sexuality of the Physically Handicapped Woman*, touch served to reveal the institutional and social pressures exerted upon them to uphold the conventions of heterosexual normativity. But it also served as a form of resistance to the hegemony of heteronormativity. The forms of subjective experience and individual history produced through these women's physical bodies highlight the need for scholars of sexuality and disability to think about touch not merely within reactive histories of social domination or sexual discipline but to think about touch as a productive entity. In other words, in what ways might we understand sexuality and disability differently, either together or individually, if we regard touch as a psychic, experiential, and epistemological category through which subjective understandings of one's body and one's self in the world are represented, refracted, and made flesh?

NOTES

Early versions of this chapter were presented at King's College London; Northwestern University; the University of Pennsylvania; the University of Toronto; the University of Washington, Seattle; and York University, Canada. Thanks to Will Smith for his research assistance and to Shawn Wilson of the Kinsey Institute for Research in Sex, Gender, and Reproduction at Indiana University, Bloomington, for help with the Carney Landis Collection. For superb comments on early drafts, thanks to A. M. Blake, Elspeth Brown, Héctor Carrillo, Steve Epstein, John Howard, Val Hartouni, Regina Kunzel, Heather Love, Mara Mills, Natalia Molina, Chandra Mukerji, Kathy Peiss, Brian Selznick, Marc Stein, and Crispin Thurlow. Special thanks to Robert McRuer and Anna Mollow for editorial guidance and abiding faith.

1. All references to case histories are taken from files, dated 1934–37, located in the Carney Landis Collection, deposited at the Kinsey Institute for Research in Sex, Gender, and Reproduction, Indiana University.

III

SPACES

8

....

NICOLE MARKOTIĆ AND ROBERT MCRUER

LEADING WITH YOUR HEAD

On the Borders of Disability, Sexuality, and the Nation

A classic team sports film rivalry consists of setbacks and springboards, moments of high drama and suspense punctuated by moments of release (laughter and tears), individual accomplishments lodged within a larger frame of homosocial and masculinist "team spirit," and personal stories from off the playing field that are later carried by viewers to the playing field. In 2004, for instance, Gavin O'Connor's maudlin *Miracle* recreated (for Walt Disney) the so-called Miracle on Ice, the 1980 Olympic battle between the United States and the USSR hockey teams in Lake Placid, New York. Such films appeal, melodramatically, to viewers' "hearts" over their "heads"; indeed, sports depicted in mainstream film is a primary arena in which unbridled nationalism is celebrated rather than regarded as dangerous, since *not* displaying patriotism around sports usually indicates a character failing.[1] Nationalities often clash in sports, and viewers' emotions are expected to soar when the assumed "home team" of the USA triumphs.[2] *Miracle* constitutes a textbook example of the cultural work performed by sports film rivalries that are played out at the level of the nation (especially when the "nation" in question is "America").

The focus of our chapter is a sports film rivalry of a seemingly different ilk, the documentary *Murderball*, by filmmakers Henry Rubin and Dana Shapiro, released in 2005—a documentary that presents the contact sport of quad rugby (developed in Canada in 1977), colloquially known as "murderball." Nominated for an Academy Award for Best Documentary Feature, and highly acclaimed in numerous Audience Awards (including Best Documentary Feature at the Sundance Film Festival in 2005 and Best Feature at the Full Frame Documentary Film Festival in 2005), *Murderball* is one of only a few disability films that show athletes succeeding not in spite of, but because of, their disabilities.[3]

A classic *academic* or *intellectual* "rivalry," we might say, following what Eve Kosofsky Sedgwick and Adam Frank call "the prevailing moralism of current theoretical writing," puts forward a vacillation between two poles, neither of which is the clear victor: "kinda subversive, kinda hegemonic" (5). What is merely a vacillation in current theoretical writing often becomes a battle in pedagogical settings: classroom debates about particular texts can generate teams defending or advancing one or the other of these two poles, as a given text is lauded or rejected as "totally subversive" or "totally hegemonic." Teach *Murderball* to a classroom full of generally thoughtful students, and you'll see what we mean. The film responds critically to some of the worst disability stereotypes and offers up what Rosemarie Garland-Thomson has called, in an analysis of *Murderball*, "fresh, feisty stories about disabled shapes and acts" ("Shape" 114). Because the film both invokes and challenges disability stereotypes, half the class will find it "subversive" for this reason and will, perhaps, turn to the graphic discussion of sexuality in the center of the film as evidence:[4] the film certainly challenges conventional images of disability as asexual; the film arguably challenges notions of what "sex" itself might be. Speaking openly about their sexuality, the athletes in the film generally focus on nonnormative practices: penile-vaginal heterosexual intercourse solely focused on a male orgasm has no prominent place here; the conversation is, rather, on autoerotics or on heterosexual sex that *could* be interpreted as more focused on female pleasure. The topics are masturbation and cunnilingus, and in the very broad sense of the term (although apparently none of the film's subjects would rest comfortably beneath the sign), the sex in the film is *kinda* queer. The other half of the class will argue that, on the contrary, *Murderball* represents a patriarchal, heteronormative, hegemonic masculinity, with bombastic male bravado in regard to sexual conquest, homophobia, and so forth. In this chapter, finding ourselves inescapably in the orbits of both kinds of rivalries, the sports film and the academic, we cannot always resist assigning scores. Even as we register decidedly hegemonic aspects of the

Nicole Markotić and Robert McRuer

film, we shall nonetheless consider some of the sexual and disability pleasures of the film. Yet ultimately, we are more interested in the materialization of other libidinal investments alongside and even through those pleasures, particularly the materialization of a libidinal investment we here call "crip nationalism." We use this term to mark an emergent, neoliberal form of nationalism that works in and through contemporary forms of disability identity, community, and solidarity.[5] Indeed, we argue that Joe Soares, who for most of the film is head coach of the Canadian team (even though he grows up in an immigrant U.S. family), becomes the ideal "extreme" coach for the crip nation. In addition, we argue that the homosocial narrative generated through Mark Zupan (perhaps the most well-known figure from *Murderball*) positions him as an ideal player for the crip nation (even though—and perhaps especially because—Soares and Zupan are ostensibly rivals for the duration of the film).

In suggesting that *Murderball* incorporates a crip nationalism, we are trying to avoid what we term "disability culturalism." Instead, we locate the film within larger transnational political, cultural, sexual, and academic economies. Crip nationalism, given that it is not founded on the assumption that disability is always and everywhere excluded or marginalized, is a strategy that, in Margrit Shildrick's terms, contests and queers "the very separation of self and other" that underpins the foundations of Western subjectivity (*Dangerous* 142), even as, we will argue, it generates other forms of dispossession. An analysis that gets caught up in whether a narrative such as *Murderball* is or is not "kinda subversive" or "kinda hegemonic" in regard to the disability identities and cultures it represents dislocates the text to an idealized space in which audiences can (supposedly) recognize disability, masculinity, athleticism, and even sex, but not the labor that continually produces or upholds the national contexts in which they currently function. The nations that Soares and Zupan represent or coach appear, at various points, to be the United States or Canada, but the phantasmatic, spectacularized crip nation engendered through that representation bears little relation to either neoliberal state, even as it is ultimately—as we shall demonstrate—quite useful to both.[6]

"Culturalism" generally, including disability culturalism and what Canadians officially deem "multiculturalism," ghosts complex questions about gender, sexuality, class, labor, and militarization. Rereading Walter Benjamin's famous assertion that "there has never been a document of *culture* which is not at one and the same time a document of barbarism," Gayatri Chakravorty Spivak insists that "a 'culturalism' that disavows the economic in its global operations cannot get a grip on the concomitant production of barbarism" (168). In this chapter, we ask what it would mean to apply Benjamin's and Spivak's words to *Murderball*. Doing so will entail, for one thing, exceeding the project of simply classifying particular cultural representations of disability as "positive" or "negative" — or relatedly, of assessing them in terms of whether they advance or impede a unitary disability movement. Benjamin's dictum, insisting as it does that *there has never been* a nonbarbaric document of culture, does not allow for what Frederick Powell passingly refers to as "an agenda of progress" (197). We shall therefore attempt to put forward a reading of the film that, to use Spivak's words, "gets a grip on" the production of barbarism. That is, although labor and economic relations are not foregrounded in *Murderball*, we will bring those relations to bear on our reading of it.

We know a few things about the flow of bodies back and forth across the U.S. and Canadian borders: both countries rely economically on immigrant labor; the workers in question are expected to be physically able (for domestic work, farm work, construction, and so forth); and they are heavily surveilled as they cross into each country and, while they are present, as "guests" or "aliens." In Canada (mostly in Alberta, but also parts of Ontario), migrant workers from south of the even more southerly border or borders (workers from Mexico, South America, and even as far as Fiji) are flown in on restrictive work visas to labor at demanding short-term jobs. They pay into social assistance programs from which they are not eligible to benefit. Various restrictive work visas have likewise been considered and implemented in the United States. And hundreds of thousands of workers cross into the country in ways that authorities deem "illegal" (often facing great physical danger and the possibility of death, particularly in desert climates). We know, then, that "ideal" bodies are desired for undesirable labor and that those bodies cross borders all the time, even as their movements are increasingly policed. We know as well that the work these bodies perform often is quite literally disabling and that subsequent recourse to national support systems is absent.

Murderball, in depicting borders and bodies, presents very different representational surfaces. First, borders are either easily crossed (as the teams travel to various national locations, or as they swap members or coaches) or are metaphorically, temporarily, and melodramatically reconstituted on the court, the metaphorical battlefield. Second, the desired bodies are not "ideal" in the sense that capital *generally* requires: something novel is clearly happening, because the rules of quad rugby insist, from the beginning, on a quantifiable level of physical

Nicole Markotić and Robert McRuer

disability. The film does, nonetheless, represent a striving for a kind of physical "perfection": a physical performance that will result in victory and be rewarded with a medal. But in this sport (and this filmic document of it), *disabled* bodies are desired, for the pleasures of competition and for the privilege of "representing" one's nation.

To sort out these disjunctions, we weave our analysis of *Murderball* with other "fresh and feisty" border and disability stories and other fresh and feisty stories of work. Our chapter was literally composed on either side of the nationally defined border that is so necessary, fetishized, and transgressed in *Murderball*. For this reason, we supplement our arguments about crip nationalism in *Murderball* with some personal reflections, which interweave in our chapter with Gramscian pessimism. Positioning our reflections has been somewhat difficult: during the composition of this article, Nicole was writing geographically from the country "on top"; Robert, from the country "on the bottom" (within the Ptolemy-originated convention of map orientation). Robert did, however, grow up in Detroit, one of the few places in which the United States is geographically "on top" (north) of Canada. Nicole grew up in Southern Alberta, north of most of the United States, but for most of the writing of this chapter, she resided just south of Detroit in Windsor, Ontario. The question of "top" and "bottom" becomes ever more complicated as our analysis and reflections develop.

NICOLE: Since Canada's "on top," I get to go first? But how to begin, when I write this in the middle of our back-and-forth discourse, interjecting these musings within the formalized academic "rivalry" we jointly compose? I'll confess: my dirty secret is that when—as Windsor residents frequently do these days—I travel across the infamous Ambassador Bridge (providing passage to over 10,000 commercial vehicles every day), I tend to whip out my U.S. passport. I'm Canadian when I return to Windsor but U.S.-ian when I enter the "north." My passport is just that, legal papers that allow me to cross borders, to send a courier package from Detroit when none of the courier companies operate in Windsor on a Saturday, and to vote in both countries. In Canada, I vote whenever an election is "called," municipally, provincially, or nationally, and always towards a labour candidate.[7] But in the United States, I vote only nationally, every four years, always from Illinois.[8] I usually vote strategically, rather than loyally, and I vote despite stories that out-of-country ballots are counted only in the event of a close race (which, at the presidential level, is rarely the case in Illinois). In Canada, I usually vote for; in the United States, I often vote against. And lately, whenever I drive "south" over the Ambassador Bridge, I smile thinking of the Canadian border guard unquestioningly believing Michael Moore in *Sicko* (2007), when Moore promises that his camera is not rolling, not capturing the moment of a U.S. citizen crossing the border because of issues of health care.

ROBERT: Joseph, my partner for most of the past decade and the center of my queer family or kinship network for all of it, often gets very, very tired and requires more sleep than many people (which he sometimes actually gets). Although his neurologist said in one annual checkup that he would be walking more slowly and with a cane within a year (so far, although he stumbles relatively frequently, he has not walked with a cane), Joseph is, nonetheless, necessarily in motion for many hours of the day. This is mainly because he is an immigrant from Brazil, caught up in the service economy of Washington, D.C., and tied to a catering job that sometimes requires twelve hours of work in a day. As with many from or in the Global South, Joseph's work conditions could be labeled "super-exploitative." Capitalism, that is, depends upon exploitation of all workers, in the form of extraction of surplus value, but increasingly over the past three decades particular forms of "super-exploitation" have been borne by particular kinds of workers from particular kinds of places. When these workers are represented in cultural criticism on the Left or—in Canada, at least, although much more rarely in the United States—in leftist-liberal journalism, the "super-exploited" immigrant is poor but robust, subject to potential injury from work perhaps, but not disabled already. Joseph's body, like those of many immigrant workers (or immigrants whose disabilities prevent them from working), does not conform to this stereotype.

"The first thing I learned how to do was jerk off." So says Scott Hogsett, a player on the U.S. quad rugby team and one of the "stars" of *Murderball*. Most of the players represented in the film conform to the stereotype of young, highly masculine athletes, and the film does much to depict their self-absorption and fascination with their Olympic-trained, physically exceptional bodies. Ironically (since it is so obviously invested in "challenging stereotypes"), the film revels in multiple "jock" stereotypes, celebrating young men who treat their bodies as if they were machines and who are obsessed with scars and injuries received on the court. Celeste Langan remarks that to "think about mobility disability is to think about norms of speed and ranges of motion" (459). The "norms" of speed and strength for these particular players are, like their bodies, exceptional. Dismissing a comparison between the sport they play and the Special Olympics, Hogsett announces: "We're not going for a hug; we're going for a gold medal."

Nicole Markotić and Robert McRuer

In complicated ways, these athletes' desire to play murderous ball and to defeat all other teams both mirrors and challenges contemporary notions of disability and capability, of team sports and nationalism. In discussing representations of mobility in films such as *Speed* and *The Straight Story*, Langan points to a model of "liberal individualism," which, she argues, "is grounded in the false premise of bodily equality as the basis of democratic justice" (463). In contrast to this model, *Murderball* repeatedly highlights the fact that bodies need not be evaluated as absolute equals: quad rugby operates through a system of classification wherein individual players receive "points" for their designated functional level; no team may exceed a total "value" of more than eight points at a time. But within the team sport as a whole, the male body paradoxically functions as a measurable synecdoche for equality that can and must be achieved for the sport to proceed.

Even more significantly, *Murderball* both preserves and contradicts the visual stereotype that male athletes project as physically superior, sexually vigorous, and conspicuously, adamantly, resolutely heterosexual. We strongly agree with Cynthia Barounis's argument that the film "figures disability as not only reflecting, but also amplifying a deeply constant heterosexual selfhood" (57). At the same time, we are equally interested in the Butlerian (queer) impossibility of that project and (even more important) in the ways in which the melodramatic management of the crisis of masculinity that the film stages—a management that results in the solidification of what Barounis terms "the link between [disabled] heteromasculinity and patriotism" (60)—is absolutely necessary for the production of the crip nationalism that we are positioning in this chapter as so useful for the neoliberal state.

Throughout the film, the U.S. players express a desire that their country, in this sport, be "on top." This desire, however, is somewhat "queered" during the scene in which the players and some of their girlfriends talk about sex and other people's assumptions about their sex lives. The men scorn any opinion that denies their (hetero)sexuality or disavows their bodies' abilities to take or give pleasure, but this decidedly does not translate into a need to be on top. In the most provocative exchange, a few of the players are asked by a woman flirting with them, "Does the girl have to be on top?" Hogsett responds, without missing a beat: "A lot of girls like to be on top." There's certainly power and control through the fetishization of the "top" position, from both the athletic and nationalistic perspective, at the same time that—sexually—there's a necessary (and flirtatious and eroticized) flexibility about who's on top.[9] We argue that the light, airy, sexual, and playful sense of "who's on top" participates in mystifying the production of crip nationalism and the more insidious neoliberal cultural work of the film. The stereotypically masculinist athletes' performance of the sexual "bottom" role, at the same time that they maintain a certain dominance, links a complicated resistance to, and reaction against, presumed notions of disability asexuality.[10] The need to present a normative (hetero)sexuality trumps the need to present an idealized masculinity. We may be crips, the athletes brag, but we're *normal* crips.

Above and beyond (although buried beneath) the more relaxed sexual banter, nationalism continues to be reinstated, and crip nationalism (also dominant, in ways we will excavate) is generated. This occurs via two melodramatic stories central to the film's project. Coach Joe Soares, an ex-player from the U.S. Murderball team, becomes coach of Team Canada after his failure to secure a slot as player for the U.S. Paralympic team in 2004. His sole sporting goal, he admits, is to defeat his former teammates. Soares, according to current members of the U.S. Murderball team, has "defected" to Canada as coach. They rant about him — "The only reason Joe went to Canada was to beat the U.S.A." — and call him a "Benedict Arnold." They shout at him across a hotel lobby: "How does it feel to betray your country, man?" Although professional athletes retire and coach other teams all the time, each U.S. player insists that Soares's "defection" was an acute betrayal, figuratively at the level of national security.

Throughout the film, Soares takes the position of the wrongly jilted beloved. Though he claims, at one point, that he's "living the American Dream," he again and again rouses his anger and disappointment at being cut from the team, vowing that he will "betray" his country the way he has decided his team, which he emotionally conflates with his country, "betrayed" him. Soares locates his situation within a melodramatic narrative of disloyalty and deception: he is the unappreciated "first wife" who has been ditched by the team so that they may achieve their trophy.[11] Melodramas present stock characters — jilted beloved, bitter first wife — on a recognizable stage. As Lisa Duggan has argued, when melodramas are played out, especially for consumption at the level of the nation, the more complex and political stories that might be narrated are obscured (*Sapphic* 20). Soares eagerly crosses the border to coach the Canadian team, and — after he has been "jilted" — proudly wears a maple leaf for most of the rest of the film. His Canadian team, likewise, easily crosses the border in the other direction — as, for instance, in one scene in which they go to Soares's Florida home for some homosocial and (Canadian) nationalist bonding after winning the Paralympics prelims in Vancouver: "In a year and a half," Joe says to the team, "we have become the strongest family I've ever had. . . . I absolutely consider you guys my boys." The jilted beloved has found new devotion in the "other," the "foreign," and seductive lover, the team that formerly occupied the role of "rival" but now offers a way for Soares to "occupy" his own former nation.[12] Soares had to leave the U.S. team because he didn't make the cut, and, in the film, he reinstates his virility by coaching Canadian athletes with, presumably, team strategies ("national secrets") that had formerly been the property of the team south of the border.

By playing this dangerous sport, pushing and knocking each other over and crashing and getting back into the game, the U.S. players, back on the court, demonstrate that they are powerful, athletically endowed, nimble men. They are young, heterosexual, all-American boys. These boys play hard and tough and don't understand defeat. "The trick to falling," Zupan advises, letting viewers in on a strategy operative on both sides of the border, is "Don't lead with your head." Lead with your body; lead with that powerful tool you need to rely on in order to succeed in this game; don't think of yourself as "special"; think of how extraordinary you are. Ironically, this court strategy sits alongside what we have been suggesting about the melodramatic schooling viewers are given: through *Murderball*'s narrative strategies, audiences are essentially told "don't lead with your head, but with your heart."

The film buttresses the Soares story of cross-border rivalry, betrayal, and devotion with a second homosocial and homoerotic melodrama aimed at audiences' hearts. Zupan's best friend Chris Igoe was the driver of the vehicle that crashed years before the events represented in *Murderball*; this was the accident that led to Zupan's disability. Both men were drunk, and Igoe was unaware that Zupan had passed out in the back of the pickup truck he was driving. When the vehicle crashed, Zupan was thrown from the back into nearby water and discovered only hours later. For years, Igoe could not bear to be in contact with his friend, much less watch him play on the court. Yet Zupan is shown in the film desiring, even needing, Igoe's gaze and approval—in many ways, more than he needs those of his girlfriend, who at one point describes herself as having a quasi-maternal bond with Zupan.[13] Zupan far more aggressively elicits the gaze of his male friend, requiring that Igoe watch his body and approve of his physically adept movements.

Igoe's appearance at the Paralympics functions both as the culmination of this melodramatic and homoerotic strand in the film and as a redemption narrative: Zupan has forgiven his friend but still needs for the person who injured him to see him playing a sport in which he can participate only *because* he is a paraplegic. Like Coach Soares, who needs his former teammates to "witness" his triumph (even as, or especially because, the triumph is over them), Zupan requires Igoe's witness (again, even as, or especially because, the triumph is in some ways over Igoe himself). It may be true, as Hogsett bragged, that the first thing players learn after a spinal cord injury is how to jerk off, but of course masturbation is usually preceded and sustained by erotic fantasies. The film, not surprisingly, does nothing to link the discussion of masturbation and other sex acts to what is the strongest erotic fantasy in the film. It is not directly spoken, but the fantasy, essentially, is "If I can only get him to watch me" (and, by extension, "If I can only get them to watch us"). An explicit acknowledgment of that homoerotic bond would force audiences to think about how that bond is functioning narratively; it would, thereby, interrupt the pleasure we are supposed to be experiencing if we are caught up in the affect of the story. Both Soares's story of betrayal and Zupan and Igoe's redemption tale thus function narratively as ways for audience members to lead with their hearts.

NICOLE: When I flash my U.S. passport on the Detroit side of the Ambassador Bridge, I am, in effect, "leading with my head," putting my best face forward and hiding my secret identity in the glove compartment (for, ironically, since the Canadian government now demands that "landed immigrants" carry various legal documents when crossing into Canada, I cannot return using the U.S. passport, but must always carry both nationalities with me when I border cross). *Murderball* fetishizes the notion of the Canadian–U.S. border by pitting ex-team member against team member, coach against player, brother (melodramatically) against brother. My ability to display documents of national belonging affords me the privilege of mobility, rendering permeable the border between two nation-states. This contrasts with the positions of Tom King's characters in his short story "Borders," who literally live in the "in-between" of the Alberta-Montana border. In King's story, the mother refuses to declare her nationality as either "Canadian" or "American," insisting that she is "Blackfoot." Border guards from both countries try to "send her back" to where she has come from. But border stations are not located exactly on the forty-ninth parallel, and each time she turns her car around, she must stop and answer the same questions at the border of the country she has just "left," only to have to answer the same series of questions and to face again the demand she choose between two nationalities. King's narrative writes a dimensional border into the geography, a landscape of in-between. Even as the Ambassador Bridge is

Nicole Markotić and Robert McRuer

owned, profitably, by Manuel "Matty" Moroun, it straddles two countries, multiple historical nation narratives, and innumerable immigrant cultures.

The complexities of national identity are further complicated by disability. When we discussed this chapter with our disability studies colleague and friend Sally Chivers, she responded with this anecdote: "I'm reminded of my former choir mate and her reasons for staying in Canada. She and her husband drove to the U.S. border on their way to start his career at Harvard. The U.S. official looked in the backseat and stated, 'No idiots, mongoloids, or morons allowed.' Her husband recoiled, 'Surely you don't mean my daughter?' Sadly, he did," and Chivers's choir friend and her family stayed in Canada.[14] Despite Shildrick's pronouncement that it is "no longer possible to distinguish between an originary body and a prosthesis" (133), some physical disabilities and many developmental and cognitive disabilities continue to be read as "alien other" by those consigned to the role of upholding some version of a conformist nation-state.

ROBERT: It's not solely the new passport requirements that mark the Detroit-Windsor border as particularly policed, but also the large Arab population in the metropolitan area that has been heavily surveilled. Although I too have crossed the Ambassador Bridge (or gone through the tunnel beneath the Detroit River) innumerable times, my own most electrified encounter with the border occurred elsewhere. Near the end of 2005, the year in which *Murderball* premiered, I was invited to apply for a disability studies and cultural studies position at the University of Toronto. Having recently received tenure at the George Washington University, I didn't relish the thought of returning to the status of assistant professor, and I expected that the position wouldn't offer a comparable salary. But, I thought, it doesn't hurt to apply.

In March 2006, I was offered the position at a level that surpassed my salary at the time. I expected Joseph to be ambivalent about the possibility of moving; I assumed perhaps that he was sentimentally (or melodramatically!) tied—as I was, certainly—to our life in D.C. I discovered, on the contrary, that he was immediately ready to pack our bags for Canada, where his work options would be multiple. Indeed, in a phone conversation with University of Toronto lawyers, I had been told, "Your partner will be issued a work permit at the same time as you." Used to receiving nothing from the state in regard to my sexuality, I asked them if I had to marry Joseph in order for him to receive a work permit. I fully expected marriage to be a condition—one that would be unwelcome to both of us for many reasons. No marriage was necessary, and it began to feel as if stepping onto Canadian soil might be that moment in which the whole documentary film of our own lives suddenly went Technicolo(u)r. With Nicole and other Canadian colleagues I began the process of sorting out what life in Canada might be like, with special emphasis—of course—on health care.

There is a clause, however, in Canadian immigration policy, suggesting that an individual might face exclusion, at a later stage, from landed immigrant status or permanent residency, if that person is considered someone who might make "excess" demands on Canadian health and social services. The real debates, with friends and colleagues on both sides of the border, began when I asked the lawyers about that clause. A day later, I heard back from them. Leading with their heads, they stated: "we think it might indeed be possible that your partner will face that exclusion at some point in the future."

"We think," of course, is no guarantee one way or the other, and now, in 2011, "we" (all of us) will never know. Canadian colleagues and friends produced stories of others on either side of the divide: "I know a heterosexual couple in a similar situation and it worked out for them," and "Yes, we've seen this clause come up before and it's been something of a problem, specifically around HIV, although we're not so sure around MS." We think it will be okay; we think it might be a problem; we don't know; we're not sure. "Minority existence," Phillip Brian Harper argues in a different context, "itself induces such speculative ruminations, because it continually renders even the most routine instances of social activity and personal interaction as possible cases of invidious social distinction or discriminatory treatment" (108). In the end, south of the border, Joseph and I decided that the question marks were too many to leave D.C., sell the apartment, give up tenure, and then wait and see. After Canada no longer seemed a viable "site" for our own emigration, Joseph and I, like so many others, watched as immigration "reform" continued (and continues) to stall and fail in the U.S. Congress (most spectacularly in the summer preceding the presidential election year of 2008).

Our personal stories have been about checkpoints, places where one starts or stops, or—more properly—where one might desire to start or might be forcibly stopped or detained. The melodramatic stories of sexuality, masculinity, and disability identity in *Murderball*, as well as the construction of Soares as the idealized crip coach (sometimes ironically, often not) for the nation, we argue, renders these other stories illegible. The personal stories we tell here are more about the state than the nation and about the ways that various institutions (including

Nicole Markotić and Robert McRuer

academic ones) are implicated in the construction of the borders that surround the state. The ease with which the disability identities and cultures represented in *Murderball* both cross borders and hypostasize, on the rugby court, those *state* borders as ultimately benign (albeit eroticized) borders between *nations*, testifies to the ways in which the construction of (disability) culture can partake of the barbarism to which Benjamin and Spivak attend. The (crip) nation is founded "on top" of these stories that are thereby (because they are on the bottom, buried, underneath) made invisible.

Some of the final images of the film continue this process of founding the crip nation on top of other, disappeared stories. One of the concluding sequences has many of the U.S. quad rugby team players working with Iraq war veterans at the now-infamous Walter Reed Medical Center (definitely not "centre") in Washington, D.C. They are not there to expose the state's failure in providing adequate care to disabled U.S. veterans at Walter Reed (the toxic, degraded state of the facility came to public knowledge only after the film's release). They are, instead, bringing the possibility of quad rugby to a group of American "heroes." The scene with Iraq war veterans is interesting not only in terms of the ongoing construction of a crip nation in *Murderball*, but also because it is the sole scene in which the film depicts women who might possibly play quad rugby. Women potentially trouble the U.S. construction of nation here; although the scene suggests the possibility of incorporation, the discourses of crip nationalism that have emerged over the course of the film, as we have detailed, are largely masculinist. The notion of the war-injured male soldier, now athlete is underscored by George W. Bush's rousing endorsement of veterans and quad rugby players in the closing credits to the film. The metonymic association of the extreme nationalism of the Bush era with the "extreme" nationalism that each player takes onto the court is troubling, to say the least. In *A Queer Mother for the Nation*, a study of the Nobel laureate Gabriela Mistral, Licia Fiol-Matta argues for understanding the flexibility of queerness. Rather than seeing nonnormative sexuality and gender as somehow essentially transgressive, Fiol-Matta instead considers how Mistral's spectacular queerness—a series of affairs with women, a paradoxical nonreproductive yet "maternal" public persona, and a widely disseminated (through photographs and other images) female masculinity—was deployed not to challenge, but to abet, state-sanctioned nationalism, racism, and patriarchy throughout Latin America. We argue here for a similar understanding of the multifarious ways in which the neoliberal state is beginning to use disability.

By portraying the U.S. team's desire to win the gold medal, depicting their desire to "defeat" Joe Soares, and filmically aligning the game itself to a Republican version of loyalty to country, "crip nationalism" is *entirely* "American," even as it is essentially offered and exported as a product that any nation might try (or buy). The U.S.-Canadian rivalry that the film works through presents a version of nation and nationalism (the other depicted as "rival," but also as so similar to the self that the camera need not distinguish individual others) that displays athletic and torqued bodies incorporated into nationalized, spectacularized global competitions. Bush's recognition of the quad rugby players conflates young, strong soldier citizens' devotion to their country with "team spirit." The final scenes effectively tie the physical therapy and rehabilitation of returning Iraq war veterans to the extreme sport of quad rugby: it may hurt, but it's good for loyal players, and—ultimately—good for the (American) team.

As we have noted, labor relations are not foregrounded in the film. We see female health care workers (apparently nurses and physical therapists) in rehabilitation centers located in the United States.[15] And we see Soares's young son, Bobby, engaged in domestic labor in Soares's home: flipping burgers for the Canadian team, polishing his father's wall of trophies. Interestingly, Soares's son (who is not a particularly good worker, in his father's estimation; he is constantly being scolded by Soares for perceived errors) provides the film with perhaps the only subtext that even approaches what we argue about the civilization/barbarism binary in circulation around the film. The subtext still fails, in Spivak's terms, "to get a grip on" the disavowal of the economic, but at the very least it might be read as a moment of rupture that opens a space in which the exclusions of crip nation might be considered. If the team is engaged in sex that is *kinda* "queer" but ultimately recuperated into a masculinist heterosexual bravado, and if the two prominent melodramatic narratives are homosocial and homoerotic but similarly recuperated, Bobby Soares—the bad worker—generates some anxiety in that he is not clearly on the path whereby traces of queerness would be topped and thereby eliminated by athleticism, heterosexual conquest, and crip nationalism.

In the middle of the narrative about the quad rugby competition, the film shows Bobby, holding a kiwi-sized trophy for a recent musical recital, staring at the rows of statuettes and sports trophies his father has won; Bobby looks defeated, simply in *not* possessing the ultra-athletic, competitive body and spirit his father so wishes to generate in him. About this pivotal moment, Roger Ebert says: "'Then an unexpected development (miraculously caught on camera) causes Soares to take a deep breath and re-evaluate his life, and his relationship with his son. Rehabilitation is not limited to the body" (par. 10). We assume that the reviewer is talking about Bobby's abject reaction to his father's opulent display of fame. But Ebert's cutesy discourse obscures the insidiousness of the connection it assumes between physical disability and moral deficiency. His review concludes: "We may not be in chairs and may not be athletes, but we all have disabilities, sometimes of the spirit" (Ebert par. 12).

The film's seeming inability to imagine anything but heterosexuality is underscored by Joe Soares's counternarrative focus, in which he worries that his son's lack of physical aptitude (depicted through viola playing) may be indicative of Bobby's heading down a questionable and, to his father, unfathomable path. Bobby Soares is arguably proto-queer. Of course, all children are proto-queer, but boys who aren't interested in sports and who play the viola have often been figures onto whom cultural anxieties about that universal proto-queerness are projected. Bobby's story is nevertheless melodramatic, and it is thus not unreadable, even according to the film's own logic. Indeed, we would suggest that this particular "queer" subplot, given how tightly it is woven into his father's, and given how clearly it works in counterposition to the heteronormativity and masculinity of the athletes, provides an autocritique that audiences (and reviewers, such as Ebert) can easily recognize. Where we read Bobby's story more fully against the grain—and, in the process, turn again toward spectral figures crossing borders completely outside the logic of this "border-crossing" film—is in our interpretation of him as one of the few bodies in the film represented as engaged in compulsory labor.

In the film's narrative logic, we suggest that one set of connections, or point and counterpoint, can be seen, while another clearly cannot: we see how Bobby's story works *against* the story of the men at the center of the film, and we thereby connect plot and subplot. The film's logic does not and cannot, for many reasons, encourage viewers to see Bobby as connected to the female workers in the hospital or rehabilitation center. We simply note here that at the very least his father degrades his labor in ways that spectrally *figure* the larger cross-border labor relations the film ghosts. Bobby's story, read in this way, effectively (and, interestingly, affectively) autocritiques the film's disability culturalism; it suggests, in other words, that the film's disability strategies have limits.

A famous photo collage by the late David Wojnarowicz presents viewers with an "all-American boy" who looks strikingly like Soares's son, without the glasses. Surrounding Wojnarowicz's "all-American" picture are these words, many of which are very much part of disability history:

> One day this kid will get larger. . . . One day this kid will feel something stir in his heart and throat and mouth. . . . Doctors will pronounce this kid curable as if his brain were a virus. This kid will lose his constitutional rights against the government's invasion of his privacy. This kid will be faced with electro-shock, drugs, and conditioning therapies in laboratories tended by psychologists and research scientists. He will be subject to loss of home, civil rights, jobs, and all conceivable freedoms. All this will begin to happen when he discovers his desire to place his naked body on the naked body of another boy.

The sex discussion the players have in front of the filmmakers, to which we keep returning, is not simply titillating "trash talk," but an engineered critique (and complaint) of the passive sexual role their visual bodies seemingly supply for viewers. The players don't simply want the audience to hear that they enjoy (heterosexual) sex acts with their girlfriends; they speak against the sexually limited role their bodies play within the confines of patriarchy and nationalized masculinity. The film and the filmmakers know this—and it is important that such knowledge be disseminated. Yet a more layered presentation about transnational queerness, disability, and labor are what the film, according to its logic, can't ask, can't tell, can't know.

US: We thought we might end with some poetic reflections on sitting drinking (Canadian) beer together in Nicole's Canadian apartment south of Detroit, flirting, bonding, but also reflecting on the dangerous geopolitics that shift culture closer and closer to barbarism. Ironically, however, that river became wider and wider and neither of us made it to the other's location during the writing of this article. We both still crave that easy crossing as much as we crave sitting around and reconstructing stories—about the worlds we live in, the ones we observe, and about the worlds we insistently desire.

NOTES

1. Even *Bend It Like Beckham*, which may be considered a more innovative film about sports, invites a patriotic reading from its audience, who is expected to root for

Nicole Markotić and Robert McRuer

Jesminder, a character who has assimilated into UK culture and whose love for football (soccer) indicates a dedication to what her parents still consider their "new" country.

2. At least, such is the assumption of most Hollywood movies. Conversely, at actual sporting events outside the United States, viewers' emotions are expected to soar when their nationality makes (or almost makes) the podium.

3. We adapt the phrase "not in spite of but because of" from Sally Chivers's recent work on the Canadian national icon Terry Fox. In speaking of a nine-foot-tall commemorative statue for the runner, Chivers writes: "This pattern of representation [of an active athletic young man making great strides *in spite* of his disability] . . . puts pressure on disabled people who can rarely convince the normative public that their achievements might occur *because of* or even *regardless of* their disabilities."

4. U.S. publishing conventions compel us to speak of the "center" of the film here (and not the "centre"), although we hope our dialogue throughout pushes these (and other) conventions.

5. This is certainly not to deny that disability has been useful to earlier forms of nationalism; veterans with visible disabilities, of course, have long been proudly put forward as national heroes (even if and as the difficult material circumstances faced by disabled veterans have often belied the symbolic function they were made to serve). Just as the "homonationalism" theorized by Jasbir K. Puar, however, "exceptionalizes the identities of U.S. homosexualities" while simultaneously queering others marked as excessive, perverse, or dangerous (4), the crip nationalism we are analyzing exceptionalizes certain (largely U.S.) disability identities and forms of solidarity even as other embodied experiences are rendered unthinkable.

6. Tellingly, the "rivalry" between nations in the film—Canada vs. the United States—is presented *only* as a rivalry between the U.S. team and an ex-teammate from the United States. Not once does the camera focus on Canadian players (in closeup), and the film's narrative strategy does not allow for the "personal story" of a single Canadian player.

7. In Canada party leaders call federal and provincial elections at Althusserian intervals, thus interpellating Canadian subjects through clerical ideological state apparatuses (ISAs).

8. In the United States, presidential elections are set for the first Tuesday of November, every four years. Most statewide elections (governors, senators, and representatives) are also held on the first Tuesday of November, every two, four, or six years.

9. The film has been well touted for its scene where players bluntly discuss sex. When a twenty-three-year-old straight male writes to the *Savage Love* columnist Dan Savage asking for advice on how to indirectly let a woman know he can "still perform," Savage quotes in his response *The Ultimate Guide to Sex and Disability*, advising the writer to take his date to see *Murderball* as a way to observe a "fairly frank discussion about sex." There is no advice for pursuing same-sex disabled dates. Yet—to keep in purview the inconsistencies and contradictions that interest us—the film repeatedly projects a

normative heterosexuality that belies the playful slipperiness of Hogsett's words. One player in fact goes into great detail explaining how he makes use of a towel as a prosthetic device to achieve the sexual "on top" position.

10. Indeed, in what other film would a male athlete gleefully relate the story of how—shortly after his accident—"one nurse got so excited I got a woody, she ran out to get my mom" (Hogsett). Barounis reads this scene as in many ways the quintessential example of how "phallic potency" is sustained in the film (59). In contrast, we read it as paradoxically suturing pride and sheepishness (who is "on top" in this scene seems particularly and comically fraught) and exemplifying the flexibly queer (in the broad sense) but nonetheless zealously homophobic new masculinities we are analyzing.

11. In one tragicomedic moment, Soares—while with his actual wife at their anniversary dinner—toasts "to Team Canada" in response to his wife's romantic toast "to you."

12. The film mirrors Soares's expectation of Canada as "enough like" the United States for one to be a surrogate for the other. Soares knows his ex-teammates' names and game strengths, yet—again—the focus on individualized Canadian players is virtually nonexistent, as it is the (easy) figuration of Canada as (*kinda*) foreign other that matters in this melodrama.

13. In one talking-head sequence, Zupan's girlfriend says that "curiosity" and "the mothering instinct" attracted her to him.

14. Our thanks to Chivers for allowing us to quote from this e-mail of 29 August 2009.

15. These rehab centers, beholden to the insurance industry, are in the United States, with low-wage workers and chronic understaffing; the film does not depict any Canadian soldiers, in rehab or otherwise, returning from active war duty.

Nicole Markotić and Robert McRuer

9

....

ABBY L. WILKERSON

NORMATE SEX AND ITS DISCONTENTS

Like members of the disability rights movement, intersex and transgender activists have illuminated the hierarchal social construction of personhood and the
significant role of medical pathologization in such categorizing.[1] They have also
fiercely resisted medical colonization of individual lives, insisting, as disability
activists have, "Nothing about us without us." These movements illustrate both
the profoundly subjugating forces arrayed in the privatization of sex and the
power of resistance through activist articulations of nonnormative sex as a basic
human right.

These concerns are all the more pressing given how globalization has extended the reach of Western medicine, exporting its troubling regimes of normalization alongside its more benign aspects. Globalization has also opened new
markets for medical tourism; in Thailand, for example, Western tourists enjoy
luxury care, while much of the local population cannot afford what is considered basic care in the richer nations of the Global North. Disability scholarship and activism is centrally concerned with self-determination for people with
nonnormative bodies. If the greater access to Western medicine (if not an end

to health care disparities) promised by development entails globalizing Western gender itself, this represents a significant issue for disability activism.

Intersex perspectives have emerged out of struggles with the medicalization of nonnormative bodies and sexualities, a concern that has been important for the transgender movement and, in somewhat different ways, for transsexuals as well. These movements have much to offer disability theorizing of sexual agency, agency in medical contexts, and agency under oppression. At the same time, disability theory, particularly through notions of interdependence, can advance intersex and trans projects of theorizing agency, as well as ongoing work in philosophy and feminist theory on *embodied* agency.[2]

But to speak in this way—of these modes of being, thinking, and acting as distinct and separate from disability—is already somewhat misleading. Disability theory and activism deal with embodied variation and vulnerability as definitive features of human existence, social landscapes shaped by hierarchies of mental and bodily functioning and morphologies, and landscapes that influence our experiences in countless ways. Intersexuality, transgender, and transsexuality are clearly part of this purview. As discrete conditions and identities, and through their larger implications, they affect the lives of disabled people. Separating disability from these concerns of gender and sex is necessarily artificial, given how sex, gender, and sexuality interact with ability and disability in the social constitution of personhood and how gender, ability, and disability are profoundly interwoven in bodily norms.[3] These converging movements raise politically urgent questions. Creating a shared language to articulate sexuality-related concerns across diverse social movements and locations is a significant and pressing rhetorical and political challenge at the heart of all questions of coalition and community.

In this chapter, I develop a critical concept of "normate sex," considering transgender, transsexualism, and intersexuality as departures from it. If a given condition can be seen as a departure from normate sex, then the primary target for intervention should be social norms and practices rather than individuals. Likewise, a critical notion of sexual interdependence calls for intervention into social conditions. From this vantage point, intersex and transgender bodies and lives underscore the importance of nonnormative sexuality as a constitutive feature of the social category of disability.

Writing about intersex and transgender sexuality through a disability lens may nonetheless seem a perverse and wayward impulse. Neither transgender, transsexualism, nor intersexuality can be readily assimilated into conventional

Abby L. Wilkerson

notions of disability; they are not motor, sensory, psychiatric, or cognitive impairments; nor are they chronic illnesses. Moreover, given cultural perceptions of disability as lack, loss, or pathology, many intersex and transgender activists vehemently refuse any association with it.[4]

Yet from a radical disability perspective, these concerns are all the more reason to proceed. Disability studies illuminates the normalization of bodies in ways that extend far beyond what might seem to be unambiguous or obvious manifestations of disability, and radical disability scholarship and activism, like the transgender and intersex movements, are based on resistance to normalization. This conjunction is a significant opportunity to explore normalization—and resistance—in and through sexuality.

Trans and intersex writers and activists have been vocal critics of projects taking up their work in the service of broader agendas, such as feminist revisionings of gender, without attending to these groups' human rights, such as legal recognition of gender identities in the case of transgender and transsexualism or the harmful medicalization of intersexuals.[5] Equally important are the ongoing debates within these communities over such issues as nomenclature, and whether intersex, transgender, or transsexualism constitute identities at all (as opposed to states, processes, or some other kind of phenomena). It is precisely because of this highly contested nature of trans and intersex that they should be addressed from a disability perspective. They present critical questions for addressing, on the one hand, the shame and stigma that hamper not only movements but coalitions across movements, and on the other hand, the co-optation of these terms and movements in the service of other theoretical projects.

As I have argued elsewhere, both oppression and liberation of particular groups generally involve a significant sexual component ("Disability"). An intersex, transgender, or disability vantage point is a particularly compelling site from which to explore: the implications of this claim and the role of conservative sexual norms in oppression more generally, as well as their frequent justifications through medical discourse; and eroticization against these norms as a means of resistance. Perversity, after all, in its deviance and opposition, can be something to be honored. Its etymology suggests a turning away from that regarded as right, good, true, for that which is "esteemed false" (OED). In a Foucauldian sense, then, the perverse impulse of this project is one of turning away from a regime of truth in search of another with the potential to release subjugated knowledges, indicating the profoundly epistemic dimension of erotic dissidence that these movements exemplify. And more than knowledge, even, is at stake in these movements: it is also the social meanings, the new social realities, they create and perform, especially through counter-erotics.

NORMATE SEX

As an initial step toward understanding how social group oppression operates through sexual dynamics, it will be useful to invoke Rosemarie Garland-Thomson's influential conceptualization of the "normate" as: "the veiled subject position of cultural self, the figure outlined by the array of deviant others whose marked borders shore up the normate's boundaries. . . . [T]he social figure through which people can represent themselves as definitive human beings . . . the constructed identity of those who, by way of the bodily configurations and cultural capital they assume, can step into a position of authority and wield the power it grants them" (*Extraordinary* 8). While Garland-Thomson's normate is indeed definitively able in body and mind, to define the figure entirely in these terms, she points out, is to miss that the normative body is simultaneously constructed through gender, race, and a complex array of other social categories.

Building on these insights, I introduce a concept of "normate sex," integrating insights from sex radicalism, disability studies, and what Judith Butler and others call the "new gender politics" of transgender and intersex (*Undoing* 4). Intersex and transgender medicalization illustrates how normate sex presumes both the sex/gender binary and conventional heterosexuality. But normate sex has many more dimensions than this. In a foundational queer theory article, Gayle Rubin identifies a social "hierarchy of sexual value," which establishes what is included within "the charmed circle" of sexuality (13).[6] Normate sex shares significant commonalities with Rubin's "Good, Normal, Natural, Blessed Sexuality" — namely, "Heterosexual, Married, Monogamous, Procreative, Non-commercial, In pairs, In a relationship, Same generation, In private, No pornography, Bodies only[, no sex toys], [and] Vanilla" (13).

But normate sex is also location specific, occurring particularly in suburban single-family homes (although *Desperate Housewives* may have put even this site into question), not on the street or in public housing projects, not in nursing homes or hospitals or rehabilitation facilities or airport men's rooms frequented by Republican senators from Idaho with wide stances. Nor can just anyone have it — certainly not Hermaphrodites with Attitude, interracial or multiracial couples, mothers receiving public assistance, adults registered as "sex offenders" because as teenagers they had consensual sex with another teenager, men with

Abby L. Wilkerson

breasts, "chicks with dicks," anyone who is HIV positive or schizophrenic or uses a wheelchair, young male immigrants from the Middle East, full-bodied women naked in hot tubs, or Bob Dole. Given current standards of attractiveness, perhaps even the young and slender cannot have it if they sport a full complement of body hair and are not muscular.[7]

Rather than an exhaustive catalog of the distinct norms that structure normate sex, this list is more of a snapshot of its recent manifestations, meant to illustrate the many social categories that constitute it, including race, class, gender, normative genital configuration, age, body size and type, citizenship, and nation—along with sexual histories and practices, and other circumstances. At any given time, manifestations can shift in relation to current dynamics, as the crisis of the moment interacts with the dominant, residual, and emergent cultural forces, to invoke Raymond Williams's categories ("Marxism and Literature" 121–27). In particular, as cultural and ideological needs shift, this will affect which already recognized social groups experience oppression, while sometimes marking out new previously unrecognized groups, exposing them as targets for oppressive practices.

The norms of normate sex, it must be understood, do not merely draw boundaries between appropriate and inappropriate desires, behaviors, identities, and spaces. They also effect a privatization of sex, regulating nonnormate sex or keeping it taboo and under wraps, through a vast array of state and cultural supports for normate sex: for example, federal policies such as tax laws and other laws benefiting married heterosexuals; or Social Security Disability Insurance and Supplementary Security Income policies that jeopardize income supports for disabled people who marry; or cultural productions such as films or television programs promoting normativity as the standard of sexiness, while depicting any departure from narrowly defined notions of normalcy as sexual tragedy, lack, loss, or threat. Normate sex continues to be culturally celebrated in its contained and appropriate channels, while young people with disabilities or the newly disabled asking parents or health professionals for information about sexuality often encounter a resounding silence or, more likely, harshly negative messages. Such obstacles are similar to those experienced with other nonnormative sexualities. The abstinence-only sex education model of George W. Bush's administration purported to celebrate "healthy" sexuality—married, monogamous, normate—and to prevent what we could see as departures from normate sex, such as teen pregnancy, single parents receiving public assistance, or even sex with condoms. This ostensible celebration of "appropriate" sexuality was one more barrier (albeit the most democratic in its imposition) to information about contraception, safer sex, and consent issues. The medicalization of nonnormate sex also plays a major role in its privatization, with "patients," isolated from others like them, treated as individuals with unique pathologies rather than as members of groups who can provide various forms of support to each other. Such support includes sharing information that is valuable, not only in making treatment decisions but also in living with one's condition more generally—or in resisting diagnosis and treatment altogether.[8]

Even these brief examples of the boundaries surrounding normate sex, the public supports for it, and the strictures against it clearly indicate both the broad social consequences of normalizing discourses of sex—and equally, I hope, the desperate need for alliance building. The very ubiquity of nonnormate sex suggested by the range of examples, the myriad ways in which sexual practices can and do depart from the norm, reveal the allure of transgressiveness, a topic to which I return near the chapter's end. Before doing this, however, I wish to examine the operations of normate sex more closely. To this end, I now turn to the examples of intersexuality and of transgender and transsexuality.

"MAKE THE HERMAPHRODITE FUCKABLE"

Lena Eckert advocates the term "intersexualization," rather than "intersexuality," arguing that "there would be no such thing as intersexuality were it not for the process of pathologization that goes hand in hand with the construction of intersexuality. . . . Intersexuality is actually an identity based on the experience of medical treatment in the West. . . . [And it is a] category which does not have any specific meaning outside of a specific medical framework" (41). This formulation resonates with disability theory notions of "disablement" as an active process of social construction.[9]

Only a small minority of the various forms of intersexuality requires treatment for noncosmetic reasons, yet the well-documented standard medical response has been to intervene on the basis of atypical appearance or physiology.[10] Medical interventions into intersex may be in a period of transition. For almost a decade, some intersexualized people have worked with academics and medical professionals in the Intersex Consensus Group to advocate substitution of the umbrella term "disorders of sexual development" (DSD) in medical contexts. As a result, the "Consensus Statement on Management of Intersex Disorders" was published in *Pediatrics* in 2006, recommending, among other things, a far more

Abby L. Wilkerson

cautious approach to surgery (Lee et al.). These efforts are possibly beginning to have an impact on medical practice. However, other intervention-resisting activists oppose the DSD terminology, some continuing to use the term "intersexuality" to signify an identity, community, and benign physiological condition, while others support the term "variations in reproductive development" for medical use.[11]

Intersex activism illustrates both how medical discourse can be inimical to sexual agency (as well as agency more generally) and how resistance is possible. Intersex activists have also demonstrated the harms of sexual privatization accomplished through medicalization: when a decision is to be made about whether an infant's or young child's genitals should be surgically altered, parents are usually presented with these questions in a highly privatized context, without input from the intersex community or from anyone else who might challenge the authority of medical professionals who have a stake in their own expertise. In addition, parents of intersex children are urged to keep silent about interventions; they are sometimes even advised to move to another town when a child's gender is reassigned, so that no one will know of any alterations.

In the extensive literature on the harms of intersexualization, survivors of these genital surgeries tell similar stories of having repeatedly been treated in childhood as medical spectacles, while being denied access to information about their own bodies and the nature and consequences of what was being done to them.[12] Thanks to intersex activist efforts, some physicians are beginning to refer parents to groups that provide nondirective, nonjudgmental counseling and support. However, there are also now efforts to eradicate intersexuality through hormone treatments and even by offering pregnancy termination to women whose fetuses are identified as intersex; these practices are similar to, and perhaps coextensive with, eugenic practices that disability theory has critiqued. In addition, until very recently many parents have, on doctors' recommendations, accepted silence about a child's conditions and medical histories as in the child's best interests. The sexual aspect of the medical scrutiny and resulting interventions only exacerbates the intense shame resulting from bodily stigma and caregivers' secrecy, leaving young intersexed people with the impression of being "the only one," a freak of nature. This isolation undermines intersex as a conceptually possible, let alone positive, identity—one more privatizing influence of normate sex.

The stigma associated with genitalia of atypical appearance has often meant that intervention is considered necessary no matter how imperfect the outcome. Cheryl Chase writes of a woman who, like many intersexuals, lacked sexual sensation as a result of the clitorectomy she had as a child because her clitoris was considered too large. When this woman sought medical help to restore sensation, "Justin Randolph, a well-known surgeon specializing in clitoroplasty . . . told her that clitorectomy had been 'all surgeons had to offer' when she was a child" ("Surgical" 150). In other words, her body had required intervention not because of organic dysfunction, but because of its departure from a morphologic ideal, and this necessity was perceived as justifying the suffering the procedure had caused her. Medical discourse constructs much that lies outside its ideal as pathological, requiring medical "correction" even when available treatments cannot restore or create the ideal. In fact, "marking" might be a more accurate term for what happens in such interventions, in which surgical scars become stigma, literal marks conveying a discredited identity, a medical seal of disapproval.

As the previous story suggests, many intersex surgeries are performed ostensibly to normalize the genitals visually rather than to correct physiological dysfunction, yet critics have reached a consensus that, as Chase writes, surgery "does not produce 'normal' looking genitals" but rather "convey[s] the clear message that 'abnormal' genitals (including surgically reconstructed ones) are unacceptable. Surgery inflicts emotional harm by legitimating the idea that the child is not lovable unless 'fixed'" ("Surgical" 155). Martha Coventry notes, "I'd be considered one of the success stories. I still have clitoral sensation, and I'm orgasmic." Yet she goes on to say, "it's taken me my whole life to come to terms with my body and not to feel such terrible shame" (qtd. in Chase, "Surgical" 155).

It is difficult to find any reports of intersexuals satisfied with their surgical outcomes. Pressure to remain closeted in this situation would be strong, yet it is striking, especially given increasing public attention, that published narratives of intersexuals consistently convey profound regret for surgical normalization procedures, especially those performed on patients too young for meaningful consent. Intersexuality is a powerful example of disruptions to agency in at least two ways: first, bodies that challenge the standard binary means of assigning sex are pathologized; second, intersexuals are then subjected to psychologically and physically damaging treatments. The combined effects are devastating.

Ideals, including medical ones, are nothing if not socially created, and medicine often relies on the quintessential traditional social concept, the heteropatriarchal sex/gender binary. Medical interventions into intersexuality reflect a necessity that is most often social in nature, rather than narrowly medical, as one can see by examining how these interventions function: Surgically altered genitalia certify that what *could* be done to bring a body into conformity with the social sex/gender binary *has* been done. Alice Dreger notes that one of the medical "rules" of gender assignment is that "genetic males must have 'adequate' penises if they are to be assigned the male gender. . . . If their penises are determined to be 'inadequate' for successful adjustment as males, they are assigned the female gender and reconstructed to look female" ("Ambiguous" 28).

It is striking that a penis is thought to require removal and its bearer to require gender reassignment simply because it is considered a few centimeters too short, and that hypospadias (in which the urethra is located somewhere other than the tip of the glans of the penis) is thought always to require "repairs"—in fact, to require interventions that often cause lasting pain and urinary dysfunction while failing to eliminate the perceived problem. These examples are based on an understanding of masculinity that requires an "adequate" penis—not in terms of erotic sensation but rather in *appearing* large enough and in enabling urination standing up, which at least in the United States is currently considered necessary for proper male identity development. Thus, the *potential* to approximate conventional sex and gender markers is prioritized not only over urinary function (which in some cases may appear unconventional) but over genital sensation as well, which can be irreparably harmed in the process.

Moreover, various types of intersex surgeries take as their objective the capacity to perform "normal" penile-vaginal intercourse. Standard treatment prioritizes this goal, cutting genitalia to shape for conventional intercourse even at the expense of genital sensation. Kiira Triea, raised as a boy but at fourteen deemed a "defective male" (i.e., a female) by John Money of the famed Psychohormonal Research Unit at Johns Hopkins, writes of being given a vaginoplasty yet being left with no clitoris or erectile tissue: "Jones [the surgeon] seems to have taken care, though, to ensure that I was able to be penetrated, as my 'vagina' seems to be deep enough to allow for that. Part of my upper left arm was pressed into genital duty here, which bothered me greatly when I came out of surgery. I wish I'd been consulted or at least informed. Of course, why would I need to be informed? The objective was to make the hermaphrodite fuckable" (143).

This medical emphasis on conventional intercourse exemplifies erotophobia, which Cindy Patton defines as "the terrifying, irrational reaction to the erotic which makes individuals and society vulnerable to psychological and social control in cultures where pleasure is strictly categorized and regulated" (103). As a host of feminist analyses have demonstrated, conventional intercourse, with all its overtones of "appropriate" gender identities, sexual identities, and the underlying biology thought to shape them, is at the center of the "charmed circle" of the "good, natural, normal, blessed sexuality" Rubin describes, leaving other structures, practices, and identities either deviant or unthinkable (13).

Clearly, then, the *medical* imperative to "make the hermaphrodite fuckable" is based on a conservative heteropatriarchal *social* imperative, one that is a cornerstone of normate sex. The disability movement has recognized and contested the medical and social imperative to bring into conformity—through correction, rehabilitation, and even sterilization and other eugenic practices—those physical bodies that constitute disruptions to the *social* body. Yet as intersex medicalization indicates, this imperative is inescapably intertwined with that which simultaneously regulates and governs sexual identities, practices, and desires, as well as outward manifestations of gender. Intersexualization illustrates the ways in which sexual disabilities are constituted in and through social environments.

Yet the social construction of sexuality is surely a more complex phenomenon than medical discourse suggests, despite the profound influence of the latter. The historian of science Christina Matta writes that late nineteenth-century intersex surgeries were based on the idea that an intersex person's anatomy, appearance, or gonads would always be the same as his or her partner's, and therefore that an intersex person's sexual behavior was inherently homosexual—and pathological. Worse yet, intersex people might have sex both with men and women, sinking to the depth of sexual depravity. Thus, the goal of surgery at this time was to eradicate sexuality in intersex people altogether, "an act of mercy" according to one doctor (qtd. in Herndon). Later in the twentieth century, the rationale for surgery shifted from preventing homosexuality or eradicating sexuality altogether to the positive demand to approximate "normal" heterosexual intercourse, as masculinity increasingly became defined by penis size and heterosexual performance.

Medical discourse, although it sometimes actively influences and sometimes passively reflects social norms, cannot ever entirely speak *for* society. This is clear, for example, in Suzanne Kessler's survey of female college students (detailed in her book *Lessons from the Intersexed*), which found that they would be unlikely to seek surgery for a clitoris perceived as too large (101). And some parents of intersex children have chosen not to comply with medical advice. Their medical noncompliance has the effect of resisting Western medicine's ongoing efforts to eradicate intersexuality, through normalizing hormone treatments or through prenatal detection meant to facilitate pregnancy termination.

Abby L. Wilkerson

WRONG BODIES, LIMINAL GENDERS, AND WESTERN MEDICINE

Like intersexuality, transgender can be considered a sexual disability in its challenge to gender norms (which, as we have seen with intersexuality, are not merely dimorphic but heteronormative), which becomes the basis for pathologization. However, its relationship to intervention is somewhat different insofar as transsexuals and some transgendered people actively pursue surgical and other interventions, while intersexuals have expressed a clear consensus in rejecting standard intersex treatments. A conflict may therefore seem to exist between the intersex and transgender movements, given that surgical procedures rejected by intersex activists are the very interventions that many transgendered individuals pursue and to which the movement seeks greater access. But as Butler argues, these differences are superficial: "Both [movements] challenge the principle that a natural dimorphism should be established or maintained at all costs," both oppose "forms of unwanted coercive gender assignment," and both demand "greater claims of autonomy" (*Undoing* 6, 7).

These movements also share a complex relation to the institution of medicine. Some people who have sought sex reassignment surgery are satisfied with their care and with the discourse upon which it is based; they find medical notions of gender congruent with their own experiences of it, despite the grueling nature of sex reassignment surgery and the entire process that surrounds it. Many transsexual and transgender activists seek improved care, better information, and enhanced agency in medical interventions, while the transgender movement as a whole challenges the authority of the medical establishment and the rigid gender binary enforced through medical criteria, treatments, and procedures. Transgender activists, like disability activists, see medicine as playing a central role in blaming and punishing them for social intolerance and discrimination — identifying them as the problem for failing to be "normal."[13]

The female-to-male (FTM) transsexual theorist Jay Prosser frames the medicalization of gender transition as an expression of transsexual agency, arguing that transsexuals have constructed and shaped this medical framework at least as much as it has shaped their bodies, minds, and identities. Reading narratives of transsexuals in the United States and Europe, he contends that this active role becomes evident through the subjective experience of transsexuals. For Prosser, the language of inhabiting the "wrong body . . . simply [reflects] what transsexuality feels like," with body image thus "radically split off from the material body" (69). "Somatic non-ownership," Prosser argues, is "not a metaphor" but rather a literal "pretransition bodily experience" for transsexuals (73). This is evident, Prosser claims, in narratives by transsexuals such as Raymond Thompson, who writes: "It felt as if I came into this world with no physical form to protect me. I was not a solid, tangible being like everyone else seemed to be. I felt vulnerable and alone" (qtd. in Prosser 73). For many transsexuals, sex change surgery is not only welcome but so deep a necessity as to be fundamental to selfhood.

At the same time, many transgendered people do not want surgical or hormonal intervention; either they do not feel the need for congruity between gender expression and somatic form (in some cases because their gender identities are not based on a unified sense of gender, but rather on a shifting play of multiple genders), or they experience a congruity in—or in spite of—transgressing conventional gender norms. Others choose some degree of medical intervention while rejecting the full standard package, such as FTMs who have "top surgery" without genital alteration (and sometimes, in order for a surgeon to perform top surgery, they are forced to pretend they will later pursue the full intervention).

To claims that medical intervention into gender can be an expression of agency, some critics object that even if transgender demand for medicalization is not medically created, it is socially imposed, insofar as cultural demands for conformity to the sex/gender binary produce felt needs for one's body to accord with one's gender expression as dictated by heteropatriarchal convention. Thus, desires for sex reassignment surgery would signal a need for social change, rather than a hormone prescription and a surgical appointment. Can the call to change punitive social gender norms be compatible with the idea that people who want medical alterations of their genders should be able to get them?

Many transgender activists call for better access to the medical interventions that are such deeply felt needs; pathologization should not be the price of this care. Gender, as one of the most fundamental aspects of identity, should be self-determined. As it is a quality strongly tied to bodily morphology and socially necessary for recognition of basic personhood, its self-determination through medical and other means should be socially supported.

Despite this deeply felt need for medical technologies, however, medical responses to transgender are by no means immune from criticism; indeed, the medicalization of transsexualism and transgender can be harmful. The psychiatric diagnosis of gender identity disorder (required by physicians in order to legitimate a request for sex reassignment surgery) has often been applied coercively to children and adolescents, causing lifelong harm. Dylan (formerly Daphne) Scholinski's *The Last Time I Wore a Dress* is a particularly compelling

Abby L. Wilkerson

narrative of adolescent institutionalization and the variety of therapeutic regimes brought to bear on gender expression. Noncoercive applications of the diagnosis are also problematic insofar as they define identities and interventions on the basis of medically predetermined, rather than self-determined, notions of gender and corresponding body morphologies.

In addition, the psychologist Katrina Roen raises concerns of ethnocentrism implicit in the Western medical discourse of gender transition; these concerns derive from her interviews with Polynesian gender-liminal people living in New Zealand.[14] Yet in addressing the important issue of cultural imperialism, care must be taken to avoid positing non-Westerners seeking surgery as merely passive dupes of the Western system.

One of Roen's interviewees, Don, identifies as Samoan and *fa'afafine*, a Samoan term meaning "like a woman." Born with genitalia conventionally considered male, fa'afafine have an accepted role in Samoan society and, to a lesser degree, in New Zealand. When Don moved to New Zealand with his family as a child, his mother warned him, "You mustn't walk like that, Don. . . . [T]hey don't do that in New Zealand" (257). Don "describes being taught from an early age that to be fa'afafine was to be valued and respected": "It's like a special woman. It's a knowledgeable woman but recognized [as] . . . anatomically male" (247).

Don states, "For me culture is always first and then sexuality . . . I'm Samoan first and foremost and . . . [secondly] I'm fa'afafine" (257). In contrast to Don's foregrounding of culture, which for him is intrinsically linked to his gender identity and sexuality, Pat, a Maori, identifies as a preoperative FTM. Transitioning because of his sense that he is in "the wrong body," Pat had "top surgery." His goal is to become a heterosexual man. His cultural identity is in many ways secondary, although at the suggestion of a fellow member of a Maori cultural performance group, getting Maori tattoos over his chest scars helped him to feel more comfortable with his changing body and served as an embodied means of honoring both his gender and his cultural identities.

Roen contends that because of the increasing influence of the Western medical discourse of gender, gender-liminal Polynesians may "seek sex reassignment surgery even though they live in a cultural context where their gender liminality might formerly have been understood in terms of a gender role for which bodily change was not considered an issue" (254). Personal narratives and anthropological accounts indicate, for example, that fa'afafine are accorded a fairly complex status in Samoan culture.[15] They are valued for perceived excellence in various kinds of work associated with women and are sought after as dramatic and musical performers, which, with increased tourism, has led to a veritable fa'afafine industry for Western consumption. Fa'afafine, as well as some anthropologists such as Niko Besnier, interpret these roles as conferring recognized cultural leadership, even as the roles trade in the stock figure of the sexually exotic native. At the same time, fa'afafine do not have the social status accorded conventionally masculine men. They are subject to some gender-based harassment, yet apparently without being considered abnormal or unnatural, as gender nonconformists have often been perceived in the West.

The increasing influence of Western medical discourse culturally and legally in New Zealand and elsewhere worries Roen. She predicts increasing difficulty for gender-liminal Polynesians in accessing traditional frameworks of gender liminality; this difficulty, Roen argues, amounts to a violation of cultural values and beliefs about "the relationship between sexed bodies and lived gender" (254). She calls for theoretical frameworks that would not simply deconstruct the gender binary but "creat[e] gendered ways of being that satisfy aspects of both racial and (trans)gendered politics" (255).

Such a goal is vitally important; Roen underscores the dangerous potential of Western medicine and culture to impose ideals that have sexually disabling consequences for gender-liminal people. It is difficult, however, to rule out the possibility that an FTM such as Pat might have wanted surgery even without the impetus of Western medicine and culture. Any analysis of transgender medicalization in international contexts should seek not only to eradicate coercion but also to recognize and foster the potential for agency in cultural exchange. An ahistorical concept of non-Western cultures as having pure and ideally fixed essences (in this case one of multiple genders) rather than being subject to change and transformation, enables a critique of one Western ideal—the medical gender binary—but substitutes another in its place: the political notion of the fluidity and multiplicity of genders. Non-Westerners may develop their own alternatives to both Western medical and political norms and to their own traditional gender categories, which may or may not continue to serve them well today.

OPPRESSED GROUPS AND NORMATE SEX

In her highly influential book *Justice and the Politics of Difference*, the philosopher Iris Marion Young explicates the term "oppression," as it is used "by new social movements in the United States since the 1960s" (40). Her positing of the differential treatment of some groups as a key aspect of injustice offers a valuable framework that can be applied to the operations of normate sex. "In its new usage," Young writes, "oppression designates the disadvantage and injustice some people suffer not because a tyrannical power coerces them, but because of the everyday practices of a well-intentioned liberal society. . . . Oppression in this sense is structural, rather than the result of a few people's choices or policies" (41). These must be disadvantages that occur differentially to members of one social group in comparison with others. Though no tyrant is necessary for such harms to accrue, "for every oppressed group there is a group that is *privileged* in relation to that group" (42). In addition, Young asserts: "No single form of oppression can be assigned causal or moral primacy. . . . [G]roup differences cut across individual lives in a multiplicity of ways that can entail privilege and oppression for the same person in different aspects" (42) — a middle-class, white gay man, for example, might experience privilege on the basis of race and class, alongside oppression on the basis of sexual orientation.

Normate sex should be understood as a powerful force contributing to social group oppression. Major social institutions — the state, medicine, popular culture, education, religion — disseminate and enforce its norms. Applying Young's framework to the context of normate sex helps to illustrate a significant aspect of social group oppression, in and through notions of appropriate expressions of sexuality. Sexual norms capture in a particularly gripping way a vast array of rules for social relations; that is, rules for relationships and interactions between and within social groups. Bodies themselves become larger than life in schemas of normate sex, representing broader states and identities, from communities to the nation. The terms of this discourse include sexual practices, identities, desires, and spaces, as well as bodily configurations, singly and in combination.

Young draws on traditional Marxist theory, while critiquing and extending it through the insights of feminism and other recent social movements, in order to propose specific "criteria for determining whether individuals and groups are oppressed" (64). Young argues that "the presence of any of these five conditions is sufficient for calling a group oppressed. But different group oppressions exhibit different combinations of these forms, as do different individuals in the groups" (64). These five "faces" of oppression — exploitation, marginalization, powerlessness, cultural imperialism, and violence — capture its systemic character and can be used to facilitate a closer look at how normate sex operates.

Exploitation occurs when "the labor and energy expenditure of one group benefits another, and reproduces a relation of domination between them" (Young 50). The concept of *sexual* exploitation, the heteropatriarchal sexual use of women and girls, is one of the founding insights of feminism, one which women of color famously contested and complicated (Young 50–51). We might also think about exploitation in terms of economies of sexual gratitude, in which sexual partners of lesser status, or those whose bodies are further from cultural norms of health, fitness, or attractiveness, are expected or assumed to feel grateful to partners of higher status or to those considered attractive or fit by conventional standards.

Being used in these ways is oppressive, yet *not* being used is also a problem. "Marginals," writes Young, "are people the system of labor cannot or will not use" (53). In the sexual economy, marginals are people the system of normate sex cannot or will not use. Young sees *marginalization* as "perhaps the most dangerous form of oppression. A whole category of people is expelled from useful participation in social life and thus potentially subjected to severe material deprivation and even extermination" (53). Sexual marginalization occurs when a group's sexuality is denied, as when disabled people are treated as asexual.[16]

Young's specific formulation of "power" involves authority, participation in decision making affecting the conditions of one's life, and the opportunity to develop and exercise skills, which in the world of work is exemplified by the status of professional work in contrast with nonprofessional labor. Because it affords ongoing opportunities for self-development, professional work has an "expansive, progressive character," as well as relative autonomy, both of which contribute to social authority and enhanced sense of self (51). These privileges "extend beyond the workplace to a whole way of life," which Young calls "respectability" (57). *Powerlessness*, then, specifically involves a lack of opportunity to make meaningful decisions over the conditions of one's life and to develop and exercise skills; it results in a deficit of respect, as when "in daily interchange women and men of color must prove their respectability" (58). Sexual powerlessness includes, but is not limited to, the lack of access to information needed to make decisions about sexuality, without which meaningful consent is impossible and which specific groups may experience differentially.

"To experience *cultural imperialism*," writes Young, "means to experience how the dominant meanings of a society render the particular perspective of one's own group invisible at the same time as they stereotype one's group and mark it out as the Other" (58–59). Cultural imperialism is expressed in the cultural products of those groups who "have exclusive or primary access to what Nancy Fraser . . . calls the means of interpretation and communication in a society" (59). Young notes a "paradoxical" effect of cultural imperialism, which generates stereotypes

Abby L. Wilkerson

of groups ("a nature which is often attached in some way to their bodies, and which thus cannot easily be denied") while at the same time rendering them invisible (59). Young points out that members of oppressed groups experience *violence* differentially; that is, they become targets as members of particular groups, often because they are perceived as presenting a "challenge to hegemonic cultural meanings" (63).

Together, Young's "five faces" help to crystallize a picture of sexually based harms as a critical aspect of the social oppression of intersexualized and transgendered people and transsexuals. The five faces sometimes overlap with and reinforce one another; it is important to note, however, that these forces are never totalizing.

Exploitation: the exoticizing of intersexualized, transgendered, and transsexual bodies results is tied to objectification by people "known contemptuously in intersex activist circles as 'wannafucks'" (Dreger and Herndon 209). In "Reading Across the Grain," Eli Clare works through the complexities of sexual objectification, which "exoticizes culture, sexualizes bodies, and distorts real lived sexuality" (*Exile* 109), hence its opposition by feminists. For disabled people, however, through its absence, "the absence of sexual gaze of any kind directed at us—wanted or unwanted—we lose ourselves as sexual beings" (*Exile* 113).

Marginalization: in heteropatriarchal terms, conventional gender identities, genital configurations, and underlying physiological structures must map onto one another conventionally to produce sexual beings. Recall the unattractively androgynous *Saturday Night Live* character Pat (played by Julia Sweeney), whose sex is not known to viewers or, in most sketches, to other characters.

Powerlessness: as the testimonies discussed earlier make clear, powerlessness is a definitive experience of intersexualization, since intersexuals have often been denied not simply participation in decisions about gender assignment or surgeries and other painful interventions with potentially serious consequences, but even information about decisions already made long before by parents and medical professionals. Transsexuals and transgendered people have experienced coercive gender identity disorder diagnoses and psychiatric treatment. And those seeking surgical and other interventions must operate within the narrow constraints of medical protocol, acceding to medical notions of gender and corresponding bodily configurations, which may not accord with their own senses of their bodies and identities. Powerlessness overlaps with *cultural imperialism*, as medical discourse enforces broader heteropatriarchal culture's norms of gender and sex, rendering those who deviate from them "other."

Violence: intersex testimonies powerfully attest to the violence of standard medical protocols, whatever the intentions of their promoters may have been, and that are not yet a relic of the past, despite recent shifts to more humane practices. Consider the practice of vaginal dilation of children, a highly painful and invasive practice that, outside of a medical context, would be seen as sexual abuse. For trans people, violence occurs in medical contexts when limited options result in bodily changes undesired by trans people, who already face a broader social climate of violence.[17]

Together, these faces of the sexual aspects of these groups' oppression reflect the systemic character of that oppression. They also indicate the ways in which being associated with a particular sexual nature (which in some cases involves a lack of sexuality) can play a significant role in being regarded as lesser than others. The question that remains is how sexual agency is possible in such contexts.

"IN THE PLEASURE GARDEN": INTERSEX EROTICS

The preceding survey of trans and intersex medicalization illustrates sexuality, specifically nonnormate sexuality, as a ground of oppression, but it is of course a site of resistance as well. Many intersexuals, transsexuals, and transgendered people experience eroticisms in distinct contrast to medicalized notions of sex—a key element of normate sex—and the creation of these erotic possibilities constitutes an important form of resistance. The very idea of intersex eroticism can be vexed, given that activists contend that medicalization has deprived many intersexed people of these potential pleasures. Some activists who had surgical interventions as adolescents speak nostalgically of the remembered and longed-for satisfactions of their unaltered bodies. In the documentary *Hermaphrodites Speak!*, Angela Moreno recalls that at age twelve, "My clitoris started to grow. . . . I experienced it as normal. . . . I not only noticed its size growing more prominent but I loved it. I had this wonderful relationship with it. I think that time that I had, maybe six months before surgery from the time that I had noticed it and started to love it to the time it was taken from me, was this time in the pleasure garden before the fall."

For others, intersex eroticism is immediate and ongoing. When Hale Hawlbecker was born, doctors told his parents that because of his small penis surgery must be performed and he must be raised as a girl. His parents refused. Now, writes Hawlbecker, "[my penis] brings me and my partner a great deal of pleasure. It grows erect, it penetrates her vagina, it ejaculates. I don't know what else I need it to do. I am just so lucky that I was able to keep it" (112). Because tests indicated that he was genetically male, his parents saw no need for intervention; a genetic essentialism thus undercut the prevailing surgical essentialism, to the ultimate benefit of Hawlbecker (and his partner) (111). Even though the sexual practices that Hawlbecker describes do not overtly vary from conventional heteronormativity, his affirmation of his own sexuality despite the size of his penis clearly indicates a resistant pleasure in refusing pathologization.

An intersexual named Kim writes of penetrating her lover with her own clitoris, a pleasure she acknowledges is possible to her only because her body has not been surgically altered, as many other intersexuals' have been. She says, "I like the fact that we are each individuals, which necessitates a wide variety of body shapes, sizes, and colors. I certainly don't feel the medical establishment has the right to determine which of our bodies are socially acceptable" (100).

Though sex-positive visions of intersex eroticism post-surgery remain extremely limited, the existing literature nonetheless indicates much about how sexual agency and pleasure can be fostered. In Sharon Preves's life history interviews with thirty-seven North Americans "whose bodies have been characterized by others as intersexed" (5), "breaking free from shame and inhibitions was often associated with learning about and acknowledging one's intersexuality" (136), whether one had experienced surgical alteration or not. Preves's participant "Claire" (survivor of a clitorectomy at age six) reports that after struggling to "accep[t] her intersexuality" as an adult, "I came to really love my sexual self. The way I felt, and the way I smelled, and the way I responded, and the way I tasted. I came to love my body that way without any judgment about how it looked in a societal way or how it performed or what it could and couldn't do" (qtd. in Preves 136). "Sherri," who had had an orchiectomy as an infant, valued her support group's help negotiating sexuality in the context of a short vagina: "I'm probably the only person in the world who, moments after [sex], would be on the phone with about thirty different women talking about it, from all over the world" (qtd. in Preves 130).

Several interrelated factors emerge from the literature as crucial for fostering sexual agency: support for positive identities (which may or may not involve embracing the term "intersex");[18] coming to terms with one's body; access to information about sexual communication and practices, delivered supportively, by others in the same boat; strategies for communicating and negotiating with actual or potential sexual partners; openness to a range of sexual practices; and expectations that partners also could be open. Intersexuals' public reflections on sexuality encompass a range of pleasures and identities, rather than evaluating the eroticism of bodily configurations and practices on the basis of their proximity to a predetermined norm. Moreover, when activists publicly claim this nonnormative eroticism, the movement challenges the medical privatization of intersex sexualities and intersex identity itself.

BOTH FLESH AND DREAM: TRANS EROTICS

The transgender movement presents a similar challenge. Contributors to *GenderQueer: Voices From Beyond the Sexual Binary* exemplify a transgendered erotics that locates pleasure in departing from gender norms. For some, this is based on a singular trajectory away from anatomical sex. "High femme" Sonya Bolus writes to her transitioning FTM lover, "I notice that much of my desire is linked to the disparity between your gender expression and your body. When you bind your breasts, pack a dick, when you wear a suit and tie, T-shirt and boxers, when you shift before my eyes from woman into man, I am aroused, excited beyond belief" (117). Bolus locates pleasure not just in her partner's masculinity but in its marked contradictions, its mutability.

Other *GenderQueer* contributors, however, eroticize their own or their partners' gender multiplicity itself. Femme Joan Nestle says to her "woman poppa," "I do long to suck you, to take your courage into my mouth, both cunt, your flesh, and cock, your dream, deep into my mouth, and I do" (177). As "a young dyke without a name yet" (223), Toni Amato overhears strangers at a restroom asking about her, "Do you think it's a boy or a girl?" (224). She takes on this indeterminacy and claims it erotically: "It's a girl, Mrs. Robinson, a girl . . . full of awe and wonder and amazement and desire thicker than the air. . . . Or it could be a boy, if that's what you want . . . a 17-year-old boy, at the mercy of hormones, full of romance and quivering lust, full of flowers and chocolates and bad poetry for the giving. It's a girl. Or a boy, if you want it. However you want it" (224).

Peggy Munson and her lover try out names for the lover's "former cock": "girlcock," "*galleros*, or cockfighter," "Jackie O" (144–45). Munson writes, "Sometimes I make her quiet, real quiet, just ozone and anticipation and *wanting*. I like it when she's my tornado girl like that, deep in the profound vortex of her own formative cunt" (145). At other times, though, "Sex with her can . . . be a *peleas de gallos*, a cockfight, pure raging animal testosterone from either one of us. . . . She confuses everything I am, shakes the change out of my pockets and makes me want to barter with foreign currency" (145). For these writers, it is the in-determinacy, the shifting range of masculinities and femininities, that provides the erotic charge.

Amato writes of her lover's response to her own claimed identity, rather than to her anatomy: "She doesn't know, my lover, what she has saved me from by her seeing and wanting what isn't there, not really, except for sometimes, when it's really, really there" (225). Gender is relational here, in the sense of being made intelligible through the erotic responses of lovers to one another. Intelligibility also emerges through public recognition. Dawn Dougherty says that her lover "is routinely mistaken for a man"; these mistakes, she knows, endanger both of them, given the constant potential for violence against gender nonconformists (222). Nonetheless, says Dougherty, "I love to be out with her. She makes me visible in my own community, and it thrills me. When I walk down the street with my lover, I am guilty by association. She makes our presence known with her swagger and muscles" (222).

CONCLUSION: A CALL FOR SEXUAL-POLITICAL INTERDEPENDENCE

In mainstream discourse, the term "sex" signifies magnetism, an inherently ir-resistible natural force that pulls bodies together the way gravity pulls us toward the ground. Paradoxically, however, particular cultural associations of sex with a given social group often serve as a wedge, separating that group from others, as we all vie for the title of most worthy and respectable. Such competition un-failingly undermines solidarity; it also keeps people silent when faced with other groups' struggles related to sexual agency. It is extremely difficult to create coali-tions around these issues of sexual oppression. Oppressed people usually have been handed more than enough shame and disgrace already to feel prepared to take on someone else's scandalous sexual predicament. Yet without facing these mainstream discourses of shaming head on, we are at an impasse when it comes to resisting the power of normate sex. Moreover, as we have seen, when we take these histories into international contexts, it is difficult not to posit our own cul-turally specific narratives—whether radical, neoliberal, or conservative—as the yardstick of others' progress or well-being, and doing so can undermine the very agency we presumably seek to foster.

The medical and social erotophobia manifested in the medicalization of inter-sexuality clearly demonstrates the centrality of sex, gender, and sexuality con-cerns to the disability movement, and thus its stake in challenging not only compulsory able-bodiedness but also compulsory heterosexuality and the sex/gender binary that supports them both. Disability studies has illuminated the importance of interdependence, both as a description of situated human life and as a social value to be promoted. If we are serious about valuing interdependence, I believe that we must push the meaning of this term further than we have thus far; in recognizing the inextricability of intersex, transgender, and disabled people's oppression, we must also envision a *sexual-political* interdependence: a politics, that is, that emphasizes our interdependence as allies and that values the potential of the sexual to enable this interdependence to flourish.

The genesis of the intersex movement illustrates the promises of sexual-political interdependence. Many intersex people who also identify as queer describe a need to also "come out" as intersexual. Chase writes: "The word 'hermaphrodite' was horribly wounding; it drove me to the brink of suicide. I thought back to my earlier process of coming out as lesbian. The way out of this pain was to reclaim the stigmatized label, to manufacture a positive acceptance of it. This second coming out was far more painful and difficult" ("Affronting" 206). In her earlier coming out, Chase recalls, her search for signs of lesbian existence paid off, and she was able to find and participate in lesbian community. However, Chase writes: "No such help was available to reclaim my intersexuality. The only images I found were absolutely pathologized case histories in medical texts and journals, close-ups of genitals being poked, prodded, measured, sliced, and sutured, full body shots with the eyes blacked out"—signaling the object of a gaze meant to travel only in one direction, in ways that are all too familiar in disability contexts (206).

Though it is now—controversially—defunct, Chase founded the Intersex Society of North America (ISNA).[19] She drew on her experience of lesbian community as a model for the kind of activism that eventually opened a space for public conversations on intersexuality, eroticizing practices, desires, and identities that had been stigmatized, thus deepening a sense of solidarity, which in turn enabled political organizing and resistance. Alliances between intersex and queer communities might be said to restore the "magnetism" attributed to sex in dominant cultural discourses and to apply this magnetism to a "perverse" end. Rather than drawing together two normatively beautiful, heterosexual, nondisabled, white, middle-class bodies to perform a specific set of predictable acts that qualify as "sex," the sexual magnetism that enables and arises from coalition building shatters the presumed supremacy of normate sex. It brings, for example, the thrill of

Abby L. Wilkerson

sexual pleasure to the guilt "by association" in which Dougherty revels when she walks down the street with her lover (222).

And coalitions are often key conditions for political change. The queer history of ISNA played a central role in bringing reform to intersex medicalization, however tentative and fledgling that reform may be. The collective action of groups like Hermaphrodites with Attitude led to modes of organizing with allies in academic and medical circles, who together are beginning to reach the medical profession. Chase's work indicates that queer and intersexual movements may be distinct but are not separate, while Naomi Finkelstein and Clare indicate the same for the transgender and disability movements. None of this is to deny the difficulties of coalition building. But disability studies and activism have demonstrated the folly of relying on atomistic visions of self-determination, which are based on autonomy at the expense of interconnection. Perhaps it is time to succumb to the perverse pleasures and challenges of sexual interdependence.

NOTES

I am indebted to Robert McRuer and Anna Mollow for providing invaluable responses to earlier drafts of this paper, as did two anonymous reviewers for Duke University Press. My writing companions Robin Meader, Pam Presser, Rachel Reidner, and Karen Sosnoski responded in extremely useful ways at various stages in this project. My partner Pat McGann and dear friends Lisa Heldke and Peg O'Connor provided ongoing discussions of issues related to the paper. Audience comments at the Radical Philosophy Association, Feminism(s) and Rhetoric(s), Society for Disability Studies, and the George Washington University Department of English benefited me as well.

1. "Transgender" typically refers to living or identifying outside of conventional gender norms, with or without medical treatment. "Intersexuality" refers to an assortment of conditions resulting in genitalia of atypical appearance or structure, in ways that tend to confound standard binary means of assigning sex to bodies.

2. See, for example, Weiss, *Body Images* and *Refiguring*; and Campbell, Meynell, and Sherwin.

3. For examples of disability studies' ongoing work on gender and sexuality, see Clare, *Exile*; Finkelstein; Garland-Thomson, *Extraordinary* and "Integrating"; Hall; McRuer and Wilkerson; and Smith and Hutchison.

4. For a discussion of these issues in relation to intersex activism, see Colligan.

5. See, for example, Koyama and Weasel.

6. While Rubin's notion of sexual hierarchy is valuable for the reasons I suggest, it is at the same time problematic insofar as she posits sexual hierarchy as operating apart

from other social hierarchies, a critique I develop in "Disability, Sex Radicalism, and Agency."

7. On Hermaphrodites with Attitudes, see Chase, "Hermaphrodites"; on "men with breasts," see Wilchins 31. In *Terrorist Assemblages*, Jasbir K. Puar considers the ways in which the sexuality and embodiment of Middle Eastern men is discursively produced as perverse and excessive. In the feature film *About Schmidt*, a naked character played by Kathy Bates invites Schmidt, played by Jack Nicholson, into a hot tub with her; the scene spawned jokes by critics and viewers alike, jokes that seemed premised on the offensive assumption that a fat woman could not be sexually attractive or inviting. The former Kansas senator and Republican presidential candidate Bob Dole's turn as a Viagra representative was likewise the subject of jokes for months after the commercial featuring him appeared; the jokes reflected widespread discomfort with sexuality among old people. The producer and screenwriter James Schamus made clear some of the compulsions facing the young and slender in our current moment when, reflecting on the making of *Taking Woodstock*, he told reporters at the Cannes Film Festival in 2009: "The biggest challenge was to get extras who were skinny but who were not working out all the time. And who still had pubic hair" (Hornaday).

8. For more of my own work considering these issues, see *Diagnosis: Difference* and "Refusing Diagnosis."

9. See, for example, Oliver.

10. In "'Ambiguous Sex'—or Ambivalent Medicine?" Alice Domurat Dreger provides an overview of the forms intersexuality takes. See Chase, "Affronting" and "Hermaphrodites," and Dreger, *Intersex* for intersexual medical narratives as well as activist responses and ethical and political analyses of intersex medicalization.

11. For a useful account of these debates, see R. Davidson; Feder; Dreger and Herndon; and Holmes, *Critical Intersex*. On one side of this debate are Intersex Society of North American (ISNA), renamed as the Accord Alliance; on another are Organisation Intersex International (OII) and the Androgen Insensitivity Syndrome Support Group UK (AISSG). See Intersex Society of North America (ISNA), "What's the History?"

12. Many of these stories are recounted in Dreger's *Intersex in the Age of Ethics*. On these harms and others recounted in this paragraph, see as well ISNA's "What's the History behind the Intersex Rights Movement?"

13. A female-to-male (FTM) transman in the documentary *Southern Comfort* lifts his shirt, revealing scars from his chest surgery so prominent as to suggest that the surgeon, known among breast cancer patients for excellent mastectomy techniques, deliberately induced the scars out of an antipathy toward this patient or transgendered patients in general.

14. Roen also identifies ethnocentrism in the Western transgender movement itself, suggesting that transgender as an identity category uninflected by race and culture is alienating and inaccurate for many people of color.

15. See, for example, Besnier; Worth.

16. See my "Disability, Sex Radicalism, and Agency" for further development of this and other examples of sexual harms differentially imposed on particular groups.

17. For an important consideration of these issues, see Wyss.

18. See Holmes, *Intersex* 109.

19. Chase was instrumental both in creating a queer and intersex alliance through founding ISNA, and later in ISNA's dissolution and reconstitution as the Accord Alliance, which advocates for the concept of "disorders of sexual development" rather than that of intersexuality. See note 11 above on debates regarding these competing frameworks.

10

CHRIS BELL

I'M NOT THE MAN I USED TO BE

Sex, HIV, and Cultural "Responsibility"

The cost of safety is to deny bodily pleasure.
—Patricia Hill Collins, *Black Sexual Politics*

Eros is a force that culture has always tried to control. For the idea of "social order" itself to exist, desire must be controlled. —Urvashi Vaid, *Virtual Equality*

In September 2003 an arrest warrant was issued for Gary Cox, deputy chief operating officer for the City of Atlanta. He was charged with, and subsequently indicted for, pandering, soliciting of sodomy, and sexual battery. The latter charge was a misdemeanor; however, the initial two were felony charges because Cox's accuser was a minor. This individual, sixteen-year-old Greg Martin, claimed that in August of that year he had arrived at the Greyhound bus station in Atlanta. His connecting bus to Michigan had been delayed, forcing him to remain at the station for several hours. Having no money for food, Martin approached Cox, who was awaiting the arrival of his nephew. Cox said that he had no money on his person but offered to take Martin to his home to acquire some. Testifying during the trial, Martin stated that while he was at Cox's home, Cox offered him $100 if Cox could perform oral sex on him. Martin rejected the offer. Cox made a counter-offer of $50 for Martin to disrobe. Martin refused and demanded that Cox return him to the Greyhound station. Having arrived back at the station, Cox touched Martin's genital area and instructed him not to tell anyone. He gave Martin $25.

The jury deliberated for one hour prior to finding Cox guilty of all charges. The judge sentenced him to seven years in prison, stipulating that he serve two years in house and be placed on probation for the remaining five. On the day the verdict was read, Mayor Shirley Franklin fired Cox, who had been on unpaid leave since his arrest.

The action was entirely unplanned.

I was in Cancun attending a conference. I had had way too much to drink at the conference's opening reception and was now stumbling back to my hotel. The walk was not too daunting; all I had to do was follow one appreciably well-lit boulevard while trying not to let the signs warning of possible alligators register too much in my consciousness.

Midway through the trek, I noticed a slightly concealed path leading from the main road to a pier overlooking the lagoon. Never one to pass up a sightseeing opportunity, I left the road and walked down the dirt path to the pier, carefully brushing aside the tree branches obscuring the trail. When I made it to the pier, I realized I was not alone. A figure had cast a line off the pier and was awaiting a bite. He turned in my direction, frowned at the intrusion, and turned away. I positioned myself away from him on the other side of the pier and gazed at downtown Cancun off in the distance. I did not think about the contrast between the relatively squat buildings in front of me and the sleek high-rise resorts behind me. I did not think about the paper I was presenting the next morning. Instead, I thought about how much scotch, gin, and tequila I had imbibed in a very short period of time and how good it felt to be alive. I could be, do, and have anything I wanted, and in that moment, I wanted him.

I abruptly turned away from the lights of downtown Cancun and approached him.

"¿Perdóneme; habla inglés?" I inquired, as if I would know what to say next if he replied in the affirmative.

"No," came the response with nary a glance in my direction.

I saw my right hand stealthily reach for this individual's package. Lucidity intervened as I forced myself to realize that my hand was not acting on its own; I was causing this to happen. I made contact.

"No." He pushed my hand away.

I sighed in frustration at this obstruction and, as if schooled in the act, reached into my pocket to extract a bill. I held it so that he could see the denomination and pushed it into the hand not holding the fishing rod. I made contact. Two hundred pesos, or twenty U.S. dollars, allowed me to. Shortly thereafter, I dropped to my knees. The money continued working in my favor for one, two, however many minutes, until he stiffened and pushed me away. I looked up—this was the first time I saw his face—and saw him gazing anxiously toward the main road. A man and a woman were staring at us through the branches. Neither my friend nor I moved. Eventually, the man said something to the woman that made her laugh. I watched them briefly as they turned away and traveled in the direction of, I can only hope, the alligators.

Having assessed the situation, he moved to the other side of the pier which was not visible from the road. He lowered his shorts past his knees and stood with his back to the lagoon, facing the Hotel Zone. He still held the fishing rod in one hand. He beckoned me over.

It did not take long to finish. His demeanor did not change even when he came. For the second time, I looked up into his face as I swallowed. I saw neither contentment, nor surprise, nor satisfaction. I discerned tolerance. That is all.

Afterward, I felt awkward, not knowing what to do or how to act. Recalling my mother's insistence on always extending common courtesy, I uttered "Muchas gracias" as I careened back toward the main road. Upon my arrival at my hotel, the bellhop smiled and touched his hat.

"I hope you had a nice evening, Señor."

I managed a weak smile as I walked past, trying to figure out how he could so cavalierly ignore the scarlet letter "P" emblazoned on my shirt.

I had barely made it to the elevator when what I had done dawned on me. As I was whisked to my floor, I replayed the events in my head. When the doors opened, I walked to my room with them still on my mind. I spent the next hour focusing on my fifteen-minute escapade: I wondered why I had allowed it to happen. I wondered about the two witnesses. I worried about Mexican penal law. Sitting alone in a hotel room in Cancun that I could barely afford, I realized I had done something that had brought me pleasure despite its illegality. It made me feel good, and it brought harm to no one, I thought. So why should it not happen again? And why could I not orchestrate events so that it would happen again?

Sleep came easily.

Chris Bell

In November 2004 Gary Wayne Carriker was charged in Fayette County, Georgia, thirty miles south of the city of Atlanta, with having consensual sex with an individual between December 2003 and May 2004 while not telling this individual of his HIV-positive status. After posting bond, Carriker returned to his studies at Emory Medical School, where he was a fourth-year student. A few months later, in April 2005, Carriker was arrested in Fulton County, where Atlanta is located, and charged with two felony counts of reckless conduct. Two men asserted that Carriker had had sex with them while not apprising them of his HIV-positive status. One of the men claimed that Carriker had participated in consensual oral sex with him throughout the month of January 2005; the other indicated that Carriker had engaged in consensual oral and anal sex with him between June and September 2004.

In November 2005 Carriker entered a guilty plea to correspond with the first charge of felony reckless conduct in Fayette County. The judge sentenced him to ten years in prison, with the stipulation that he serve two. The balance of the sentence would be served on probation, and he was also mandated to undergo counseling. During the initial two years of his probationary period, Carriker was required to honor a 10 p.m. curfew as well as fulfill five hundred hours of community service with an AIDS service organization. He was expelled from Emory Medical School and ordered to reimburse scholarship funds to that school as well as to his undergraduate institution, the United States Air Force Academy. He voluntary relinquished his commission as an Air Force Officer. Later that month, Carriker entered a guilty plea in Fulton County for the two indictments for reckless conduct there. His accusers testified that they did not think Carriker should receive additional prison time, especially since he informed them of his HIV-positive status, albeit after the acts. The judge agreed, sentencing him, despite the prosecutor's insistence on a harsher penalty, to ten years—two in prison, eight on probation—just as the judge in Fayette County had, with the sentences to run concurrently. None of the individuals contracted HIV from Carriker.

It happened seamlessly, almost as if it were meant to be.

Summer was waning, although you would never know it this particular night in Chicago, where the temps were in the 70s even at 4 a.m.

I was returning home from a party at a friend's house where I had had quite a bit to drink. Since it was such a nice night, I opted to take a quick stroll up Milwaukee Avenue. This meant that after disembarking from the train, I did not exit at the turnstile adjacent to my apartment; rather, I walked to the other end of the platform and exited from there.

There were few pedestrians out at that time of morning, although the occasional taxi meandered by. I reveled in the silence of this block that in the daytime was abuzz with energy. As soon as I saw him standing under the awning of the Washington Mutual at the end of the block, I knew what was about to happen. I walked past him and heard him call after me "¿Cerveza?" I crossed the street and turned in his direction when I had reached the other side. One glance was all it took. He followed me across Milwaukee and accepted the twenty dollar bill I offered him. For a split second I contemplated the observational reach of the cameras outside of Washington Mutual, my bank, but then I cast those thoughts aside. As I walked toward my building, he wordlessly fell into step behind me.

I entered the courtyard of my apartment building, and he followed suit. I keyed into the building and held the door for him. We walked up the three flights of stairs to my apartment. As soon as we entered, I led the way to the kitchen, where I frowned and said "¿Cerveza? No más." (I felt a pang of regret in that I did not know how to say "I don't have any" in Spanish. I don't drink beer; thus, stating that there was no more, when there had never been any in my apartment, felt morally wrong.) I reached into the cupboard and extracted two glasses and a bottle of rum I'd picked up in Puerto Rico not long before. This satisfied both of us.

And then it happened. The TV cast its glow on us as we maneuvered on the couch. I marveled at the swiftness with which he put the condom on much more so than the fact that he put it on. And then it was over.

I closed the door behind him, presuming he would know how to find his way back to the courtyard, then the street, then the bank, and then wherever. I made my way back to the couch. As the sun came up, I closed my eyes and slept.

It was entirely uncomplicated.

Both the Cox and Carriker cases are fitting points of departure for an examination of not only the politics of HIV disclosure but the contexts (or social spaces) in which that disclosure does or does not occur. Although Cox was HIV positive, this fact was barely reported in the media and was not focused on during the trial proceedings. The central issue was his propositioning of a minor individual. The charges against Carriker, in contrast, pertained wholly to the nondisclosure of his seropositive status. In his analysis of the Carriker case, "Policing Positives," the journalist Kai Wright traces the history of partner notification laws in the United States:

Western efforts at disease control have been firmly rooted in paternalism and policing from their inception. The German doctor Johann Peter Frank first spelled out the state's responsibility—and authority—for maintaining a healthy citizenry in a series of groundbreaking, turn-of-the-19th century volumes, aptly titled *A System of Complete Medical Police*. It was a soup-to-nuts guide on what people needed to do to stay healthy, and how the state should encourage that behavior. Predictably, moralism was a recurring theme—one infamous section urged local officials to place time limits on dances that seemed too erotic, like the waltz.

That top-down perspective on prevention has persisted, and it informed government's initial response to HIV. . . . [W]hen, in 1990, Congress passed the Ryan White CARE Act, which is now the federal government's primary vehicle for funding AIDS services[, lawmakers] included a provision demanding that every state have a criminal code that allows it to prosecute a person's failure to disclose an HIV diagnosis to someone who may be put at risk by it.

Ultimately, for all the talk about sending messages to people who are positive, the real message of criminalization laws may be to everyone else: this troubling and complicated epidemic isn't your problem, it's that of monstrous outsiders who we can simply wall off from regular folks' lives.

The history of AIDS criminalization laws in the United States is the history of marginalization, demonization, and scapegoating. It is also a history that has precedent in other countries.[1] In essence, the history of AIDS criminalization laws is an instructive one based on the rigorous disciplining and punishment of ostensibly deviant bodies.

On an April evening following the uncomplicated September night, I found myself walking down Listopada Street in Bielsko-Biala, a city in southwestern Poland. I had moved to Bielsko that January to teach cultural studies classes at the university and to undertake disability-related research at Auschwitz and Birkenau.

I had been drinking this evening at my favorite restaurant, Mimoza. Having polished off a trout, a side of leafy-green szpinak, and the better part of a bottle of red wine, I knew what I needed.

As I walked down Listopada, my thoughts turned to a conversation I had had in Warsaw with a friend a few weeks prior:

"I've taken to prowling the streets looking for men to pay to have sex with me."

"You what?!"

"You heard me."

"But why?"

"Why not?"

"Because it's prostitution, and you can go to jail for it."

"Actually, I think the legal term is 'pandering.' But in any event, you don't have to be so negative."

"Christopher! How often do you do this?"

"Oh, every once in awhile. The first time was in Mexico, and it happened again when I was living in Chicago, and I tried to make it happen last night here in Warsaw over by the train station but the guy freaked out and ran away. It was really dramatic, too. I mean, he was the one who came up and asked me for money. But then he got all weird when I told him I'd give him some if he let me suck him off. I don't understand some people."

"This happened last night?! Here? I left you at a bar. Why couldn't you just pick someone up there? Or go to the sex club? You certainly know where it is."

"True. But it's not the same. And don't get me wrong; I still have standards. Like last night while walking through the train station, a guy approached me and asked for money. I could have taken him back with me to the hotel, but he looked drugged out. So I declined. Surely there must be something said for that."

"Yeah, but I don't know what. In any event, I think you should stop it. What happens if you get beaten up?"

"But I haven't."

"But you could."

"But I haven't."

"You should stop."

"I know I should stop. But I can't. It feels nice to be in control."

That night on Listopada, I went home alone.

The next afternoon, I was walking down the same street, having spent the better part of the morning sipping tea and reading Trollope, when I felt a tug on my arm. I glanced over to see a dark-skinned individual looking at me inquisitively. All around us, the locals tried to disguise their amazement at the sight of two nonwhite people on a street in southwestern Poland. "What's going on in our world?" they most likely thought to themselves. "I'm going to have him," I vowed to myself.

We walked back to my flat near the City Hall. As we entered the foyer, the landlord's son did a double take. I greeted him more cheerfully than usual and entered my flat uninhibitedly.

Chris Bell

We shared a bottle of Zubrowka vodka and, despite the presence of three chairs, sat on my bed, talking for some time. He spoke no English but I knew enough Polish to grasp most of what he said. He was a security guard at a bank in a small town outside of Bielsko and also a bouncer in a club in that same town. Although he was shorter than me, he was heavily built and carried himself with evident ease.

"What happens if you get beaten up?"

"But I haven't."

"But you could."

He told me he was from Romania. It seemed more of a confession than an addition to the conversation. Then he explained that he was a Roma gypsy and that Polish people tend to look down on these individuals. "Not me," I said. "Not me."

I noticed that he drank faster than I did (which rarely happens), so I was quick on the refills. Our conversation was interesting, and I tried to act animated as I talked about myself and listened to him, but I had something else on my mind.

An hour after our arrival, I noticed his movements had slowed. I allowed the conversation to taper off. He closed his eyes. I quietly stood up, turned off the overhead light, and sat back down next to him. His eyes fluttered open. "Co to jest?" he asked, gesturing toward the darkened light. "It's okay" I assured him. I placed my hand on his crotch. "No" he said, displacing it. I reached into my pocket and pulled out a fifty zloty note. I extended it to him. He looked at it for what seemed like a very long time. Then he sighed, took the fifty (eighteen U.S. dollars), stood up, walked to the center of the room, took out his wallet, carefully folded the note, placed it into his wallet, and then repositioned himself next to me. The orchestrations, while impressive, did not obscure the realization that he was mine.

He moved well, doing things that I did not expect him to do or to allow me to do. Toward the end our eyes met. To my surprise, he leaned in and kissed me, passionately, lingeringly.

When it was over, he once again became his talkative self. He wanted to have a drink in the city center. I declined. "I'm tired now, and I must travel to the United States tomorrow for a quick visit. I need to rest." He seemed genuinely sorry to leave.

The experience was nice, but I could have done without the kiss, which I enjoyed a little too much.

Laws change to take into account modifications in cultural norms. The Cox case bears this out. During the course of his trial, the prosecution unsuccessfully attempted to include evidence of an earlier arrest. In 1991 Cox had been arrested at a rest stop in Gwinnett County, which is adjacent to Atlanta and includes many of the city's suburbs. He had been arrested for propositioning an undercover Georgia Department of Transportation officer. He entered a "no contest" plea to the charge and was issued a fine of five hundred dollars and a one-year suspended sentence. During the Cox and Martin trial in 2004, the judge refused to hear this evidence on the grounds that the more recent case involved soliciting a minor for pay, while the previous one involved an adult with no offer of remuneration; and in 1998 the Georgia Supreme Court invalidated the state's sodomy law, allowing the act to occur when it involved consensual, noncommercial sex between adults in private.

The kind of jurisprudential rethinking evidenced in the Georgia Supreme Court's decision in 1998 is an incentive to reevaluate the state's AIDS criminalization law, the same law that penalized Carriker. One major problem with the current law is its failure to distinguish among types of sexual practice. The Centers for Disease Control (headquartered, ironically, in Atlanta, in the same county in which Carriker was convicted) has differentiated among sex acts along the lines of risk. Performing oral sex on an individual—which Carriker did and which Cox offered to do—does not carry the same risk as anal or vaginal sex. Nonetheless, the acts are prosecuted in the same manner. This is indicative of a failure in policy. The law should be updated to reflect biomedical knowledge about risk and transmission.

The time had come to leave Poland. The train was scheduled to depart Bielsko at 3:45 a.m., arriving in Warsaw at 8 a.m. From there I would fly to Zurich for a conference. After that I would begin my new life as a PhD student in England.

I had spent the day saying goodbye to friends, cleaning up my flat, and reading Wilkie Collins. Now, at 2 a.m., all I had to do was take out the trash, give the flat one final once over, and allow time to pass.

The street was as quiet as usual; the air crisp, courtesy of a cool mountain breeze. I deposited the bag into the trash receptacle at the end of the street and turned back in the direction of the flat. I saw him watching me. He was walking across the street in the same direction I was headed in. Without hesitation, I approached him and flashed the fifty zloty note. I gestured for him to follow me, holding onto the note. We entered the foyer and proceeded into the flat. Once inside, I closed the door, tossed the keys and the note on the table, and dropped to my knees. I unzipped him and put him in my mouth. "I like women," he protested weakly. He spoke in English but I did not pause to ponder this. I kept moving, working on his balls now. "I like women," he reiterated when I indicated that he should lower his pants. "I believe you," I mumbled, appreciating how readily he complied with my unspoken demand while simultaneously placing his hand on the back of my head to guide me.

Before long, I was on the bed with him beside me. He was clothed, although his shirt was pulled up and his pants were pulled in the opposite direction. I wasn't wearing anything. I began to finish myself off. As I did so, I noticed him watching my technique. This was a turn-on: a man who "likes women" lying with me on a bed and watching me jack off. I came quickly, placing my mouth on his neck as I did. He did not protest, nor did he take his eyes off of the spectacle I was creating. I was very proud of myself.

He took his time buckling up. Then he took a spin around the flat. He seemed quite comfortable and began to strike up a conversation. I half participated, explaining that I would be leaving for Zurich shortly. I was still reveling in the impossibly simple seduction, while also thinking back to a conversation I had had earlier that summer with Darek, an individual I'd dated for a short time.

"You pick men up on the streets here in Bielsko? How? It's impossible."

"It's not as difficult as you might think. I mean, if you think about it, that's how we met."

"What are you talking about? We met because Jacek introduced us."

"And I met Jacek one afternoon when I got off the train and walked past him on my way home. I'm telling you, it's simple. People just want to be with someone, to touch someone, for a short time. I provide that with no strings attached. What's wrong with that?"

When it came time for me to leave, I walked out with my baggage. He preceded me into the hallway. I placed my baggage on the floor and locked the door. I explained that I had to go upstairs to place the key in my landlady's mail slot. Without waiting for a response, I dashed up the stairs. On my way back down, I heard the front door slam; the echo reverberated throughout the hallway and the stairwell. I wondered if he had taken the bag with my laptop in it or the one with my passport. He had claimed neither. I can only guess that he had had enough for one night and was on his way home to fail to remember. I picked up my baggage and headed into the night. It wasn't until I was an hour into The Woman in White on the train to Warsaw that I realized I still had the fifty zloty note.

In the 1980s and 1990s, social spaces in parts of the United States underwent a dramatic change from relatively liberal environments wherein pleasure could be sought and found to increasingly staid environments wherein pleasure might be sought but at the risk of not being found and incarceration. The prime example of this sanitizing of public spaces is New York City's Times Square, often referred to as the crossroads of the world. Whereas Times Square had previously toggled between a destination for families (the Broadway Theater district and the host of hotels and restaurants surrounding the district) and a destination for sexual hookups (peep shows and strip joints), by the twenty-first century, the white-washing of Times Square was complete. The crossroads of the world had erected barriers at its borders, which aimed to keep sexual perversion out.

In *Times Square Red, Times Square Blue*, Samuel Delany comments on the sociocultural shift that occurred in Times Square in the late twentieth century:

> As a sign system, what the neon visibility of sex shops and peep shows and porn theatres signaled to people passing by was: Unattached men (or men whose attachments are, however temporarily, not uppermost in their mind), this is the place for you to spend money. Such men have tra-ditionally spent freely and fast. Though some of them are gay, as we all know most are not. Remove those signs in an area where once they were prominent, and it's like reversing the signal: Now it means that men *with* attachments can spend their money here—which is often men with a great deal more money, men who want to spend it in business. (95; emphasis in original)

The Times Square of the pre-1980s allowed men of all races, ages, and sexual orientations to come together. But once it was determined that the site was not honoring its potential as *enough* of a revenue-producing force, it had to be re-invented: "the city wanted to get the current owners out of those movie houses, 'J/O Clubs' (Jack Off Clubs, advertised as just that on the marquees), and peep shows, and open up the sites for developers" (Delany 91). But where were the patrons of these venues supposed to go? In the 1980s and particularly in the pre-combination therapy 1990s, an era in which AIDS scapegoating often operated in an unabated fashion, this was not a question that warranted discussion, let alone a comprehensive response from city officials. Out of sight, out of mind, conven-tional wisdom dictated.

Arguably, for those who did patronize the now-vanished sex clubs and movie theaters in Times Square, the shuttering of those establishments did not cre-ate a catastrophe insofar as access to each other. Public parks and washrooms retained their appeal, and later the Internet would also facilitate the search for casual sexual encounters. However, the loss of the Times Square sexual free zone

Chris Bell

should not be casually dismissed. Indeed, as Delany argues, it might be viewed as an immensely effective salvo against freedom of sexual expression.

"I'm not happy here," I kept repeating to my PhD supervisor. "I need to be somewhere else in order to be productive." That "somewhere else" ended up being Poland once more. After a depressing three and a half months spent in the UK, I was returning to my adopted country to write my thesis.

But I would not leave for another week. It was the New Year and Nottingham was decked out accordingly. I walked through the Old Market Square, desperately attempting to ignore the crush of activity. "It's two o'clock in the afternoon," I thought. "Shouldn't these people be home nursing hangovers?" As I walked past McDonald's, I saw him: cute, young, and asking for assistance. He was the perfect target, but something held me back. He asked me for money, and I brushed past him without making eye contact.

I thought about him throughout the afternoon. Around 5:30, curiosity got the best of me. I realized that there was no likelihood that he'd still be there. I also realized that I had lived in this city for months and never seen him before, a fact that decreased the likelihood of his presence even more. But he was there. And I was prepared.

As I approached, he made his plea. I flipped him a two pound coin. He clasped his hands together, performed a little bow, and thanked me profusely. I walked around the block. As I came up on him again, he began to make his plea. When he recognized me, he stopped and thanked me again for the money. I recognized his sincerity as a performance, but I was taken in. I stepped up to him and, sotto voce, in the midst of the activity in Old Market Square, said, "I'll give you twenty pounds more if you'd like." His eyebrows raised and his lips parted in reply but no words came out. Finally, he nodded and said, "Yes. Thank you." We began walking homeward.

His name was Jon; I'll never forget that. He had been living on the streets since his stepfather had thrown him out of the house several months earlier. He had had a few run-ins with the law in Sheffield but was trying to do the right thing by relocating to Notts. His father was in Spain, and he hoped to go there someday to be with him. As he talked, I couldn't help but want to hear more. I found him fascinating. I wanted to protect him.

"What is this place?" he asked as we entered the rambling home I shared with eleven other individuals.

"Oh it's a place where a bunch of students live. We're all from different countries, and we study here."

"It's nice."

"C'mon," I said, beckoning to him to follow me upstairs to my room.

"No, I'd better stay here. I, ah, don't want to get blamed if something comes up, um, missing."

I did not tell him that all of my housemates were away for a few more days and that we would be alone for some time. It's not that I thought something untoward would happen if I told him, so much as that I had the confidence that nothing would happen as a result of my disclosing this. So why waste the words?

I bounded to my room and pretended to retrieve the twenty-pound note that was already in my pocket. Back downstairs, I handed it to him. Again, he thanked me with unfailing politeness, and I felt something for him again.

"Would you like something to eat?"

"That's right nice of you, but I don't want to be a bother."

"It's no bother. Come in here."

We entered the kitchen and I listened to him marvel at its size. I reminded him that twelve college students lived in the house; hence, the dual refrigerators, stoves, and ovens, and the massive space in general. I began to make him a sandwich, spreading black currant jelly on the bread. When I began to do the same with the peanut butter, he intervened, saying that he did not like peanut butter.

"Would you like more jelly then?"

"Yes, I would."

I handed him the knife and encouraged him to make his sandwich as he saw fit.

"Thanks a lot. You're cool, and you're also really photogenic. You should model."

This caused me to laugh and protest.

"You're American, aren't you?"

"Unfortunately."

"From whereabouts?"

"The last place I lived while there was Chicago, although I'm originally from St. Louis."

"Chicago. I'd like to go there someday. I'd like to go to a lot of places someday."

I never saw anyone down a sandwich that swiftly. I urged him to make another. He did and ate it just as swiftly, while talking about Michael Jordan and the Chicago Bulls. Despite the large size of the room, we stood next to each other at the counter. He emitted the stale odor of sweat and desperation. This detracted from his appeal.

"I should go now. But thank you for being so nice to me. And good luck with your studies. Maybe I'll see you around someday and I can thank you."

I didn't really want to do it, but I couldn't think of anything else to do or say that would make him stay. And so I caressed the outside of his sweatpants and explained that he could thank me in that moment if he wanted to. I regretted it instantly. His expression clouded and he seemed genuinely disappointed. I had changed in his eyes.

"I'll do it, I mean, I've done it before. But you'll have to pay me."

He was a businessman through and through.

"What about the twenty quid I gave you?"

"You said that was mine! You said I could have it!"

He was insistent and, for once, was making me uncomfortable.

"But I didn't get anything for it."

He began to pace back and forth, looking at his watch.

"Look mate, I gotta go. I gotta take this money and go get a hit. I like to shoot up."

He raised the sleeve of his jacket to display a line of deeply embedded track marks along the length of his left arm.

"I gotta go score with this dude before it's too late. It's twenty-five quid and I got it. But I can come back later."

His agitated mood had turned me off almost as much as my propositioning him. I was no longer interested, just curious.

"What do you do when you shoot up?"

"Heroin and crack."

"Oh."

He provided detailed instructions on how to mix the concoction with a spoon and what to do with it. And then:

"Do you want me to come back later?"

"No, that's okay."

"I can come back later tonight or tomorrow."

"I leave for Scotland in the morning and I won't be back for a few days. After that, I'm going to Poland for several months. Don't worry about it."

"Oh."

I could not let him leave with the memory of his arm so firmly embedded in my memory.

"Do me a favor though. Just show me your dick."

He thought about this for a few seconds and then he slowly began to untie the

white ribbon of his sweatpants. As he lowered them as well as his shorts, he gri-
maced, allowing, "It's not very big." I looked, and then he left.

I thought about Jon for some time afterwards. Occasionally, I still do. I smile
when I recall his reference to me as "photogenic." I wonder if he ever made it to
Spain. I'm awaiting a resolution that will probably never come.

In viewing the space of the city as a sexual free zone, it is not uncommon to
view it as an incubator of AIDS as well. From *Boys on the Side* to *Longtime Com-*
panion to, of course, *Philadelphia*, the city is often depicted in AIDS narratives
as "too free" a sexual free zone. The city as AIDS incubator in contraposition to
the rural town as protected terrain is a theme briefly alluded to in Delany's text.
Describing one of the city's "AIDS tragedies," he recalls this conversation: "'You
remember your little hustler friend Mark?' a redheaded hustler, Tony, in black
leather pants and black leather jacket, who specialized in heavy S&M topping,
told me one evening, elbow to elbow with me. . . . 'Two weeks before he died, we
all got together and sent him home—upstate to Binghamton. He wanted to die at
home. So we sent him there. And he did'" (48). While it may not be accurate to
describe Binghamton, New York as "rural," the space is certainly not as urban as
New York City. Accordingly, it is not enough to report that Mark was sent home.
It should also be stressed that he was sent out of the city. The return of Times
Square and other urban locales in the United States to spaces not of sexual pleasure, but of "family values," is, in a sense, a return to the model of the colonial
and settler family, whose members kept each others' best interests in mind and
shunned outside interference. Rural areas, although they can be depicted as wild,
unexplored terrain, are most often envisioned as wholesome spaces of peace and
tranquility. Rural life is assumed to be safe life. Judith Halberstam notes, "Delany
suggests that we break away from the cozy fantasies of small-town safety and big-
city danger, and reconsider the actual risks of different locations in terms of the
different populations that inhabit them. Specifically, he recommends that we not
design urban areas to suit suburban visitors" (*Queer Time* 15).

Within spaces where public sex is accessed—bathhouses, movie theaters, sex
clubs—the disclosure of an HIV-positive status does not always occur. This is not
surprising given the emphasis on anonymity in these venues. As Stephen Murray
observes: "Even in metropolises with venues for male-male sex, many men who
have sex with men seek to keep their desires from being known (i.e., as part of
their public persona) and do not reveal their names to sexual partners. Anony-

Chris Bell

mous sex can be seen as more private than sex in bedrooms shared by people in ongoing relationships in that most everything about the self remains unknown to sexual partners in anonymous encounters" (161). To reiterate, people do not always disclose their status in sexual free zones (or elsewhere for that matter). But that does not mean they are lacking in moral fiber. It implies that those acting in sexual free zones realize that they are occupying a space in which the rules (read "family values") of the outside are not in effect. Within the sexual free zone, a different (but not necessarily inferior) code of conduct is practiced.

I'm in St. Louis, having come from the doctor's office. I had spent six additional months in Poland. One day, during the sixth month, I noticed lesions on my left leg. I had been waiting for this moment for nearly eight years; the moment when AIDS began to make its presence unmistakably known. I thought about contacting Darek, the doctor I'd dated the year before, but I opted not to. I decided the best thing would be to return to the States, where it all began.

Having no health coverage, I was forced to rely on the services of the Ryan White CARE program. Prior to accessing those services, I was required to have an intake with a case manager.

Our meeting was fairly mundane, involving lots of paperwork and signatures. One of the forms I was obligated to sign prior to receiving services pertained to Missouri law RSMO 191.677, which reads, in part:

> *It is your responsibility to alter your behavior so that you do not expose other people to the HIV virus. Criminal charges could be filed against you if you know you carry the HIV virus and you create a risk of infecting another person (for example: your partner) with the virus through sex, needle sharing, biting or other established means of transmitting the virus.*
>
> *Violation is considered a Class B Felony, punishable by five to fifteen years in prison or if the other person contracts HIV, a Class A Felony, punishable by ten to thirty years or life imprisonment. The use of condoms is not a defense to this violation.*

At the conclusion of our meeting, I received a copy of all of the paperwork. I took it and used it to attain a doctor's appointment. The lesions were biopsied and were revealed to be nonharmful. Shortly thereafter, I successfully interviewed for a teaching position in Baltimore, which would have me leaving the state of Missouri, and its laws, behind.

Prior to leaving for Maryland, I discarded all of the case management parapher-
nalia except for my copy of RSMO 191.677. It came with me to Baltimore, where I
still have it tucked away.

Restricting access to sexual freedom in Times Square, Delany asserts, rendered the space "safe" in fraught ways: "Desire and knowledge (body and mind)
are not a fundamental opposition; rather, they are intricately imbricated and
mutually constitutive aspects of political and social life. . . . [W]e might give more
thought to the necessary and productive aspect of this imbrication of knowledge
and desire as it expresses itself so positively in so many forms of contact, before—with a wrecking ball and even more sweeping legislation—we render that
central structure asexual and 'safe' in the name of family values and corporate
giantism" (168–69).

The politics of containment are alive and well as evidenced in: the Cox and
Carriker cases, the questionable laws in Atlanta (which is often referred to as "the
New York of the South") specifically and Georgia overarchingly, and the (mis)
management of urban spaces such as New York. It is not enough to cleanse mainstream culture of individuals such as Cox and Carriker; it is not enough to reinvent sexual free zones as sanitized playgrounds for the mainstream masses. As
John D'Emilio has argued regarding the gay liberation movement: "The acceptance of our erotic choices ultimately depends on the degree to which society is
willing to affirm sexual expression as a form of play, positive and life-enhancing.
Our movement may have begun as the struggle of a 'minority,' but what we
should now be trying to 'liberate' is an aspect of the personal lives of all people—
sexual expression" ("Capitalism" 474).

These individuals and those zones offer opportunities to interrogate the codes
that sustain us to our delight and constrict us to our disadvantage.

I have lived in Baltimore for nearly two years. Picking up men on the street here is
amazingly easy. I remember:
The first one, the one who passed me on the street one Friday night and asked for
help. I replied that I'd give him twenty dollars. We walked to my apartment, which
was just steps away. While I relieved myself of the alcohol I had just imbibed, he sat
in my living room. When I finally returned, I gave him the twenty and made my
request. He agreed and even gave me instructions on paying particular attention
to the head because that made him feel good. He also apologized for not being as
fresh as he could be due to sweating while sitting in jail most of the day. We wound

up in my bed for a few brief moments, but he grew uncomfortable because he kept thinking about getting home to his young son.

Another one, whom I passed in an alleyway. He offered to sell me a watch. When I asked the price and he replied seven dollars, I made him an offer of twenty if he'd do my bidding. He agreed immediately. As we walked back to my place, he kept asking if I was a cop, because this was "just too good to be true." I was chagrined when he couldn't perform. He was too, and he chided me mildly for not having any porn for him to view, because "that's how you're supposed to do it." He left without the twenty and in somewhat depressed spirits since, as he termed it, he "could have used a good nut."

The one on Thanksgiving who whistled after me while I walked down an alleyway. I stopped and said "What up?" to which he ineffectually replied "You." I began to walk away when he called after me. "I've got ten inches." "Show me," I countered. And there, against the wall in the alleyway, he started stripping, first removing his shirt. When I saw the muscles, I stereotypically began to think of prison gyms, but I quickly pushed that thought from my mind. Before he had a chance to unzip his jeans, I said, "You're coming with me." He was very friendly on the short walk home, apprising me that he'd come up from Virginia with a girlfriend who had left him and how he too hated Baltimore and wanted to go elsewhere. At my place, he spent time in the bathroom soaping himself up and then came into the bedroom and sug gested I do the same. "I tend to stay clean," I replied. After a sufficient period of time with him in my mouth, I was ready to move on, but, as he claimed in suggesting I continue, "We've got all night." "Actually we don't, so let's fuck and get on with it." This put pressure on him and he remained soft. He grew angry, and I asked him to leave. He became belligerent and loud when I declined to pay him. I finally got him outside where he stood in front of my apartment for several minutes banging on the window, declaring, "I know where you live." "Obviously," I said to myself. I'm sure my neighbors loved this.

The hairy one who wanted to screw with the lights on so he could see me. He tried very hard, and even broke a dripping sweat. But try as he might, he could not insert part A into part B. "The tightest ass I've ever seen," he repeated over and over. He too got nothing.

The failed one whom I approached outside of the Central Library on one exceptionally hot afternoon and offered twenty dollars to perform. "How 'bout I give you an ass whipping for free?" I threw up my hands in resignation and walked away to the sound of "I hate fuckin' faggots" over my shoulder.

The eager one who seemed so happy to have me pick him up and made no secret *of being impressed by the luxury apartment I struggle to live in. As we entered the building, I was thankful the doorman was elsewhere, although I felt tense sharing the elevator with my visitor and another tenant. The act itself was swift and to the point. Afterwards, he asked for forty dollars. I offered thirty and a Pellegrino, which he accepted. As he left, he commented, "You're a good guy."*

I've resigned myself to the fact that this is the way my life is. Perhaps these dalliances will decrease in frequency; perhaps they will increase. I doubt they'll ever stop. The action is a part of me now. I'm making myself happy by making other people happy. It's what I do because I'm a good guy.

The aims to legislate codes of conduct of HIV-positive individuals under an ideology of "responsibility" may have been effective when modes of transmission were still unknown, but that time has long since passed. This is the HIV age of reason when HIV transmission laws should be categorized by measurable level of risk and, even then, reconciled on a case-by-case basis. Denying the HIV-positive subject access to a variety of sexual experiences through the threat of litigation and incarceration is supremely ill-advised because doing so, initially, does not work and, more importantly, forecloses possibilities of pleasure. In the final analysis, it is important to be mindful of the health status of *both* the HIV-negative and the HIV-positive partners as, drawing on an early safer sex slogan, protection is the priority. In the case of negative individuals protection pertains to not contracting HIV, while in the case of positive individuals protection pertains to preventing reinfection. But this is not all. It is also important to consider the oft-maligned and rarely discussed wishes of HIV-positive individuals because the protection of sexual desire must be a priority too.

An additional conclusion is warranted.

I was twenty-three years old when I was diagnosed as HIV-positive; I am now thirty-four. Previously, I never would have imagined that I would pay individuals for sex or that I would do so while not, in some instances, disclosing my status. I'm not the man I used to be. Admittedly, I may not be "responsible" as determined by conventional norms, but that doesn't immediately relegate me to the realm of "irresponsibility." Some of my behaviors might dwell in that realm, but I don't have to be positioned there, or position myself there, in totality or permanently. I can occupy a middle space, moving toward and away from responsibility and irresponsibility as circumstance, agency, and desire dictate. While I would prefer to remain as rooted as possible in the realm of responsibility (because I have been socialized to believe this is what I should do), there are aspects of that other place that I find fetching. Sometimes irresponsibility works for me and, I believe, is not as harmful as it is posited as.

In a similar vein, just as I do not always have to perform responsibility (or responsibly), mainstream culture does not always have to demonize me for engaging in sex practices. To reiterate, I was twenty-three when diagnosed; I'm thirty-four now. It is ludicrous to imagine that I have not engaged in sexual activity during the intervening years, and it is foolish to categorize all of those actions under the umbrella term "sex." Indeed, I wonder, what is sex? It's a given that oral sex is not the same as anal sex, but that fact does not stop them from being equally criminalized in some locales. If I engage in mutual masturbation with an individual, which may or may not involve our bodies actually touching, must I disclose my status? Redefinitions are called for and a discussion about the applicability of those redefinitions is in order as well. We can also realize that we live in a culture of risk in which engaging in sexual activity with any individual, with or without consent, can lead to complications. On that score, I wonder what happens if an HIV-positive subject makes it a point to disclose his status prior to the sex act, but the partner claims he did not? It's very clear to me who will be penalized in this instance.

Writing in Fearless Speech, Michel Foucault summons the Greek concept of parrhesia, "frankness in speaking the truth" (7). He explains that "the commitment involved in parrhesia is linked . . . to the fact that the parrhesiastes [one who uses parrhesia, thus one who speaks the truth frankly] says something which is dangerous to himself and thus involves a risk" (13). Risk is at the heart of this chapter. Of course there is the obvious risk: the question of individuals placing others in danger of contracting a deadly virus. There is, as well, the risk of having pleasure stymied. But there is another risk as well: the risk an individual takes by speaking of his actions truthfully. As Melvin Dixon asks: "What truthtelling are you brave enough to utter and endure the consequences of your unpopular message?" (200). Perhaps in telling stories of my life I'm tired of being good; maybe I'm trying to be and do better. I wrote this; I inserted myself into it; I admitted knowledge of wrongdoing; but mostly, I have tried to reach for, to access, the truthtelling Dixon imagines. I call upon others both in and out of mainstream culture to truthfully examine their own actions and to try to follow the same path.

NOTES

Chris Bell died on December 25, 2009, while final revisions were being made on this chapter and volume. The version printed here was prepared for publication by the editors, based on conversations with Bell prior to his death. Beyond minor copyediting, the words are his own.

1. Recall the treatment of HIV-positive subjects in Cuba in the 1980s who were quarantined in state-sponsored camps.

IV

....

LIVES

11

·························

RIVA LEHRER

GOLEM GIRL GETS LUCKY

THE CASTLE

The keys are already in my hand as I come home again. The sight of the long iron fence in front of my building makes my spine prickle with metamorphosis. The big security key turns easily in the first lock, but the gate itself is so heavy that I have to throw my whole body against it to swing it open. It feels good to press my skin against the cold, simple rods. All those thousands of iron gates all over our city; every one a testament to the fact that iron has been used as a divider between worlds for centuries. Iron is an ancient, eldritch charm against demons and faeries, able to divide the world of monsters from the world of men. This iron threshold marks the line between the hard-shell body I wear in the street and the soft stitched-up skin of my animal self.

The sounds of coming home—the turn of a lock, the squeak of metal, the closing clank—are my quiet incantations for the protection of monsters.

Most days, my building's gauntlet of security gates and doors grants me sanctuary. Each one that closes behind me lets me drop another defense. But not today; today I'm not alone. You're coming to my house for the first time. I glance at you from the corner of my eye and feel all over again the fierce hopes you have raised in me.

We walk together through the lush courtyard full of plants all waving a shrubbery green welcome. They're offering you the warmth I can't quite give, yet. The courtyard echoes with our footsteps—one even beat, one erratic tattoo. More keys, more doors, both of us quiet, small words and sideways looks.

You look tense. Maybe you're just spooked by the elevator, which scares the bejesus out of everybody. It's an antique birdcage with a positively carnivorous brass scissor gate. The machinery does its menacing clatters up to my floor, laying on a full repertoire of horror movie sound effects. At least this makes us both burst into laughter. After all that my actual door is a bit of anticlimax—an ordinary dark wood slab festooned with an urban compilation of locks, chains and deadbolts. The only oddity is that the peephole is set very low.

Three last twists of the key, and we're in.

Oh. Wait. No, we're not. Where did you go? When did you go? I guess, after all, you were spooked by me.

THE STREET

I try to be surprised, but this is hardly the first time that someone couldn't quite cross the line. At least now the door is locked behind me, and I can finally forget my size, my shape, and my way of walking. The street armor falls off in layers and dissolves on the floor. I am naked with relief and angry at the safety of solitude. In reprieve from the sidewalk.

Safe for now from the narrow strip of pedestrian road where Us collides with Them. My unpredictable gait turns it into a slalom course. I zigzag through the crowds with my eyes fixed on my traitorous feet. Even the empty sidewalks skirmish with my body. They're angled toward the traffic so that rain and litter tumble toward the gutter. But my ankles are unstable, and this slant can pop the tendons right out of their sockets. I have to keep changing what side I walk on to keep the stresses even. This must make me look either lost or paranoid, like I think I'm being followed.

On the other hand, my ankles provide an excellent reason not to look up. I can pretend not to see the staring, the gaping, the swiveling, opaque, one-way eyes. To maintain ignorance of the necks whiplashing back and forth with instant judgment. True, ignoring them often results in some sharp pebble of public cruelty, such as the always popular "What's wrong with you? Hey ugly chick. Are

you a midget? Are you a dwarf? Man, lookit her shoes. Hey if I looked like you, I'd kill myself."

Even the stares of children go in deep. Innocence leaves its own burns. So I pancake myself into the brickwork or move in oblique angles to the traffic or shove through the crowd hard as an icebreaker. Walking through a tangle of eyes. Eyes raise, eyes meet, eyes slide away, eyes widen, eyes lock, and eyes are cast down.

We animals learned to stare at each other millennia ago, before we were humans, when we were still prey and predator both, leaping through trees and running over savannah. Where learning to tell pack mate from interloper, carnivore from herbivore, alpha from omega was a matter of immediate survival. But in the modern city, we don't worry too much about nonhuman eyes.

Today we navigate a daily pageant of human variation. The fear is more abstract and the judgments more subtle. The pageant teaches us both desire and repulsion. All those different bodies offer a catalogue that lets us discover the shape of our lusts. Our libidos become engorged on memories of bodies we've briefly seen. Shapes flicker like flash cards strobing a route between head, heart, and pelvis.

All women know that the sidewalk is a catwalk. From before the first faint ringing of puberty we are judged on the quality of our flesh. And my entry in the pageant is a body that's more Z-shaped than S-curved. Soft tissue hung from angular and wayward bones. Not built for the performance of Womanhood. She should sway with a spine strung in a sinuous rosary of bones, with brain at one end and cunt at the other. She should undulate with a hide-and-seek of the hips and the breasts. Animate her armature of fertility. Sometimes we punish her for the power of her gravitational field and call her a Streetwalker.

Some women opt out of the pussy dance and choose kinetic defenses, stomping like battle-limbed warriors or pulling a shroud around their sex. Old women disappear into a slow molasses of obscurity, even when they fight to be seen. I can see the day coming when the shape of my body will be chalked up to age and I will join the ranks of the Invisible Women.

Until then, I will be one of the crip girls whose bodies scare the panel of judges. They are afraid that our unbalanced shapes hint of unsanctioned desires. On both sides of the bed.

My friend Eli says that any three crips walking together is a parade. That's because even though we've always been here, we lived in back rooms, in attics, and nursing homes, trapped by stairs and manual chairs and sheer bloody prejudice.

We began to appear along with curb cuts, electric doors, and kneeling buses. Our slow emergence seemed to engender a confusion. The long absence meant that society never evolved a social contract that interprets the movement, the language, and the culture of gimps. Some of us are structurally remarkable; some of us move or speak or stare back in ways that are Different. Canes and chairs and dogs disrupt the pedestrian flow. The crowd streams around us like rocks in the river, staring at and ignoring us in strange proportions.

In the sidewalk mating dance we're winnowed out as undesirable breeders. They don't look long enough to decide whether we're attractive or not. The pack just knows prey when it sees it. We bear the eyes of primates whose curiosity has turned toxic.

Up inside my apartment I look out the windows and watch the people seven floors below. I trace the path through the courtyard that we took inside. It was so hard to look you full in the face. Would you have followed me all the way in if I had? It's a very sexual problem, this custody of the eyes. Because, after all, a lover's regard begins as a stranger's gaze. When I saw you for the first time it was an accident. Some momentary unguarded glance in the park, at a party, in class, I can't remember. And I don't know how to flirt with you if I can't look at you. Your eyes promise both transcendence and disaster. I wait for your words to make it safe to see you. Until then, my peripheral vision is sensitive as a bruise.

MY MOTHER'S HOUSE

I was a frozen child in my mother's house. She was frantic to protect me from what might happen when and if I did grow up. After she tried so hard to help me survive, the future slowed down and became a place where I was not allowed to ripen. My puberty threatened to elide straight into Sleeping Beauty's cryogenic coma. She tried to keep me in her maternal stronghold so that I could remain unthreatened by the desires of men.

My mother used to sew me clothes that matched her own outfits, even making identical doll clothes from the leftover scraps. As a little girl I was so proud of these outfits, and of looking just like Mommy. But as I grew older her creation of me did not change. Mom was a big woman and downscaled her own caftans and muumuus into little tents that hid me completely. And it was clear that everyone—Dad, Grandma, Grandpa, Aunt Ruth, Aunt Sarah, Uncle Barry, Uncle Lester, all my cousins, doctors, nurses, teachers, housekeepers, neighbors, milkmen, and the Rabbi—all agreed that my safest place was in hiding.

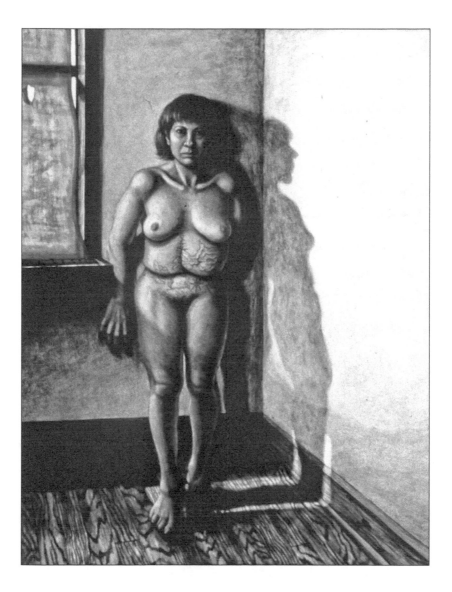

Despite the mummification by wardrobe, there was recognition of my gender. My bedroom had pale-pink walls, white-and-gold French Provincial furniture, a flowery duvet and pink chiffon draperies. Ironically, I hated all of it and repainted everything black and yellow when I was twelve. This made my grandmother utterly distraught. Then there were the pretty girl attempts; for parties, Mom would curl my hair with heated tongs into a style that looked like it had been dropped onto my head. But my gendering had a vestigial, dead-end quality. My family assumed that any relationship with a boy was either a hopeless prospect or murkily dangerous. I was told, with dreadful kindness, that I should never expect to marry. In the darker versions of my fairy tale, where sex actually loomed, the Big Bad Wolf would use my body simply for its unacceptable, discardable help-lessness.

The one great hope was that I'd find a "nice crippled boy," and we would take care of each other in sweetly platonic fashion.

As I became a teenager my mother insisted that I never shut my bedroom door. I suppose this was in aid of keeping me from getting in touch with my hormones. She snooped around my room all the time (calling it "housekeep-ing"). One day she discovered that I had a crush on a boy; she found I'd cut his picture out of a yearbook and put it in a locket. She made jokes about that locket to everyone—jokes that seemed to say that I had done something totally bizarre and inappropriate by even having a crush—until I was completely mortified. People would ask my female cousins and my female friends if they "liked" any-one. Never me. My feelings about boys turned ingrown and confused as a toenail.

Even when Mom stopped making my wardrobe, I still was not allowed to pick out my own clothes. Mom and Grandma filled my bedroom closet with unisex polyester shirts and elastic old-lady double-knit pants in "mod" diamond patterns. For special occasions there were deeply traumatic dresses: a clutch of brownish plaids and infantile flowered cottons, all of them smocked, puff-sleeved, and baggy as hell. It wasn't even necessary for me to be along when these items were purchased since "fitting" was a relative term. Grandma sewed me floor-length elephant bell-bottoms in order to hide my orthopedic shoes. But since I'm under five feet tall, the pants made me look like I was walking around in a trench. My outfits formed a spectacular camouflage of puerile design.

Unsurprisingly, when I finally started buying my own clothes at eighteen, I dressed like a hooker in a storm cellar. After that phase I promptly retreated into bulky disguises of my own devising. It took me years to figure out what looked good on me, since I panicked every time I saw my body actually defined by my clothing.

And still I have no idea what I look like outside my fears. All I think is: I protrude.

THE CLOSET

Crip girls wear plunging necklines to draw the eyes away from our bent backs. Long velvet skirts cascade over our leg braces. Short skirts skim away from the scars on our bellies. Tight pants deflect your gaze from the tremble in our arms. Gold and silver ornaments advertise the charms we are allowed to flaunt. We'd like a great tumble of hair to hide in. We know, completely, whether our breasts or legs or hands or eyes or maybe just our voices are our "best features." Our hopes of desire are condensed into these segregated, illuminated parts. We use magic spells and incantations to make the rest of us disappear.

THE CLASSROOM

I knew plenty of other children mired in parental wardrobe witness protection programs. Both boys and girls came to school in garments meant for giant infants, at Condon School in Cincinnati, an elementary school for disabled children. By sixth grade we presented a picture. It was the 1960s, after all, and kids our age were not wearing potato sacks.

As we reached puberty there was mass adult panic whenever we acted our hormonal age. We played out a round robin of infatuations in our tiny classes. My earliest crushes were on boys with: spina bifida, cerebral palsy, achondroplagic dwarfism, and spina bifida, again (hey, it's a popular birth defect). Also I had a crush on a girl with juvenile arthritis and cataracts. We acted out our crushes as far from teachers, therapists, or the dreaded school nurse as possible. Otherwise, we were subjected to long, mutually embarrassing lectures about "appropriate" behavior, which amounted to self-neutering lessons. When it came to sex, everyone forgot that we were children with full medical educations in the human body. Sex was the one incongruous area where we were kept rigorously uninformed. The school even fired our art teacher for giving us informal sex-ed lessons, which mostly meant that he let us hide in the art room during free periods so we could talk a little dirty, say "penis," and have shrieking hysterics. It followed that the art

Riva Lehrer

room became the rumpus room, where boys on crutches would chase after girls in wheelchairs in laps around the craft tables.

Outside of "special" school, I saw the normal girls being prepared for womanhood. Early gifts of kitchen toys and playtime makeup led to prom frocks and high heels. Women's studies has taught us to see the damage caused by rigid gendering. But there is a different kind of confusion and hurt caused by its absence, when it's clear that you're not being included because you've been disqualified. Disabled women must continually claim their gender in the face of active erasure. Equally, disabled boys are often deprived of routes to masculinity. Parents of disabled children get inculcated with the message that letting us enter the sexual marketplace will only cause us pain and rejection.

Crips of my generation grew up without knights in prosthetic armor, without deaf princesses, spastic vixens, or any inkling of future X-Men. Dolls were monotypes. GI Joe was built of ruthlessly working parts and had yet to experience TBI or PTSD. Not that we're awash in gimpy role models now, but there were none outside of a telethon then. I vividly remember a few made-for-TV movies in which a normal person (usually female) would be attracted to a disabled person (usually male). Especially popular was the blind girl next door, given that she could be beautiful and wear a mysterious expression (and stylish shades). Attraction to a crip was a display of the hero and heroine's moral perfection. Or in the horror flicks, either the crip or the "normal" was damaged or sick, in thrall to unnatural desires. I can't think of one love story from back then that led to a believable happy ending.

ART SCHOOL

Even now, no one is more amazed than I that I don't actually live in my mother's pink castle. But circumstance blew the door open; my mother died and my family fell apart when I was seventeen. It was a bitter and terrible freedom.

In the silence, I finally began to hear my body speaking. Since I'd never expected to lose my virginity, I hadn't really thought about who was or was not a suitable object of desire. I was a cocoon of a girl whose naiveté emerged as bisexuality. I rather doubt that's what Mother had in mind.

In the 1970s bisexuality had glamour and mystery. It was a way of claiming my difference that did not have the stigma of disability. I was surrounded by art school kids who were trying to invent themselves just as frantically as I was. The central project of my reinvention was an absolute denial of my disability.

Riva Lehrer

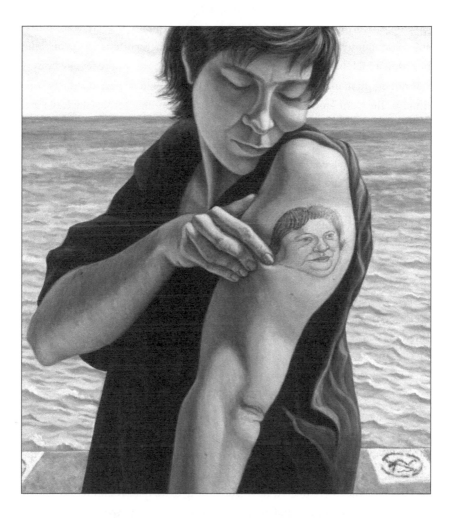

It's amazing what I was able to deny. If something was too obvious I treated it as some kind of punk rock quirk. When I talk to people from back then they all say they didn't know what the hell was going on with me. Art and queerness both gave me space without shame—at least inside of art school. There was no disabled community to offer another perspective. The other glorious aspect of being bi was that I felt liberated from the unattainable standards of the female body. I was not meant to interlock with a single gender but could be part of a misty continuum. The word "queer" captures—better than any other term—the way I feel about my body.

The day that my first college boyfriend asked me out, I literally thought he was talking to someone behind me. I spun around to see what she would say. I was baffled when there was no one there. Poor guy, he never quite knew what to make of me. I hid from him even while we were tangled up together. I was so damn grateful when he finally ended my terrified virginity, as I had no idea how to let it happen. Not the how of it, but how to let it go. During all the years that we were together, both of our families tried to break us up. His felt I wasn't enough of a woman for him. Mine thought he was just being nice and that I should set him free. Alas, I didn't disagree.

I didn't begin school aware of being bi. Even though I was happy with The Boyfriend, in my second year I also fell in love with my best female friend. My first reaction was, "Jeez, don't I have enough problems?" When we actually became lovers that all changed. I was more disoriented by my lack of guilt.

I explored various kinds of erotica in my new status as two kinds of nonvirgin. When I stumbled over images of disabled women, they were often very upsetting. In straight pornography they were simply fetish objects. While that doesn't sound any different from porn per se, these women did not seem to be connected at all to their own eroticism, but were acting out a desperate bid for any sexual recognition. They were offered up as something extra queasy and taboo. In lesbian porn I did find stories and pictures of disabled woman expressing their own desires. Unfortunately, those stories were less than hot, as they were as interested in making a feminist theory point as in making a girl horny. It would be years before I believed that someone could truly love the imperfect, not just jerk off to it. Or close their eyes and imagine some other body pressed close in bed.

I wonder how many disabled people find their sexuality through a covert, nameless, grand experiment in undefined love. Disability can act as a radical alchemist's laboratory of relationship possibility. A place where love might be in-

vented beyond the roles of gender, and leave behind inherited, failed mimicries of intimacy.

TWO PEOPLE WALKING DOWN CLARK STREET

A Friday night early in the story of us: two wary, giddy people walking down Clark on their way to dinner. It's hard to walk down the street with you. Being together fractures my vision into pieces like an insect's compound eye. I am utterly magnetized by the sight of you; I can't stop wondering what you see in me; I'm watching us being watched; I'm hovering above us; I'm completely out of my body. I am ashamed, too, because you quickly see that being my companion means becoming one-half of a two-headed freak in a sideshow. On the other hand, most of those people staring at us don't think we're a couple. They think you're my attendant, my brother, my sister, or my savior.

Sometimes you check with me about the reactions you see on the street. Sometimes you try not to show what you've seen.

I asked: "What did you see the first time we met?"

You said: "I thought you were very serious."

FOUR ROOMS: A TRAVELOGUE

This time we're going to your house.

The minute you invite me in, it's as if my skin erupts with cat's whiskers, all of them quivering and investigating for danger. This place suits your needs, which are so different from mine. I feel like I've parachuted in with just a knife and a Hershey bar.

The place I live is so built to my idiosyncrasies that it virtually wraps itself around my body. Home lets me forget myself. Everything fits my scale and my senses. The furniture is smallish and low to the ground. The light comes from half a dozen ornate chandeliers, which are oddly practical since they hang low enough that I can change my own light bulbs. There are no rugs, carpets, or any other snares for the unwary on my floor.

On the other hand, your house is a challenge from the get-go. First we have to climb three flights of stairs anchored by very shaky banisters. By the top I'm lurching off balance. So I enter unprepared for the wall-to-wall shag carpeting that grabs my ankles and nearly throws me across the room. I seem to have entered an episode of *When Apartments Attack*.

Riva Lehrer

I wobble through the living room trying to keep a tight rein on my limping. And I say, here, I'll help you get the drinks. But Whoops, no, the wine glasses are in cabinets somewhere up near the ceiling. And oh, no, please don't ask me to open the Chardonnay. That's not a crip thing. I'm just plain old bad with corkscrews.

The only place to sit in the kitchen is on backless leatherette barstools. These do unfortunate things to my posture while dangling my feet several inches above the floor. I feel about as sexy as a dachshund—but, alas, nowhere near as cute. Not sure if this is turning out to be romantic comedy or farce.

One frazzled hour of cooking later, and we finally settle down at the dinner table. We're not doing tasks. Just talking. Meanwhile our hands move the dishes and silverware around in silent patterns of approach and withdrawal. Eating dinner has taken on as much coded meaning as a geisha's painted fan.

We take our coffee cups into the living room where it's time for a new round of Close Encounters of the Furniture Kind. This room is dominated by an enormous velour couch. It poses the immediate question of where to sit. All the way at one end? In the middle, hoping you'll head that way yourself? I try to arrange myself in an elegant position and avoid being consumed by the cushioning.

I've been expecting you to flinch at all my flailing around. I suddenly realize that you've been very calm all night. Incredible. For whole moments I forgot to be awkward. True, I am still trying to make shapes with my body that pass for normal. But you're radiating something that is imploding my fears. The cushions dip as you do sit down close to me. My eyes rise up and travel the length of you. I find myself imagining how the pieces of us might find a way to fit together.

All through this evening I'm wondering what will happen if—when—I can't hide my oddity from the truth of your hands. Every inch that we move closer goes off like sirens in my head. They nearly drown out your words, which I need to hear so badly, since we have not touched yet and I still don't know if we ever will. The space between us waxes and wanes. All night I've been telling you the scariest things about me and waiting for you to run. Now I'm letting myself hope I won't see an echo of those stories in your eyes.

Desire plants me inescapably in my body. The shields are falling against mutual lust. The truth under my clothes is whispering loudly, *urgently*, asking how will I explain myself to you. I am most comfortable with the language of medical records. With convoluted, opaque terms that let me speak as if I were on display in the next room. Terms meant for an examining table, not a bed. You see, my family was right, after all: to have warned me about desire when I was a child. Because I've been destroyed in other bedrooms, just the way they foretold. I'm trying not to remember the lover who said I was beautiful from the waist up, but too deformed from the waist down. Or the lover who said my disability was never a problem, until it suddenly became the reason for our breakup. Or the lover whose parents said that their child shouldn't be "taking care of a cripple." Or all the lovers that no one ever believed were really my lovers.

You pull me up toward the farthest doorway. I can see a smoothly made up double bed with a gray cat asleep on its cover. She sees us and leaps for the floor.

Beds are complicated places. Pain and illness, sanctuary and isolation all reside in bed. Pleasure these days is mainly a distant promise. During nights alone in the darkness, I've wrestled my sheets into chains. I think that touching you could break the Möbius strip that binds me only to myself.

Or, if I lie down with you, you could cut me into pieces better than any surgeon. I'm already divided into parts. Dissected by other lovers' words, hands, and eyes into acceptably erotic portions or into no one's land. When we lie down I will beg you to ignore whole parts of me. I will promise to hide them. I will hope you can forgive them. I'll ask you to show me which fragments I can keep, and what I must disown. I will wonder how much of me will get to stay this time.

I can feel your breath on my face. You are dreadfully perfect. Somewhere, dimly, I know that your nose is a bit too . . . and your teeth are just a little . . . but those are thoughts from another galaxy.

Is it possible that I look like this to you, also clad in a molten glaze of beauty?

You pull me up, and into the center of your home. Into the dark. A door sways lightly closed. Even as we fall into your bed, I am prepared to be tossed back into the sea of strangers.

THE SHEETS

Your hands are on, are in, are under my clothing.

A Panic Inventory: There. Is. Not. One. Inch. Of. Me. That. Is. Normal. I have a painter's honesty: knowing that not skin, not hair, not eyes, or mouth or bone or joints or muscle or fingers or fingernails are untouched by strange variations. Monster on the outside, and monster on the inside where the bone, the muffled thump, and the secret details live.

I feel your hands finding me. Running down my swerve of unruly spine. My spine is a parade of vertebrae in all four dimensions. Your palms grip the vaulting barrel of my ribcage. My terrible ribs that make clothing grapple on me like

Riva Lehrer

cats clawing a boulder. But now that clothing falls. Your fingerprints snag on my pale hidden skin, startled at the basket weave of scar tissue. Your hands trace the palimpsest of forty-three surgeons' signatures and the imprint of three hundred hospital bracelets.

Without the scars there is no me; with them, I am in a negotiation with your hands.

The places I want to be touched are shoved up hard against the forbidden wastelands. Not a finger's breadth apart. There are Klaxons of trespass in my voice. I'm afraid that being with me is like fucking a butcher's chart.

But—

It's been so long that I forgot. Skin is not a shell; it reverberates in me like ringing a bell. My skin sings in one dense chorus. In loneliness it had been broken into soloists. Now my fingers speak to your skin. My tongue says other, more primal things, and everything it says is wet. Your blood-colored places are as fluent as mine, as ready for the choir. You make me remember that skin deep is deep indeed.

It's enough for once, that all of the secrets I have to offer aren't grim. My body surprises us both with its ability to be joyous.

And you said: "You laugh with your whole face."

EMPTY BED

You unmade the bed; now no one lies in it.

You were my first disabled lover. Not my first lover: I'd had partners for twenty-five years before I met you. Yet somehow you were the one to end my virginity, over and over again.

Sometimes when we were out on the street together you let your disability show. That made me so happy. It freed me, too; we weren't running from anyone's scrutiny. It's horrible to admit that I was indebted for your accident. Breathtaking selfishness, I know, but through it you understood my own somatic craziness. We met at just the right time after your injury. If it had been too soon after the trauma, you would still have been trapped by shock. A bit later and someone else would have helped reconcile you to your remade body. We even met at our first disability conference. Both of us in a state of flux that led to erotic experiment.

My crip lover, in both senses, you are the first one who ever got me to completely take off my clothes.

So this is my thanks to you, for that gift, the union of our full-length skins.

Riva Lehrer

When we were naked together, I stopped being the Bride of Frankenstein. I stopped being a living-dead collection of stitched together body parts. I stopped being a creature whose only home was the doctor's theater.

You made me your Golem, instead. If you wonder, is that better, let me say, Yes. Shaped and reshaped by your hands, formed as a being of breathing clay. You carved the truth on my forehead and animated it with the imprint of your lips on mine.

And reconsecrated me every night in bed.

The Golem of Prague was made through love, magic, and daring, and so were we. I am trying not to fall into dust now that you are gone.

I miss your scars and your patience with mine. But I walk a little less defended in the world.

Because of what you said, with your fingers: I have assembled you in the night. Felt the edges of the puzzle pieces, the keloid map, and the flinching, sleeping bones. I know what you look like, and I know what we look like together. Watch my eyes, so we can both be visible. In total darkness. With the lights on.

THE STREET

This morning I swung open the black gate onto Balmoral. Stepped out onto the sidewalk behind two slender blondes. Per usual, I felt like a troglodyte lurking behind their thoughtless, easy gait. But then for a moment, I remembered your lips against my forehead. The scar where you kissed me burned, and I thought: feel sad for them. These two will pass and leave no startled mark on the eye. Perhaps, after all, it is a melancholy thing to be forgettable. Whatever else I may be, I am a memory walking into view. I am a new shape on the street.

PRAYER OF THE GOLEM

Protrude is to walk in all directions at once
is muscle stronger than bone
is tendon rigid as cables
that raise the circus tent
is limbs that turn back to the body halfway
to reach for you sideways

is eyes that can't be caught
is ears that keep secrets

Riva Lehrer

is silence in the wiring
is shoes built for mutants
is tongue writhing like an eel in the mouth.
when the mouth mumbles love.

protrude is falling down everywhere
everywhere. anytime.

protrude is my shoulders at your waist
my waist too low and thick to cradle
my cradle in the riverbank
my breasts, mysterious, hidden in reeds.
my feet tangled with your legs,
legs tangled with furniture,
bucked down to the ground
by a crouching pebble.

protrude in the expanding wingspan of crutches
protrude in the flying shul of a wheelchair
protrude is emet carved on my forehead,
a scrawl that holds both truth and death.

protrude is desire thrusting from darkness
protrude is clay that runs wet as blood.

Wet as the coming of the Bride
at last, in joy,
stripped bare.

THE BELFRY

Your friends don't like that you call yourself monster
Monster
But they too, just as you, pull me in, pull me over
On top of their sheepish skins.
Watch me shiver the silver from the back of the mirror
Weave it into my sky-black fur.

I am the one who crashes through walls
I am the one who flies out of windows
I bring the bed with me

Riva Lehrer

On top of my crooked back.

I give your words fangs
I give your touch claws
To hold, to hold in, to hold on.
Hold him. Hold her. Let go. Come.

We will only move forward
Our dance clears the room
Shadow crossing the moon
Without me, love would be
a
small
pink
candy
heart.

12

···················

LEZLIE FRYE

FINGERED

"You're a freak."

It started out sly and emboldened and triple-dog-daring style, dripping with eight-year-old arrogance in the bulk bin aisles of the PC Market on Franklin Avenue.

"Your hand is so freaky, you are a freak!" It got louder and more urgent as the investigation continued, less controlled, less confident, more desperate to convince me and more fearful that the project would not be carried out. It's interesting how a young child can so effectively enact repression on an adult person twice his size with about 207 more college credits focused on the topics of privilege and oppression and big plans to change the world, and this power—it fascinated me.

"Well whataya mean, freak?" I ask him. "What's that mean, huh?"

"You know, it's just weird-like, just creepy-like."

"Like bad or like different?" I query in the most neutral voice I can conjure up for someone who isn't entirely responsible for the epithets he spews. About eighteen "like"s get lobbed between us in a matter of four minutes.

And then he starts pulling this capital "P" Progressive bullshit I know is hangin' out in his momma's back pocket, who's standing behind us with her eyeballs bugging out, scooping already stale, dried apricots nervously into a plastic bag that won't open quick enough to make it look the slightest bit natural. 'Cause after I say "I dunno if that's so nice to call someone a freak. How do you think you might feel if someone called *you* that?" he starts this backpedaling business of, "Well, I don't mean it in a *bad* way, it's just freaky that's all," and I know very well this kid's been called a freak before, and I know very well how good it feels to him to identify someone else even freakier than him. I could sense it from the onset of our "interaction." I am his discovery, like a lost action figure caked in dirt or a cracked blue robin's egg or a clover with exactly four leaves, only I am a real live human being ripe for the finding and right in the middle of an everyday trip to the grocery store. And I'm a better find too, 'cause seeing me changes the way he can look at himself; with the titillation of realizing with his pin-the-tail-on-the-new-freak find, he is momentarily off the hook. I am a tool for him to shape himself against, because if I define the borders of freakdom, he can easily slide under the "normal" wire. So there is a sigh of relief in his attack, a calm and easy sense of himself that indicates he has instantly absorbed this new visual information offering him an automatic improved status in the hierarchy of weirdness. I am a temporary and irresistible get-out-of-jail-free card.

"I mean, you can't do anything," he informs me bluntly.

And I appreciate this. The way I often appreciate children who lack the skills or desire to censor themselves in such a way that might make them appear particularly likable. And there's a kind of caustic satisfaction when somebody says something nobody ever says but everyone always means. His words are shiny raw meat on a piece of dry white butcher paper and they're bleeding all over us both. "Sure I can," I tell him calmly, but he is not convinced.

"I betcha can't eat with that hand," he conjectures. "You can't hold onto a fork."

"Well, maybe not." I tell him, "I prefer to use this one, and I can eat a *lot*, OK."

"I bet you can't play ball," he spits at me with a glimmer of vindictiveness that unsettles my patient and generous posture. So I try not to look at mom who's closing in on us to remind him how "we talk about this at home, darling." Ya, sure. That's why I'm being held hostage by the freak police in aisle seven, right lady, 'cause y'all talk about this aaaaaaall the time.

"Ah haaah, I can," I spew back instead.

"I bet you can't jump rope."

"Oh yes, I can." Suddenly I am nine years old, and I'm in the playground behind St. Clement's parish on Orchard Street in Chicago, playing a fierce and spitefully educational game of foursquare and beating Jason Wheeling at arm wrestling because crutches make your muscles real big and I'm a Feminist arm-wrestler too, "Lezzie the leeeeeez-bee-anne," in fact.

"But you can't hold things with it."

Against my better judgment I am illustrating my incredulous capabilities to precariously balance a wine bottle, two cans of over-priced black beans, and a bag full of peanut butter pretzels. And after a second I realize I have just made myself into a goddamn circus seal and everything I just read about the historical significance of freak shows is flooding my limbs and "*discourse: acting on the body*" is blinking on and off in fluorescent orange light across my forehead, leaving the hot buzz of embarrassment itching inside my ears.

"Betcha can't ride a bike," he says.

Sucker. "Oh yes, I can. And fast and hard and up big hills too," I add. "I can outride you any day, kid." "Kid" is not something I usually call children, but this guy is grating on me, so I go for the low blow and ride on our substantial age difference until I can collect myself and offer a remotely more mature counter-argument.

"Betcha can't throw this." He grimaces with a fat orange in his hand.

"How do *you* know?" My mean second-grade self is rearing out, rolling up her sleeves, and coming in for the bitch serve that will knock me right into the Queen box, where I intend on staying for the rest of recess. This is considered "poor sportsmanship when used against a novice" and can "result in the other players ganging up against the server," but I am becoming agitated and grasping, grasping to get a hold on the trajectory of our meeting.

"Betcha you can't write homework with that hand."

He's got me there and then suddenly for every bad reason I am saying "So what!" and the words puncture every possibility in my mind that we are going somewhere with this line of accusations. "And anyways," I tell him "I write better with this hand . . . what hand do you write with, huh?" And he says his right hand too, and when I point out that this is similar about us, he bristles. He can write with any hand he wants, it seems.

"I dare you," I say. "I just *dare* you to think of any *one* thing I gotta do that I can't." His brain is turning, turning but before he can come up with something, I'm tying up my bag of pepitas, writing in black crayon the number 7–4–0–2 with my oooooooonly writing hand, and goading him further, "Betcha I can kick yer butt at any video game too."

He protests loudly between whiny requests for raisins, also stale, like everything else in the bulk bins at this store, but I can tell he's unsteadied by my appropriation of his "betcha" weapon.

"And I betcha I can tie my shoe faster than you can find the chocolate malt balls," I say, further escalating the absurdity of this conversation.

And then, in an entirely unmeditated gesture toward my own unexpected mini strategic essentialist grocery shopping project, I suddenly hear myself saying, "There's a lot of things I can do that you can't, you know."

"With that hand," he smirks.

"With this hand, yes."

And then the dreaded, inevitable, and unintentionally invited nasty edges of disbelief surface in his words: "LIKE WHAT?"

"Well . . ." I say, cloaked in a pause that is all plastic security.

Think, *think*!!! Of everything I couldn't imagine in the last twenty-six years, right—now. This is, after all, as good a time as any for a critical epiphany between the dried pears and sesame sticks.

I'd been moving through the better part of the last two months in a foggy panic that seeped into every spare moment *try*ing to figure out just exactly what was so great about disability and ability, and this fucking kid was illustrating the whole dilemma of coming out. Coming out to the store at 9 p.m. and not hiding my hand in the left-hand pocket of my hoodie. To be visible, it's tiresome. All I wanted was some pepitas and pretzels, damn it.

"HUH!? Like *what?!*" Pressing, pushing there's suspicion and triumph in his voice. I feel sniffed and found out and I am sweating and he's swinging a long clear sack of raisins back and forth and balancing on one foot, expectant and ready to pounce. This boy, freak making, smells me and encroaches, eyes sparkling and dirty laces dragging underfoot.

I feel the weight of weeks of rummaging around in myself, "What is *good* about my body, about my 'difference?'" Doing a strategic inventory of coming out as queer, showing up to accept my prepackaged, preappropriated identity with all this history and community and culture and logos and prancing around at PRIDE upon permanent graduation from the depths of heterosexual despair. Juxtaposed with the first time I use the word disability and my family tells me, "*You're* not disabled. You're perfectly capable." "You're normal, just like me," my sister insists. That's a bad word, see, and I'm not bad. But I keep trying to claim it through the prickly protest and awkward explanations and the more I identify with people like me, the more I wonder, "Where's the party?" "There *must* be something about my hands that I can hold onto, that can help me through these ugly moments with eight-year-olds and twenty-four-year-olds and fifty-two-year-olds," I think. There's gotta be something about my body that can help me out of this.

Frantically I am scanning the surroundings: identifying exits, registering the contents of plastic bins, searching the carts of passersby for some tool, a route of escape. The elevator music tempo rises and sweat is accumulating every place. I survey the produce desperately, pausing over gnarly ginger roots and carrots that mirror the unruly direction and growth of my limbs, seeking the sexy chaos of organic fruits, the escapees of genetic testing and modification, dirty and un-symmetrical in the shadow of their absence belied by the shiny, perfect symme-try of tens of waxy, odorless apples stacked upon each other. These errors in the (re)produce regime are spoiled only by the aberrant viewer and put to the most incredible and productive use by more adept reception; I remember, then, the first time I discovered this, sitting on the side of the road with a broken down Geo Prism, bored to the point of obscenity. Having untangled the stem of a Granny Smith I realized that the tip of my hand, with its knotty pointed corner and angled curve, fit perfectly into the nook at its top. When I applied pressure I noticed the stretching, slow at first and then with a sound, not violent but a sort of spreading sound, not the clean cutting of a well-sharpened knife but a less precise separation, dripping and marked by fingerprints my hands leave behind.

All of a sudden I am very calm and I'm looking the boy who is not the freak right in the eyes and again I hear myself talking, saying, "like, I can fit my hand into very small spaces," and his mother glances over at me and her mouth has dropped open a little and the word "hush" is hanging out below her bottom lip. But this garners a certain fascination from the boy and so he skips a beat and smiles at me sideways, the sticky plastic bag hanging limply from his fingers.

They're gaping, these two with their excess extremities, and now I want them to notice, to see me; I demand it of them the way I have of so many lovers, to look at my body in its startling familiarity. I let them memorize the way my arm wraps around itself, twists into my wrist, bends in two directions at the elbow. I will them to imagine all the places my hand has been, between which cracks suiting just its shape, into which crevices only it can fit, the openings it meets and how deeply it may slip unhindered by the endless redundancy of knuckles and joints and fingernails crowding and poking in every which direction. On the edge of my limb leak suggestions: where it frequents my body, how it visits bodies like theirs; invitations offered up by each crease, fold, sphincter, each contracting muscle, each liminal space between. I let my hand hang, taut and heavy before

Lezlie Frye

their gaze, erect, bent, unpredictable. I move slightly by way of directing them. This fantasy, of locating their focal point, mapping the frame, timing the impact, tightens up to the extent that I exist only inside the crack in this moment.

I am not choosing this, I remind myself. This is not mine, this contact. It does not belong to me even as it makes each of us, the boy, his mother, me. But in it is a thin slit of space fitted for the knotty end of my limb. Curving methodically along its edges, I push up against it, applying pressure, flirting with the dangerous possibility of being submerged completely, slowly, then faster, disappearing and reappearing as a repetitive dialectic motion into which I breathe. Here, against the fleshy insides of this painful confrontation unfolds the world-making power of seeing myself another way. Flanked by the confines of this repressive accusation that I am something less than whole or human, I begin to find a way in.

"It can come in handy sometimes," I brag shamelessly to the boy and his mother. My hands were born to be inside these cracks, I remind myself. They were born to roam beyond the rims of them. My hands were born to be inside of cunts, to reach in, bring babies forth; I've always known this. A small and winding, dexterous hand, smooth with no nails protruding. Not sharp, but worn like driftwood or clear glass rubbed on coarse sand. Another knotty, sturdier one, stubby like a carpenter's hand, like my father Richard's. Working hands. Welcoming hands. Walls of vagina-hugging, tight-slipping, lining-gripping hands, like my four fingers sighing on the way through another's five. My hands don't lie. My hands.

I ask this boy where he's heard the word freak. "School . . . everywhere," he retorts. He won't say it's been hurled at him before but I know. He is tiring of my questions and has resigned himself to staring. And then I learn that his momma has already taught him to appropriate the feminist rhetoric of safety in lieu of teaching him about human difference, because he says, "this conversation is making me uncomfortable. I'm done talking about this," all attitude and blame.

But instead of telling him that I'm the one that gets to say that and how his raggedy little blue corduroy ass will stand here and wait until I'm good and ready to call it quits, I kneel down and look into his eyes with my hand raised between us and say, "Well that's OK, because this is a *very* small town; I know we'll see each other again soon and we can finish this conversation then." I wonder who will be more punished by this always-incomplete project to which I have nonetheless promised to return.

Course I don't wanna look at his sorry face any time soon, seeing as how it is not legitimately the responsibility of the "object" to give the "object lesson," and since I have no desire to negotiate his mother's reaction to what has been perceived as an indictment of her parenting, which it in fact is. Though I'm not sure she understands this 'cause as I turn to leave, she leans toward me. And as if it were my choice to postpone a perfectly ordinary activity like eating to justify my presence in a public space, as if I in fact had consented to absorb the burdensome task of educating eight-year-olds by way of corporeal display, and as though I had seamlessly anticipated the absent lesson plan showcasing the multicultural inclusion of the cripple, she silently mouths the highly exaggerated words, "*Thank you.*"

13

....

RACHAEL GRONER

SEX AS "SPOCK"

Autism, Sexuality, and Autobiographical Narrative

In recent years, the media has been inundated with narratives about autism, including best-selling autobiographies, films with prominent autistic characters, and even scholarly work that belatedly confers "diagnoses" of autism on artists such as Michelangelo and characters such as Melville's scrivener, Bartleby. The popularity of these narratives parallels an increase in attention to autism over the past twenty years in the medical and educational communities as well as in the popular imagination.

Despite the wide-ranging attention to autism, also known as autism spectrum disorder (ASD), there has been very little attention to sexuality among people with ASD. And when sexuality is represented, it is usually depicted as abnormal. Even a casual survey of clinical, medical, and education literature reveals that sexual behaviors are to be discouraged or "managed" among autistic people, especially those who live in group homes or institutional settings. The language of these and other texts, popular and scholarly, assumes that all people with ASD, no matter how high functioning on the autistic spectrum, are or should be asexual, presumably because their sexuality is inappropriate and potentially harmful to others. For example, myriad articles discuss how to keep a person with ASD from engaging in public masturbation or inappropriately touching another person. These texts, which tend to be written in a condescending manner, perpetuate the false assumption that autistic people should refrain from sexual behaviors altogether. The European Charter for Persons with Autism, adopted by the European Parliament in 1996, also illustrates this lingering assumption about autistic asexuality. The charter reads: "Many people with autism, particularly those who are more severely afflicted, show little interest in sexual relationships and will consequently show little interest in such activities" ("European").

Wendy Lawson, a prolific writer and an autistic woman herself, recently attended an academic conference on autism at which a well-known speaker said that "[s]exuality is not a problem for individuals with ASD. They don't seem aware of their sexuality. If sexuality does present a difficulty then the best thing to do is to redirect the individual . . . keep them busy." Lawson was furious. "'Actually, I am a sexual person too,' I wanted to say. 'I have the right to be a sexual person, just like you do'" (*Sex* 27–28). She reports that many of the other conference attendees privately disagreed with the speaker, but the public and dominant story was and still is that asexuality is and should be the norm for people with ASD.

In this chapter, I examine representations of sexuality within autobiographical narratives of people with ASD. I am particularly interested in how people with ASD construct and describe sexuality, despite being labeled asexual by family, friends, and doctors. My title, "Sex as 'Spock,'" refers to one of the metaphors most often used by these authors to explain their autism, that of half-human and half-Vulcan Mr. Spock from *Star Trek*. More recent variations of the original *Star Trek* series have featured similar human-hybrid characters, such as the android Data and a half-cyborg named Seven of Nine; like Spock, they are relentlessly logical beings who do not recognize or feel human emotion and rely instead on facts and figures to negotiate social relationships. For this reason, many autistic writers compare themselves to these characters. As the autistic author and animal scientist Temple Grandin explains, "I need to rely on pure logic, like an expert computer program, to guide my behavior. . . . I can't read subtle emotional cues. I have had to learn by trial and error what certain gestures and facial expressions mean" (*Thinking* 135). Like the android character Data, who experiences significant confusion about sexual and romantic relationships, Grandin feels that she cannot express her sexuality in conventional relationships because, she says, they are "too difficult for [her] to handle" (133). As I will argue, Grandin and other people with ASD may choose relationships and sexual expressions that are unconventional, but they are definitely not asexual; in fact, the personal narratives

Rachael Groner

written by and about autistic people form a complex challenge to heteronormativity and to mainstream cultural assumptions about sex and disability.[1] Much as an autistic person is often illegible to the non-ASD, or neurotypical (often abbreviated as NT) world, autistic sexuality is illegible to heteronormativity. In a sense, autistic sexuality is always and necessarily queer, even if the people involved are not gay, lesbian, bisexual, or transgender in identity or practice. Judith Halberstam wrote in the early 1990s that "[t]here are no transsexuals. We are all transsexuals" ("F2M" 225). I take this to mean, in part, that the term "transsexual" is simultaneously useful and useless, a postmodern cipher. I will extend this formulation to claim that all people with ASD are queer and, simultaneously, that there are no people with ASD who are queer.

In making this claim, I am also following Robert McRuer, who writes that there is a crisis around heterosexual and nondisabled people that manifests itself in "complex processes of conflation and stereotype: people with disabilities are often understood as somehow queer (as paradoxical stereotypes of the asexual or oversexual person with disabilities would suggest), while queers are often understood as somehow disabled (as an ongoing medicalization of identity, similar to what people with disabilities more generally encounter, would suggest)" ("As Good" 94). For McRuer, the goal is not to simply notice the parallels between representations of disabled and queer bodies, but to *do* something with those parallels, for "[n]either gender trouble nor ability trouble is sufficient in and of itself to unravel compulsory heterosexuality or compulsory able-bodiedness" (95). He says, and I agree fully, that we need to actively perpetuate the crisis; if compulsory heterosexuality and compulsory able-bodiedness are always already failing systems, as Judith Butler, McRuer, and numerous other queer theorists suggest, we need to push at those moments of failure and suggest multiple alternatives. In this chapter, I wish to perpetuate the crisis and to complicate it further by emphasizing not just able-*bodied*ness, for autism is not located solely (or even primarily) as a physical disability. Perhaps a key aspect of a critically queer methodology is to push at the distinctions of the mind and body split in disability studies at the same time that we push for the destruction of able-bodied privilege.[2]

Before turning to specific autobiographical narratives, let me introduce some of the key terms that will appear throughout my discussion. First, I will use the terms "autistic people" and "people with ASD" interchangeably to describe people along the autism spectrum. There is controversy over which term is most appropriate; rather than becoming mired in that controversy, I will alternate between the two terms used most often by people with ASD. I use the term "NT" to refer to neurotypical or nonautistic people or cultures, though some argue that this term implies that there are two neurological categories, typical and atypical. Some scholars of autism even insist that we should order the neurological spectrum according to diverse abilities and not social norms. For example, Simon Baron-Cohen writes that "people with [ASD] might not necessarily be disabled in an environment in which an exact mind, attracted to detecting small details, is an advantage. In the social world there is no great benefit to such a precise eye for detail, but in the world of math, computing, cataloguing, music, linguistics, craft, engineering or science, such an eye for detail can lead to success rather than disability" ("Is Asperger's" par. 1 of summary).

Because media representations of ASD are limited and stereotypical, I wish to describe the autism spectrum for readers who are unfamiliar with it. In general, medical and psychological literature on autism describes it as a disorder that manifests itself as a range of cognitive, sensory, and social behaviors that are usually considered atypical by people in the NT world and the medical community. For example, some people with ASD are described as having unusually heightened or diminished reactions to sensory stimuli (touch, sound, smell, etc.). Another oft-described characteristic is the development of obsessive physical fixations, or tics, and the pursuit of seemingly irrational repetitive activities. Some autistic people seem to have what are called photographic memories and can absorb large amounts of information more quickly than NT people; others are cognitively impaired, especially in the area of verbal skills. Most autistic people report difficulty communicating with others, and it seems that this occurs because they tend not to conform to unspoken NT rules of communication. For example, people with ASD tend not to look other people in the eye; they say that they cannot read others' facial expressions or understand emotions as concepts or experiences; and they are considered by many in the medical community to be uninterested in other people, sometimes being described as treating others as inanimate objects. The autism spectrum is wide-ranging and includes those who are considered to be severely debilitated and require full-time care, as well as those who achieve high levels of intellectual and social success (the latter are often labeled by their peers as merely eccentric rather than disabled). Most autistic people report difficulty creating and maintaining interpersonal relationships with acquaintances, friends, lovers, or family members. There is generally no physical limitation or disability that prevents people with ASD from participating in sexual activity, though some individuals with heightened or diminished sen-

Rachael Groner

sory abilities have to adjust normative sexual activities for their bodies, a process that NT people engage in also, albeit in less conscious ways.

The demographics of people with ASD are difficult to ascertain, largely because autism is occasionally misdiagnosed or, more commonly, goes undiagnosed, especially on the "high-functioning" end of the spectrum, also known as Asperger's syndrome. In addition, because of the attention autism has garnered, the numbers seem to grow each year, so any demographic information is necessarily incomplete. According to Victoria McGeer, 75 percent of diagnosed autistic people are "mentally handicapped in a general way [and] the remaining twenty-five percent—often identified as having Asperger's syndrome—show average to good cognitive functioning as measured in standard intelligence quotient tests. But even those with Asperger's syndrome display these characteristic abnormalities to some degree" (235). McGeer's pathologizing language, it should be noted, is typical of the descriptions of people with ASD in popular, medical, and scholarly literature.

The relationship between autism and gender is fairly unclear at this time, but medical literature reports that the ratio of men with autism to women with autism is estimated at 3:1. It has also been reported that "many of autism's manifestations . . . echo types of behavior with which we are all familiar in a certain type of 'normal' male" (qtd. in S. Smith 245). When it comes to sexual identity, Donna Williams, a writer with ASD, has posited that the autism spectrum contains a higher percentage of gay, lesbian, bisexual, queer, and transgendered people than the NT community. Dawn Prince-Hughes, the author of an autobiography about autism, agrees; she argues that "most autistic people do not see gender as an external or internal category that is important or even applicable, especially to themselves" (Songs 59). When discussing her husband Danny, Barbara Jacobs notes that he always had an "affinity with transgression" and that, although heterosexual, he "loved the feeling that he was in the company of those who might be marginalized by the majority, just as he was" (159).

Few people with ASD write autobiographies, and most of these are written by women on the "high-functioning" end of the autism spectrum. Thus, I make no claims that the texts I examine here represent the ASD population. Nor would I claim that there are great similarities among this group of authors and texts, for autism affects each of them in very different ways. In a discussion of autobiographical narratives, it is important to note that the very concept of autobiographical narrative presents problems for autistic writers and readers, because autistic people seem to conceive of themselves in a way that is very different from

NT writers and readers. Medical professionals seem to agree that an autistic person does not conceive of herself or himself as a distinct, coherent, and knowable self, though most readers assume that writers have some semblance of self when they create a narrative. Further, most literary criticism about autobiographical writing is founded in part on the assumption that even if the authenticity of the narrative is questionable, the existence of an author is a given. Indeed, narratives by people with ASD do tend to be significantly less organized, if you will, than those of NT writers. In one of the first essays to focus on these autobiographies, Sidonie Smith explains that people with ASD "do not appear to get together an 'I' and a 'you' through which to develop a concept of a narrative subject and a narrative life" (232). For example, Williams, in one of her autobiographical books, describes her difficulty in seeing herself as a subject when she explains that at the age of six, she wrote graffiti on a wall that said "Donna is a nut." As she explains, "it took me four more years to realize that normal children refer to themselves as 'I'" (*Nobody* 23). Although this quote does not indicate it, Williams consistently challenges the concept of "normal" in her writing and her other work (as a blogger, a singer-songwriter, and an educational consultant). But she recognizes that language is one place where "normal" is hard to shake.

One of the challenges posed by a lack of a subjective sense of self (an "I") seems to be that it also precludes a sense of an other (a "you"); this is one of the reasons that people with ASD may often seem unaware of other people's existence. Jacobs, an NT woman married to a man with ASD, writes that a friend with ASD told her, "I was eighteen before I knew other people were *real*! It blew my mind" (69). Researchers like Baron-Cohen and Uta Frith argue that the biomechanics of an autistic person's brain prevent the development of an NT subjectivity. Such scholarship has given rise to therapeutic models that attempt to teach autistic people how to conceive of themselves as discrete, concrete, and knowable. According to these models, autistic people, even if they are not able to "overcome" their brain structures in full, may nonetheless be able to develop an NT-like subjectivity. The stated goal of such therapy is to help autistic people feel more comfortable and be more successful living in an NT world; NTs, in turn, might be more comfortable and successful interacting with autistic people who are assimilated to NT conventions. Frith and Baron-Cohen are controversial, to say the least. I find their therapeutic model to come dangerously close to advocating a form of neurological and behavioral passing. Numerous scholars maintain that Frith and Baron-Cohen have drawn questionable conclusions about ASD. For example, in 2004 the authors of a special issue of *Philosophy, Psychiatry,* and *Psychology*, edited by Richard Gipps, disagreed vehemently with Frith and Baron-Cohen, positing that autism does not demonstrate a lack of subjectivity at all. Instead, they claim that autism produces alternative forms of subjectivity for which the mainstream Cartesian theories of Frith and Baron-Cohen do not account. Stuart Shanker, one of the issue's featured authors, suggests that "what autism may really represent is not a window into the hidden mechanisms involved in a theory of mind, but rather a window into the conceptual problems involved in Cartesianism that lead one to postulate a theory of mind" (220). Shanker and his fellow authors are proposing something akin to the spectrum of subjective experiences, wherein NTs are not the standard against which all other theories of mind are compared. Instead, the NT world is just one of many, and the ASD world is equally complex and valuable. I am squarely in Shanker's camp.

Frith and Baron-Cohen aside, there are people with ASD who have come up with their own personal therapeutic models to help them cope with the challenges of confronting the "normal" world. Williams explains that she literally wrote herself into existence in the NT world by teaching herself how to write in a subjective narrative voice, even though this voice was utterly foreign. Anne Fleche, echoing the title of Williams's memoir, *Nobody Nowhere*, usefully argues that Williams "enables us to 'read' the way a body becomes a subject, [or how] a nobody becomes a somebody" (111). Further, Fleche writes, "Williams shows the contradictory ways in which it is possible to embody a self precisely by performing autism; that is, by vocalizing the need to embody a self" (118). In a similar vein, Sidonie Smith concludes that autobiographical narratives by people with ASD "hint at a different subjectivity" (244). For Smith, narratives by people with ASD provide a valuable opportunity to intervene in the existing debates in scholarship on autobiography about authenticity and claims to truth. She persuasively argues that memoirs by autistic people demonstrate the very limits of autobiographical writing, scholarship about autobiographies, and perhaps narrative itself.

Autobiographical narratives by people with ASD began to appear in the early 1990s. Most of the texts I analyze were published in the early 2000s, which is when a boom occurred in such publishing. The narratives examined in this chapter include: Temple Grandin's *Emergence: Labeled Autistic* and *Thinking in Pictures and Other Reports from My Life with Autism*; Wendy Lawson's *Life Behind Glass: A Personal Account of Autism Spectrum Disorder*; Dawn Prince-Hughes's *Songs of the Gorilla Nation: My Journey through Autism* and an edited collection, *Aquamarine Blue 5: Personal Stories of College Students with Autism*; Chris and

Gisela Slater-Walker's *An Asperger Marriage*; and Donna Williams's *Nobody Nowhere: The Extraordinary Biography of an Autistic, Somebody Somewhere: Breaking Free From the World of Autism*, and *Everyday Heaven: Journeys Beyond the Stereotypes of Autism*. Rather than discussing each narrative one by one, I explore them thematically, so as to demonstrate relationships among them. My goal is not to provide a comprehensive analysis of these texts, but rather to demonstrate how narratives of people with ASD are resisting heteronormative prescriptions and proscriptions and creating new, potentially queer, forms of sexuality and relationships. Along the way, I also discuss several texts that are not autobiographies but that provide context and/or feature some ethnography and biography. These include: Maxine Aston's *Aspergers in Love: Couple Relationships and Family Affairs*; Barbara Jacobs's *Loving Mr. Spock: Understanding an Aloof Lover*; and Wendy Lawson's *Sex, Sexuality, and the Autism Spectrum*.

STRANGE RITUALS: PERFORMING HETERONORMATIVITY

Dawn Prince-Hughes is one of many autistic women who compare themselves to the popular half-cyborg and half-human *Star Trek: Voyager* character named Seven of Nine. She writes that "[l]ike Seven of Nine, I find that I am only part 'human' and very much something altogether different. . . . I don't understand the strange rituals associated with attraction or why people are obsessed with certain physical characteristics" (*Songs* 85). In the next pages, I analyze Prince-Hughes's and other ASD writers' encounters with the "strange rituals" of NT sexual life. I argue that their narrations of these encounters might productively be read as queer: not simply because some describe same-sex sexual interactions, but also because, by highlighting the strangeness and unintelligibility of gendered and sexual norms, these texts point to the fictiveness of NT heteronormativity. As I will show, the notions of neurotypicality and heteronormativity are linked; much of what renders ASD a "disability" in the sexual realm arises from a perceived failure to read and correctly perform heteronormative codes of sexual behavior — or, from an intractable awareness of the illogic and arbitrariness of these codes.

Prince-Hughes explains that in high school she "had no overtly sexual feelings for anyone, male or female, but I had to admit a desire to be near some women because they made me feel good" (*Songs* 54). Her lack of sexual interest in boys during high school prompts fellow students to call her a "faggot." Straight boys and men are particularly threatening to her during this period. Prince-Hughes is raped numerous times, after getting drunk or stoned at high school parties as a means of coping with feeling so different and socially awkward. She finds refuge within the gay and lesbian community, asking her parents to drive her several hours to the nearest queer support group. During this time, Prince-Hughes has no interest in a sexual relationship but believes sexuality runs on a continuum; she even wonders if "one could be 'lesbian' in one's orientation to the world but choose never to have sex" (*Songs* 58). The support group provides many benefits to Prince-Hughes as a teenager; the most important of these is information about sexuality, which feels to her like a foreign language.

In early adulthood, Prince-Hughes begins to have sexual and romantic relationships with women almost exclusively, but she still does not identify as a lesbian. She works as an exotic dancer for several years in her twenties and describes feeling "confronted . . . by [her] expanding sexuality" (*Songs* 78). Her female coworkers express attraction to her and make sexual advances, but Prince-Hughes finds that, even after years of exploration with the queer support group, she still does not understand what is happening for her coworkers. In response, she decides to approach sexuality as if it were a research project. "To me, sex was an exercise to be mastered. . . . [It was] intellectual in nature" (*Songs* 86). She watches pornographic films, reads sex manuals and erotic literature, and asks her coworkers detailed questions, all of which she compiles in her head, so as to at least act the part of a sexual being, even if she does not feel comfortable with the many "rules" that govern sexual relationships. Eventually, she tries out her knowledge to great success, easily starting sexual relationships with a number of women and, as she describes it, achieving a high level of sexual satisfaction in her partners.

But as she continues to learn and practice her new skills, it becomes clear to her that even when she flawlessly applies the logic of sex and love, just as popular films might have scripted it, she fails. For example, it appears to her that in popular culture and in the stories of her friends, women are after love, not sex, and their ultimate goal is marriage or, in her case, a long-term relationship. In relentlessly logical form, Prince-Hughes wakes up the first morning after each sexual encounter planning to move in with her new partner and start a life together, often to the surprise and dismay of the woman in whose bed she has awoken. Over and over this occurs, for, Prince-Hughes says, she could not adjust her methodology after learning it so thoroughly and, she thought, so well. Although she looks beyond heterosexual stories for inspiration, she finds that the lesbian and bisexual world is not so different from its heterosexual cousin and that human relationships are much more complex than a set of rules or skills could explain. Prince-Hughes feels more mystified than ever and experiences panic and rage attacks as a result of her repeated failures to create the idealized version of love and sexual compatibility. Sexual "research projects" such as Prince-Hughes conducts appear often in autobiographies of people with ASD.

As is the case with many NT adolescents, some autistic people report retreating into isolation to avoid sexual (and other interpersonal) activity altogether; others react in an opposite manner and report engaging in sex often and with multiple partners. A good example of both extremes is Danny Jacobs, whose story is told by his wife, Barbara, in her book *Loving Mr. Spock: Understanding an Aloof Lover*. When Barbara first meets Danny, he is regularly having casual sexual encounters with many different women because "[s]ex, he said, was meaningless. An act he rarely got anything from" (29). He calls casual sex "The Game," describing his encounters as "robotic" challenges that are not about sexual or social pleasure but about the successful accomplishment of a task. After the couple marries, their sexual relationship vanishes, and Danny swings to the other end of the sexual spectrum. Barbara writes: "That [sex] means something to me was irrelevant to him. If I wanted him to go through the motions, he said he would, for my sake, but I would have to initiate it, because, unless he was playing The Game, he was completely sexually passive, a sexual object, and always had been" (169). Like Prince-Hughes, Danny Jacobs studies and masters the rules of sexual and social engagement as if they appeared in a playbook. But as was the case for Prince-Hughes, the rules of the game are not adequate for his real-life relationship.

Prince-Hughes's and Barbara and Danny Jacobs's stories reveal the fault lines in heteronormativity. Although both writers initially expect that their thorough research will result in social and sexual literacy, it ultimately leads to frustration and, eventually, to physical and emotional pain and stress. This occurs not because either fails in adequately performing feminine and masculine gender roles, but rather because they perform these roles too well: in Prince-Hughes's narrative, the "feminine" valuation of love over sex; in Danny Jacobs's story, the "masculine" experience of sex as a "game" without emotional significance. By taking gendered norms to their logical extremes, Prince-Hughes and Jacobs reveal the absurdity of these norms and thus, as Butler might argue, threaten their undoing.

Gisela and Christopher Slater-Walker's book, *An Asperger Marriage*, focuses squarely on heternormative assimilation and doesn't dwell on sexual failures and exclusions. Yet it, too, undermines some of the foundations of heteronormativity. The book describes their experiences as a mixed NT (Gisela) and ASD (Chris) couple. Many of the challenges they face seem quite common among

NT and ASD couples alike: problems negotiating private space while living in the same household, making financial decisions jointly or individually, and handling interactions with extended family members and friends. When they go to couples counseling to address these issues, the counselor tells them that Chris's diagnosis of ASD must have been wrong; she is certain that people with ASD never marry. The Slater-Walkers are slightly uncomfortable with the counselor's questioning of Chris's diagnosis, but they seem to accept it and move on with the counseling.

In a narrative that is detailed about the many challenges the couple faces, sexuality is the one issue neither author is comfortable discussing. Gisela writes that the only problem they have never had is with "the 'physical side' of our marriage, although I understand that this is not always the case for people with Asperger Syndrome" (91). The single additional comment that they make about sexuality, in a short jointly written chapter (most of their chapters are written individually), is a similarly vague statement that although many couples, ASD or otherwise, do not enjoy happy sex lives, "fortunately, this part of our marriage is very happy, and . . . we do not have the urge to make it public, so we are keeping this chapter short and discreet" (100).

The Slater-Walkers conform here to one of normative heterosexuality's most important requirements: that sex be kept private and "discreet." Paradoxically, though, the compliance with this requirement risks rhetorically erasing the "happy" — and, readers seem meant to assume, normative — sex to which their text alludes. That is, if the imperative to keep sex private were to be taken to its extreme (if, for example, the Slater-Walkers had taken their adherence to this rule a step further and entirely omitted any mention of sex), sex would risk disappearing into unrepresentability. As we have seen, the erasure of sexuality is common in professional and medical accounts of people with ASD. The Slater-Walkers' discretion in regard to sex might therefore prompt the question: how far removed are heteronormative ideals of privacy from the pervasive assumption of asexuality that informs dominant cultural representations of autism?

BREAKING THE GLASS WALL: CREATING ASD SEXUALITY

As we have seen, people with ASD are neither asexual nor asensual. Yet, certain aspects of ASD — in particular, an intolerance for being touched that some autistic people experience — make some conventional sexual acts unpleasant or undesirable and thus necessitate alternative modes of sexual and sensual expression.

Temple Grandin is an autistic writer who chooses to be celibate. Grandin makes a conscious choice to avoid the sorts of "games" and rituals that Prince-Hughes and Jacobs work so hard to understand. As a teenager, Grandin says, she felt that when "hormones hit, [her] life revolved around trying to avoid a fear-inducing panic attack" (*Thinking* 88). She and her parents notice early in life that Grandin cannot stand being touched; even hugs from loved ones make her skin crawl. This is a common experience among people with ASD; each autobiography explains the difficulties in finding tolerable ways to touch and be touched by others. Grandin researches the topic and discovers that other autistic people also experience an unpleasant heightening of the senses; one woman describes rain as sounding like "gunfire," and a man says he can hear "blood whooshing through [his] veins" (*Thinking* 72). As I have mentioned, many people with ASD avoid looking directly at another person's eyes or face. Williams describes seeing colors and shapes that NTs insist do not exist, and she has great difficulty with fluorescent lights because they make her temporarily blind. Others report being drawn to certain tastes or smells such as soft, bland foods or the smell of aluminum pans. As in Prince-Hughes's experience, panic attacks are frequent reactions to sensory triggers; in order to avoid such attacks, many autistic people say that they stay indoors to avoid new experiences and people. One of the issues repeated in several autobiographies by people with ASD is that certain acts of affection, or of a sexual nature, are off-limits, such as kissing or sharing a bed. Darius, one of the authors in *Aquamarine Blue 5*, a collection of personal stories (edited by Prince-Hughes) about the lives of college students with ASD, writes that he doesn't like soft touches, and he refuses to kiss anyone, no matter how much affection he may wish to express. Darius has sex with both men and women, but he explains that he sets the physical terms of the encounter so that he can tolerate being so close to another person's body and performing sexual acts he generally finds uncomfortable.

One of the few seemingly universal sensations that many people with ASD tolerate, and even crave, is intense pressure. Grandin discovers this when, as a child, she wraps herself tightly in blankets; later, when she works as an animal scientist designing slaughterhouses, she is especially concerned that the animals feel no stress or pain at the facilities she designed. One device—the squeeze chute—seems to calm animals down dramatically, even in the most stressful of environments. It consists of two side panels that press into a cow's sides, holding it immobilized while being vaccinated or receiving medical treatment. In fact, Grandin writes, "gentle pressure on the sides of a piglet will cause it to fall asleep, and trainers have found that massaging horses relaxes them" (*Thinking* 83). Copying the design of the squeeze chute, Grandin builds a smaller scale squeeze machine to fit her human body; over time, she arrives at a design that gives her control over the level of the pressure the panels provide, though she describes being completely immobilized: "As I developed my squeeze machine, I designed it to enhance the feeling of being embraced. Now, if I suddenly resist, I cannot pull my head out of the softly padded neck opening. In order to open the latch, I have to relax and lean forward. I am never locked in the machine, but I am prevented from suddenly pulling away from the soothing pressure" (*Thinking* 80). While Grandin would probably not make this connection herself, someone who read her description of the squeeze machine out of context might easily assume that it is intended to produce sexual pleasure. Readers may note the similarities, indeed, between the descriptions of Grandin's experience and those of BDSM and other sexual practices that involve restraint and/or physical pressure. The "embrace" of Grandin's squeeze machine may not be explicitly sexual, but her description of the experience reads very much like sexual pleasure.

The squeeze machine performs an additional function for Grandin beyond physical stimulation. There is, for her, a "language of pressure" that the machine "speaks" to her. The slightly varying sensations of the machine are "the tactile equivalent of a complex emotion and [it] has helped me to understand complexity of [human] feelings" (90). Grandin's career is focused on nonhumans—cattle and other farm animals in particular—and she describes learning about complexity and about human relationships through her animal relationships. She writes of cows, for example, that "[b]eing autistic has helped me to understand how they feel, because I know what it is like to feel my heart race when a car horn honks in the middle of the night. I have hyperacute senses and fear responses that may be more like those of a prey-species animal than of most humans" (*Animals* 155).

Athough Grandin disavows sexuality, she nonetheless embraces a form of sexual or sensual expression. And because her expression of sexuality or sensuality is disconnected from heteronormative narratives of sex and love, it seems to me that it is strikingly queer. Grandin is not only undoing heteronormativity, by showing it as something she can refuse, but also creating an alternative sexuality and sensuality that has its own language, its own set of practices, and its own equipment. Queer theories of performativity call for repetitive citations of mainstream discourse as a means of disrupting it. By rearticulating sex and sensuality in denaturalized, new, and potentially queer forms, Grandin and other

ASD writers may contribute to the undoing of normative sexual identities and practices, which are inaccessible or undesirable.

In creating a new language or practice of queerness through ASD, these narratives also unsettle heteronormative assumptions about the role of emotion in sexuality and sensuality. The traditional assumption that sexuality is intimately related to love is not upheld in these autobiographies; as is common in queer theory, concepts such as love and pleasure are questioned. What is love? What is pleasure? How do I know that what I feel as joy is the same as what another person feels when he or she uses the same word? Grandin writes that she has never felt the emotion of "joy" and that the closest she comes to it is the feeling she has when she completes an intellectual challenge. Many people with ASD have written that safety and security are perhaps the most descriptive words for what they liken to NT emotions such as love or passion. Danny Jacobs, for example, told his wife that for him, love equals security; he believes "safe" is the best word to express his feelings for her (74). Maxine Aston, who has interviewed many people with ASD about sex, tells the story of a couple, composed of one NT person and one person with ASD, who told her about the first time they had sex. Aston writes that the NT woman "disclosed to [her partner] how special it had been to her and asked him how it had been for him. He replied in all honesty that he had felt disappointed at the time. She was shocked by this and asked why he was disappointed. He said because he expected her to have bigger breasts and that he was surprised that one breast in particular was not as big as the other. She was absolutely devastated by this remark and her confidence and self-esteem took a severe knock" (47). The man did not understand how his words might be interpreted, and his partner did not understand that he, like many people with autism, was being "normal" for him by being very literal and direct with his language. In troublingly ableist language, Aston calls this phenomenon "feeling deafness," even arguing that some people with ASD literally lose their hearing when encountering words that express or describe emotion (48). One productive avenue for discussion (beyond the scope of this chapter) is to find ways to describe and discuss emotion among ASD people as valid in and of itself. As yet, there are only the beginnings of a movement for ASD pride regarding emotional and cultural differences. The ASD autobiographies and other texts I discuss in this chapter participate in this movement by advocating acceptance and valuation of a wider spectrum of emotional expression than NT culture recognizes.

Prince-Hughes is one writer with ASD who attempts to formulate a sense of pride in her difference from the NT world. In her autobiography, she recounts that she initially takes a job as an exotic dancer because it affords her the ability to stop living in the streets of Seattle and to get an apartment and other basic necessities. She continues dancing, however, because it allows her to explore her burgeoning sexuality in a relatively safe environment. The club where she works is owned and managed by fellow dancers, and there is an atmosphere of support and care among her peers. Further, she usually dances on a stage behind a glass wall; a curtain goes up or comes down based on a customer's payment. One of her most insightful points is that the objectification of women by the male customers seems to reflect a lack of feeling and emotion; Prince-Hughes assumes that these men show emotion elsewhere, but that in order to fully objectify another person as they do at the club, they turn off emotions temporarily. For her, this kind of disconnection is dangerous and disrespectful. Although people with ASD often describe being disconnected from emotion, there is a distinct difference between her cold male customers and people with ASD: "These 'respectable citizens' were doctors, lawyers, city council members" and had a choice in how to express emotion and sexual desire, but she was without choice, trapped behind an emotional glass wall that echoed the physical glass wall around the dancer's stage (78). The metaphor of a glass wall is common in autistic people's descriptions of their lives, as in Wendy Lawson's *Life Behind the Glass: A Personal Account of Autism Spectrum Disorder*. When she is a dancer, Prince-Hughes has not yet been officially diagnosed with autism—that happens in her thirties, as a result of her own research about why she feels so different from other people—but she has chosen a profession whose trappings make literal a metaphor that she and others with ASD frequently use to describe themselves.

It is not until Prince-Hughes begins to work at the Seattle Zoo that she feels truly "liberated." Through another powerful metaphor she reveals more about herself as a sexual and sensual being. She writes that when she first begins to visit the zoo, she "heard the clang and moan of the opening door down the hall and woke up from the dream I was in. It was a dream about waking up, and it was coming true" (110). Prince-Hughes works directly with gorillas, as a volunteer and then an employee. The moments she describes with the gorillas are those in which she begins to truly understand the NT world for the first time. Her first intimate encounter with a gorilla occurs when, as a zoo volunteer, she is feeding strawberries to Congo, a large silverback male. Although she is under strict orders to keep her hands away from his, their fingers touch, and their eyes meet: "I relaxed into his touch and his nearness. This is what it is, I thought. This is what it means to love and be loved. This is what it is to touch and look at another person and feel its meaning. This is what it is to not be alone in the vastness of the space we hurtle through among the coldness and the dying. This is what it is to live, I thought" (6).

Unlike any physical, sexual, or emotional connection Prince-Hughes has ever made before, even with family members, her encounter with Congo allows her to break what she experiences as the glass wall of her autism. She immediately decides to work with gorillas full time and to return to school; she dives into yet another learning experience, this time about gorilla and human culture. In the gorillas, Prince-Hughes sees much of herself: like her, they have difficulty remaining calm when there are loud noises; they dislike crowds of people; and when people invade their carefully monitored public space, they create small nests in which to hide, for comfort or solace. Prince-Hughes says that gorillas are also awkward around human beings, and, although they seem intellectually capable of learning human behaviors, they usually refuse to do so.

Over time, Prince-Hughes realizes she is learning how to be an NT human being through her relationships with the gorillas. For example, she learns from them how to "put other people at ease with quick sideways glances and smiles — which evolved from submissive primate grimaces and are intended to convey that no harm is meant" (136). Such cues, which NT people had seemed to know instinctively, Prince-Hughes was previously unable to learn or practice. Perhaps most important, she writes that she learns how to feel and express something like NT emotion through her sensual interactions with the gorillas. Prince-Hughes does not quite claim that ASD emotion is as valid as NT emotion; but among other autism narratives, hers comes closest to doing so.

COMING OUT: WRITING AUTISTIC, WRITING QUEER

Numerous historical and political commonalities exist between the ASD and LGBTQ communities. One of the commonly held beliefs about autism, for example, was Bruno Bettelheim's now-rejected theory of the "refrigerator" mother, in which autism was thought to be caused by a cold and unloving mother. Similarly, cold and unloving mothers were once thought to be the cause of homosexuality. An even more striking coincidence between the two communities is that one of the main treatments for symptoms of autism is applied behavior analysis (ABA), a system founded by Dr. O. Ivar Lovaas in the 1960s and practiced today by doctors, therapists, and educators. With funding and support from

Rachael Groner

the National Institute of Mental Health, among other mainstream organizations, Lovaas and several of his followers developed programs aimed at training children to replace "bad" behaviors with "good" ones. ABA was initially used in the UCLA Feminine Boy Project, in which boys who preferred "feminine" behaviors, like playing house or nurturing dolls, were forced to play in "masculine" ways, such as with toy guns. The project's tactics included "aversives," such as physical restraints, slaps, pinches, hits, hair pulling, electric shocks, and exposure to noxious odors or tastes (Dawson). While ABA is still practiced today in fields such as child and educational psychology, there is a general consensus that severe aversives are inhumane and ineffective. Lovaas was not the sole pioneer of what is often called the ex-gay movement—a movement to "cure" or "convert" homosexuals through ABA methods—but his work was significant in bringing it to the mainstream. Lovaas was also not focused solely on homosexuality; he believed that ABA could help people address any and all "bad" behaviors. Proponents of ABA argue that it can reduce the stress on autistic children and adults by training them to assimilate their behaviors to normative standards. For example, the Autism Resource Foundation, among other organizations, says in its online "Frequently Asked Questions about ABA" that "[a]lthough ABA does provide the best methods for managing problem and aberrant behavior such as self-injurious, ritualistic, repetitive, aggressive and disruptive behavior, it does this through teaching alternative *pro-social* behavior."

As the numbers of people diagnosed with ASD have grown in recent years, so have the organizations dedicated to supporting people with autism. A loose conglomerate of people, an autism community, has sprung up. The autism community has begun to organize politically and, in the process, has looked for models to emulate, such as the Deaf community. But it is the gay community that seems to have the most influence within the ASD community, perhaps in part because of the common history with ABA. The autism activist Phil Schwartz, for example, writes that the gay community has built and leveraged large numbers of straight allies; he suggests that the autism community would do well to practice similar techniques. In a similar parallel to the LGBTQ movement, a group named Aspies for Freedom petitioned the United Nations in 2004 for recognition as a social minority group (a minority based on something nonbiological or physical, but recognizable all the same). Not unlike many segments of LGBTQ communities who see homosexuality not as the opposite of heterosexuality but as a point on a sexual continuum, members of Aspies for Freedom are vocal proponents of a "neurodiverse spectrum," in which autism is a variation of neurological function, not a separate or pathological category.

As I have argued, the sexuality and sensuality of people with ASD may indeed be read as queer, regardless of partner, activity, or intention. To again adapt a phrase from Halberstam's "F2M": all people with ASD are queer, and no people with ASD are queer. In demonstrating the nonheteronormative performativity of sexuality in these autobiographies, my intention is not to reify a new category of queerness or disability that is stable or simplistic; nor is my point that queerness and ASD are equivalent. But I certainly hope, again following McRuer, to have perpetuated the crisis in heteronormativity by recognizing texts written by people with ASD as doing similar work to that of queer texts, even when the ASD texts in question are not representing same-sex sexual desires or practices. The autobiographical narratives I have explored here are starting to write autism into existence as queer, disallowing a discourse in which autism is solely defined as a medical and neurological disorder. In fact, these narratives complicate what we mean by disability in yet another layer than just the mind and body split, for by writing themselves as queer, they provoke further consideration of how disability studies itself is queer.

NOTES

I am grateful to Anna Mollow, who provided rigorous and supportive comments on multiple drafts of this chapter, and to Gabriel Wettach, who gave me comments on this chapter in its earliest draft form.

1. By "heteronormativity," I mean to describe a set of hegemonic practices, norms, and institutions of heterosexuality in contemporary American culture. A good working definition of heteronormativity is articulated by Lauren Berlant and Michael Warner: "Heteronormativity is more than ideology, or prejudice, or phobia against gays and lesbians; it is produced in almost every aspect of the forms and arrangements of social life: nationality, the state, and the law; commerce; medicine; and education; as well as in the conventions and affects of narrativity, romance, and other protected spaces of culture. It is hard to see these fields as heteronormative because the sexual culture straight people inhabit is so diffuse, a mix of languages they are just developing with premodern notions of sexuality so ancient that their material conditions feel hardwired into personhood" (554–55).

2. Cal Montgomery, although she has referred to her cognitive disability as an "invisible" one, argues that there should not be a distinction between visible disabilities, which are often physical, and invisible ones, which are often cognitive. There are

Rachael Groner

exceptions to each category: some physical disabilities manifest themselves without obvious visible markers, and some cognitive disabilities have visible physical manifestations. Even more important, Montgomery says, we must account for diversity within the disability community so that we can remove all of the barriers mainstream society presents.

V

....

DESIRES

14

ANNA MOLLOW

IS SEX DISABILITY?

Queer Theory and the Disability Drive

ANGRY_KITTEN

On a June afternoon in 2004, I logged onto *Nerve* magazine's online personals site. Perhaps because my as-yet-unwritten talk for that year's MLA panel on sex and disability was in the back of my mind, my eye was caught by one of that day's "featured profiles." It belonged to "angry_kitten," a young woman who wrote that the "Celebrity I resemble most" is "Larry Flynt as a girl. Except not overweight or in a wheelchair." Clearly, this witticism implies that if references to *Hustler* magazine are sexy, especially when made by a "girl," then disability is not: being "overweight" or "in a wheelchair," that is, constitutes the antithesis of desirability. Angry_kitten's self-representation thus performs a disavowal of disability that the genre of the online personal ad seems to demand; health, slenderness, and the regular pursuit of athletic activities are among the most heavily advertised attributes on online dating services.

But angry_kitten's quip can also be read in another way. Her insertion of the phrase "in a wheelchair" into a personal ad arguably augments the transgressiveness that her self-comparison to Larry Flynt seems designed to signal; it may have the effect not only of distancing her from wheelchairs and other ostensibly unsexy images but also of metonymically linking the wheelchair, through its association with Larry Flynt, with the pornographic. By connecting disability to both sexual excess and sexual lack, angry_kitten's personal ad encapsulates two apparently opposing ways of thinking about sex and disability. Both of these modes are familiar to disability scholars, who have pointed to ubiquitous cultural representations of disabled people in terms of sexual deficiency, while also calling attention to pervasive associations of disability with excessive sexuality. For example, cognitively disabled people are commonly depicted as childlike and asexual but are also often feared as uncontrollable sexual predators.[1] Similarly, websites for "amputee devotees" present disabled women in terms that evoke sexual excess (a photo of an amputee woman shopping or washing dishes is sufficient to provide "compelling erotic entertainment") and simultaneously emphasize lack ("A woman is not whole if she does not have something missing!" www.amputee-devotee.com announces) (Gregson 2).[2]

These contradictory constructions of disability create a double bind for people with disabilities: if disability can easily be interpreted as both sexual lack and sexual excess (sometimes simultaneously), then it seems nearly impossible for any expression of disabled sexuality to escape stigma. A liberal politics of disability might respond to this problem with a reasoned refutation, pointing out that people with disabilities are as sexual as nondisabled people and are no more likely to be "freakishly" or "excessively" so. In support of this claim, one might observe that a person with a spinal cord injury has not "lost" his or her sexuality, or that there's nothing inherently pornographic or kinky about an image of a short-statured person engaging in sexual intercourse.[3] Yet the culture's unwillingness to accept these eminently reasonable claims, its persistent insistence that disabled sexuality is somehow both lack (innocence, incapacity, dysfunction) and excess (kinkiness, weirdness, perversion), suggests that something more than reasoned discourse will be necessary in order to understand and respond to the energies that drive this illogical, intractable conception of sex and disability.

These energies might usefully be read in relation to what psychoanalysis terms the "death drive." In making this argument, I am drawing on writing by Leo Bersani and Lee Edelman, which is often cited as exemplifying an "antisocial" or "antirelational" thesis in queer theory. Bersani and Edelman do not theorize "disability" as such, but as I will demonstrate, their arguments about a destructiveness that may be both inherent in sexuality and incompatible with

Anna Mollow

liberal politics—or perhaps even with any form of politics or sociality at all—are highly relevant to disability theory.

In choosing the term "disability theory" rather than "disability studies," I mean to signal a possible difference between these two discourses. For disability *theory*, I propose, sex can no longer be conceived of as a subfield or specialized area of investigation (to which a new anthology might be devoted); rather, disability theory insists, through its sustained engagement with theories of sexuality, that it is impossible to think about either term, "sex" or "disability," without reference to the other. This is because, as I will demonstrate, sex in a sense "is" disability: the concepts of "sexuality" (as it is elaborated in psychoanalytic theory) and of "disability" (as it is figured in the cultural imaginary) share profound structural similarities; in some instances, they could even be described as two names for the same self-rupturing force. Psychoanalysis calls this force the death drive; in this chapter, I propose that it might also be named the "disability drive." To foreground associations between disability and the death drive means, as we shall see, theorizing disability in terms of identity disintegration, lack, and suffering. Such terms may seem inimical to a politics of disability liberation. But in this chapter I critique politics of disability that emphasize identity formation and pride, exploring instead the benefits of highlighting those aspects of sex and disability that undercut and perhaps even preclude assertions of humanity.[4]

CAN DISABILITY THEORY HAVE *NO FUTURE*?

"The Child whose innocence solicits our defense": this ubiquitous cultural figure is the target of *No Future*, a polemic against an ideology that Edelman defines as "reproductive futurism" (2). "We are no more able to conceive of a politics without a fantasy of the future," Edelman argues, "than we are able to conceive of a future without the figure of the Child" (11). The invocation of this figure—which, Edelman makes clear, is "not to be confused with the lived experiences of any historical children"—invariably serves to uphold "the absolute privilege of heteronormativity" (11; 2). Therefore, "impossibly, against all reason," *No Future* "stakes its claim to the very space that 'politics' makes unthinkable" (3). Queerness, Edelman asserts, "names the side of those *not* 'fighting for the children'"; that is, the social order ascribes a fundamental negativity to the queer, who is structurally defined in opposition to "the Child" (*No Future* 3). While liberal politics, putting its faith in reason, seeks to refute this characterization of queerness, Edelman proposes that queers might "do better to consider accepting and even embracing" it (*No Future* 4). Queers, Edelman maintains, should respond to homophobia not only by insisting upon equal rights within the social order but also: "By saying explicitly what Law and the Pope and the whole of the Symbolic order for which they stand hear anyway in each and every expression or manifestation of queer sexuality: Fuck the social order and the Child in whose name we're collectively terrorized; fuck Annie; fuck the waif from *Les Mis*; fuck the poor, innocent kid on the Net; fuck Laws both with capital *l*s and with small; fuck the whole network of Symbolic relations and the future that serves as its prop" (*No Future* 29).[5]

This impassioned polemic is one that disability theory might well take to heart. For the figure that Edelman describes as "the disciplinary image of the 'innocent' Child" is inextricable not only from the cultural politics of queerness but also from those of disability (*No Future* 19). After all, it is in the name of the "Child whose innocence solicits our defense" that ritual displays of pity regularly demean disabled people: "Please, I'm begging for survival. I want my kids alive," Jerry Lewis implores, countering disability activists' protestations against his assertion that a disabled person is "half a person" (qtd. in Johnson, *Too Late* 58, 53). "You're against Jerry Lewis!" a surprised passerby exclaims to Harriet McBryde Johnson as she hands out leaflets protesting the Muscular Dystrophy Association, his surprise likely informed by a logic similar to that which, in Edelman's analysis, undergirds the use of the word "choice" by advocates of legal abortion: "Who *would*, after all, come out *for* abortion or stand *against* reproduction, *against* futurity, and so against *life*?" (Johnson, *Too Late* 61; Edelman, *No Future* 16). Similarly, why *would* anyone come out *for* disability, and so against the child who, without a cure, might never walk, might never lead a normal life, might not even have a future at all?

The logic of the telethon, in other words, relies on an ideology that might be defined as "rehabilitative futurism," a term that I propose might operate alongside, and often in intersection with, Edelman's "reproductive futurism." Because if the future, as Edelman maintains, is always imagined in terms of a fantasmatic "Child," then the survival of this future as the Child is, as the telethon makes clear, threatened not only by queerness but also by disability. Indeed, futurity is habitually imagined in terms that fantasize the eradication of disability: a recovery of a crippled (or hobbled) economy, a cure for society's ills, an end to suffering and disease. Eugenics' sterilization and "euthanization" of disabled people is an instantiation of a futurism grounded at once in reproductive and rehabilitative ideals: procreation by the fit and elimination of the disabled, eugenicists promised, would bring forth a better future.

Consider also Edelman's argument that "the lives, the speech, and the freedoms of adults face constant threat of legal curtailment out of deference to imaginary Children whose futures . . . are construed as endangered by the social disease as which queer sexualities register" (*No Future* 19). Replace the words "social disease" with "disease," and "queer sexualities" with "disabled bodies" and Edelman's remarks precisely articulate the connections disability activists and scholars have made between the proliferation of images of pitiable disabled children and the curtailment of actual disabled people's freedoms: in the United States today, nearly two million disabled people are confined to institutions, while poster children and their contemporary correlatives fixate a culture invested in the fantasy of a future without disability.

Given all these interconnections, it is tempting to advocate that disability theory adopt *No Future* as one of its own canonical texts. But of course adoption, in its many forms, has well-known pitfalls. Noting that it is often LGBT people themselves who deliver the "message . . . of compulsory reproduction," Edelman cites Dan Savage's self-congratulatory claim that adopting a child means choosing "something more meaningful than sit-ups, circuit parties, and designer drugs. For me and my boyfriend, bringing up a child is a commitment to having a future" (qtd. in Edelman, *No Future* 75). Textual adoption also has downsides, which Ellen Samuels highlights in her critique of "the wholesale adoption of [Judith] Butler's theoretical framework by disability scholars" ("Critical" 64). "Is it not necessary," Samuels wonders, "to at least ask if there is a difference between disability/impairment and gender/sex—and, since there obviously is, how that difference operates in the present situation?" ("Critical" 64). Also relevant in this context is Trina Grillo and Stephanie M. Wildman's famous critique of "like race" analogies, which, they argue, often have the effect of "stealing" the "center stage" from people of color (621).

In this chapter, rather than treating queerness and disability as definable categories whose differences might be elided by the imprecise use of analogy, I am interested in confounding the meaning of each. In many ways, *No Future* seems to invite such an approach: Edelman steadfastly resists the framing of queerness as an identity whose claims might be diminished by other groups' appropriations. Queerness, he maintains, refuses "every substantialization of identity" (4). However, Edelman's claim to eschew identity politics is regarded by some queer theorists as specious. In *Cruising Utopia: The Then and There of Queer Futurity*, José Esteban Muñoz characterizes *No Future* as a form of "white gay male crypto-identity politics" (95); Edelman's work (and Bersani's), he suggests, practices "a

distancing of queerness from . . . the contamination of race, gender, or other particularities that taint the purity of sexuality as a singular trope of difference" (11).

Such particularities, it is true, receive relatively marginal attention in *No
Future*. Race is mentioned in a brief footnote; in another note, Edelman observes
that the "*sinthom*osexual," his text's privileged figure for imaging queerness, is
most frequently imagined in our culture as being "embodied by machinelike men"
rather than women (165, n. 10). A marginalization of topics such as race and gender, Edelman might seem to imply, is a crucial aspect of his argument: after all,
queer theory "marks . . . the 'side' outside all political sides" (*No Future* 7). Yet
No Future's argument unfolds against a backdrop of references to issues of clear
political relevance to LGBT people: gay marriage, domestic partnership benefits,
antidiscrimination ordinances for LGBT employees, papal pronouncements about
homosexuality, queer-baiting of children, and hate crimes against queers. The embrace of queer negativity may, as Edelman insists, entail a refusal of any "determi-
nate stance or 'position,'" but *No Future*'s argument against reproductive futurism
would be far less compelling without its repeated references to—and indeed its
implied positionality in relation to—these recognizably political issues (4).

Does this lend support to Muñoz's charge that *No Future* is invested in a form
of "stealth" identity politics (94)? If, according to Edelman's argument, queers are
"singled out," or "distinctively called," to perform the rather glamorous-sounding
work of figuring "the availability of an unthinkable jouissance," then are the particular concerns of women, people of color, and disabled people (who may, of
course, also be queer) hopelessly mired in the political (109; 26; 39)? Is queer
antifuturism, as Judith Halberstam argues of "gay shame," a "White Gay Male
Thing"—and perhaps, by extension, also a "nondisabled thing" (220)?[6] "It has
been clear to many of us," Muñoz writes in an earlier critique of *No Future*, "that
the antirelational in queer studies was the gay white man's last stand" ("Thinking" 825).[7]

But in pointing to a possible dearth of discussion of race and gender (and,
one might add, disability) in *No Future*, its critics have not established that its
arguments depend upon such exclusions. On the contrary, *No Future*'s claims
about queerness's relationship to negativity and the death drive can be enhanced
through an analysis of their potential application to, and intersection with, other
minoritizing discourses. Focusing primarily on disability (perhaps one of the
"other particularities" toward which Muñoz gestures?), I argue that queer "antisocial" theory should be—and in many ways, already is—a "disabled thing." In
making this argument, I take seriously Edelman's "insistent refusal of identity

Anna Mollow

politics" and his expansive definition of queers as "all so stigmatized for fail-ing to comply with heteronormative mandates" (*No Future* 165, n. 10; 17). I thus understand *No Future* as suggesting that the embrace of negativity it advocates for queers must also be available to all subjects whom our culture abjects. Such an embrace may indeed be ethically imperative, Edelman argues, because "those of us inhabiting the place of the queer may be able to cast off that queerness and enter the properly political sphere, but only by shifting the figural burden of that queerness to someone else" (*No Future* 27).

Nor, according to my reading of *No Future*, does "choosing to *accept*" the "*structural position* of queerness," as Edelman advocates, mean abandoning all political projects (27; emphasis in original). It is "politics *as we know it*," or "every *acknowledged* politics," that Edelman refuses (*No Future* 3; emphasis added). In turning away from what "will *count* as political discourse," *No Future* assigns to queer theory an "impossible project" that might, despite itself, be described as political: that of imagining "an oppositional *political* stance exempt from" the imperatives of reproductive futurism (11; 27; third emphasis added). Moreover, Edelman would have queer theory undertake this project without wholly relin-quishing the politics we do know, that is, while continuing to insist "on our equal right to the social order's prerogatives" (*No Future* 29).

I therefore read *No Future* not as advocating that goals such as gay marriage or accessible workplaces be surrendered, but rather as insisting that the work of queer theory—and, I propose here, of disability theory—is also to unsettle the assumptions that underlie these goals. *No Future* issues a troubling challenge: can we envision a politics not framed in terms of futurism or a futurity not grounded in reproductive (or, I ask here, rehabilitative) ideology? Insofar as reproductive (and perhaps also rehabilitative) futurism seem invariably to give shape to "the only politics we're permitted to know," Edelman's refusal of the political cannot easily be dismissed (*No Future* 134).

TAKE TINY TIM

Before disability theory considers taking *No Future* as a text of its own, we may first wish to consider Edelman's take on disability. In support of his argument, in the second chapter of his book, that "acts that make visible the morbidity in-herent in fetishization" (such as antiabortion activists' penchant for displaying photographs of fetuses) are "by no means outside the central currents of social and cultural discourse," Edelman's Exhibit A is Tiny Tim:

Take, for example, Tiny Tim—or even, with a nod to the spirit of the late Henny Youngman, "take Tiny Tim, *please!*" His "withered little hand," as if in life already dead, keeping us all in a stranglehold as adamant as the "iron frame" supporting his "little limbs" . . . ; his "plaintive little voice" . . . refusing any and every complaint the better to assure its all-pervasive media magnification, in the echoes of which, year in and year out, God blasts us, every one . . . and his "patient and . . . mild" . . . disposition so thoroughly matching the perfect humility of its coercive self-display that his father with "tremulous" voice recalls how Tiny Tim "hoped the people saw him in the church, because he was a cripple, and it might be pleasant to them to remember upon Christmas Day, who made lame beggars walk, and blind men see." . . .

Very pleasant indeed. And more pleasant by half than remembering, instead, who made lame beggars lame (and beggars) and who made those blind men blind. But then, *A Christmas Carol* would have us believe that we know whom to blame already, know as surely as we know who would silence the note of that plaintive little voice and require that the "active little crutch" . . . kick the habit of being leaned on. (*No Future* 41–42)

The preceding passage may not at first appear to bode well for a disability theory adoption. For one thing, it evinces no particular interest in the politics of disability oppression: the implied referent to the "who" that made "lame beggars lame (and beggars) and who made those blind men blind" is, presumably, "the same God who putatively made them walk, and see"—rather than, as the social model of disability would insist, social structures and architectural and attitudinal barriers. And the "who" that might "require that the 'active little crutch' kick the habit of being leaned on" is not, as this formulation might suggest in another context, a rehab counselor or occupational therapist. It refers rather to Scrooge, Edelman's first example of a "canonical literary instantiation" of what he calls "*sinthom*osexuality," his neologism for an "antisocial force" that he identifies with queerness (*No Future* 39).

Given the frequency with which disabled people are portrayed as Tiny Tims, the cultural opposition that Edelman identifies between the Child and the *sinthom*osexual might seem to indicate a fundamental opposition between queerness (or *sinthom*osexuality) and disability (or the Child). But the relationship among these terms in *No Future* is more complex than this schema would suggest. In order to gain a fuller view of this complexity, we must turn to Edelman's explication of Lacan's concept of jouissance. Lacanian jouissance, Edelman writes, entails "a violent passage beyond the bounds of identity, meaning, and law" (*No Future* 25). According to Lacan, jouissance is "unnamable," and for this reason it is "akin to the quintessential unnamable, that is to say death" (qtd. in Edelman, *No Future* 25). Jouissance can take two very different forms. In the first, Edelman explains, "it gets attached to a particular object or end," thus "congealing identity around the fantasy of satisfaction or fulfillment through that object" (*No Future* 25). The death drive is manifested in this first version of jouissance when it "produces identity as mortification" (as it does, for example, in fetishizations of "fetal photos" or of the "withered little hand" of Tiny Tim) (*No Future* 25; 41). Lacan's second version of jouissance, as Edelman describes it, "tears at the fabric of Symbolic reality as we know it"; it "evokes the death drive that always insists as the void in and of the subject" (*No Future* 25). "Bound up with the first of these death drives is the figure of the Child"; "bound up with the second is the figure of the queer" (*No Future* 25–26).

If the Child and the queer occupy opposing sides of this paradigm in *No Future*, where is disability? It is everywhere. Disability is bound up with the Child, as suggested not only by Edelman's analysis of Tiny Tim but also by his description, in an earlier version of *No Future*'s first chapter, of an antiabortion billboard as a "poster child for children" and by his characterization, in his book, of the Catholic Church as "blindly committed to the figure of the Child" ("Kid" 24; *No Future* 29). And disability figures importantly in the reading of *Silas Marner* that follows Edelman's discussion of *A Christmas Carol*; the "sightless eyes" and "catalepsy" of George Eliot's protagonist aid in making the apparition of the child Eppie seem miraculous (*No Future* 55).

But disability is also enmeshed with the queerness to which, in Edelman's analysis, the Child is opposed. It can be seen in Scrooge's "stiffened" "gait" and in the figure of Captain Hook, whom Edelman describes, along with Scrooge, as embodying "a drive toward death that entails the destruction of the Child" (*No Future* 44, 21). And according to Edelman's analysis of *North by Northwest*, the film's villain, Leonard, embodying *sinthom*osexuality, is "deaf to claims of human fellowship" (*No Future* 20). Then there is irony ("that queerest of rhetorical devices" [*No Future* 23]), which, according to Paul de Man, produces "dizziness to the point of madness" (qtd. in Edelman, *No Future* 87). Tropes of disability are also present in what Edelman reads as Jean Baudrillard's "panicky offensive against reproduction without heterogenital copulation," in which sex is described as devolving into a "useless function" and humans are distinguished (unsuccessfully, Edelman argues) from "the order of the virus" (qtd. in Edelman, *No Future* 64, 62).

Edelman's apt reading of these remarks of Baudrillard in relation to what was once called "the gay plague," as well as his own plays on the word "bent," suggest that it can often be difficult, in homophobic and ableist culture, to distinguish between queerness and disability (*No Future* 62; 90).[8] Antigay religious leaders, Edelman notes, characterize queer sexualities as "unhealthy" and "ugly," and "ministries of hope" offer cures to those who have "grown sick-to-death of being queer" (*No Future* 91; 47).[9] Against the "pathology" or "social disease" as which queerness is diagnosed, queer-baiting of children, Edelman argues, functions as a form of "antigay immunization," while the narrative of *A Christmas Carol* serves as an annual "booster shot" (*No Future* 143; 19; 49).

These repetitive references to disability suggest that disability, along with irony and queerness, might be another name for what Edelman calls "the remainder of the Real internal to the Symbolic order" (*No Future* 25). Indeed, disability metaphors often seem to be the closest approximations to a name for the "unnamable" that Lacan posits as the death drive. The terms Edelman uses to describe the death drive include "wound," "fracture," "stupid enjoyment," "mindless violence," "lifeless machinery," "senseless compulsion," "disfiguration," and a "shutdown of life's vital machinery" (*No Future* 22; "Kid" 28; *No Future* 38; 23; 27; 38; 37; 44). Although these signifiers do not directly refer to specific impairments, they do, taken together, evoke the physical and mental injury and dysfunction as which disability is commonly understood.

And then there is Edelman's term "*sinthom*osexuality," a neologism formed by "grafting, at an awkward join," the word "sexuality" onto Lacan's term "sinthome." Lacan's "sinthome" is an archaic way of spelling "symptom" (qtd. in Edelman, *No Future* 33). The etymology of Edelman's term, then, is something like "symptom-sexuality." However, the Lacanian "sinthome" means more than simply "symptom"; as Edelman explains, it refers to "the particular way each subject manages to knot together the orders of the Symbolic, the Imaginary, and the Real" (*No Future* 35). The sinthome is the only means by which the subject can access the Symbolic order of meaning production; but paradoxically, because of its "stubborn particularity" (each subject's sinthome is as individual and as meaningless as a fingerprint), its unintelligibility or untranslatability, the sinthome also threatens the Symbolic order to which it provides access (Edelman, *No Future* 6; 36).

Both this access and this threat are figured as disability. In order to be constituted as a subject and to take one's place within the Symbolic order, one must be metaphorically blind: the cost of subjectivity is "blindness to this determination by the sinthome," "blindness to the arbitrary fixation of enjoyment responsible for [the subject's] consistency," "blindness" to the functioning of the sinthome (Edelman, *No Future* 36; 38). The alternative to subjectivity as disability would be, according to Lacan, "radical psychotic autism" (qtd. in Edelman, *No Future* 37). That is, whatever might alleviate our constitutive "blindness" by exposing "the sinthome as meaningless knot" must effect a "disfiguration," the consequences of which would be "pure autism" (Žižek 81, qtd. in Edelman, *No Future* 38). On the one side, blindness; on the other, disfiguration, psychosis, autism: when it comes to recognizing the senselessness of one's sinthome, it seems we're disabled if we do, disabled if we don't.

All this is enough to make one wonder why the death drive—which has less to do with literal death than with figuring a strange persistence of life in death, or of death in life (perhaps like the "living death," or "life not worth living," of which disability is often supposed to consist)—is not called the "disability drive." Writing of the contingency of disability as an identity category, Michael Bérubé observes: "Any of us who identify as 'nondisabled' must know that our self-designation is inevitably temporary, and that a car crash, a virus, a degenerative genetic disease, or a precedent-setting legal decision could change our status in ways over which we have no control whatsoever. If it is obvious why most nondisabled people resist this line of thinking, it should be equally obvious why that resistance must somehow be overcome" (viii). Might part of this resistance be attributable to a fear that, in the car crash or other identity-shattering event, it might be the driver's own hand that makes that disabling turn; that is, that the driver might be driven by an impulse, unwanted and unconscious, toward something beyond the principles of pleasure and health? Adding the name "disability drive" to the terms for this "beyond" might enable us to understand the means by which images of disability seem so powerfully to both excite and repel, to become, as Tobin Siebers writes, "sources of fear and fascination for able-bodied people, who cannot bear to look at the unruly sight before them but also cannot bear not to look" ("Disability in Theory" 178).

Signs of a disability drive may be manifested in Edelman's discussion of Tiny Tim. Take, for example, Edelman's contention that "the pleasurable fantasy of survival" in Dickens's story requires the survival of the fantasy that Tiny Tim "does not excite an ardent fear (or is it a fearful ardor?) to see him . . . at last cash in his chips" (*No Future* 45). It's a familiar cultural fantasy: cure 'em (as Dickens might hope) or kill 'em (as Edelman suggests readers must secretly wish). In this unacknowledged wish, however, there may be more at stake than either killing or curing. In the chapter that follows his reading of *A Christmas Carol*, Edelman adduces Lacan's discussion of the legend of Saint Martin, who was said to have cut his own cloak in two in order to give half of it to a beggar. "Perhaps," Lacan suggests, "over and above that need to be clothed, [the beggar] was begging for something else, namely that Saint Martin either kill him or fuck him" (qtd. in Edelman, *No Future* 83). Drawing upon this passage in his analysis of *North by Northwest*, Edelman proposes that as Leonard (played by Martin Landau) attempts to push Cary Grant's Roger Thornhill to his death from atop Mount Rushmore, he "enacts . . . the one [killing] as displacement of the other [fucking]" (*No Future* 85). Killing as displacement of fucking: might a similar displacement be at work in Edelman's attribution, to Dickens's readers, of a "fearful ardor" to see Tiny Tim "at last cash in his chips" (*No Future* 45)?

As evidence for this suggestion, take the mode by which Edelman introduces his discussion of *A Christmas Carol*: "Take Tiny Tim, *please!*," "with a nod to the spirit of the late Henny Youngman" renders Tiny Tim wifelike—clearly undesirable in this context, but not wholly uneroticized (*No Future* 41). And then there is the word "take," which, particularly when followed by the word "please," as it is here, has a meaning other than the ones Edelman seems deliberately to invoke: "take" means "fuck," and so Edelman's directive to "Take Tiny Tim, *please!*," which echoes his earlier injunction to "fuck Annie; fuck the waif from *Les Mis*; fuck the poor, innocent kid on the Net," seems to authorize an additional imperative: fuck Tiny Tim. "Fuck" here means, of course, "remove" or "the hell with," but it also means fuck.[10]

And don't these two ways in which *No Future* says "fuck Tiny Tim" coincide with what disability theory most ardently desires? "Fuck Tiny Tim, *please!*": rid us, please, of this most reviled textual creation. And also: if it is our cultural mandate to embody this pitiable, platitude-issuing, infantilized, and irritating figure—well, then fuck us, every one. Fuck us because figuratively, we are already "so fucked" by our culture's insistence, through this figure, that the disabled are not fuckable. And this insistence, *No Future* gives us the tools to understand, must be understood as a displacement; propelling every cultural representation of disability as undesirable, I propose, is a "fearful ardor," an unacknowledged drive.

Sex, linguistic convention suggests, is inseparable from disability: we speak of being blinded by love or going mad with desire; we say we suffer from lovesickness and succumb to fits of passion. Lust renders us dizzy and weak in the knees. In the throes of desire, we tremble, stammer, forget our words, and lose our memories. But in other ways, common sense indicates that sex is *not* disability: a sensory impairment is not the same as an orgasm; a building without ramps is not equivalent to the merging of bodies in sexual acts; the experience of chronic pain differs from the sensation of a first kiss with a new lover. Such literal correspondences are not what I have in mind when I ask, as I do in the remainder of this chapter, whether sex "is" disability. In particular, I wish to be clear that I am not suggesting, as Freud claimed, that individuals become sick or disabled as a means of fulfilling unconscious desires. On the contrary, I consider Freud's theories of "primary gain" (according to which ill people derive erotic enjoyment from their ailments) and "secondary gain" (in which disability is desired because it confers social rewards) as themselves symptomatic of the disability drive, that is, of the ways in which, in the cultural imagination (or unconscious), disability is *fantasized* in terms of a loss of self, of mastery, integrity, and control, a loss that, both desired and feared, is indissociable from sexuality.

This argument is analogous to those Edelman makes in relation to queerness. Noting that our culture ascribes to queer sexualities an intrinsic murderousness and suicidality (as evident in some right-wing commentators' assertions that male homosexuality constitutes "a culture of death," a natural outcome of which is serial killing),[11] Edelman advocates more than a simple refutation: "Without ceasing to refute the lies that pervade these familiar right-wing diatribes," he asks, "do we also have the courage to acknowledge, and even to embrace, their correlative truths?" (*No Future* 40; 22). For Edelman, these "correlative truths" are twofold: *all* sexuality is destructive, not in the sense of effecting literal death, but in the threat it poses to the integrity of the subject and thus to the social order; and for this reason queers, onto whom the dominant culture projects the destructive aspects of sexuality it refuses to acknowledge in itself, should welcome their association with the death drive. Edelman thus responds to a minoritizing, essentializing, and homophobic formulation (gay men as murderers) not through disavowal (really, our sexuality is gentle and loving) but through a nuanced reworking of it (all sexuality is destructive in complicated ways that should be embraced).

I take a similar tack in my argument about a disability drive, a term that I posit not as a name for a new "instinct" that could empirically be validated or disproved, but as another appellation for—and thus another way of understanding—what psychoanalysis calls the death drive. At the same time that I contest the widespread ableist and minoritizing assumption that people with chronic pain and illness enjoy and perhaps even cause their impairments, I also ask: what would it mean to embrace this assumption's "correlative truths"? As a way of beginning this exploration, I turn to Bersani's essay, "Is the Rectum a Grave?" Published in 1987, during the early years of the AIDS pandemic, this still highly influential essay seeks to understand the phobic, hostile, and blaming attitudes directed at gay men during this time. These attitudes, of course, remain in play today. Indeed, I would propose that "Is the Rectum a Grave?" should be considered a key text for contemporary disability theory. Although Bersani's essay doesn't employ terms such as "ableism" or "disability," it powerfully articulates connections between ableism and homophobia; that is, it analyzes the ways in which ableism—manifested here as a murderous hatred directed at people with a particular impairment—has "legitimized" an unleashing of "homophobic rage" ("Rectum" 28; 19).

Drawing on psychoanalytic theory in order to account for this convergence of ableism and homophobia, Bersani asks why, in dominant cultural discourses about AIDS, gay men are represented as "killers" ("Rectum" 17). This question brings up issues that intersect both with Edelman's concerns in *No Future* (gay men as murderers) and those I am raising here (disabled people as blameable for impairments ostensibly resulting from perverse sexual enjoyment). "What is it exactly," Bersani asks, "that makes [gay men] killers?" ("Rectum" 17). "Everyone agrees that the crime is sexual," but "the imagined or real promiscuity for which gay men are so famous," Bersani suggests, may be less important than cultural fantasies surrounding anal sex: "Women and gay men spread their legs with an unquenchable appetite for destruction. This is an image with extraordinary power; and if the good citizens of Arcadia, Florida could chase from their midst an average, law-abiding family, it is, I would suggest, because in looking at three hemophiliac children they may have seen—that is, unconsciously represented— the infinitely more seductive and intolerable image of a grown man, legs high in the air, unable to refuse the suicidal ecstasy of being a woman" ("Rectum" 18).[12]

"But why 'suicidal'?" In part, Bersani proposes, because "*To be penetrated is to abdicate power*" ("Rectum" 19; emphasis in original). Writing against what he refers to as "the *redemptive reinvention of sex*," Bersani contests the common assumption that sexuality is "in its essence, less disturbing, less socially abrasive, less violent, more respectful of 'personhood' than it has been in a male-dominated, phallocentric culture" ("Rectum" 22; emphasis in original). This notion, Bersani argues, informs an entire range of positions on "the battlefield of sexual politics," from antipornography activism to celebrations of bathhouses and SM ("Rectum" 22). Against this redemptive project—a project inspired, he maintains, by a "profound *moral revulsion* with sex"—Bersani asserts that sex is, "at least in certain of its ineradicable aspects—anticommunal, antiegalitarian, antinurturing, antiloving" ("Rectum" 22; emphasis in original). Eschewing redemption, Bersani asks, as Edelman does in *No Future*, what it would mean to insist upon, and even to celebrate, sexuality's imbrications with the death drive: "if the rectum is the grave in which the masculine ideal . . . of proud subjectivity is buried, then it should be celebrated for its very potential for death"—not the biological death brought about by AIDS, but rather "the risk of self-dismissal, of *losing sight* of the self" ("Rectum" 29; 30; emphasis in original). Sex, Bersani argues, threatens "the sacrosanct value of selfhood, a value that accounts for human beings' extraordinary willingness to kill in order to protect the seriousness of their statements" ("Rectum" 30).

This argument is highly relevant to disability theory, not only because Bersani articulates it here in relation to AIDS phobia but also because— even more important for my purposes in this chapter—much of what Bersani claims that sexuality ineradicably "is" could be understood as disability. This can be seen, for instance, in Bersani's argument that "a gravely *dysfunctional* aspect of what is, after all, the *healthy pleasure* we take in the operation of a *coordinated and strong* physical organism is the temptation to deny the perhaps equally strong appeal of *powerlessness*, of the *loss of control*" ("Rectum" 23–24; emphasis added). In this formulation, what might be termed able-bodiedness (health, pleasure, coordination, strength) seems, on the one hand, to be opposed to terms commonly associated with disability ("powerlessness," "loss of control") but, on the other hand, to be itself disabling (there is a "gravely dysfunctional"—or, we might say, "severely disabled"—"aspect" of this "healthy pleasure").[13] Similarly to Edelman, Bersani seems to be arguing that what stabilizes and gives coherence to the subject is in a sense disabling (metaphorically "blind" for Edelman, literally "dysfunctional" for Bersani) and yet, paradoxically, that these disabling congealments of identity serve as defenses against a more radically disintegrating force, which I have been calling the disability drive, in which sexuality and disability begin to merge.

In *The Freudian Body* (which was published in 1986, one year before "Is the

Rectum a Grave?"), Bersani argues that "the most radical originality of psycho-analysis . . . has to do with a *disabled* consciousness" (6; emphasis in original). The *"disabled"* aspect of consciousness to which Bersani refers is sexual; psycho-analytic theory and therapy resist, but cannot escape enacting, "the devastat-ing pleasures of an eroticized" and "inherently dysfunctional consciousness" (*Freudian* 6). This eroticized and dysfunctional (or sexual and disabled) con-sciousness is manifested in "a certain type of failure in Freud's thought," which Bersani wants to "celebrate" in *The Freudian Body* (3). This "failure," or "theoreti-cal collapse," Bersani figures as disability: "psychoanalytic reflection on desire," he writes, is "paralyzed" and "madly excessive"; a "beneficent discursive paraly-sis—or at the very least, a beneficent discursive stammering" is "at the heart of Freudian discourse" (*Freudian* 5; 31). Such beneficent symptoms appear, Bersani argues, when what Freud wants to be saying about topics such as sexuality and the death drive comes into conflict with the conclusions to which, apparently de-spite his intentions, his arguments seem to be leading.

This can be seen, for instance, in *Three Essays on the Theory of Sexuality*, in which Freud's teleological argument (according to which orality and anality are stages of development on the road to a mature heterogenitality) is undermined by a competing characterization of sexuality that Bersani draws out, according to which the "abortive, incomplete, and undeveloped beginnings of our sexual life constitute and exhaust its essence" (*Freudian* 40). This "abortive, incomplete and undeveloped" "essence" of sexuality can be understood as disability; it refers to what Bersani calls a "biologically dysfunctional process of maturation" in which "we desire what nearly shatters us" (*Freudian* 39). According to the strand of thought that Bersani isolates in Freud, "the pleasurable unpleasurable tension of sexual excitement occurs when the body's 'normal' range of sensation is ex-ceeded, and when the organization of the self is momentarily disturbed" (*Freud-ian* 38). Thus, "sexuality would be that which is intolerable to the structured self" (*Freudian* 38). "Sexual pleasure enters the Freudian scheme," Bersani quotes Jean Laplanche as noting, "within the suffering position" (qtd. in *Freudian* 41). "The *mystery* of sexuality is that we seek not only to get rid of this shattering tension but also to repeat, even to increase it" (*Freudian* 38; emphasis in original). For this reason, Bersani famously asserts, "sexuality . . . could be thought of as a tau-tology for masochism" (*Freudian* 39).

Might it also be thought of as a tautology for disability? Disability, not nec-essarily in any phenomenological or ontological sense, but rather as it is com-monly figured: as "undeveloped," "abortive," or "unpleasurable," as "loss of self," "failure," "dysfunction," "collapse," the "suffering position." Sex is disability: we desire what nearly shatters us; we desire what disables us. But, it might be objected, doesn't such a claim derive from precisely the model of disability that we should be contesting? After all, disability scholars and activists have insisted that disability is *not* failure, dysfunction, loss, or suffering—that instead it is merely a form of physical or mental difference—or rather, that it is the social process by which benign human variations are stigmatized *as* failure, loss, or lack. And so one might argue that, in the interests of upholding this redefinition, we should critique, rather than embrace, Bersani's and Edelman's uses of disability as metaphor for these abjected states.

Is it possible, though, that the project of reinventing disability as difference rather than suffering or loss is informed by a "*moral* revulsion" not unlike that which inspires the "*redemptive reinvention of sex*" that Bersani critiques ("Rectum" 22; emphasis in original)? The "redemptive reinvention of sex," like the redefinition of disability I have been describing, emphasizes the value of diversity. "The revulsion," Bersani characterizes this project as arguing in relation to gay male sexuality, "is all a big mistake: what we're really up to is pluralism and diversity, and getting buggered is just one moment in the practice of those laudable humanistic virtues" ("Rectum" 26). Or: the pity and fear are all a big mistake; what we're really embodying is variation and difference, and suffering and loss, if they are present at all, are insignificant aspects of the disability experience.

It "is perhaps necessary," Bersani writes, "to accept the pain of embracing, at least provisionally, a homophobic representation of homosexuality" ("Rectum" 15). Might we consider, analogously, embracing a representation of disability that some would consider ableist? "Sex" and "disability," I am arguing, can be read in psychoanalytic discourse as two names for, or perhaps two sides of, the same process: that which Bersani calls "the terrifying appeal of a loss of the ego, of a self-debasement" ("Rectum" 27). Although we are more likely to call that which is "terrifying" about this "self-debasement" disability and that which is appealing "sex," the profound imbrication of these two terms is evident in the multiple instances in Bersani's and Edelman's work (and in the writing of Freud, Lacan, Laplanche, and others whom they cite) in which disability is called upon to figure the self-rupturing aspects of sex. The "redemptive reinvention of sex" denies this imbrication, seeking to move sex away from disability as it is commonly understood ("what nearly shatters us"); a redemptive reinvent of disability may move disability away from sex, at least as sex is understood in psychoanalytic accounts ("that which is intolerable to the structured self") (Bersani, *Freudian*

39; 38). Therefore, if revulsion or disavowal characterize our responses to constructions of disability as that which debases or nearly shatters our selves—that is, if we insist instead on our personhood and pride—we may risk contributing to an already pervasive cultural desexualization of disability. And in refusing sex as disability, we also risk obscuring what Bersani perceives as "the inestimable value of sex" (and, I would add, of disability): the threat they pose to the integrity of the self, or ego, in defense of which humans have been so willing to kill ("Rectum" 22). Moreover, in seeking to cast off stigma, in asserting proud disabled identities, the "best" we can hope for may be, to adapt Edelman's words, "shifting the figural burden of [disability] to someone else" (*No Future* 28).

Edelman, as we have seen, posits queerness as the name for the "*structural position*" that bears the burden of figuring the negativity of the death drive (*No Future* 27; emphasis in original). This structural position could also be understood as disability. Indeed, sex—or, more precisely, the negativity that Bersani and Edelman each describe as inhering in sexuality—is, their work makes clear, always also disability: the stammering, paralysis, autism, blindness, psychosis, deafness, dysfunction, loss, lack, suffering, incompleteness, and disease as which, in their writing and the psychoanalytic discourse that informs it, this negativity is repeatedly figured.

PITIABLE OR DISREPUTABLE

I wish to be clear that the argument I am making about the disability drive is not a minoritizing one, according to which some people (whom we call masochists) find disability erotic—or, conversely, some people (whom we call disabled) are secretly masochistic. Rather than thinking of sex and disability primarily in relation to identities (such as the masochist or the disabled person), I want to examine the ways in which these identity categories function to cordon off, as the particular concerns of a minority group, what I am arguing are better understood as ubiquitous mergings of sex and disability. Reading the disability drive in this way, I suggest, may have important implications for how disability is understood in a range of contexts, including those not immediately legible as "sexual." In particular, the concept of the disability drive may provide a way of responding to problems that have beset disability studies' construction of disability as a minority identity.

This construction, in its emphasis on visible difference and its downplaying of suffering, has sometimes had the effect of marginalizing invisible impairment

Anna Mollow

and illness, as writers such as Samuels, Liz Crow, and Susan Wendell have observed.[14] Chronic illness, pain, and depression, according to these writers, don't always conform to disability studies' dominant models. Indeed, they may even seem to contradict them. For example, people with chronic pain, rather than contending with maudlin displays of pity, must often labor to convince others that they are genuinely suffering, not just "looking for attention."

These critiques persuasively demonstrate a need to differentiate between common cultural responses to disabling illness (which is often "invisible") and visible disability (which often does not involve sickness). Interestingly, though, even some forms of visible bodily difference don't quite fit disability studies' foundational paradigms. For example, fat people are less likely to be pitied as victims suffering from a tragic disease than to be blamed for "overeating" and other forms of self-indulgence.[15] Indeed, the question of blame seems crucial here: in which contexts are disabled people regarded as victims, and in which are they seen as agents, of their impairments? With this question in mind, I propose that alongside arguments distinguishing between illness and bodily difference, or between visible and invisible disability, we might consider, as an additional heuristic, a distinction between representations of disability as "pitiable" or as "disreputable."

Disability studies has had much to say about figurations of disability as pitiable, in which unwanted sympathy precludes recognition of any enjoyment disabled people might find in lives assumed to be "not worth living." The field has had less to say about an inverse process, often operating in relation to disabilities that contemporary culture deems disreputable, in which sympathy that may be desired (as well as accommodation) is withheld from disabled people who are blamed for impairments imagined to derive from "unhealthy" enjoyments (e.g., fatness, alcoholism, addiction, HIV, AIDS, psychiatric disability, or chronic illness with no clearly defined medical cause).[16] Yet these apparently divergent cultural responses to disability—imaged as precluding enjoyment or, alternatively, as deriving from excessive enjoyment—are shown to be interconnected when, reading sex and disability together, we understand the enjoyment in question as erotic—and when, using the concept of the disability drive, we take measure of the complex ways in which the eroticism infusing cultural figurations of disability circulates. Pervasive cultural fantasies of (pitiable) disability as foreclosing possibilities of pleasure, and of (disreputable) disability as arising from indulgence in destructive pleasure, have something crucial in common: they each eroticize disability (or, we might say, they fantasize it in sexual ways), and they each do so without acknowledging the enjoyment such fantasies afford to those who indulge them.

Take, for example, the father of psychoanalysis, who is also a likely progenitor of the "it's all in your head" skepticism that many people with chronic illness or pain confront. Where "hysteria is found," Freud asserts, "there can be no question of 'innocence of mind'" (*Dora* 42). Thus, his patient Elizabeth von R. appears to experience a "voluptuous tickling sensation" when Freud touches her painful leg (*Studies* 137); Dora's sore throats derive from a history of childhood masturbation and an unconscious desire to fellate her father; and Freud suggests that the nosebleeds of another patient are due to her "*longing*" for him (qtd. in Masson 101; emphasis Freud's). In what might be interpreted as the analyst's desire for his disabled patients to desire him, we can discern signs of a disability drive. That is, what might appear as merely a stubborn refusal, on Freud's part, to allow for any distinction between his patients' disabilities and their sexualities may point us to the stubbornness of a drive—a drive that insists, as we have seen, on the indisseverability of sex and disability. And I suggest that the enjoyment such a drive may afford—notwithstanding Freud's oft-quoted protestation that he is "simply claim[ing] for [him]self the rights of the gynaecologist," not "gratifying sexual desires"—is by no means confined to the "hysterics" (or their contemporary correlatives as "somatizers" or "hypochondriacs") whose bodies and minds are made to figure this indisseverability (*Dora* 3).

Sex as disability, figured as the pathology of a disabled minority, can be made to signify a sexualized disreputability, in regard not only to "hysterics" or "hypochondriacs," whose deviant desires can putatively be read on their bodies, but also to those termed "promiscuous," "addicted," "compulsive," or "queer," who are blamed for "spreading AIDS"; the "obese" or "overweight," who supposedly can't get enough of the food they are said to substitute for sex; and the "mentally unstable," whose sexual urges, it is feared, are unchecked by "normal" inhibitions. Paradoxically, though, sex as disability also infuses the minoritizing construction of disability as pitiable. "I know what they're all thinking. My dick doesn't work," John Hockenberry writes (87). He recounts being asked by a flight attendant: "I guess you are the first handicapped person I have ever seen up close. Have you ever thought of killing yourself?" The airline worker then voices "her other big question": "Can you, I mean, can your body, I mean are you able to do it with a woman?" (Hockenberry 97).

The flight attendant's excited questioning evinces signs of the disability drive, which we might also refer to as a compulsion toward, to adapt Bersani's words, "the suicidal ecstasy of being [disabled]" ("Rectum" 18). Disability, it seems, is erotically charged, even (or especially) when it is imagined to negate the possibility of sexual enjoyment. Indeed, the argument I have been making, that sex in some ways "is" disability—that is, that "sex" and "disability" often serve as different signifiers for the same self-disintegrating force—enables us to perceive elements of sexual fantasy in the familiar statement, "I'd kill myself if I were disabled."

DISABLING "THE HUMAN"

Not wishing to be seen as either disreputable or pitiable, disabled people have protested: those with chronic fatigue, chronic pain, or chemical sensitivity insist that their impairments have biological, rather than psychosocial, causes; wheelchair users explain that they value and enjoy their lives; blind or deaf people reiterate that they don't necessarily long to see or hear; some people with psychiatric disabilities emphasize that theirs is an organic disease of the brain, not an alibi for laziness or other character flaws, while others argue against the construction of "mental illness" as a category of disease. Taken together, each of these ways of reframing disability can be seen as participating in a broader project, articulated by disability studies and the disability rights movement, of allowing disabled people to be recognized as human beings (rather than merely the objects of the dominant culture's fantasies, sexual or otherwise). Hence, the title of the Berkeley poet and journalist Mark O'Brien's autobiography: *How I Became a Human Being*. O'Brien's answer to the question his book's title implies is unequivocal: it was the disability rights movement that enabled him to escape "the living death of nursing homes" and to be treated, for the first time, "as a human being" (*Human Being* 3; 4).

But here a problem emerges: as we have seen, the writing by Bersani and Edelman that I have examined forwards powerful arguments against the project of becoming human. Urging queers to embrace the "inhumanity of the *sinthomosexual*," Edelman observes that the liberal goal of expanding the category of "human" to encompass those presently excluded from it will not "stop the cultural production of figures" made to embody the inhumanity of the death drive (*No Future* 107).

What would it mean for disability theory to embrace disabled people's figuration as inhuman? As we contemplate this possibility, a moment from *How I Became a Human Being* may give us pause. After a presentation by the physicist Stephen Hawking at the U.C. Berkeley campus, O'Brien posed the following question: "Doctor Hawking, what can you say to all the disabled people who are stuck in nursing homes or living with their parents or in some other untenable situation and who feel that their life is over, that they have no future?" (*Human Being* 230). A response that might be derived from Edelman's book—that there is, and can be, no future, since the future, by definition, can only ever be a fantasy ("always / A day / Away," in Annie's paean to "Tomorrow")—hardly seems more adequate than Hawking's reply: "All I can say is that one must do the best one can in the situation in which one finds oneself" (*No Future* 30; *Human Being* 231).

In light of O'Brien's question, Edelman's embrace of the death drive, or Bersani's celebration of what he calls "the breakdown of the human itself in sexual intensities," can easily appear as irresponsible theoretical indulgences ("Rectum" 29). Indeed, the word "irresponsible" is one that Bersani himself uses when he reflects, at a distance of thirteen years, on "Is the Rectum a Grave?": "Much of this now seems to me a rather facile, even irresponsible celebration of 'self-defeat.' Masochism is not a viable alternative to mastery, either practically or theoretically" ("Sociality" 110). This remark highlights important shifts and ambivalences in Bersani's thinking over the course of his career, which may serve as an entry into the question of the status of the human in disability theory.

Bersani and Edelman are often cited, as if in the same breath, as proponents of an "antisocial" or "antirelational" "thesis" in queer theory, in opposition to which some critics of their work, such as Muñoz, have defined their own projects as "utopian."[17] But Bersani's work, rather than conforming to either side of a utopian/antirelational binary, often reveals an interest in thinking in both of these ways at once. For example, writing of passages in his book, *Homos* (published in 1995) that are frequently cited as the origin of the "antirelational thesis," Bersani describes the "performance of antirelationality" that he celebrates in Jean Genet's *Funeral Rites* as a "*utopic* form of revolt" ("Sociality" 103; emphasis added). This joining of the utopian and the antirelational corresponds to what Bersani describes, in an essay published in 2004, as a central concern throughout his career: "a dialogue (both conciliatory and antagonistic) between" Foucault and Freud ("Fr-oucault" 133). In this essay and other recent writings, Bersani moves away from the "Freudian" and toward the "Foucauldian." Worrying that the psychoanalytic (or antirelational) side of this paradigm may be politically irresponsible (insofar as its insistence on the intractability of the death drive seems "resistant to any social transformations whatsoever"), Bersani has become increasingly interested in the creation of what, invoking a phrase of Foucault's, he calls "new relational modes" ("Fr-oucault" 134).

Interestingly, this "admittedly utopic" project often employs a rhetoric of futurism, both reproductive and rehabilitative (Bersani, "Fr-oucault" 134). For example, in a reading of Plato's *Symposium*, Bersani approvingly observes that "the goal of a love relation with Socrates" is "the bringing to term of the other's pregnancy of soul" ("Sociality" 110; 117).[18] Not only a pregnancy but perhaps also a rehabilitation of the soul is at stake at moments in which a utopian impulse is evident in Bersani's work—as when, for example, he speaks of effecting "a *curative* collapse of social difference," or of enabling a future enjoyment of "as yet unarticulated pleasures" that have thus far been "suppressed and *crippled*" (*Homos* 177; "Fr-oucault" 137; emphasis added).

If, as these examples suggest, Edelman is correct in asserting that we cannot think of the future without reference to the Child—and if I am right in suggesting that the overlapping ideology of rehabilitative futurism is equally pervasive and insidious—then how *should* disability theory answer O'Brien's question? The disability rights movement, of course, has already provided compelling responses: protestations against the injustice of institutionalization, critiques of the nursing home lobby, and advocacy for attendant programs. Theoretically, it could be said that the goal of de-institutionalization is merely a liberal one, as it aims only to include disabled people within the social fabric. Yet in this instance (and many similar ones), an imperfect politics clearly seems better than no politics at all.

But what is the role of disability *theory* in relation to this politics? Is it, as Paul Longmore described disability studies in 2003, to serve as the "academic counterpart to disability rights advocacy" (*Burned* 2)? Or should disability theory conceive of itself as sometimes in tension with this movement (as queer theory often is in relation to the mainstream LGBT movement)? Insofar as it has acted as a "counterpart" to the disability rights movement, disability studies has made crucial contributions to what might be called a humanizing enterprise. It has offered, for example, myriad analyses of the reasons for our society's willingness—its desperation, even—to dehumanize and exclude disabled people, even to the point of locking them up.

But when sex enters the picture, things get complicated. Consider, for example, the following remark, made by a doctor to a group of patients at one of

O'Brien's rehabilitation hospitals: "You may think you'll never have sex again, but remember . . . some people do become people again" (*Human Being* 80). The doctor's comment points to a paradox that inheres in any conversation about sex and disability: disabled people, it is implied here, are less than fully human because they are presumed not to "have sex"—but sex, psychoanalysis shows us, is radically *de*humanizing, effecting a "shattering" of "the structured self" rather than its entrenchment in personhood or identity. This paradox is at the root of the double bind I discussed in the introduction to this chapter, in which disability simultaneously figures sexual excess and sexual lack: disabled people are regarded as sexually deficient and therefore not fully human, but at the same time, disabled people register as less than human because disability is the ubiquitous figure for a dehumanizing, identity-disintegrating force that resembles sex.

If, as the second half of this paradoxical construction suggests, assertions of humanity are in necessary conflict with expressions of sexuality, then perhaps disability theory should, rather than seeking to humanize the disabled (insisting that disabled people be treated "as human beings"), instead ask how disability might threaten to undo, or disable, the category of the human. It might do so in part by attending to the insights Bersani's and Edelman's readings of psychoanalytic theory yield, according to which sex, far from enabling us to "become people," ruptures the self and dehumanizes us all.

But what, then, would become of disability politics? Critics of *No Future*—despite Edelman's insistence that its argument pertains to "figurality," not to "being or becoming" the death drive—tend to read the book as advocating, on a literal level, the abandonment of hope and political goals (*No Future* 17; 25).[19] As noted earlier, however, it is "politics *as we know it*" that Edelman refuses, and even this refusal does not mean that queers should stop insisting on "our equal right to the social order's prerogatives" (*No Future* 3; 29; emphasis added). Edelman further clarifies this point in his essay "Ever After": "Without for a moment denying the importance that distinguishes many [political] projects, I want to insist on the need for an ongoing counterproject *as well*: a project that's willing to forgo the privilege of social recognition" (473; emphasis added).

Such a counterproject—one that can be read as possibly opposing the humanizing impulse behind O'Brien's narration of *How I Became a Human Being*—may take shape in some of O'Brien's own poetry. While the title of his autobiography speaks of becoming human, his unpublished poem "Femininity" disrupts this trajectory. O'Brien writes of lying:

Anna Mollow

Naked on the gurney
in the hospital corridor,
surrounded by nurses,
tall, young, proud of their beauty,
admiring my skinny cripple body.
"You're so thin,
you should've been a girl."
"I wish my eyelashes
were as long as yours."
"Such pretty eyes."
I thought
or think I thought
or wish I'd said,
"But your bodies work.
Get scissors,
cut my cock and balls off.
Make me a girl,
without anaesthesia,
make me a girl,
make me a girl."[20]

Much of the unnerving intensity of these lines derives from what, invoking Bersani, we might refer to as their embrace of "the suicidal ecstasy of being a woman" (or a girl, or queer, or disabled); from their rejection, that is, of the ideology of rehabilitative futurism, and from their refusal to engage in a "redemptive reinvention" of sex or disability. O'Brien's speaker does not plead with the nurses who admire his "skinny cripple body" to "cure me" or "make me walk again." Nor does he attempt to redefine his body (which does not "work") as merely a manifestation of human variation. Suffering and lack, rather than being dissociated from disability, are amplified and eroticized: "cut my cock and balls off . . . without anaesthesia," the speaker implores, the repetition of his plea ("make me a girl, / make me a girl") evoking the repetitiveness of a drive.

"Femininity" can indeed be read as an instantiation of the disability drive: disability in this poem, like "the rectum" in Bersani's essay, "is the grave in which the masculine [and nondisabled] ideal of proud subjectivity is buried." It will of course be tempting to evade this "nightmare of ontological obscenity" ("Rectum" 29), this fantasy of *un*-becoming human.[21] But the dehumanizing double binds that so persistently structure cultural representations of sex and disability suggest that such evasions may be futile. Intrinsically obscene, yet inherently asexual: rather than attempting to assume a different position within this impossible paradigm, disability theory should perhaps underscore its pervasiveness as evidence of a disability drive; as a sign, that is, that our culture's desexualization of disabled people functions to defend against a deeply rooted but seldom acknowledged awareness that all sex is incurably, and perhaps desirably, disabled.

NOTES

This chapter benefited greatly from thoughtful comments from Robert McRuer, Ellen Samuels, and Joshua J. Weiner.

1. See Michel Desjardins's and Michelle Jarman's chapters in this volume for discussions of social perceptions of cognitively disabled people's sexualities.

2. For a thorough discussion of the sexual politics of "amputee devoteeism," see Alison Kafer's chapter in this volume, as well as her essays "Amputated Desire, Resistant Desire: Female Amputees in the Devotee Community" and "Inseparable: Constructing Gender through Disability in the Amputee-Devotee Community."

3. Barbara Faye Waxman-Fiduccia discusses websites that equate disability with kinkiness ("Sexual"). For a personal narrative about his friends' assumptions that his spinal cord injury rendered him "sexually dead," see Hooper.

4. To take up influential arguments in queer theory regarding the self-rupturing aspects of sex—as well as disability, I propose in this chapter—would move disability theory away from the identity politics that has predominated in disability studies. The status of identity politics in the field is a central concern in two recent books that each contain the word "theory" in their titles: Robert McRuer's *Crip Theory: Cultural Signs of Queerness and Disability* and Tobin Siebers's *Disability Theory* offer two contrasting accounts of what crip and disability theory should look like. Disability theory, as I construe it in this chapter, has more in common with McRuer's "crip theory," which entails a critique of liberal identity politics, than with Siebers's "disability theory," which involves "a defense of identity politics" (*Disability Theory* 14). In this chapter I retain the term "disability" (although I do also like "crip"), because I appreciate its grammatical negativity ("dis") and because, in different ways from "crip" (which, despite its increasingly flexible uses, does nonetheless, as it derives from "cripple," seem to privilege certain forms of impairment), "disability" has an extremely expansive definitional capacity. For a critique of Siebers's earlier arguments in favor of identity politics, see my essay "Disability Studies and Identity Politics: A Critique of Recent Theory."

5. "Laws with capital *ls*" refers to former Boston Cardinal Bernard Law's contention

that health care benefits should be denied to same-sex partners of city employees on the grounds that "society has a special interest in the protection, care and upbringing of children" (qtd. in Edelman, *No Future* 29).

6. Halberstam seems to imply this when she writes, in her blurb of Muñoz's book: "Muñoz insists that for some queers, particularly queers of color, hope is something one cannot afford to lose and for them giving up on futurity is not an option."

7. Muñoz's response to *No Future* was part of an MLA panel in 2005, "The Antisocial Thesis in Queer Theory," that was moderated by Robert Caserio and also included Edelman, Halberstam, and Tim Dean. The panelists' positions were published the following year in *PMLA*.

8. The online journal *Bent*, which features "True Stories of Disabled Gay Men," plays on the dual connotations of this term. For analyses of the inextricability of ableism and homophobia, see McRuer's *Crip Theory* and Kafer's "Compulsory Bodies."

9. Susan Schweik's *The Ugly Laws: Disability in Public* offers a thorough analysis of the connections between disability and "ugliness," as manifested in the "ugly laws" (antivagrancy ordinances that targeted visibly disabled people) in late nineteenth- and early twentieth-century American cities.

10. Performance artist Greg Walloch's film, *Fuck the Disabled*, plays on these two meanings of "fuck."

11. Referring to the serial murders committed by Andrew Cunanan, whose victims were mostly gay men, Gary Bauer and Peter A. Jay each called male homosexuality a "culture of death" (qtd. in Edelman, *No Future* 39–40).

12. Bersani refers to an incident in Arcadia, Florida, in which the house of a family with three hemophiliac children believed to have HIV was set on fire. The community's hostility toward the family was defended by the town's mayor and his wife (Bersani, "Rectum" 16–17).

13. See McRuer's *Crip Theory* for an intriguing argument about the critically queer work that the phrase "severely disabled" might perform (30–31).

14. See Crow; Wendell, "Unhealthy" and *Rejected* (19–22); and Samuels, "My Body." See also Mollow, "Disability" and "When."

15. Among fat scholars and activists, there is disagreement as to whether fatness should be included under the rubric of "disability." See Solovay 128–70.

16. My pairing of the terms "pitiable" and "disreputable" is meant to serve as a flexible heuristic, not a rigid binary; neither term always attaches in predictable ways to any given form of disability. For example, a person with a mobility impairment might be regarded in different contexts (or even simultaneously) as a pitiable victim and/or as the deserving recipient of divine retribution, while someone with a terminal illness might be pitied and/or blamed for "unhealthy lifestyle choices."

17. See, for example, Muñoz, *Cruising* 11.

18. This observation is part of a series of birthing metaphors Bersani adduces in order to critique aspects of psychoanalysis. Similar metaphors appear in *Homos*, as

when Bersani writes approvingly of Genet's narrator being "orally impregnated" by his lover (178). These images, in conjunction with an emphasis on futurism ("only what society throws off . . . can serve the future") complicate Edelman's characterization of the passage in which they appear as a "profoundly influential analysis of the anticommunalism of eros" (Bersani, *Homos* 180; Edelman, *No Future* 176, n. 30). Also noteworthy in this regard is Bersani's contention that SM "is fully complicit with a culture of death" (*Homos* 97); as noted earlier, in another context Edelman forcefully critiques the uses of the phrase "a culture of death" to describe queer sexualities (see note 11 above and *No Future* 39–40).

19. See Halberstam's comment, note 6 above. According to Muñoz, Edelman "recommends that queers give up hope" and advocates "abandoning politics" (*Cruising* 91). Lynne Huffer seems to have *No Future* in mind when she writes, "Call me Pollyanna, but I want a future: not a heteronormatively reproductive future-as-prison, but an erotic, yes-saying queer heterotopia" (186). Such responses, Teresa de Lauretis suggests, do not account for what, in a textured analysis of *No Future*, she describes as the book's "two discursive registers": "the ironic and the literal, the figural and the referential, the literary or speculative register of theory and the empirically or fact-based register of politics" (258).

20. This excerpt was provided by the Mark O'Brien papers, the Bancroft Library, University of California, Berkeley.

21. An example of a humanizing reading of "Femininity" can be found in Siebers's *Disability Theory*. Siebers provides extended and appreciative analyses of O'Brien's poetry, which are valuable for their nuanced considerations of the poet's complex reworkings of conventional constructions of gender, sexuality, and disability. However, the conclusion to Siebers's discussion of "Femininity" may obscure some of that complexity. "The poem represents disability identity as acceptance of lack," Siebers acknowledges, "*but only insofar as* lack appears as a marker of sexual power" (*Disability Theory* 173, emphasis added). And, Siebers continues, "The poem understands femininity as symbolic of lack, *but only insofar as* lack appears specifically as the enactment of sexual attractiveness" (*Disability Theory* 173, emphasis added). Thus, Siebers concludes, "O'Brien uses disability to confuse gender categories with sexual ones for the purpose of rejecting the stereotypical asexuality of disabled people and asserting that they desire to be both sexually active and attractive" (*Disability Theory* 173). In order to make the argument that countering stereotypes and asserting disabled people's power, agency, and attractiveness are central activities of "Femininity," Siebers must attempt to contain the effects of the poem's eroticization of lack (lack is present, according to Siebers, "only insofar as" it indicates sexual attractiveness or power). This reading thus elides some of the most salient aspects of O'Brien's poem: its staging of a "nightmare of ontological obscenity" in which sex and disability come together to negate, or disable, potential assertions of pride, power, and humanity.

Anna Mollow

15

....

LENNARD J. DAVIS

AN EXCESS OF SEX

Sex Addiction as Disability

I was a loving, caring man alright, but that loving and caring *had* to have its focus on a woman who fed the loving and caring back to me in the framework of a sexual relationship. Without that I was, figuratively, a polio victim without an iron lung.
—Anonymous, *Sex and Love Addicts Anonymous Handbook*

Erotomania, or de Clérambault's syndrome, is the only sexual obsession that is listed in the American Psychiatric Association's *Diagnostic and Statistical Manual of Mental Disorders*, fourth edition, text revision (*DSM-IV-TR*), the bible of psychiatric diagnosis. According to the *DSM-IV-TR*'s definition, an erotomaniac is a person who is obsessively in love with someone, usually famous or out of reach, known either slightly or not at all. The erotomaniac believes either that the desired person shares this passion too, or that given the right conditions, including stalking, the beloved can be convinced to love the erotomaniac. Erotomania is a medical diagnosis; the *DSM-IV-TR* lists it under the heading "Delusional Disorders" (American Psychiatric Association 324–25). John Hinkley Jr., who stalked Jodie Foster and shot Ronald Reagan, and Margaret Mary Ray, who stalked David Letterman, could be diagnosed as erotomaniacs.

Erotomania is a psychiatric disorder, but is it a disability? It seems to fit the medical model of disability as a pathology in need of rehabilitation or cure. It also appears compatible with the Americans with Disabilities Act's (ADA) definition of disability as "a physical or mental impairment that substantially limits one or more of the major life activities." But erotomania is not covered by the ADA; nor are its relatives, sexual addiction and sexual compulsivity, which, although they are not listed in the *DSM-IV-TR*, are recognized by many practitioners as categories worthy of professional treatment. Later in this chapter, I will discuss the differences among these terms and explain why sexual addiction is not included in the *DSM-IV-TR*. For now, I wish to ask: What would it mean to understand sex addiction as disability? If we genuinely regard psychiatric disorders as within the spectrum of disability, how can we make our established concepts of disability fit with these disorders? For example, the identitarian model of American disability studies, articulated by Simi Linton in *Claiming Disability*, celebrates disability; "I am proudly disabled" is a statement imaginable according to this model. Might the "sex addict" also proudly claim his or her status? Should disability scholars and activists fight stereotypes or negative media portrayals of adulterers, sex workers and their clients, and users of pornography?

One possible objection to viewing sexual addiction as a disability is that to do so would mean condoning violent or threatening behavior such as stalking, sexual assault, or sexual abuse of children. Yet most people who define themselves as sex addicts, or who receive treatment for related disorders, do not engage in violent behavior. Moreover, many other psychiatric disorders, despite being associated (usually incorrectly) with violence, nonetheless receive protection under the ADA and have been shown to be compatible with social models of disability.

Applying the social model of disability to sex addiction, we might therefore fight to remove the barriers that prevent sexual addicts from fully participating in society. Should we contest the medicalization of sexual diversity? Decriminalize prostitution? Forbid employers from discriminating against workers who have multiple sexual partners, dress provocatively, or attend Sex and Love Addicts Anonymous (SLAA) meetings? Are these concerns properly framed as disability issues?

There are no easy answers to these questions. They show that our models of disability are unsuited for describing many psychiatric disorders. They also highlight a need, articulated by Shelley Tremain, for understanding not only disability but also specific impairments as socially constructed categories. That is, in addition to asking what social barriers oppress sex addicts, we must also ask how sexual addiction came to be understood as a disorder and what ideological work its construction as such performs.

What "is" sexual addiction? According to popular and medical literature, sexual addiction—or the related category, sexual compulsivity—is characterized by an undue or abnormal focus on sexual activity. Sex addicts may masturbate, copulate, or fantasize too much and/or with the "wrong" sort of people. The masturbation may be so frequent, ten to twenty times a day, that it causes damage to the genitalia. Sex addicts may seek out gratification with sex workers or engage in "risky" behaviors. Or they may simply engage in the garden variety of adultery, serial partners, or scopophiliac or exhibitionist behaviors, some of which are defined as criminal. It is also possible to be a sex addict simply because of a "codependent" relationship with one person—or even with no person. A sex addict may simply have a self-perceived excessive focus on sexuality as a mechanism for providing relief or comfort. In all cases, the sex addict finds that his or her sexual activity is so great that it interrupts the "normal" flow of his or her life and the lives of other people.

Here are four first-person accounts of self-described sex addicts, all taken from the *Sex and Love Addicts Anonymous Handbook*:

> Before I was twenty years old, I had slept with more than a hundred men, suffered from VD, had three suicide attempts, been sent to a psychiatrist by the police and my parents, and had a baby whom I gave up for adoption. . . . My husband and I had sex every day, but it was never enough. I could not be happy or satisfied, and masturbated sometimes several times a day (SLAA 165)

> My sexual acting out continued at graduate school in Ohio. But my acting out became much more compulsive. I spent hours going from men's room to men's room on campus, seeking brief encounters with men. . . . I found my life taking on a pronounced split. By day, I was a graduate student/teacher, respectable, intelligent, and urbane. By night, I was a driven sex addict. I hung out in the bathrooms; I drank at the bars, I couldn't get enough. (SLAA 173)

> I knew that I was out of control. . . . [M]y sexual activities were more than simply cheating on my wife. I was filling every available moment with sex and spending a lot of time developing relationships, with sex as the sole

purpose. . . . Even more important than the sex was the thrill of the chase, the excitement of seeing whom I would be with the next weekend on a business trip. . . . But it was beginning to wear thin again and I realized that I was once again counting how many women I had, how many in the last month, etc. (SLAA 180)

Much of what these men talked about [in SLAA meetings] I initially mistook for blatant (hetero)sexism. "Of course *men* would sexually objectify women or try to make them into their mothers," I told myself. "But I'm a political, conscious lesbian. *I* don't do those things." Only I *did*, and in much the same manner as the men did. . . . Because I'm an addict, I have looked to lovers and sexual partners to fill a void in me that cannot be filled by another person. (SLAA 188–89; 190)

Certain key words stand out in these sexual addiction narratives: "abnormal," "too much," "wrong," and, of course, "normal." The point is that any discussion of sex addiction will bring us back to a set of central concepts in disability theory: the related ideas of normality, abnormality, deviance, difference, and so on, as applied to the human body and the human mind. Sex addiction cannot be separated from the normalizing discourses that, in the nineteenth century, came to dominate thinking on sexuality and physical and mental difference. The great sexual awakening (or disciplining, if you are a Foucauldian) of the nineteenth century was informed by a proliferation of ideas about sexual morality, encouragement of reproduction under the protection of marriage, and many theories relating sexuality to health.[1] Moral physiologists and, as the century progressed, sexologists lectured the public through marriage manuals and medical texts — now written in English for the general public rather than in Latin for specialized medical audiences — on the eugenic, negative, and positive aspects of sexuality. Such books were for the most part prescriptive, attempting to define deviant or perverse sexuality and to instruct readers, mostly men, on how to have "ideal" marriages with healthful and proper sex lives. The sexual awakening movement was a strange blend of progressive ideas about educating a sexually ignorant population of men, so that they could give pleasure to their wives, respect women's rights, protect the health of the couple, and understand a growing body of knowledge about human sexuality and physiology. Deeply intertwined in this narrative was a eugenic strain, which included birth control and selection of partners for better breeding.[2] On the whole, these works saw sexuality as something that had normal and abnormal parameters and that increasingly had

Lennard J. Davis

proper and improper techniques. The readers of such works were encouraged to know about the normal body, genitals, and sexual function and how to do the right things to the right body parts. Moralism and medical certainty governed and disciplined sexual behavior.

This was more or less the state of affairs until the mid-twentieth century. Our own time, ensuing from the sexual revolution of the sixties, offers fewer prescriptive and descriptive norms. In many contexts, sexuality is seen as a good in and of itself, although health and happiness are concomitant benefits, and the issue of choice and negotiation between consenting adults is a new standard of correct behavior. The old questions—how many times a day, week, month—seem fairly banal. Which orifice, which genital, which person—all have increasingly become open to question and acceptance. Fetishistic and sadomasochistic practices are no longer universally derided as deviant. In some locations, sadomasochism (SM) and its codes of morality and behavior (safe words, negotiations of scenes, etc.) are arguably almost mainstream; sexual toys, bondage equipment, and erotic clothing are now available in suburban shopping malls. As a number of sex researchers indicate, we have shifted from a discussion of the morality of sexuality to a supermarket of sexual choices and a language of negotiation. No longer is anything wrong in sexual relations, as long as whatever one desires is negotiated to the satisfaction of the participants.

Notwithstanding this free-market, neoliberal approach to sexuality, aided by the growth of the Internet, sexuality is not without its governing mechanisms.[3] In response to the efflorescence of sexual choices, a new obsessive category has been created: the sex addict. As we have seen, sex addicts are said to be too interested in sex or to have sex too much and often with the wrong kind of people—notably other sex addicts, children, animals, or sex workers. Yet, in the language of addiction, the problem is not so much the behavior per se but how you feel about it. If you feel shame, guilt, or as if the behavior is taking over your life and causing financial or emotional ruin and so on, then you are an addict. But "how you feel about it" is, of course, far from an individual matter. One's feelings of shame and guilt are deeply dependent on the social milieu that defines acceptable and unacceptable behaviors, however openly or subtly.

Although the sex addict language tends to be gender, class, and race free, framing the problem as one of individual choice and reform, there are certain ways that gender, race, and class are inextricable from this discussion. The paired concepts of nymphomania and satyriasis were among the earliest disorders the discipline of sexology defined. While both of these conditions constituted what

William Cullen in 1827 called "localized disorders of the genital organs," it was nymphomania that stayed in the klieg light of medical attention, since women were the focus of massive discussions around issues of chastity and desire in the nineteenth century (qtd. in Berrios and Kennedy 386). As middle-class white women were expected to be pure and chaste, the extreme of sexual excess was seen as more unseemly in them. For a middle-class white woman, to have the "disorder" of nymphomania meant to bear too strong a resemblance to poor women and women of color, who were assumed to be excessively sexual.

In the twentieth century, the concept of addiction took up some of the regulation of desire that sexology's concept of nymphomania had enforced in the nineteenth century. Late twentieth- and early twenty-first-century sexual imperatives for women are complex and often conflicting, demanding sometimes that women be highly sexual, but also stigmatizing inappropriate or excessive female sexuality. The notion of sexual addiction is one mode of regulating too much, or the wrong kind of, female sexual desire and activity.

To understand how "sex addiction" does this regulatory work, for women and men, and even transgendered people, alike, we must turn to the history of the broader concept of addiction. The term "addiction," in the sense of being addicted to drugs or other substances, began to be used in the twentieth century. People in the nineteenth century had a range of opiates and other drugs available to them without regulation or proscription. Anthony Giddens asserts that in a traditional society, where one's behavior is socially determined, there is no addiction; but in a society based on individual lifestyle choices, the idea of addiction arises (74–75). In fact, it is most likely that many of our grandparents or great-grandparents were, according to modern-day definitions, "addicted" to opiates or alcohol through the use of patent medicines, easily available through local stores, peddlers, and pharmacies. Such opiates included the overused "gripe water," a tincture of opium used to quell fussy babies. The modern concept of addiction arose in tandem with the banning of alcohol and then opiates, barbiturates, and other drugs. In the United States, regulation of drugs occurred during Prohibition when people turned from alcohol, now difficult to find, to marijuana, opium, cocaine, heroin, and barbiturates. Given the logic of prohibition, if alcohol was banned, surely drugs should follow.[4]

Sexual addiction, as a concept, came out of the twelve-step program for alcoholics, which itself began in 1936 with Alcoholics Anonymous (AA). The twelve-step message entered the American and English-speaking public awareness through word of mouth; two books written by the founder of AA, Bill W.; jour-

Lennard J. Davis

nalism; and a number of popular films from the 1940s through the early 1960s.[5] During this period, alcoholism morphed from a personal problem to a medical one; it became well established as such by the 1960s. We first start seeing books on sexual addiction in the 1970s, coinciding with the founding of SLAA, which held its first regular meeting in Cambridge, Massachusetts, on December 30, 1976. Once the idea had been assimilated that alcoholism might be understood as a disease—a form of chemical dependence predicated on the proclivity of some people in the population to be hyper-susceptible to alcohol or other chemicals— then it was possible to entertain the notion that people might be addicted to the chemicals involved in sexual arousal and satisfaction: endorphins, norepherine, dopamine, serotonin, and oxytocin. Like alcoholics or drug abusers, sex addicts might become dependent on particular neurochemicals.

The positing of sex addiction as a disease took part in a larger social trend during the late twentieth century, which removed the onus of moral judgment from certain behaviors by redefining them as medical problems. Yet sex addiction does not have the same legitimacy as psychiatric impairments like "schizophrenia" or "manic-depressive disorder" or even alcoholism. Because it began with twelve-step programs, its origin is nonmedical and, in a profound sense, demotic. Unlike alcoholism, it is not listed in the DSM-IV-TR; it is therefore not considered a psychiatric disorder by the medical profession.[6] Sex addiction hovers between a popular interest in obsessive behavior and a clinical suspicion of an addiction to something as "normal" as sexuality. Yet after the idea of sexual addiction permeated the popular press, practitioners began to apply it to their patients.

The genesis of sexual addiction presents some knotty theoretical problems for disability studies. The social model of disability depends upon a distinction between "impairment" (a physical condition) and "disability" (the social barriers that disable people with certain impairments). The notion of impairment generally rests upon medical diagnosis. If a person "has," say, chronic fatigue syndrome (CFS) or multiple sclerosis (MS), this means that a medical diagnosis has been made, which places the person within the protected class in regard to legislation concerning disability. Impairment, then, is not a "given"; it is conferred by medical professionals. Moreover, the process by which it is conferred is often contested. Frequently, people who have CFS, or are in the early stages of MS, have "normal" medical tests and no visible signs of disease; they are therefore often assumed to be malingering or "somatizing." Indeed, many medical professionals still maintain that CFS is not a "real" illness. Sex addiction is arguably an even more unstable category. Because it began as a popular movement, it in a sense poses a populist challenge to the medical elite, who have not yet chosen to include this disease entity in their official, professional diagnostic handbook. In the absence of a medical diagnosis, should sexual addiction be permitted to enter the safe confines of the disability category? If we say "no," are we ratifying the medical profession's authority to define disability? This problem raises another question: the postpsychiatry movement is challenging the foundational categories of psychiatry, much as disability activists have challenged similar issues relating to physical impairment. Members of the psychiatric survivor movement assert that they, not psychiatrists, are the best authorities on their bodies and minds. If disability studies refuses to accept a disease entity like sexual addiction because it is named and defined by the people who "have" it, would the field be dismissing the very tenets of the psychiatric survivor movement?

The answers to these questions are far from clear. Moreover, because of its heterogeneous origin, sex addiction carries various, sometimes conflicting, definitions. One writer claims that addiction is "a psychic state that often predates the addict's first encounter with his drug and that remains unchanged throughout the career of his substance abuse" (Trachtenberg 28). Others write, "the addict is a person who never learns to come to grips with his world, and who therefore seeks stability and reassurance through some repeated, ritualized activity. . . . The true addict progresses into a monomania" (Peele and Brodsky 27). The major organization that formulated sex addiction as a disease is SLAA. Its website contains the following information: "Addiction can take many forms, including, but not limited to, a compulsive need for sex, extreme dependency on one person (or many), and/or a chronic preoccupation with romance, intrigue, and fantasy. Sex and love addiction may also take the form of anorexia, a compulsive avoidance of giving or receiving social, sexual, or emotional nourishment." One of the immediate questions that arises is: can we say that addiction to sex is a valid form of addiction? No illegal or legal drugs are used. Ostensibly, the addiction is to one's own biochemistry and predilections. But then why can't we say that happy people are addicted to serotonin, or that sad people are addicted to the lack of serotonin? Or why not say that nursing mothers are addicted to oxytocin or prolactin, or that athletes are endorphin addicts? As one book puts it, "addiction has as much to do with love as it does with drugs. Many of us are addicts, only we don't know it. We turn to each other out of the same needs that drive some people to drink and others to heroin. And this kind of addiction is just as self-destructive as—and a lot more common than—those other kinds" (Peele and Brodsky 13). If people are addicts without knowing it—are they addicts?

Giddens takes a more sociological approach to neoliberal capitalism and sees addiction as a function of a society that encourages identity through choice. Modern societies, he argues, react to discursive control by creating new options and knowledges. Giddens uses the phrase "institutional reflexivity" to refer to a process that creates a society based on endless choices, in which "any pattern or habit can become an addiction" (75). Since choice becomes central to neoliberal consumer society, addiction is defined as the inability to choose. That is, you do something over and over again because you can't choose, because you are compelled to perform and re-perform, think and rethink. In this way, obsession is not about choosing what you are doing; it is about the fact that you can't choose to stop doing it. And the not being able to choose is finally about losing the much-valued centerpiece of neoliberal possessive individualism—the ability to choose among a variety of consumer options. Because the addict is unable to choose, he or she lives an unfulfilled life. According to SLAA, "the guilt of prior deeds and passions or missed opportunities gave way to the deepest, most pervasive guilt of all: that of having left life unlived, or having turned our backs on the possibility of fulfilling a meaningful destiny" (70). In this case, "unfulfilled" lays an accumulative metaphor—having enough to fill one—over the requirement to live a fulfilled life. Obviously a fulfilled life is one that conforms to all kinds of norms. A fulfilled sexual addict, by definition, cannot exist.

But how do we define the sex addict as opposed to any other addict? The projects of Kinsey, Masters and Johnson, and other sex researchers of the 1950s and 1960s were largely descriptive, not proscriptive or pathologizing. This trend continued through the 1980s. At the beginning of that decade, researcher John Money wrote: "It hardly needs to be said that there is no fixed standard as to how often is too often in sex, whether in terms of total orgasmic frequency, masturbation frequency, copulatory frequency with or without orgasm, homosexual or heterosexual frequency, or number of partners. The range of variations is wide, from extreme apathy and erotic inertia to a plurality of orgasms on a daily basis" (94). Money's distanced observation, presented along with the phrase "it hardly needs to be said," reflects the generality of the claim that you can't insist on a norm for sexual behavior. If you can't have a norm, how can you describe the point at which normal becomes obsessive, at which sexual activity becomes addiction?

Money's neutral, descriptive account of sexual behavior in 1980 contrasts with the language used to describe sexual addiction in other texts in the years that followed it. Indeed, the replacement of nonjudgmental analysis with patholigizing moralism is the hallmark of the sexual addiction accounts. Writing in 1988, Peter Trachtenberg defined "the Casanova Complex" as the "compulsive" addiction of males to multiple partners. Far from a distanced and scientific description of human sexual variation, Trachtenberg's approach, as is common in the more contemporary literature about sexual addiction, tends toward the moralistic. Trachtenberg says he interviewed about fifty men, whom he found by placing classified ads. He wanted to speak to men "whose relations with women were characterized by brevity, instability, and infidelity" (18). Of these men, he writes, "Their happiness seemed strained and self-willed. . . . [O]ne encounters an underlying hunger and impoverishment of spirit and an unconscious view of women as faceless instruments of pleasure, ego gratification and relief" (19). By calling their condition a "compulsion," Trachtenberg emphasizes, "I have implied that Casanovas are sick people" (29). The author offers, at the end of his book, "options available to Casanovas who wish to achieve 'sexual sobriety'" (21).

Once sexual activity is framed as a disease or addiction, it moves from the realm of a neutral descriptive narrative to another kind of recuperative narrative. It becomes, in effect, a disability. How does this happen? One way to think about this question is to consider briefly the history of Casanova, the figure Trachtenberg evokes, and see how that history changes from his own time to ours, a movement that parallels the move from descriptive to proscriptive. Reading through the writings of Giaccomo Casanova, one notices a complete absence of any medical notion of sexuality. The earliest reference to Casanova in print was written in 1823, the year the book appeared in German. Countess d'Albany writes: "Have you read, Madame, the Memoires of Casa Nuova? It is a book worse than the *Confessions* of Rousseau, but an observer and philosopher can make discoveries there not to be made elsewhere. One cannot understand how an old man of seventy could write such a confession without blushing and without remorse. He makes me detest both men and women at the same time" (qtd. in J. Childs 218).

While this assessment certainly expresses moral concern, it conveys no sense that Casanova had a medical or a psychological problem. In a letter from 1822, Heinrich Heine writes that Casanova's "autobiography stirs up much interest here." Of Casanova's work, he writes, "I would not recommend it to a woman I cherish but would to all my male friends. Out of this book there emerges a breath of sultry Italian sensuality. . . . There is not one line in the book which is in harmony with my sentiments but there is also not one line which I did not read with pleasure" (qtd. in J. Childs 285). By 1835 a writer links Casanova's sexuality with his interest in learning: "equally thorough and learned in voluptuousness and science, such is the motto I would place under the portrait of this Jean-Jacques who, without doubt, was the most remarkable figure in the social life of his century." That same writer sheds possible light on how some viewed Casanova's sexuality, noting that "a questionable mock modesty of our century has rejected his *Memoirs* with moralizings, and the police have come to the aid of this prudery by forbidding in this or that German State, the most remarkable of all books" (qtd. in J. Childs 322).

Before the late nineteenth-century emergence of sexology as a distinct field of professional knowledge, reactions to experiences such as Casanova describes might include blushing, pleasure, moralizing, and even police repression. Sex, however, was not yet subject to notions of normal, abnormal, diseased, or healthy.[7] In Trachtenberg's late twentieth-century account of a "Casanova Complex," moralization and medicalization function together; the "Casanova's sickness" and "spiritual impoverishment" are inseparable. Popular trade books such as this, along with self-help manuals, have played a very important role in developing social concepts of disease in the past century. These books, along with journalism and other media, disseminate the parameters of disease entities through the general public so that ordinary people acquire a language for describing some of the complex and ineffable features of emotional and behavioral life. Many of these books involve a first-person involvement and often a conversion experience. So Trachtenberg, along with the anonymous author of the "basic text" of *Sex and Love Addicts Anonymous Handbook*, Caveh Zahedi (who made the movie *I Am a Sex Addict*), and Michael Ryan (who wrote *Secret Life*), all tell their own stories, ending up with salvation or at least the prospect of cure through the twelve-step program. There is a strong sense of personal salvation, gratitude to the process, and a sense of occupying a moral high ground at the end of these works.

The self-help books often use scientific sources, studies, and surveys, which they cherry-pick, but mostly rely on composite fictionalized accounts of people who are usually given first names like Sam or Beth. As one book explains its method: "This is in some ways a personal book. . . . As the book has broadened in scope, I have developed the theme wherever possible in the form of psychological vignettes. These are fictional accounts, inspired not so much by clinical observations as by normal experience. Although fictional, the characters in these accounts are in a sense familiar to us all" (Peele and Brodsky 14). Another writer laments the absence of psychological studies and research, saying "we are aware that we are jumping ahead of research by describing as clearly as could be what we have gleaned from our personal and clinical experiences" (Mellody viii). Such books do not operate exclusively in the realm of the factual; they work in the area of the ideological, the imagined, the narrativized. People become types; behavior loses any ambiguity and becomes clear and knowable. Race, gender, physical and cognitive disability, and sexual orientation all disappear behind the universalized façade of the addiction. Despite a veneer of scientism, there is also a strongly detectable moralizing: addiction, we learn, "is a malignant outgrowth, an extreme, unhealthy manifestation, of normal human inclinations" (Peele and Brodsky 16).

There is a link between moralizing in the self-help books and in the twelve-step programs, which require the acknowledgment of a "Higher Power." While all programs stress that the Higher Power doesn't have to be God—it can be Nature or the Universe or even the group itself—the God model comes up in many of these books, as it does in the conclusion of Pia Mellody's *Facing Love Addiction*, when she says, "We have found that with the help of a Higher Power, whom we call God, we *can* stand the pain of reality" (225). God turns up in the *Sex and Love Addicts Anonymous Handbook*, where participants are told that a "reliance on God or some other source of power beyond one's own resources" is necessary (SLAA vii). And although the non-God alternative is permitted, the rest of the handbook simply expresses thoughts like "And it is here that true love, which is of God . . . is found and expressed" (SLAA vi). Even poet Michael Ryan's worldly and well-written memoir ends with relief at "stopping my most shameful sexual behavior (through the grace of God)" (353). And Toni Bentley, former ballet dancer, details in *The Surrender* how her obsession with anal sex led her to find God, a journey that might seem counterintuitive, but ends with her religiosity and the obsession's end. My point here is not that one should or shouldn't believe in God, but that a quasi-religious and thus moralistic approach seems to be embedded in the sex-addiction program.

Yet throughout the development of the idea of sexual addiction, there is an imprecision in explanatory systems. Is the disorder moral or spiritual? A problem of psychological origin? A chemical addiction to certain neurotransmitters that are produced during sexual arousal? Such uncertainty pertains not only to sex addiction but to addiction more broadly. Stanton Peele and Archie Brodsky claim in 1977 that: "Addiction is not a chemical reaction. Addiction is an experience—one which grows out of an individual's routinized subject response to something that has special meaning for him—something, anything, that he finds so safe and reassuring that he cannot be without it. If we want to come to terms with addiction, we have to stop blaming drugs and start looking at people" (18). In this account, addiction is expanded away from drugs to food, sex, work, and such a wide variety of activities that "addiction is not an abnormality in our society. It is not an aberration from the norm; it is itself the norm" (Peele and Brodsky 18). But if it is the norm, can it then be a disability? Or what would it mean for a disability to be a norm?

In a post-Stonewall era, sexual addiction texts do not characterize gay, lesbian, or bisexual experiences as abnormal. We need to recall that the whole thrust of the sexology movement was to include and describe the variety of sexual experience. In theory at least, promiscuous gay sex doesn't look any different from promiscuous heterosexual sex. But if generalized gay or lesbian experiences escape pathologization in the sex addiction literature, queerness does not. If queerness is seen as including polyamorousness and other nontraditional notions of sexuality, then the normative nature of the sexual addiction language steers a wide arc around such practices. This can best be seen by the 1990s, as the addiction model for sexual behavior was refined with a parallel notion of "compulsivity." The use of the term "sexual compulsivity" is intended to bridge the gap between the nonmedical self-help programs and the practitioners of sex therapy. Indeed, one professional journal links both terms in its title: *Sexual Addiction and Compulsivity: The Journal of Treatment and Prevention*. The term "compulsivity" gets the issue out of the demotic self-help, twelve-step programs where it began and into the psychiatrist's, therapist's, and mental-health practitioner's offices.

No doubt partially in response to the rise of managed health care, the need for diagnosis, and the now ever-present requirement to use standardized diagnoses developed in the DSM-IV-TR, compulsivity has become a measurable phenomenon, whereas love addiction was more of a conceptual category. One of the first instruments for measuring sexual compulsivity was a scale that could be used, as the title of one journal article put it, for "predicting AIDS-risk behavior among homosexually active men" (Kalichman et al.). In this context, the boundaries between queerness and disability seem porous indeed; it's difficult to say whether sexual compulsivity is a disability or a form of queerness, since both might be said to involve too much sex, or the wrong kind, with the wrong kind of people.

Furthermore, the disability and queerness that is diagnosed as sexual compulsivity must be measured, quantified, and regulated because it is believed to produce more disability (HIV and AIDS).

Yet if in the context of cultural panic about AIDS, sexual compulsivity seems both queer and pathological, in other contexts, the disorder bears an uncanny resemblance to normative ideals of heterosexual masculinity (and of heterosexual feminine desire). The title of a *Glamour* magazine article in June 2006, drawing on research that links sexual compulsivity to risk-taking behavior, asks: "Is there a Casanova Gene?" According to the article, "guys with a lot of the chemical [dopamine] tend to be spontaneous, risk-taking and highly sexual" (Fahner 138). As genetics develops, we may well see an assertion that there is a gene for sexual promiscuity. In that case, will there be a medical foundation to sexual addiction? Interestingly, for Darwin, survival was based on finding the best sexual scenario for reproduction. In an evolutionary sense, the "Casanova gene" would be the desired mutation to help further the progress of the human race, illustrating the reproductive force of the "selfish" gene.

Sexology created a science of human sexuality, but there also needed to be a science, or at least a philosophy, of love in order to develop a notion of obsessive, addictive, or compulsive sexuality. In the mid-twentieth century, notable books like Erich Fromm's *The Art of Loving* developed models about what love is and should be. Love is not a spontaneous feeling, a thing you fall into, according to Fromm, but it is something that requires discipline, concentration, patience, faith, and the overcoming of narcissism. It isn't a feeling; it is a practice (92). Fromm and others developed a notion of the right kind of love—a normativity of love that was coupled with a hypothetical entity called "the healthy couple" or a "healthy relationship." Love and sex went together like the proverbial horse and carriage. Books like Eustace Chesser's *Love Without Fear: How to Achieve Sex Happiness in Marriage*, published in 1947, equate the happy marriage with love and with heterosexual normality. Love addiction would lie outside of this normative bubble.

Self-help books about the problematics of obsessive love often note that a healthy sexual relationship should be predicated on the idea that a couple accept limerance as a temporary state and that a long-term relationship will not have the ardor of a first night or the honeymoon period. The *Sex and Love Addicts Anonymous Handbook* points out that "the sex and love addict would come to substitute the thrill of sexual adventure or intensity of 'love' for the more encompassing satisfactions, founded first and foremost on self-respect, and later realized in family, career and community" (SLAA viii). In this scenario, the thrill of sexuality, the lure of ecstatic sex between two people, is supposed to cool down to the more tepid communal, networked satisfactions of career, marriage, and community. In this scenario, there is no civilization of discontents, no conflict between eros and psyche. The high-tension electrical charge of sexuality is supposed to run down to the apparently less distracting and more comforting low-wattage baseline of the domestic space and the workplace. In much of the literature on sex addiction, what is essentially a neoliberal, bourgeois vision of life, rife with work-ethic values and utilitarian views of human relations, receives a degree-zero camouflage as simply the right way to live.

Codependence—a variation on the addiction scenario added in the 1990s—is part of this scheme. It too comes directly out of AA, part of a dawning realization that the problem was not solely the addicts but also the family and friends who constitute a network for the alcoholic. Codependence is like sex addiction, in that the codependent person is fixated on another person for approval, sustenance, and so on. Thus, Mellody can use the terms interchangeably: "Love addiction, therefore, is an addiction that often becomes visible to the codependent only after some work has been done on the core symptoms of codependence" (7). In *Facing Love Addiction*, Mellody insists that the Love Addict (her capitalization) is a person who is fixated on another: "Love Addiction, like other addictive processes, is an obsessive-compulsive process used to relieve or medicate intolerable reality. Caught in the throes of withdrawal pains [when the Avoidance Addict—the other half of the codependency model—pulls away], Love Addicts start obsessing" (27). According to Mellody, love addiction is a gateway addiction leading to additional addictions: to sex, food, drugs, alcohol, and so on.

Love addiction apparently leads to obsession and compulsion—but it is not always clear which is the cart and which is the horse. Indeed, the problem of causation has beset theories of obsession for centuries. In the eighteenth and nineteenth centuries, as I show in my book *Obsession: A History*, obsession developed from doing one thing too much. The disease and etiology were the same: you did one thing too much, and you ended up obsessed, that is, doing one thing too much. The addiction scenario, in our own historical moment, is involved in a similar dance of causality. Why is one person a sex addict and another not? Does having too much sex make you a sex addict; or do you have too much sex because you are a sex addict? Until the 1990s, when the brain chemistry model began to replace a psychodynamic model, sexual addiction was believed to be caused by childhood abandonment and narcissism. Craig Nakken distills these ideas down to their most common elements: "There are persons who are more susceptible to addiction. These are persons who don't know how to have healthy relationships and have been taught not to trust in people. This is mainly because of how they were treated by others while growing up, and they never learned how to connect" (26). Nakken further explains: "Addiction is a 'pathological relationship.' What does this mean? To be pathological is to deviate from a healthy or normal condition. When someone is described as being ill, we mean that this person has moved away from what is considered 'normal.' The 'pathological,' therefore, means 'abnormal.' Consequently, addiction is an abnormal relationship with an object or event. All objects have a normal, socially acceptable function" (10). This passage makes clear the contemporary modality of addiction speak. There are obviously normal people, who live natural and healthy lives. Then there are addicts, who are abnormal and live unhealthy, ill lives. In addition, the world is itself bound up in this fairly obvious natural path of life, because it is part of a scenario that is subject to the Higher Power. Nakken explains that "with a spiritual Higher Power we learn to perceive and accept a natural order, a natural flow" (22).

The swirl of confusion continues. If addiction is an abnormality, a pathology, then clearly it is a disability. Given a psychodynamic or a biological or chemical explanation of addiction, what addicts and society seek is a cure. So this disability isn't one to be celebrated, or even linked to a political and social model; it is simply a state of being that requires cure. But cure can only come, in the parlance of the twelve-step programs, from a belief in God or a Higher Power and the willpower that comes from group interaction. The pathology model then reverts to the most ancient attitude toward disability, the religious one. Medical conditions require divine intervention linked with personal devotion and self-discipline. The fugue of explanatory models in this view is disconcerting to dizzying.

What I want to suggest is that the formation of a disease, in this case sexual addiction, is at base a social and political process. This is what I would call a biocultural explanation in the sense that it is a result of biology and culture. Certain behaviors come under disciplinary and moral scrutiny. Aspects of the behavior are isolated and then compiled into syndromes or disorders, which comprise a list of possible symptoms. Groups of people, whether doctors, self-help group members, or larger segments of the public, begin to group these symptoms or behaviors under the rubric of the disease entity, which comes into being itself from this very social, biopolitical process. As we've seen in this case with sexual

Lennard J. Davis

addiction, a series of categorizations had to come first. In the beginning was the pinpointing of the consumption of alcohol as a problem. Then the disease of alcoholism had to come into existence, with its own cure modalities. Along with this, the notion of addiction had to develop and become accepted, and finally a range of addictive behaviors had to be described and expanded. Moving from the more obvious chemical dependencies (and these too are somewhat arbitrary — why opiates, barbiturates, and alcohol, but not caffeine, nicotine, or serotonin?), a generalization occurs in which behaviors not previously seen as pathological (work, sex, food) become seen as linked to pathology. After the disease entity is established with the most egregious cases, a kind of me-too malady adoption occurs, in which lower-frequency or lower-intensity behaviors begin to fall under the larger rubric. In this expansion, as we've seen with depression, erectile dysfunction, obsessive-compulsive disorder, situational affective disorder (formerly known as shyness), and other disorders, a consumer-driven, corporatist push casts the net of the disease entity wider, so that people who are merely sad, recreationally sexual, emotionally needy, or overly neat and orderly see themselves as "having" the disease entity. In synchrony with this expansion, family members and friends suggest, based on publicity and other rather simplified conceptualizations of illness, that a person might be in need of medical care or a twelve-step program. Peer pressure to stop certain kinds of disturbing behaviors can be easily cast into being concerned about the person who is displaying this behavior. This kind of social surveillance is very much what Foucault had in mind when he described regimes of biopower.

In this scenario, which I'm not prepared to defend in this short chapter but which I merely suggest as a way of thinking of disease, impairment is not merely acquired but is, in effect, generated by vast social processes — the same social processes, sometimes, as those that then disable individuals seen as "having" particular impairments. The old impairment and disability gap begins to collapse, though, when we consider these complex forces at work in the creation, deployment, consumption, and proliferation of disease entities and cure rationales. Particularly in the case of cognitive and affective disorders, our models of disability need to be rethought. In the rethinking of these models, we will have to come up against the question of whether lifestyle disorders like sexual addiction are disabilities. In doing so, we might want to move from the individual to the larger social, cultural, political milieu. Can we say that an individual "has" a sexual addiction, or should we say that a society has produced a therapeutic community around addiction? Do we attempt to provide accommodation to those with sexual disorders (including impotence along with nymphomania)? Or would it be more logical to accommodate the larger world to the behaviors of its members? There is no easy answer to this problematic, and we might have to end up rethinking what we mean by disability and accommodation by considering the errant categories of difference, the ones that don't fit so easily into our ideas about the social model.

NOTES

This chapter was previously published as chapter 6, "Obsessive Sex and Love," in *Obsession: A History*, by Lennard J. Davis (Chicago: University of Chicago Press, 2008), 161–81.

1. See Foucault, *History*; D'Emilio and Freedman; Giddens; and Laqueur.

2. One of the main publishers of such material in the early twentieth century was the Eugenics Press.

3. See Cooper for a clinical analysis of the role of the Internet in shaping contemporary sexual behavior.

4. For a detailed history of this subject, see Boon.

5. These films include *Lost Weekend* (1945), *Come Fill the Cup* (1951), *Come Back Little Sheba* (1952), *Something to Live For* (1952), *I'll Cry Tomorrow* (1955), *The Voice in the Mirror* (1958), and *Days of Wine and Roses* (1962).

6. It may well be that the DSM-V will list sexual addiction along with addictions to shopping, work, and so on. There is an active debate now going on about whether one can be addicted to behaviors rather than substances.

7. Masturbation was perhaps an exception. It was first critiqued in the eighteenth century, but it wasn't until Tissot's book in the nineteenth century that it came to be seen as a disease entity. Its existence as a disease was predicated on the fact that it wasn't sexual intercourse, which was seen as healthful, while chastity was regarded as a problem. See Laqueur for a much more detailed account.

16

....

ALISON KAFER

DESIRE AND DISGUST

My Ambivalent Adventures in Devoteeism

Dear Alison,

. . .

Because of an overall almost total void of amputee women, when one does show herself, it is a major event. For instance (and please don't take this personally), if I were to see you unexpectedly, walking down the street, chances are good that it would send me into a state just short of shock — the adrenalin would start to flow, the heart rate would quicken, the palms would start to sweat, etc. This really happens! And, I would, in relishing the moment, do everything UNOBTRUSIVELY possible to savor it.

In the past, I've turned my car around . . . to have another look. I've followed someone around in a store/shopping center (at a safe and non-threatening distance) for a few minutes, stealing quick glimpses now and then. . . .

I just don't want you or any of your disabled sisters to perceive people like me, who have a genuine interest in you, as well as your "predicament," shall we say, and who could provide the love and care you deserve, as a bunch of wolves moving in for the kill. Nothing could be further from the truth! To win the love and trust of a disabled lady by meeting her needs and providing for her in every way possible . . . would be the ultimate!

. . .

Give us a chance, and you'll reap the benefits IN SPADES!
A friend and admirer,
"Steve"

"Steve" and I have never met; our one-sided relationship consists solely of this e-mail and another like it a week earlier.[1] Lengthy descriptions of one man's sexual self-understanding, both messages offer a personal account of "devotee-ism," a sexual attraction to disabled people, often amputees. For Steve, this desire for amputees "ebbs and floods, . . . but IT IS ALWAYS THERE," and he carefully explains the nature of this attraction. Noting that devotees "would infinitely rather go out with an amputee of average looks and build than a gorgeous 4-limbed woman," Steve encourages me to think kindly of devotees because they "can't get enough of [my] beautiful looks." For Steve, my "beautiful looks" are the result of my two above-the-knee amputations; the fact that he knows nothing else about my appearance, or my life in general, does nothing to dampen his desire.

It is a desire that others apparently share: although Steve was among the most articulate and thorough defenders of devoteeism to enter my inbox, he was not alone; over the course of a few years, beginning in September 2000, several other devotees wrote to me about their desire for bodies like mine.[2] Reading those e-mails, I did exactly what Steve had politely asked me not to do: I took them personally. Who were these men tracing me through the Internet? Was I one of the women they were following surreptitiously? I became increasingly suspicious of strangers, particularly those interested in learning about my disabilities.

My suspicions were shared, and expanded upon, by my friends and family. "There are people called devotees," I would explain, "who are sexually attracted to amputees." Their responses were immediate and unequivocal: "Ewww, that's weird. What's wrong with those people?" Although I confess to following this train of thought myself, wondering what was "wrong" with devotees, hearing it expressed with such consistency troubled me. What were my friends and family finding reprehensible—the surreptitiousness of devotee behavior or the desire for disabled bodies? The fact that many of them condemned devoteeism immediately, hearing only about the existence of the attraction and not its manifestations, led me to worry that what troubled them was the very casting of disabled bodies as inherently attractive. And if so, where did that leave me? Did my friends and family unconsciously find my body so freakish that anyone attracted to it was immediately suspect? Did I share their derisive attitudes? What would it say about my self-image if I dismissed as disgusting and suspicious anyone who desired me? On the other hand, what would it say about my self-image if I were so desperate for sexual recognition that I accepted the kind of behavior mentioned in Steve's e-mail? Were these two choices my only options? Was devotee desire the only desire available to me?

Like many people, I initially discovered devoteeism when doing an online search for "amputee."[3] It was 1996, fourteen months after my injuries, and these websites seemed to confirm my worst fears: my new body was apparently disgusting to all but a select few—the "devotees"—and even they felt the need to hide their feelings behind pseudonyms and nicknames.[4] Their secrecy seemed evidence that there was something wrong and shameful about an attraction to bodies like mine. Otherwise, why not be "out" about their desires? After reading through several websites, I quickly shut down my computer, studiously avoiding any such pages in the future.

A few years later, in 1999, I returned to the question of devoteeism—this time with a slightly different lens. I wanted to examine why some women actively engaged in amputee-devotee communities, what benefits they derived from their involvement, and how they understood themselves in relation to devotees. What were they finding in amputee-devotee communities that I had missed? What motivated their involvement in something that many other disabled people had condemned as exploitative and ableist? My interest was partly a result of frustration with existing approaches to the phenomenon. Until very recently, medical journals contained the only analyses of devoteeism, analyses that relied heavily on the notion that a desire for disabled women is a pathological trait requiring therapeutic intervention.[5] What are the cultural assumptions that ground such characterizations? If we cast devotees as "pathological," then what are we saying about the desirability of disabled women? What might the stories of disabled women contribute to these discourses of inappropriate desire?

What I found in the stories of amputees involved in devoteeism were tales of renewed self-assurance and empowerment. Women who had felt profound shame about their bodies reported significant gains in their self-confidence after discovering devotees. Such changes in self-perception then led to dramatic changes in behavior: one woman reported no longer feeling too embarrassed to leave her house, while another abandoned her practice of hiding her stump underneath baggy clothing and wraps.[6] Hearing these stories, I realized I could no longer simply dismiss devoteeism. In 2000 I wrote "Amputated Desire, Resistant Desire" as a way of thinking through these issues. This piece, although it contained ambivalences, was largely an argument for attending to the experiences of women in amputee-devotee communities; the essay challenged the assertion that a desire for disabled bodies is, in itself, a marker of pathology.

Once that piece went online, with my e-mail address attached, I began to receive e-mails much like the one with which I began this chapter. Devotees wrote to describe devoteeism, to detail their desires, and even to request dates with me and other amputees. As my inbox filled with messages from devotees, my initial discomfort with devoteeism returned. Although the e-mails were intended to flatter me, their constant refrain that devotees were the only people capable of desiring bodies like mine was disconcerting. This repetition, coupled with frequent accounts of devotees stalking amputees, made me increasingly uncomfortable about continuing any involvement in devoteeism, even as an outside observer.

Indeed, part of my discomfort stemmed from the fact that I was finding it increasingly difficult to locate myself "outside" of devoteeism. My inbox regularly turned up e-mails from strangers discussing my body with a disconcerting intimacy, an intimacy borne not of explicit descriptions of sex but of explicit reflections on my appearance and others' (alleged) reactions to it. Devotees discussed my stumps with a troubling familiarity, even possessiveness, as if their (allegedly) unique desire granted them some kind of claim over my body. Whether I wanted it or not, I was being written into devoteeism through these e-mails. By the end of 2001, I decided to abandon this research. I could not bear the way this work was making me feel about my body, as if my stumps belonged more to the devotees in cyberspace than they did to me.

My discomfort remained coupled, however, with feelings of necessity. Amputees continue to wrestle with the complexities of devoteeism, and there is scant research addressing the topic from feminist or queer cultural studies perspectives.[7] Thus, years later, I return to the topic yet again, this time to trace the root of my continued ambivalence. Although I remain deeply troubled by my interactions with devotees, I have encountered too many stories of female amputees finding pleasure and opportunity in devotee communities to accept such communities as exclusively exploitative. Moreover, as someone who is routinely met with hostile stares because of the oddness of my body, I can't help but be intrigued by the notion of finding eroticism in bodies typically marked as undesirable. The form this eroticism takes in devoteeism, however, worries me, and I cannot shake my uneasiness about the phenomenon. Over ten years after my

Alison Kafer

first exposure to devoteeism, what is it about the devotees' desire that continues to trouble me? Why do I remain so ambivalent?

In this chapter, I attempt to answer that question, arguing that the rhetoric of devoteeism relies as heavily on *disgust* for disabled bodies as it does *desire*. Devotees typically define themselves not simply as people sexually attracted to amputees but as the *only* people sexually attracted to amputees. "Unlike everyone else," they claim, "we find you not disgusting but desirable." In so doing, they establish the groundwork for a devotee exceptionalism, according to which only devotees are capable of desiring amputees. I begin by tracing the logic of desire and disgust that pervades devoteeism, arguing that devotees' descriptions of their attraction often perpetuate the ableist assumption that disabled bodies are properly objects of disgust. In the second half of this chapter, I examine my own entanglement in this logic of desire and disgust, reflecting on the assumptions, fears, and desires that drive my research. Part of this self-reflection involves a turn to queercrip relationships, specifically the writings of lovers Eli Clare and Samuel Lurie, in the hope of articulating other models of desiring disability that are not reliant on fetishistic representations or the binary logic of desire/disgust.

Demographic analyses of devotees are rare and reliant on small sample sizes, but they suggest that devotees in the United States tend to be white, middle- to upper-middle class, well-educated men between the ages of twenty-five and sixty-five; anecdotal evidence provides the same profile.[8] Most devotees are non-disabled men interested in disabled women, but, judging from the numerous websites catering to gay male devotees, there seems also to be a significant population of gay men involved in the attraction.[9] I focus here exclusively on heterosexual male devotees, nondisabled men attracted to disabled women, for reasons that will become clearer below.

Throughout the chapter, I train my attention on "devotee discourses": websites produced by and for devotees, e-mails and conversations with self-identified devotees and amputees, and other community-generated texts. Concentrating on this material allows me to discuss devotee exceptionalism and its logic of desire and disgust without necessarily condemning any individual devotee's attraction to amputees. As someone whose own desires are too often cast as deviant—the sexualities of disabled people have long been rendered inappropriate, and queer sexualities continue to be derided as immoral—I am wary of preemptively dismissing another's desire as in need of correction. Rather, my goal is to highlight the dense undercurrents of disgust found in devotee discourse. How is devoteeism represented and constructed by people who identify with the attraction? What cultural assumptions undergird such constructions, and what are their effects?

DESIRE AND DISGUST: UNPACKING THE LOGIC OF DEVOTEEISM

According to *OverGround*, a devotee website, a devotee is "a person, male, female, straight, or gay, who is sexually and emotionally attracted to people . . . who have a specific disability, and whose reaction on encountering such a person is massive and overwhelming" (Child and King, "OverGround's Manifesto" par. 1). This kind of reaction to disabled bodies is assumed to be limited to devotees; devotee discourses typically insist that amputees are attractive only to devotees. J., one of the most frequent contributors to *OverGround*, puts it bluntly: "We know we're unusual, but your physical alteration doesn't disgust us. So you have a stump . . . , we don't find it disgusting. . . . Of all the people you meet, we are the ones who will never ever say, 'Apart from that she's very attractive'" ("Devotees" par. 10).

As evidenced in J.'s remarks, the interplay of desire and disgust plays an integral role in devotee logic. Within this framework, the site of an amputation can never be neutral: it is always the determining aesthetic factor of an amputee. Depending on one's perspective—namely, whether one is a devotee—an amputation is charged either with desire or disgust.[10] According to this logic, the key difference between a devotee and a non-devotee is the value afforded an amputation: devotees bestow attractiveness and desirability upon it; non-devotees are disgusted by it. But both are assumed to cast the presence or absence of an amputation as the determining factor in a woman's sexual attractiveness. To desire her is to find her attractive solely on the basis of her amputation, and thus to be a devotee. Anyone who does not identify as a devotee is, by definition, a person disgusted by amputees. Within this logic, there is no position outside of the desire/disgust binary.

Once amputation is cast as the sole marker of attractiveness, then devotees become the only people capable of feeling that attraction. Devotee discourses constantly remind amputees that "no one else will ever love *all* of you, the whole woman" because, for devotees, the amputation is primary in constituting who the "whole woman" is. In the logic of devoteeism, "amputee" becomes a woman's primary identity, an identity that ostensibly elicits disgust from all non-devotees. Indeed, non-devotees, as constructed within devoteeism, are incapable of feeling anything but disgust toward an amputation. Bette Hagglund, an amputee who founded the amputee-devotee social network *Fascination*, recommends that amputees avoid relationships with non-devotee men for this very reason. "It may be better," she suggests, "to get romantic with someone who is attracted to you without reservation and with full acceptance of your physical limitations" ("Fascination" conclusion, par. 1). These qualities, presumably, only devotees can provide.

This construction of devoteeism places the partners of amputees at risk of misrecognition. If my lover desires me, then she must be a devotee, even if she has never understood herself as such. But if she disavows devoteeism, refusing to ground our relationship on my status as an amputee, then her very desire for me is dismissed as inadequate. Despite any claims to the contrary, her refusal to identify as a devotee is cast as a rejection of my disability. According to the exceptionalist logic of desire and disgust, to love an amputee is to be a devotee; to refuse such an appellation is to love an amputee only partially, ashamedly, reluctantly.[11]

Within this framework, self-loathing is seen as the only reason an amputee would refuse a relationship with a devotee. As one devotee explained to me, "I've found that it's the amp ladies who don't have confidence in themselves who are uncomfortable with the idea of devotees. They don't like themselves and they think there must be something wrong with someone who likes them."[12] J. takes this position one step further, arguing that women who reject devotees are so disgusted by their own disabilities that they need partners who share their revulsion. He writes on the website *OverGround*: "Some people who are physically impaired feel ashamed of their impaired bodies. . . . Despising themselves, they will tend to despise those who find them attractive, and will value the attentions only of those who feel an equal disgust" ("Twins" par. 8).

This logic casts sexual desirability as the only real problem facing disabled women; issues such as unemployment and underemployment, social marginalization, poverty, discrimination, and inaccessibility rarely appear in devotee discourses. In an *OverGround* interview with W. and K., a devotee-amputee couple, J. repeatedly asks K. about her experiences in rehab. His primary focus is the issue of "attractiveness": "Were you concerned about losing personal attractiveness . . . ? Did you feel that your personal attractiveness was severely reduced by your amputation?" ("W. and K."). K.'s answers are telling. Each time J. poses this kind of question, she explains that she had more pressing concerns: "As you know I had other problems . . . and at that time you don't care much about [your attractiveness]. We were kept quite busy all day so my aim was learning to walk again." When J. asks about the loss of attractiveness yet again, she chides, "as you might remember this was secondary to me. I tried hard to walk again, and to work again. That was my main focus."[13] Rather than pursuing these issues, J. turns the conversation to K.'s feelings about devotee desire, suggesting that within the logic of devoteeism, desire and disgust are the only lenses through which to view disability.

LeRoy Nattress draws on this closed logic in his call for further research on devoteeism. He suggests that "more and better information" on the attraction will eventually lead to "increased awareness" and "reasoned acceptance" of devoteeism. Amputees will learn to recognize their "unique attractiveness to some men" and will thus be "helped to develop to [their] fullest potential, based not on the expectations of society, but on [their] choices and abilities" (4). But can the dating obstacles faced by disabled women best be addressed through increased acceptance of, and dependence upon, devotees? And, more importantly, are such obstacles the only hindrances to women's full development? According to the devotee logic of desire and disgust, the answer to both of these questions is a resounding "yes."

It is certainly true that the impact of an amputation or other impairment on a woman's social life can be staggering. Many feminist and queer disability studies scholars have focused their research on sex and sexuality among people with disabilities: some have concentrated on issues of representation; others have explored political, economic, attitudinal, and architectural barriers; and still others have examined the effects of these histories and disabled people's responses to them.[14] What distinguishes this work from Nattress's position is that it contextualizes these "dating obstacles" within a larger analysis of ableism and political oppression, recognizing that sexual marginalization is deeply connected to political and social marginalization.

In the devotee worldview, in contrast, amputees struggle because they hate themselves and lack suitable lovers, not because they live in a society structured around the needs of the nondisabled. Nattress, J., and others suggest that all an amputee needs to flourish is self-acceptance, a self-acceptance that can best come from a relationship with a devotee. By discussing an amputee's well-being only in terms of physical attractiveness and romantic relationships, devotee discourses present disability as an individual problem. In so doing, they perpetuate one of the most entrenched assumptions of an ableist culture: that disability is a problem to be addressed only on an individual or familial level, not a social, political, or legal one. And within the closed logic of desire and disgust, it is a problem that can be addressed satisfactorily only through participation in devoteeism; anything else is a recipe for self-loathing, denial, and inadequate relationships.

Perhaps most disturbing about the closed logic of desire and disgust is the way it serves to excuse exploitative behavior. Because devoteeism is presented as an amputee's only path out of disgust, practices that might otherwise be seen as threatening are cast as harmless, even beneficial. For example, many of the essays featured in *OverGround* describe individual devotees' encounters with amputee women. Often called "sightings," these stories are collected and shared among devotees, and they occasionally note the general location where a specific amputee has been spotted. In "Sightings," for example, John mentions that "a petite blond with a left BK [below-the-knee amputation] can often be found in a particular neighborhood shopping district" (par. 11). R. Amy Elman notes that *Amputee Times*, another devotee publication, explicitly urges its readers to report on the whereabouts of amputee women; one issue calls for a "national (or international) register of attractive amputees. This means that readers must report their sightings and the names and addresses of women they know about" (qtd. in Elman 266–67). Records of such sightings are popular because many men neither know any amputees nor have regular exposure to them. Reading about the sightings of other devotees not only offers them the vicarious pleasure of an amputee experience but also may guide them toward a sighting of their own.

These encounters are often as much "followings"—if not "stalkings"—as "sightings." Steve's e-mail, with which I introduced this chapter, provides an excellent example of this expansion: "[I]f I were to see you unexpectedly, walking down the street, . . . I would, in relishing the moment, do everything UNOBTRU-SIVELY possible to savor it," including trailing at a "safe distance." Later in the e-mail, Steve bemoans "the nut cases" and "the dangerous ones" "who give a bad name and reputation to the devotee community" by failing to be as cautious as he is. Quick to distance himself from those "other devotees" who inconsiderately frighten amputees by following too closely or too overtly, he positions his behavior as harmless, even flattering. As Steve's disavowal suggests, the complaints of unhappy amputees have not gone unnoticed by devotees, and many have been quite explicit in their condemnation of abusive behavior.[15] The problem, however, is ascertaining which kinds of behaviors constitute harassment; as illustrated by Steve's e-mail, many devotees do not consider tracking women to be harassment if it occurs at a "safe distance."

In his dissertation about devoteeism, Nattress offers a list of common strategies for meeting amputees, including: following an amputee in order to photograph her and learn about her life; participating in organizations that serve amputees, such as shoe exchange or support groups; corresponding with a female amputee via e-mail, often pretending to be a female amputee oneself; and creating detailed records of amputee sightings (18–19).[16] As this list suggests, taking surreptitious photographs, sharing stories about amputee sightings, secretly following women, and lying about one's identity are seen not as harassment but as acceptable behavior, presumably because such manifestations of desire are expected to be a welcome respite from the disgust an amputee typically experiences. The presence of such activities on this list—as well as the very existence of such a list in a dissertation by an "out" devotee—suggests that these behaviors are expected and accepted within devoteeism. Admittedly, most devotees acknowledge that if taken to extremes, these acts can be considered abusive. At the same time, they are quick to insist that such harassment is less the fault of the devotee and more the fault of an intolerant society that forces devotees to keep their desires hidden.

Thus, according to this framework, the way to eliminate such harassment is to increase awareness about devoteeism. Once men are more comfortable making their desires public, they will no longer pursue amputee women in such clandestine ways. This assumption may indeed be true; with greater social acceptance, many devotees may change their secretive behavior. The problem with this position, however, is that devotees are absolved of any culpability in sexual harassment. If disabled women would accept devotees, the logic goes, then devotees would no longer need to lurk in support groups or secretly photograph them. The *OverGround* contributor J. is quite explicit in attributing the responsibility for ending harassment to amputees. "Once you [amputees] put behind you the prejudice that . . . devotees are disgusting creatures," J. writes, "you can understand why [they behave the way they do]. . . . And if you're friendly perhaps they will stop lurking and behave better" ("Why Devotees" par. 8). Interestingly, J. employs the language of disgust—typically used to describe the way non-devotees feel about amputees—to talk about devotees. In so doing, he accomplishes two things: first, he constructs a bond between amputees and devotees on the basis of their shared rejection by non-devotee culture as "disgusting"; second, he perpetuates the opposition of disgust and desire common to the logic of devoteeism, assuming that once devotees are no longer seen as disgusting, they will be seen as desirable.

Note that the disgust aimed toward devotees is assumed to be temporary; once society develops a greater understanding of devoteeism, it will no longer cast the phenomenon as disgusting or pathological.[17] Such optimism regarding the possibility of attitudinal change reveals a striking double standard considering devotees' pessimism regarding amputees. The disgust that non-devotees feel toward amputees is portrayed not as something that can be alleviated by increased awareness or social change but as something immutable, even natural. Changes in social practices and beliefs affect amputees only insofar as they alter the behavior of devotees, alleviating them of the need to pursue their desires undercover; non-devotee disgust toward amputees, on the other hand, is apparently so profound and far-reaching that it cannot be overcome.

Casting harassment as innocent, something devotees do only out of unrequited desire, completely ignores the ways in which such acts can disempower women. Some amputees express reluctance to see their prosthetists, whom they fear may be closet devotees getting secret thrills.[18] Other amputees have tried, without success, to ban devotees from amputee-oriented activities and organizations (such as the Amputee Coalition of America) in an attempt to eliminate devotee harassment.[19] For many women, organizations that could serve as valuable resource centers have become sites of potential exploitation.

Months after attending an amputee support group in 1997, I learned that the convener of the group was a devotee, and that he had given my name and physical description to other devotees. I discovered these facts when I met someone who already "knew" me through the organizer; my one-time attendance at the support group had apparently been enough to introduce me to an entire network of devotees. I felt exposed, vulnerable, and betrayed; since then, I have been wary of unknowingly sharing my stories with devotees. This wariness has, in turn, affected my encounters with amputees. Female amputees occasionally send me e-mail, asking me how I have adjusted to life as an amputee, what my daily routine is like, and what advice I would give them about devotees. I have yet to respond to a single one of these e-mails. I wish I could say that my feminist desire to support disabled women compels me to respond, but my sense of self-protection—justified or not—triumphs every time. After my support group experience, and after hearing numerous stories of devotees masquerading as amputees online in order to ask exactly these kinds of questions, I am too suspicious to reply with sincerity to a stranger. I am painfully aware that if these are real amputees writing me, then my cynical silence may appear as cruel indifference. In my lack of engagement, I may be cutting myself off from potentially productive relationships with other amputees. Even so, the risks of replying to these e-mails feel too great. Simply knowing about common practices of devotee subterfuge places me in what seems like an untenable situation: open myself to potential exploitation or close myself to community.

Given experiences such as the ones I have described, it is not surprising that devoteeism elicits suspicion from many disabled women. This suspicion is not based in self-loathing, as some devotees claim, but in a rejection of the desire and disgust dynamic that pervades devotee discourse. That is, the ambivalence of devotees' own desire elicits such negative reactions. Disabled women understand how devotee exceptionalism—"we are the only ones who could ever love you"—perpetuates ableist assumptions about their presumed undesirability; it leaves unchallenged the notion that amputees are properly objects of disgust. Moreover, disabled women recognize the ways in which this exceptionalism is then used to excuse, if not to produce, exploitative and potentially dangerous behaviors: "I'm the only one not disgusted by you, so you should welcome my attention, whatever its form."

DESIRING DISABILITY: MY GORDIAN KNOT

I began this chapter by reflecting on my ambivalence about devoteeism and devotee-oriented research, detailing my trepidation about this topic. To depict this work as fraught with misgivings is to tell only part of the story, however, for desire factors into my experiences as well. I have not only had the intellectual pleasure of making connections among different texts and histories, I have also experienced the much more visceral pleasure of exposure to amputee bodies, bodies similar to my own. Analyzing devoteeism has exposed me to a world I otherwise would never have known existed, and I can't pretend to know the full effects of this encounter on my sense of self. Through this research, I have seen dozens of pictures of amputee women on the Internet. For someone who rarely sees a body resembling her own in other media, such an experience has been profound.

Analyses of devoteeism tend to overlook the access amputees gain to other disabled women through their involvement in amputee-devotee communities. Typing "amputee" into an Internet search engine brings up more sites about devoteeism than anything else; women who have no other connection to disabled people or disability organizations, and who are looking online for support and community, may very well find it on these amputee-devotee sites. While the ASCOTworld website is focused primarily on hosting amputee-devotee chats and selling photographs of amputees to devotees, the site often features infor-

Alison Kafer

mation on shoe-exchange groups and health care, serving as a support network for amputees. Similarly, although the primary goal of an ASCOTworld conference might be to introduce amputees to devotees, amputees will likely spend at least part of the weekend socializing with other women. Through this virtual and physical community, a new amputee might meet other disabled women who can serve as powerful mentors for her, modeling how to adjust to life with a disability.

This kind of mentoring may prove to be particularly important when it comes to sexuality, as studies suggest that a lack of role models dramatically affects the sexuality of disabled women. For many women, particularly those who become disabled later in life, it is difficult to learn to incorporate wheelchairs, prosthetics, scars, and stumps into their ideas of a "sexy" experience.[20] The photographs and videos of female amputees circulating throughout amputee-devotee communities might offer disabled women a powerful resource for integrating sexuality and disability. Devotee websites might be the only places where an amputee can easily find images of women who look like her, images of women being "sexy" while seated in a wheelchair, leaning on a cane, or donning a prosthetic. Indeed, prosthetics are often cast as more erotic than medical on these websites, a radical shift in meaning that could encourage amputees to incorporate medical equipment such as wheelchairs, canes, and prosthetics into sex play.[21] Moreover, they might begin to recognize amputated bodies themselves as sources of pleasure. K. tells *OverGround* that she enjoys looking at the pictures of other amputees because "it's interesting to see how other amputee women look" (J., "W. and K.").

Sometimes, when I get dressed, I think about these women who insist upon the sexiness of their stumps. Over the years, I have become increasingly comfortable exposing the burn scars on my arms and back, and I like to flaunt my wide, wheelchair-pushing shoulders, but I still carefully conceal the ends of my stumps underneath skirts and shorts. What lessons could I learn from these women featured on the Internet? What lessons have I already absorbed from them? Thinking about my body while thinking about their bodies, and their relations to their bodies, is itself a kind of desire.

This pleasure—my pleasure—in both the sight and site of female disabled bodies raises difficult questions about my own entanglement in ableism and objectification. How am I objectifying the bodies of amputees in my quest for images that reflect my existence?[22] How has discovering their photographs transformed the way I live in the world? Is my own empowerment a vicarious result of these women's participation in devoteeism? How does my desire—for sexual recognition, for identification, for community—rely on networks established to serve devotee desire? What are the effects of my research on these women's lives, desires, bodies? What, if anything, do I owe them for the many pleasures I receive? My pleasure in seeing these bodies does not exist apart from power relations.

Nor does yours in reading this chapter. As an amputee, you may recognize yourself in my ambivalence; as a devotee, you have experienced an increase in your visibility; as a nondisabled, non-devotee, this exposure to devoteeism may have affirmed your physical and sexual "normality." Reading about amputees and devotees may bring the pleasure of recognizing that you are not like "them," that you are not "other," thereby buttressing your own ableist privilege in a nondisabled world. Rather than being trapped between the two poles of desire and disgust, nondisabled non-devotees are the unmarked norm within the framework of devoteeism: those whose bodies do not disgust, those whose desires require no justification.

Amputee, devotee, nondisabled non-devotee: even these designations are too simple, too narrow. What about the disabled person who isn't an amputee—how might other disabled people locate themselves in this logic?[23] What about the nondisabled non-devotee whose lover is disabled? Or what about a relationship between two amputees: one disabled body finding pleasure in another? Or, for that matter, an amputee discovering pleasure in her own body, incorporating her stump or stumps into her own sexual fantasies and desires? For me to ignore these possibilities would be to accept the devotee logic that only devotees can desire amputees; it would be to perpetuate the ableist notion that desiring disability can always and only be pathological.

The desire and disgust dynamic is hard to escape, however, as it is articulated within an ableist culture in which disability is used to justify social, economic, and political inequalities. In this context, devoteeism is like a Gordian knot: the more I attempt to unravel the strands of desire and disgust, the tighter the pieces hold together. This complexity, this tangle of desires and motives, is overwhelming, as illustrated by an encounter I had at the Oakland airport. Waiting outside baggage claim for my ride, I was approached by a well-dressed man in his thirties. After saying hello, he commented on my smile and asked me for my name and number: "Maybe we could go out for a drink sometime." Caught off guard, I said something about not living in the area. As he continued to make small talk, it suddenly crossed my mind that this man might be a devotee. I could feel myself immediately shutting down, wary of telling this possible devotee anything about myself. I gave vague answers to his questions and explained that I was involved with someone else. Sensing my discomfort, he apologized and quickly walked away.

After he left, I began to question my assumption that he was a devotee. At that moment, I realized how implicated I was in the logic of devoteeism. I had somehow managed not to hear his praise of my smile and my self-confidence, assuming that it had to be my amputations—and only my amputations—that attracted him. In hindsight, this reaction seems like such a loss, not of a date (many women, I imagine, would hesitate before giving a stranger at the airport their names or phone numbers) but of something more profound: an awareness of myself as a sexual being, a recognition of my desirability. How sad that I was unable simply to feel flattered in his offer, to feel pleasure in this man's desire. How disconcerting that I was so quick to buy into the ableist assumption that my impairments eclipse all other aspects of my life. Do I subscribe to the notion of devotee exceptionalism, the idea that only devotees can find bodies like mine desirable? I want to say no, but my reaction to this man suggests otherwise.

The Gordian knot pulls tighter: assume for the moment that my reaction was correct, that this man was a devotee. Would it have been wrong for him to have been drawn more to the shape of my stumps than the curve of my smile? Is one desire, one attraction, inherently better than the other? Is there something wrong with finding it sexy the way my skirt skims the edge of my stumps, or the way my stumps shift when I push my handrims? Is it pathological to fantasize about moving one's hands across the ends of my stumps, or to desire that more than the feel of my breasts? To be clear, I'm not suggesting that I was wrong to be wary of this stranger, especially given my experiences with devotees. But I do want to acknowledge the ways in which this encounter has forced me to recognize my discomfort with seeing my stumps as sites of desire. Am I wary of such desire because of the ableist dimensions of devotee rhetoric, because of internalized shame about my body, or because of an assumption that desiring disability can only be pathological?

The questions continue, pulling the knot still tighter: why have I so consistently focused my research on heterosexual male devotees? Is it simply that these are the devotees I have encountered, or am I trying to insure that the image I associate with "devotee" bears no resemblance to the image of my female lover, no similarities to my queer communities? And if so, what or whom am I trying to protect? Would I have to alter my definitions of devoteeism if the term suddenly had to include my lover? Am I so reluctant to situate myself within devoteeism that I have drawn artificial boundaries around my research? Even more troubling, has my attention to heterosexual amputee-devotee relations been a way to distance myself from the *amputees* in these communities, a way to reassure myself that I am not like them? Has my focus on heterosexual devotees allowed me to ignore my own unwillingness to accept my amputations as sites of desire?

Conversely, how much of my wariness of devoteeism stems from the relentless sexism and heteronormativity of devotee discourses? If devotees were not so insistent on describing women as "ladies," or so certain that all of disabled women's problems could be solved by a good man, would I be more accepting of their position? And would I be more open to devotees if they seemed more queer, more open to other "deviant" desires?[24]

I have no easy answers to any of these questions.

It is this lack of easy answers that leads many disabled people to share in my ambivalence about devoteeism. We are reluctant to condemn the phenomenon, cognizant of the implications of condemning people who find disability attractive. Few of us want to deny the experiences of those disabled women who have found the attraction to be life affirming and empowering. Simultaneously, however, many of us feel a lingering sense of discomfort with devoteeism, as we are equally cognizant of the implications of devotee exceptionalism. People with disabilities are not eager to endorse the assumption that disabled bodies are inherently disgusting to all but a select few, or that abusive expressions of desire are better than no expressions of desire. These complexities have everything to do with the seeming monopoly devotees hold over representations of sex and disability. For an amputee like myself, almost the only place I can find images of bodies like mine is on devotee websites. To find traces of desire, I must wade through narratives of disgust, and that is what makes devoteeism so troubling.

But I continue to wrestle with these complexities because I continue to find the promise of desiring disability compelling. As I have argued here, current constructions of devoteeism are too wrapped up in exceptionalist logic, fetishistic reductions, and exploitative practices to meet this promise; devotee discourses too often cast disabled bodies as disgusting, accepting ableist rhetoric about the asexuality of disabled women rather than resisting it. Instead, I want to imagine a sexuality that is rich and robust not in spite of impairment, and not fetishistically because of impairment, but in relationship to it. How have disabled people crafted sexual identities and practices that take our impairments into account, not in order to overcome them, but to capitalize on them? How might impairments enhance sexual encounters, opening up new possibilities and experiences? How might the absence of an arm or a leg make maneuvering easier? How might

Alison Kafer

it enable new positions or closer touches or longer embraces? How can impairment be recognized in our discovery of potential erogenous zones or sites of erotic pleasure? And how might that eroticization happen without a simultaneous reification of disgust, or without the reduction of one's lover to an amputation, in which the absence of a limb is cast as the sum total of identity, existence, and worth? In other words, are there other models for desiring disability that don't rely on the closed logic of devotee exceptionalism?

I find one possible answer to that question in the work of Eli Clare and Samuel Lurie, lovers who explore the territory of disability and desire. Lurie is nondisabled, and he writes about Clare's hand tremors (Clare has cerebral palsy), not as something to be overlooked or passively accepted, but as something to be desired. For Lurie, each of Clare's tremors is a gift across his skin. "Immediately, my body started begging for that exact tremoring touch," he writes. "When I discovered that his right hand tremored more than the left, that's the one I pulled to me, to rub my chest, cheek, thigh. I didn't want a single bounce to go to waste" (84). In this language of desire, a dramatic reimagining of cerebral palsy, tremors become touch, each "bounce" a source of pleasure and delight.[25]

The tremors that bring Lurie such pleasure had often been a source of psychological pain for Clare. In an essay lamenting the ways in which bodies marked by difference are "stolen" through physical violence and social isolation, Clare confesses, "Sometimes I wanted to cut off my right arm so it wouldn't shake. My shame was that plain, that bleak" ("Exile" 362). Clare describes the theft of his body, condemning the effects of ableism, classism, sexism, homophobia, and transphobia on his life; "gawkers," discrimination, and misrecognition have too often found their way under his skin. This shame, however, finds a powerful antidote in Lurie's desire: "*He cradles my right hand against his body and says, 'Your tremors feel so good.' And says, 'I can't get enough of your shaky touch.' And says, 'I love your cerebral palsy.' . . . Shame and disbelief flood my body, drowning his words. How do I begin to learn his lustful gaze?* Believing him takes more than trust" ("Gawking" 258; emphasis in original). Reading their essays together makes clear how both make themselves vulnerable to each other, mutually negotiating the terrain of their desire. Lurie recognizes this interplay, writing, "there was an utter magic in the combination of my wanting that very specific thing that for Eli was the root of so much of his own struggles with his body" (84). Seeing his tremors register as erotic touch, Clare began to see himself through a lens of desire rather than shame.

What, if anything, makes Lurie's desire different from the desire of the devotees I've sketched here? And what, if anything, distinguishes Clare's response to it from the welcoming responses of some amputees to devotees? These are not simple questions, but they are ones that disability studies and disability rights activism need to engage seriously: how can we desire disability, disabled bodies, without falling into the exceptionalist logic of desire and disgust that pervades devoteeism? How can we eroticize extraordinary bodies without fetishizing impairment, without reducing human beings to spare parts and effacing the lived experiences of disability?

One key distinction between Lurie's and Clare's narratives and the narratives circulating within devoteeism is their engagement with the larger culture. Disgust appears in Clare's essays as a political reality, mutable and debatable, rather than as a natural and inevitable reaction to disability, as it is figured in devoteeism. He acknowledges that many people may approach disabled bodies with more disgust than desire, but he insists that such reactions be understood in terms of larger cultural histories and practices of representation. Questions about sexual desirability and self-esteem are seen as directly related to questions about social recognition, political power, economic access, and sexual autonomy. Clare not only challenges the gawkers but also condemns the institutionalization of disabled people in nursing homes, the coerced sterilization of people with cognitive impairments, and the segregation of disabled children in "special" classrooms. In stark contrast to devotee discourses, which present sexual desirability as the only real problem facing people with disabilities, Clare's narrative positions sexual oppression as inextricable from political oppression.

Versions of the tremor and touch story appear in several of Clare's recent essays, suggesting that Clare recognizes the revolutionary potential in his exchange with Lurie. What is exciting about this narrative, and what moves this exchange away from the realm of devoteeism, is Clare's hope that others might come to feel a similar desire, might begin to recognize tremors—or stumps, or scars, or sensory impairments—as sensual gifts. In a series of questions that refuse to posit disabled bodies as properly objects of disgust, Clare writes, "*If I touch you with tremoring hands, will you wince away, thinking* cripple, *thinking* ugly? *Or will you unfold to my body, let my trembling shimmer beneath your skin?*" ("Gawking" 260; emphasis in original). "Let my trembling shimmer beneath your skin": finding the erotic in his tremoring touch, Clare refuses the exceptionalist logic of devoteeism. He speaks directly to his readers, tempting them with the promise of his touch, encouraging them in their desires, never once suggesting that devotees are the only ones who could ever find him sexy. Disgust isn't seen as naturally adhering to particular bodies, and desire isn't assumed to be the province of only a select few.

I recognize myself in Clare's narrative of shame and desire; I am painfully aware that I too have sometimes yearned to be free of a visibly different body, have wanted to shield my broken parts from public view. As with Clare, however, my shame is countered by a desire to reclaim my body from the gawkers, to revel in the bumpy scars that move across my skin or in the ease with which I can curl up into myself, and into my lover, with my abbreviated body. I am moved by Clare's and Lurie's accounts, excited both by the details of their specific negotiations and by the larger implications of those negotiations. I hear revolution in this "extra touching," an opening of possibilities in this reframing of cerebral palsy. I want more such stories that make my skin tingle with possibility, that demand recognition of my desires and desirability, that refuse to separate political oppression from sexual marginalization. I no longer want to wade through devoteeism's narratives of disgust, narratives that erase the specificities of my life and the breadth of my experiences, in order to find traces of desire. I want alternatives to tales of devotee exceptionalism; I want to imagine the possibility of radical social and political change that affects all of us. Devoteeism would then represent only one choice out of many, a choice that would no longer seem so fraught with ambivalence.

For now, however, the ambivalence remains, settling in deep around me, and my wanting only brings with it more questions. Even now, years and pages later, I cannot answer all the questions I've posed in this chapter, the questions I've tossed at you, the questions I imagine you have for me. These questions are lodged in my bones, prickling beneath my skin, poking at my desires. Even now, informed by feminist and queer theory, by the poetics of lovers like Lurie and Clare, by my own experiences of desiring and being desired, I remain gut-wrenchingly uncertain. This is an uncertainty fed by the stares I receive on the street; an uncertainty stoked by the threats of disgust and promises of desire I find in devoteeism; an uncertainty nurtured and tended by my own struggles to come to terms with the substance of my desires and the terrain of my body.

Maybe this is all I can give you, this gut-wrenching, knotty ambivalence. Maybe at this point we are served more by a willingness to sit with the complexities than by an insistence on fixed positions or definite answers. If a feminist and queer disability studies is about fundamentally questioning the processes by which certain bodies, desires, and practices become normalized, then perhaps searching for a single answer to the question of devoteeism is a misguided approach. And an answer to what exactly? The question of devoteeism's appropriateness? The question of the desirability of my body? To give an answer would be to suggest that I'd untied the knot, when all I have are these strands, turning and twisting in my hands.

NOTES

I want to thank all of the amputees and devotees who have shared their thoughts and experiences with me. For helping me navigate these complexities, I am grateful to the participants in the Ed Roberts Seminar in Disability Studies at the University of California, Berkeley, 2006–2007, and, especially, Sarah Chinn, Anna Mollow, and Dana Newlove.

1. "Part II," e-mail to the author, 25 November 2000; "Your Article," e-mail to the author, 17 November 2000.

2. Although I still occasionally receive such e-mails, I received a large number of them on a fairly consistent basis from 2000–2002.

3. See Raymond J. Aguilera's "Disability and Delight: Staring Back at the Devotee Community" for another example of an amputee first encountering devotees online.

4. Contributors to devotee websites seldom post under their full names, relying on pseudonyms or disclosing only their initials. This practice stems from the stigma many men experience as devotees. Fearful of rejection or ridicule, they prefer to keep their desires private, identifying with devoteeism only among other devotees or under other names. As a result, many devotees use the language of passing and coming out to describe their participation in devoteeism; devotee discourses are full of "coming-out stories" in which devotees describe having first realized the nature of their attraction and/or how they explained it to their friends, coworkers, and family. Some devotees explicitly align themselves with LGBTQ populations, arguing that devotees deserve the same kind of social recognition and acceptance that has been granted to LGBTQ people. (Of course, the degree to which queers have attained—or desire—such recognition is debatable, and, as I suggest below, devotee discourses are marked by a heteronormativity that renders any allegiance to queer communities suspect.)

5. For an example of the medical approach to devoteeism, see Bruno. In the last few years, both the popular press and the field of cultural studies have discovered devotees, pretenders (nondisabled people who want to pass as disabled and/or use adaptive technologies such as braces or hearing aids), and wannabes (nondisabled people who feel they were born into the wrong bodies, often undergoing elective or self-surgery to impair themselves). Like the medical accounts that precede them, many of these stories are concerned primarily with tracing the etiology of these "conditions" (e.g., Elliott). While amputees figure in the medical texts almost exclusively as the unwilling and unwitting victims of devotee exploitation, they appear in these more recent texts as envy-

inducing reminders of the beauty to be found in fragmentation and separation (e.g., Lingis). None of these accounts of disability and desire attends seriously to the material effects of ableism on the lives of disabled people.

6. See Duncan; Duncan and Goggin; Hagglund; and Storrs, "Caveat" and "Amputees" for accounts of these kinds of behavioral and attitudinal changes.

7. Margrit Shildrick and Fiona Kumari Campbell provide two exceptions, each briefly addressing devoteeism in their recent examinations of disability and subjectivity.

8. On devotee demographics, see D. Dixon; Nattress.

9. For a discussion of devoteeism among gay men, including personal reflections on the phenomenon, see Aguilera; Aguilera et al.; Guter. Some nondisabled straight women identify as devotees, but they are in the minority; almost all of the postings on devotee websites involve male devotees, and only a few female devotees have attended amputee-devotee conferences hosted by organizations such as ASCOTworld. I can find very little mention of lesbian devotees, and several Internet hits on the topic consist of requests from male devotees for "sexy dyke amps" or feature explicit photographs of sex between nondisabled men and disabled women. I obviously cannot rule out the existence of lesbian devotees, but they do not play a role in the devotee discourses under discussion here.

As even a cursory Internet search of devoteeism makes clear, devoteeism is by no means limited to the United States or English-language websites and communities; as far as I know, however, there are no studies of the global devotee population.

10. It is this siting of desire in an amputee's stump that leads most outsiders, including medical professionals, to cast devoteeism as a form of fetishism (a form of sexual desire in which sexual gratification is tied to the real or fantasized presence of an object or body part, often to the point of obsession). Devotees, however, resist this characterization for two reasons: first, they object to the medicalization of their desires, asserting that there is nothing pathological or diagnosable in their attraction for amputees; and second, they insist that they are not fixated on stumps, but are attracted to the "whole person," so the label does not accurately apply. Although I am sympathetic with their first complaint—I, too, am reluctant to cast their attraction (as opposed to their behavior) as pathological—I have my doubts about the second; as I suggest here, their understanding of the "whole person" seems completely bound up in the stump itself.

11. When Paul McCartney's (now defunct) relationship with Heather Mills first became public, devotee websites buzzed with the news that McCartney had finally "come out" as a devotee. Despite the fact that McCartney had never expressed a particular desire for disabled women, the mere fact of his involvement with an amputee was seen as irrefutable evidence of his "true" identity. In this characterization of the McCartney and Mills relationship, her status as an amputee is the only factor that matters.

12. Personal communication, 26 October 2000. For a brief reflection on the use of

the term "ladies" in amputee-devotee communities, and an extended analysis of gender roles within devoteeism, see Kafer, "Inseparable."

13. I want to caution against reading K.'s remarks as an argument about the irrelevance of sexuality to rehabilitation. Disability rights activists and disability studies scholars have argued persuasively about the importance of holistic approaches to rehab, including information about sexual function and attention to sexual self-awareness. K.'s comments are noteworthy for their challenge to J.'s single-mindedness; I read them less as an argument about the place of sexuality in the recovery process than as a rebuke of J.'s approach.

14. See, among others, the work of Block; Clare; Kafer; O'Toole; Shakespeare et al.; Waxman-Fiduccia; and A. Wilkerson for examinations of sexuality and people with disabilities.

15. ASCOTworld, for example, bans from future events any person who "acts out" or "maliciously causes trouble," discouraging members from taking unauthorized photographs and loitering uninvited at amputee events.

16. Nattress's complete list: (1) Seeing a woman on crutches or limping, following her to verify her status as an amputee, and then learning as much as possible about her. (2) Sitting in a public space where others have seen an amputee in the hopes of seeing, photographing, and possibly meeting her. (3) Collecting photographs and articles about female amputees. (4) Drawing pictures of amputee women or modifying existing pictures to make the featured woman into an amputee [a process known as "electronic surgery"]. (5) Keeping a detailed list of female amputees. (6) Developing programs or starting organizations that serve amputees. (7) Calling female amputees whom one has read about in order to learn what their lives are like. (8) Carrying on extensive correspondence with a female amputee, often pretending to be a female amputee oneself. (9) Asking an amputee one already knows for the names and numbers of other female amputees. (10) Writing fiction starring amputee women or women who become amputees. (11) Researching the amputee-devotee community or disability issues in order to meet disabled women. (12) Possessing and providing information on wheelchairs, prosthetics, and other assistive devices to women with disabilities (18–19). Few devotees, Nattress stresses, partake in all twelve. The difficulty in ascertaining which behaviors constitute harassment within devoteeism, and the ease with which secretly following and photographing women is accepted, is evident in the wide range of behavior in Nattress's list. Writing fiction about amputees is a completely different kind of activity from following an amputee home, yet they are presented here, side-by-side, as if no such difference existed.

Number eight in Nattress's list—masquerading as an amputee—begins to blur the line between "devotees," "pretenders," and "wannabes." Pretending in Nattress's schema, however, is more a means to an end—a way to meet female amputees, the object of a devotee's desire—than an end in itself. For most pretenders and wannabes, the erotic attraction is to appearing and/or being disabled oneself, rather than to being sexually or romantically involved with another disabled person (Bruno; Elliott; Harmon, this edited volume).

17. Opinions are mixed as to the best way to accomplish this increased social acceptance, but there appears to be agreement that such an increase is necessary. Although I do not have space to explore it here, the question of a possible link between the devotees' desire and the social taboos surrounding that desire merits exploration. Would devoteeism be as appealing for some of these men if it were no longer so esoteric or taboo? Are they as drawn to the possibility of social and sexual transgression as they are to disabled bodies? Is part of the pleasure of devoteeism found in bonding with other men around secret desires?

18. Gregson profiles an amputee who experiences this fear.

19. During the annual meeting of the Amputee Coalition of America (ACA) in 1996, female amputees held an emergency women-only meeting to discuss "the devotee problem" at the convention. Some women felt they were being harassed; others felt uncomfortable not knowing whether they were secretly being watched. During the meeting, attendees voted to urge the ACA to ban all devotees from future conventions and events. Immediately afterward, they invited LeRoy Nattress to present his research on devotees. Nattress explained to the assembled women that an outright ban on devotees was not only inappropriate but unfeasible. According to his research, 80 to 90 percent of the devotees in attendance were either spouses of amputees or professionals working at the conference (prosthetists, therapists, etc.). Based on Nattress's recommendations, the women decided to abandon their call for a ban and resolved instead to hold two women-only meetings at future ACA meetings (Nattress).

20. For a discussion of these difficulties, see Shakespeare et al. 74.

21. Non-devotee versions of such imagery might be easier to access for amputees involved in queercrip communities. For two queer meditations on the use of medical equipment in and/or as sex play, see Nomy Lamm's description of prosthetic legs as dildos (152) and Robert McRuer's analysis of performance artist Bob Flanagan (*Crip Theory* 181–94). For a sexually explicit and defiantly queercrip example of making a wheelchair sexy, see Loree Erickson's film *Want*, which powerfully combines footage of Erickson, her attendants, and her lover with a voice-over about living in an ableist society.

22. Most of the women depicted in professional pictures, such as those produced and sold online by ASCOTworld, CD Productions, and other amputee-owned image sites, receive payment for their services. Unfortunately, many of the images that circulate among devotees were not produced under those circumstances. Collectors often have pictures of unknown amputees that they either bought from other devotees or downloaded off the Internet, and the Internet is littered with photographs of anonymous amputees. Because there are reports of amputees having their pictures taken without their permission, it seems likely that at least some of the pictures in circulation were obtained under false pretenses. Indeed, the proliferation of unauthorized

photographs renders it nearly impossible to determine whether or not the photo trade exploits amputees. Images that might initially appear the most exploitative—pictures of naked or partially clad amputees in sexually suggestive or explicit poses—may actually be less exploitative than the "candid" images of fully clothed amputees involved in mundane activities.

These facts render my pleasure in viewing these images particularly problematic. Most of the images that I find most intriguing are the ones of unidentified women smiling at the camera as they sit in the grass or work in their kitchens or move down the street. These photographs, unlike the "swimsuit and lingerie" and "donning and doffing prosthetics" photographs, are much more likely to have been obtained without the women's permission.

23. Indeed, people with disabilities are not all similarly located in the rhetoric or logic of devoteeism. Amputation, paralysis, and deafness are commonly represented in devoteeism; autism, depression, multiple chemical sensitivities, and anxiety are not. Perhaps nonapparent impairments are more difficult to fetishize than those that mark the body or that necessitate some kind of adaptive (and readily apparent) technology. Perhaps also the rhetoric of disgust on which devoteeism relies so heavily requires some kind of visual marker. Thanks to Jen Patterson and Anna Mollow for bringing this difference to my attention.

24. For reasons that I hope are clear in this chapter, I have always been vigilant about not disclosing any details of my personal life to people involved in devoteeism, including my queer identifications. My silence, of course, is read as a sign of both heterosexuality and an acceptance of heteronormativity; as a result, I have been exposed to devotee discourses about the "causes" of homosexuality among disabled women. Amputees, I am told, occasionally turn to female lovers because they are unable to find men who will accept disabled partners. The specter of lesbianism thus serves as justification for increasing social acceptance and awareness of devoteeism; the proliferation of devotees would render lesbianism unnecessary, a goal "we" all are assumed to share. This twist on the sexist and heteronormative position that all lesbians are failed heterosexuals unquestionably affected my stance toward devotees, making it more difficult for me to accept them as "fellow deviants." For a brief examination of heterosexism within devoteeism, see Kafer, "Inseparable." For a satirical take on the assumption that disabled people turn to same-sex relationships because of an inability to find heterosexual partners, see Walloch.

25. Clare's and Lurie's stories are part of a small but growing number of memoirs, essays, and manifestos that present sex and sexuality as an integral part of the lives of disabled people (e.g., Finkelstein; Kleege; Linton, *My Body*; Lamm; O'Toole; *Want*). I focus on this particular example rather than others because it explicitly addresses the issue of desiring disability, of finding the erotic in a particular bodily sign of impairment.

17

....

KRISTEN HARMON

HEARING AID LOVERS,

PRETENDERS, AND DEAF WANNABES

The Fetishizing of Hearing

This is a special meeting place for people who have a deep felt desire to wear hearing aids for pleasure, even though not deaf, and for those who find that hearing aids and deafness have erotic and fetish qualities.

It is also a place to discuss the more radical topic of being a deaf wannabee, and a meeting place for those who have decided at some time in their life to "cross the bridge" and choose to become deaf by impairing their hearing.

—"Description," Deaf-Wannabee Yahoo Group

At first glance, phrases such as "hearing aids for pleasure," "gaining hearing loss," and "acquiring deafness" seem out of place, potential typos in the social text. "With a hearing aid, really? You wanna be . . . what?" Desiring deafness questions what we consider to be "authentic" physical, social, and cultural indicators of hearing status; desiring disability renders unintelligible our constructs of the normate body and its pleasures.[1] "Embodiment," Judith Butler writes, "is not thinkable without a relation to a norm, or a set of norms" (*Undoing* 28). Social norms are grounded in binary constructions such as ability/disability, in which disability is the contested and stigmatized opposition of ability. Because desiring disability "undoes" a person, in reference to existing bodily integrity norms, perhaps the thorniest discussion here has to do with this binary, whether or not such desires are transformative, or reiterative, and of which norms.

It seems clear from the outset that a fetishistic interest in hearing aids—assistive devices—is necessarily predicated upon, or is a product of, the medical model. Because of the medical model, the sense of hearing is made over into a commodity or magical fetish. However, disability and deafness and the Deaf cultural and linguistic community are generally conceptualized as separate, socially bound categories; interrogating the fetishizations generated by the medical model alone cannot quite address the questions posed by those who choose to deafen themselves.[2] Can such a person say, "I don't feel so hearing no more," and simply begin a life in a deafened body and/or initiate a Deaf identity? This chapter explores some of the theoretical, ethical, and rhetorical issues surrounding the desire of deafness, first as object and then as subject.

Sexologists argue that there are three general categories of disability fetishists: devotees, pretenders, and wannabes. According to Richard L. Bruno, "*Devotees* are nondisabled people who are sexually attracted to people with disabilities, typically those with mobility impairments and especially amputees; *Pretenders* are non-disabled people who act as if they have a disability by using assistive devices (e.g., braces, crutches, and wheelchairs) in private and sometimes in public so that they 'feel' disabled or are perceived by others as having a disability; *Wannabes* actually want to become disabled, sometimes going to extraordinary lengths to have a limb amputated" (243–44). These groupings also appear in the Internet discussion group Deaf-Wannabee. However, they are descriptions of very general and fairly porous principles of attraction; members may transition from one group to another or simultaneously self-identify with more than one "deaf fetish" label. In the discussion group, there is considerable overlap between devotees and pretenders; many of the devotees post pictures of hearing aid wearers and also chronicle their own experiences with wearing hearing aids in private and in public. Devotees and pretenders tend to be (but are not exclusively) male, professional, educated, and—judging from contextual information or self-disclosure—white and heterosexual.[3] In contrast to the wannabes, the pretenders and devotees tend to have more erotic sex play regarding use and sight of hearing aids; they also are more likely to self-identify as having "fetishes."

Despite the title that emphasizes the "wannabe" portion of the membership, Deaf-Wannabee desire is generally focused upon the wearing and use of hearing aids (by devotees, or "hearing aid lovers," and pretenders). Some members do, however, focus primarily upon "crossing the bridge," or self-deafening (and for lack of a better term, I will refer to them as "wannabes" in this chapter). This particular English-language Internet discussion group began in the spring of 2000, and by the fall of 2006, the mostly British and Western European members had exchanged over two thousand messages (and at the time this chapter was written, there were over seven hundred active and inactive members from several countries, including the United States).

While it is difficult to generalize from the group members' sporadic interchanges and the fluctuation in participation, it seems that in the Deaf-Wannabee group, a slight majority of those who describe—or at the very least, articulate—self-deafening desires are women, particularly young women. A large percentage of both male and female wannabes already have some degree of naturally occurring hearing loss; of those, many express interest in exerting some level of "control" over the process. Still others intentionally deafen themselves for reasons that are more aligned with identity and/or body integrity.

Motives for deafening vary; some cite desire for membership within the Deaf community while others want the deafened body and sensory state. As a variegated grouping, those who desire, simulate, and choose disability do not easily align with academic and political efforts to "refram[e] 'disability,'" as Garland-Thomson puts it, "as another culture bound, *physically justified difference* to consider along with race, gender, class, ethnicity, and sexuality" (*Extraordinary* 5; emphasis added). Even in Lennard Davis's call to "reverse the hegemony of the normal and to institute alternative ways of thinking about the abnormal," the normal/abnormal binary remains intact, as will always be the case in an ableist and audist society (*Enforcing* 49).[4] In such a context, desiring and crafting an "abnormal" body or persona raises uneasy questions about embodiment, authenticity, and the sociopolitical aspects of deafness and identity.

From the Duke in Mark Twain's *Adventures of Huckleberry Finn* to a man pretending to be "hearing impaired" in order to get released from a speeding ticket, Deaf imposters or pretenders are nothing new. When it comes to men and women who wear hearing aids or who pretend to be deaf or hearing impaired on occasion, public consensus suggests that this behavior, although suspect and perhaps "perverted" or "fetishistic," is nonetheless legible, from an academic or empirical perspective. Perhaps the use of hearing aids is a sign of displacement or projection (as theorized by Sigmund Freud), or perhaps this fascination with hearing aids is part of the fetishization of many objects in our culture associated with the feminine or the vulnerable, such as high heels. Perhaps such fixation upon or use of hearing aids is another incidence of a paraphiliac fascination that can then be explained in the terms of the social science and medical discourses. Perhaps fetishists "have" a psychiatric disorder that causes the fixation; perhaps such obsessional thinking and use of objects is a marker of psychiatric disability. Fetishists of the body modification and cyborg tradition might add, ironically or not, that hearing aids are a technology that can be worn as a marker of the body's sensory limits or excesses.

Most of these theories of the fetish stress the retroactive or repetitive nature of meaning making from within a particular individual, and as such, fetishistic desires resist regulation. As the literary critic Rebecca Comay notes, "the 'happy' pervert is not motivated to seek analysis, just as the enraptured consumer is mollified by the gleam of things" (55). Comay goes on to say: "These versions of the fetish therefore involve a similar temporality of stasis. By freezing time—at the moment *before* the traumatic insight (Freud) or as the abstraction of inert exchangeable instants (Marx)—the fetishist seeks to pacify the restless *Nachtraglichkeit*: the incessant self-rupturing of history" (55). In this context, such actions are stigmatized, to be sure, but they are socially legible, as deferred or reiterable actions. One can make meaning out of these object fixations, feel turned off or turned on, as the case may be, and call them "deviant desires." One can even look up Curtin University of Technology's rather proper-looking Department of Podiatry on the Internet and see a lengthy and resourceful web page on the "The History of Footwear: Foot Fetishism and Shoe Retifism," complete with etymologies ("retifism" being a more precise term for sexual attractions to shoes). As idées fixes, certain object fetishes have entered into the public discourse in ways that the disability fetishes and "wannabe" desires have not.

As one "Deaf-Wannabee" member pointed out, a foot fetish is relatively tolerated as a fetish; most people, she notes, consider foot fetishes to be strange desires, but not out of the realm of possibility for other people. This member wonders why, when foot fetish erotica is easy to find and when one can fairly easily find amputee erotica—a fetish that she acknowledges most people would find difficult to comprehend—deaf erotica is difficult to find ("BBC Show—a good idea???," Deaf-Wannabee, July 2006).[5]

Despite the context this writer provides for understanding fetish, the notion of what constitutes "deaf erotica" for members of this group is not uncomplicated, and the members sometimes feel the need to clarify their motives or to point out differences among desires. After a posting entitled, "Fetish or . . . ??,"

Kristen Harmon

(Deaf-Wannabee, July 2006), both male and female members responded by clarifying their own positions in reference to the other members: some noted that they get "excited" but are not responding sexually, while others noted that the attraction is sexual or erotic. Still others noted that they wanted the silence of a deafened experience. A list member who identifies herself as a pretender gave an interview on "Ouch!," a disability oriented BBC podcast, noting that, "By the way, it's not a sexual thing for me although it is for most of the other pretenders I know. I just think it's cool . . . like 'wow, I wish I could be cool like deaf people'" ("Ouch! Podcast" 18).

Pretender and devotee postings are more common from the men in the group. These run the gamut between the overtly prurient, asking for pictures and videos ("Any pictures and/or video . . . ," Deaf-Wannabee July 2002), to wistful postings, such as the one from a married hearing man, who confesses to a huge attraction to women with hearing aids; he continues his musing and notes that he would not hesitate to have an affair with a woman with hearing loss, but because he's not a person prone to cheat, he will have to wait and see if his wife ever develops a loss. He adds, in a confessional tone, that if he did meet a hard-of-hearing or deaf woman who wanted to play around, his commitment to his wedding vows would be severely tested ("One More Comment," Deaf-Wannabee, March 2006).

Despite the fact that several of the devotees and pretenders describe being in relationships with hard-of-hearing or deaf people, perhaps the projective element inherent in fetishistic fantasies would account for the oddly asexual (in the sense of being described independently of sexual acts), yet furtively excited, nature of many e-mail exchanges between group members, particularly in relation to sensation and to the "thing-ness" of deafness and hearing loss: "From an early age I had a deep fascination with ears. As a child I was absorbed by the sight of [a] girl's ears, and with putting objects in my own ears" (qtd. in Suggs 45).[6] "I'm very interested in the body hearing aids," and "I think they look 'cool' on girls" are also common sentiments. Often these postings are accompanied by a request for photos of "girls" in hearing aids. The photo gallery consists almost exclusively of "photo albums" containing close-up photographs of white men, and the occasional woman, wearing behind-the-ear (BTE) hearing aids or up-close shots of the hearing aids themselves. The exception, a series of photographs of a glamorous white woman's face, pouting and posing for the camera, is jarring, particularly as her relation to hearing aids or deafness is not made observable. Notwithstanding the connotation that the model has possibly had plastic surgery and the corollary fetishizing of female body parts, the normative and normate values the photograph expresses in relation to objectified or eroticized beauty seem out of place in this discussion group's photo gallery.

The fetishists in the Deaf-Wannabee group generally use the group as a confessional, a resource room, or as a source of fetish-related erotica of sorts — including a picture gallery of hearing aids — rather than as a "hook up" site, though, to be sure, that does happen. Similarly, as Raymond Aguilera points out in relation to the Dragonworks Devotee Community, "pictures [of amputees] were relatively soft-core, and could in fact barely be called pornography at all . . . notably less explicit than mainstream pornography. . . . In the written stories too, there seemed to be a surprising lack of actual sex" (256; 257). Instead of overt or explicit sexual or erotic identification with deafness, a new member typically expresses profound relief and delight for having found that he or she "is not the only one in the world" who has "felt this way" about hearing aids and deaf people.

On the whole, from within and from without, there seems to be a lack of conceptualization of what it might mean to have a fetishistic interest in a wearer of hearing aids or a (fetishistic) desire to have sexual encounters with a person with an altered sense of hearing. Such conceptualization might point to the limitation of using reified labels for a singular fetishistic behavior or interest, particularly because fetishes for particular disabilities or disability accoutrements can sometimes coexist; for example, the hearing aid fetish can coexist with a fetish for braces, or for eyeglasses and leg braces. (While some members mention membership on other online disability devotee communities or mention co-occurring fetishes, most often fetishes for hearing aids or hearing aid wearers are discussed as isolated desires.) In any case, one has only to look at the long lists of names of particular fetishes, borrowed from sexological studies and then placed in titillating contexts such as the *Encyclopedia of Unusual Sex Practices*, to see that the fetish is, in the public eye, "a curiosity and source of amazement." As a descriptive term for pretender and devotee desire, "fetish" offers up surprisingly little, other than connotation and stigma.

The use of fetish terminology is further complicated when one looks to see the formal use of the word in psychiatric discourse. In the American Psychiatric Association's *Diagnostic and Statistical Manual of Mental Disorders*, fourth edition, text revision (*DSM-IV-TR*), fetishes are found under the general category of "Sexual and Gender Identity Disorders" and finally under the diagnostic category of "paraphilias" or "recurrent, intense sexually arousing fantasies, sexual urges, or behaviors generally involving 1) nonhuman objects, 2) the suffering or humiliation of oneself or one's partner, or 3) children or other nonconsenting persons that occur over a period of at least 6 months" (566). The diagnostic terms for the identified paraphilias are: exhibitionism, fetishism, frotteurism, pedophilia, sexual masochism, sexual sadism, transvestic fetishism, voyeurism, and paraphilia not otherwise specified (American Psychiatric Association 567). While it seems that "nonhuman objects" are descriptive of hearing aid fetishes, this is complicated by the commodification of hearing aids; as products readily available from online sources and dealers, and as products that are presented as desired devices for deaf children and the elderly to wear, hearing aids are nonhuman objects that have taken on the magical stance also associated with cultural fetishes.

A fixation with a wearer of hearing aids could, however, be very loosely construed as a fascination with a "nonconsenting partner," and this certainly has relevance for people who wear hearing aids and who have been approached by people who seem rather too interested in the fact of one's hearing aids. However, as fetishes are currently construed, this emotional or social discomfort does not have psychiatric bearing. According to the *DSM-IV-TR*, "Paraphilic imagery may be acted out with a non consenting partner that may be injurious to the partner," as in sexual sadism or pedophilia (American Psychiatric Association 566); the further refined criteria outlined under "Fetishism" focuses upon "nonliving objects," with no mention of a nonconsenting partner (American Psychiatric Association 569–70). "Nonliving objects" are carefully distinguished from the use of female clothing, as in "transvestic fetishism," or when an object is "genitally stimulating" because it has been designed for that purpose (American Psychiatric Association 570).

The *DSM-IV-TR* also insists, in bold type, on the distinction between these disorders and the "nonpathological use of sexual fantasies, behaviors, or objects as a stimulus for sexual excitement in individuals without a Paraphilia" (American Psychiatric Association 568), noting as well that "many individuals with these disorders assert that the behavior causes them no distress and that their only problem is social dysfunction as a result of the reaction of others to their behavior" (American Psychiatric Association 567). Because "self-reports" are subjective, and because there are not clearer, more empirical criteria for a diagnosis, one wonders where the specification lies between an individual with a paraphilia and an individual without paraphilia: what does one do with a noncriminal, "happy pervert" who physically harms no one other than perhaps himself or herself?

The diagnostic criteria for a fetish paraphilia also require that fetish-related "fantasies, sexual urges, or behaviors cause clinically significant distress or impairment in social, occupational, or other important area of functioning" (American Psychiatric Association 570). Though the devotee and pretender members of the Deaf-Wannabee group share stories about the difficulties of "coming out" and share fears of disclosure, they generally do not express "significant distress" (the case is perhaps different for some of the "wannabes").

On the whole, in a system where "normality is broadly equated with desirability," where "move[ment] towards the norms of sexual function is framed as an 'improvement'" (Downing par. 2), one wonders—uncomfortably, given the context of disability fetish—about the limits of measuring sexuality. Writing about LGBT sexuality, Butler makes a point that has provocative implications for a discussion of deaf and disability fetishism: "Sexuality is not simply an attribute one has or a disposition or patterned set of inclinations. It is a mode of being disposed toward others, including in the mode of fantasy, and sometimes only in the mode of fantasy" (*Undoing* 33). Object fetishes are accepted—even celebrated as subversive or liberatory—within queer and SM communities. Can fetishes for hearing aids and attempts at self-deafening be placed within the same category? In addition to the sociopolitical ramifications of perceived "foul play" done to one's body, the sticking point seems to be the opposition of ability and disability, and the exclusion of disabled and d/Deaf people from "compulsory heterosexuality" by way of "compulsory able-bodiedness" (McRuer, *Crip Theory* 2).[7]

Yet because these pretender and devotee fetishes tend not to harm the physical body, and because this particular use of hearing aids reflects consensual behavior or a private decision, does this mean that co-opting of deaf apparatuses—hearing aids, or even a "deaf voice"—is ethically unproblematic, particularly in regard to "real" deaf and deafened bodies? Kath Duncan, a double congenital amputee and activist, suspects that "the distance between the biomedical gaze and the adoring one . . . is not so very far. The devotee gaze is enabled by dominant, powerful envisioning of different bodies" (11). In her famous essay on visual pleasure in narrative cinema, Laura Mulvey (by way of Freud) contends that the first source of pleasure in looking, scopophilia, arises from "using another person as an object of sexual stimulation through sight" (and as such, scopophilia is one helpful way to define the fetishistic qualities of a fascination with a "non-living" object that is worn by a "nonconsenting partner"). The second source of pleasure, for Mulvey, "comes from identification with the image seen" (441).

The significant point here is that the "pleasure in looking has been split between active/male and passive/female" (Mulvey 442). The phallic principle and gendered oppositions upon which Mulvey's theory depend certainly do not easily explain (or they invite a too facile explanation of) queer and straight women's uses of hearing aids. Yet Mulvey's general theory of the gaze does indeed open up some of the general ethical questions raised by the pretender and devotee fetishes.

The "idealization" here seems less about the disabled body per se and more about the use of a common prosthesis as a trope. Instead of correcting a deficiency, the use of hearing aids supplies a deficiency, and in doing so, the gaze "fill[s] a gap, but . . . also diminish[es] the body and create[s] the need for itself" (Jain 44). So this use of hearing aids endlessly refers back to the medical definitions of impairment, but arguably fueling the relations of looking are two idealized subject positions not wholly unlike those Mulvey theorizes: one subject whose gaze puts her or him in a position of mastery, and another who becomes merely a sensate body (with a prosthesis). In ways that perhaps exceed Mulvey, however, devotees, pretenders, and wannabes position themselves on both sides of this exchange.

One pretender and wannabe writes, "Another method I have used is to place cotton wool deep in my ear canal. Pretty effective, and it allows a longer term assessment. . . . After several months of simulated deafness I have removed it and then spent several days with normal hearing, and then returned again to the trial. It's totally controllable and safe." She continues by noting her decision to "adopt" hearing loss, "I have decided that I really do want to take on board a mild hearing loss which is sufficient to justify the enjoyment of wearing a second hearing aid" (qtd. in Suggs 52). Similarly, another pretender and wannabe writes, "I want to use hearing aids, and have the enjoyment of doing so and knowing I need them. As near as possible I want 'normal' hearing with my hearing aids" (qtd. in Suggs 63). In addition to "creating the need" for hearing aids, these members place emphasis upon "normal" and "control" over the process, which seems to suggest that the weight lies upon the hearing aid as prosthesis, supplying disability.

Another pretender, one who writes prolifically about his experiences with hearing aids, by turns warns and titillates other members by noting that the first experience with using hearing aids could disappoint because the listening experience is so new and different. He then instructs his fellow pretenders, with liberal use of exclamation points, to look in the mirror in order to see how wonderful the new hearing aids appear ("How to Wear Your BTE," Deaf-Wannabee, August 2004). The writer's use of a mirror seems scripted, it fits so well with the scopophiliac process Mulvey describes.

Homi Bhabha's conception of the "racial fetish" is also useful for exploring the implications of a member of a majority population taking on characteristics of a minority. Bhabha draws upon the logic of Oedipal conflict and castration fears, and he argues that the resultant fetish provides a mechanism for understanding the nature of displacement, in that the logic of stereotyping in the public domain draws upon the same mechanisms that underlie the fetish in the private domain. In this paradigm, the fetishist, or the "dominant individual," then "projects otherness and difference . . . upon the disparaged group" (Straker 412).

According to Bhabha's theories, in the fetishist's mind the assumption of otherness applies to all in the same group. In the context under consideration here, the resulting stereotype could allow for the use of deaf people, in particular, or hearing-aid users in general, as a fetish to "suspend belief in Otherness even while being cast as Other" (Straker 412). One Deaf-Wannabee group member, describing how he developed a "hearing aid fetish" due to a mild hearing loss as a youth, wrote that with the new aids "I suddenly received an unprecedented amount of attention . . . My hearing aids had changed me from a zero to a superhero" (qtd. in Suggs 67). This writer shows the same inverted logic in a later post, in which he both is Other and desires Other: "Yes I'm most DEAFi-nitely turned on by the feel and sight of myself in hearing aids . . . In fact I'm convinced I perform far better sexually when I have them in! This belief is essential to my fetish" (qtd. in Suggs 68). This writer mentions that his sexual partner is hard of hearing and that he has dated "real deafies" before (without disclosing his fetish). His comments could read as confirming Bhabha's link between stereotypic representation and fetish as process of displacement: "For fetishism is always a 'play' or vacillation between the archaic affirmation of wholeness/similarity—in Freud's terms: 'All men have penises'; in ours: 'All men have the same skin/race/culture'—and the anxiety associated with lack and difference—again, for Freud 'Some do not have penises'; for us 'Some do not have the same skin/race/culture'" (74). Substitute "all men have hearing" and "some do not have hearing," and the result is a similar recognition and disavowal; that is, the use of hearing aids to enact a "hearing-impaired" persona or, alternately, to select sexual partners on the basis of prosthetic machinery.

In a similar fashion to pretenders selecting sexual partners based upon their "lack," fairly common are devotee testimonies that describe early fascinations with a fellow child or teenager wearing hearing aids. Because this group's membership seems to skew toward members older than thirty-five, descriptions of "body aids" are not uncommon. One member remembers dating a girl who wore such a body aid, and he notes that the wiring and size of the objects in her ears and on her body amazed him; he recalls her as an attractive girl, if not particularly smart, and he doubts that he would have dated her if she had not been wearing a body hearing aid ("Re: New Here, Wife is HOH," Deaf-Wannabee, September 2005). She was a "pretty girl," one whom he wanted to have, but perhaps only because she provided a simulacrum of other pretty girls, reduced to—but paradoxically powered by—a pretty, plastic machine.

Regressive and culturally hegemonic elements recur in more explicit comments—such as "I have a youthful female ears-wearing-hearing-aids fetish"—and in requests for pictures of girls and women wearing hearing aids. Similar postings make it clear that pictures of "girls" wearing hearing aids are sexier than standard pornographic fare ("deaf wannabee," Deaf-Wannabee, February 2001). And a particularly baroque (and relatively rare, insofar as prurience goes) posting notes that what is desired are young men who have been forced into wearing diapers, coke-bottle bottom glasses, wheelchairs, and braces; this group member loves to see young men in body casts and who are forced—with great embarrassment and discomfort—into wearing diapers. He also notes that he likes young lovers in clearly visible hearing aids, particularly when these young men learn to depend on the aids and can no longer function without them ("Greetings DW-group," Deaf-Wannabee, September 2001). Other sentiments along these lines go in more detail into motivation, making it clear that what is attractive, especially in the cases of multiple disabilities, is the element of pervasive "dependence."

In one particularly memorable exchange, a writer with a fascination with deafblindness engaged in a dialogue with a woman who was already blind and was "working on" deafness. In his response to her post, he thanked her because reading her post gave him the feeling that he could understand her from the inside and outside and that what attracted him to her was the permanence of her situation, and the fact that she will always be dependent upon others. This particular fashioning of an erotic scenario struck him as very appealing because of everything that he could do to help her ("More Questions to L," Deaf-Wannabee, August 2003). This "dependence" amplifies passive gender roles and robs the disabled woman of independence, as the deafblind woman noted, in lengthy responses to this and other group members' attraction to "dependence" ("Question to L" and "More Questions to L," Deaf-Wannabee, August 2003). Her points were well received by the man who initially expressed a romantic interest in extreme dependence; in addition to a cheery acknowledgment, he signed off with an affectionate closing.

In discussions of fetishistic fixations, it has been suggested "that because disabled women and girls inherited ascriptions of passivity and weakness, pornographers and others sometimes selected them to portray as ultimate compliant sex objects" (Lowenstein 138). Sex play such as the following scenario pops up occasionally in the narratives that women pretenders or wannabes post: one woman with a devotee husband describes how, when she catches him gazing at her ears, she'll make a performance out of taking out the hearing aids, softly rubbing her ears, and then, after close inspection of her earmold, slowly pushing the hearing aid back into her ear. If he says something while the hearing aid is out, she pretends not to understand and indicates to him that she cannot hear without her hearing aids. He smiles sympathetically and calls her his deaf wife ("K.'s Side of the Story," Deaf-Wannabee, November 2005). Another husband and wife play with the notion of "deaf wife" and dutifully post their adventures online; this time the woman tells him that he will have to speak louder on account of her hearing loss, and her husband responds enthusiastically, with gratifying results for both. She adds that playing the deaf wife was the performance of her life, a role she was destined to play ("New to Group," Deaf-Wannabee, September 2003).

In contrast, for the few men who described the erotic effects of wearing hearing aids in a sexual situation, the locus of pleasure was turned inward. One man writes, "I . . . have a fetish of a 'turn on' when someone plays with my hearing aids while they are in my ears." Another confides, "I would encourage intimate partners to touch and if willing to 'play' with my hearing aids while they were in my ears. Those who were willing to do so gave me quite an 'EarOtic' experience" (qtd. in Suggs 66–67). Neither of these men divulged whether or not their sexual partners also perceived this as role play.

At times, the juxtapositions among the eroticized interests of the pretenders, the fascination expressed by the devotees, and the "serious consequences" of intentional deafening created an uneasy dialogue among this group of people brought together by a compelling need or desire for deafness. At one point, the juxtaposition is jarring: a long and heartfelt personal narrative about progressive hearing loss is followed by a different member's long and rather eroticized and objectified description of various techniques and tools for inducing deafness, including a discussion of "thresholds of pain."

Kristen Harmon

Becoming "deaf by choice" (or desiring self-deafening acts) is to risk what Butler calls "unintelligibility," in that "the laws of culture and of language find you to be an impossibility" (*Undoing* 30). Perhaps in response to the threat of unintelligibility, then, the "wannabe" members reverse pathologized phrases in their descriptions. They write of "gaining hearing loss" as opposed to losing hearing, "acquiring deafness" instead of "having" hearing. In their surprisingly positivist impressions of an absence, these phrases seem to enact a contradiction. However, it is important to note that the terms of embodiment in both "losing" hearing and "gaining" hearing loss endlessly refer back to the medical model. Other phrases such as "tuning" a hearing loss in order to attain the desired decibel loss appear to depart from this phraseology, and yet continue to point back toward audition.

While these particular semantic changes are made for the purposes of normalizing and incorporating self-deafening, a central observation of this chapter is that this use of terminology stands in contrast to sociolinguistic and community-oriented descriptors used by those in the culturally Deaf, signing community. Deaf people use the construct of a "Deaf World," as opposed to a "hearing world"; "Deaf" and "hard of hearing," as opposed to hearing impaired or deafened; and "fluency in American Sign Language (ASL)" to describe users of a full-fledged language, as opposed to "manual communication." These descriptors consciously insist upon a conception of self that is not ableist or audist, not medicalized or pathologized; instead of focusing upon the absence of a sense, these terms assert a holistic identity, grounded in language and community, in visuality instead of (the lack of) audition. For Deafblind people, this sense of self is mediated through the tactile. This is not to say that all of the wannabes use medicalized terms of description; some of those who elect deafness, particularly the women, also use the sociolinguistic descriptors for their desires; they want a Deaf body and self.

Little wonder that there is such a visceral response to the description of self-deafening; the act, or the desire for it, confronts head-on both essentialist (and often medicalized) and social constructionist definitions of what it means to be a deaf person. Does one desire the deafened body, the fact of deafness, or is it the stereotype—the role play—of a deafened person that appeals? Does one desire a culturally Deaf identity and community, or is it a (possibly psychological or physiological) desire for separation, disengagement from the noisy, intrusive, *hearing* environment?

The Deaf community eventually discovered the presence of the Deaf-

Wannabee discussion group, and several Deaf people joined the list to express their outrage and to raise pertinent points about the political relationships that are obscured in the acts of "elective deafness" or passing as deaf. One new list member, for example, wrote "Enjoying yourself now, eh? Changing your identity from hearing to HoH for 'kicks'? Do you realize that d/Deaf people can't even try to change themselves from d/Deaf to Hearing even if their lives counted on it?" ("Pretending," Deaf-Wannabee, June 2004).

What's wrong with becoming deaf or Deaf? Nothing, as long as "you are already losing your hearing," as one respondent noted. For many Deaf people, including those who joined the Deaf-Wannabee list, this is the boiling point. Pretenders and devotees are generally avoided or dismissed. Hearing-aid fetishists are seen as being fascinated with markers of "oral deaf," or "hearing impaired," and as such, do not have much bearing on the discussion of cultural identity. In a Deaf paradigm, however, it is the Deaf wannabes that present the biggest difficulty—or, some would argue, affront.

Even though some Deaf parents may see a desire for deafness in their own hearing children, there are some important differences in how these desires are perceived. For one, there is the assumption sometimes made by wannabes that learning sign language will gloss over the origins of elective deafness. Fluency in sign language is an important marker of Deaf identity, but fluency is difficult to attain and does not automatically entail membership. There is also the set of beliefs and values embedded within the "Deaf World," a concept used by Deaf people in the United States to describe "relationships among themselves, to the social network they have set up, and not to any notion of geographical location" (Bahan et al. 5). As a social entity with embedded cultural and social ties, the community resists hegemonic and stereotyped representations of deafness, Deaf people, and signed languages.

Perhaps this is what one woman faced in her initial encounters with Deaf people; she states that being Deaf is not what she imagined, and that Deaf people can be just as complicated and as unfriendly as (hearing) people. Because of her experience, she'd begun to rethink "crossing the bridge" ("Random Thoughts," Deaf-Wannabee, October 2005). She does not describe how she met or approached Deaf people, how fluently or clearly she signs, or any other contextual information, so it's difficult to surmise, but one does wonder how her images of Deaf culture as being nice, sweet, and happy influenced her reception.

What is particularly problematic is valorizing or glamorizing a community without recognizing historical forces of social, economic, and linguistic oppres-

Kristen Harmon

sion. Hearing privilege in an ableist and audist society does not simply (or completely) vanish upon one's desire not to be hearing anymore. Despite the renunciation of the sense of hearing, erasure of a privileged subject position is not as easily accomplished. To better understand this difficulty, one only has to reverse the direction of ability and disability. Consider that a deafened person who longs and aches to be hearing and who spends countless hours in "learning to listen" and in speech therapy in order to better sound like hearing people (regardless of whether or not a hearing person can make himself or herself understood to a deaf person) is approved in his or her desires to assume something closer to the privileged subject position. It is also revealing to look at the ways in which deaf and deafened people are encouraged to view hearing aids and cochlear implants as that which will "restore hearing" (note here the logic of "compulsory able-bodiedness"). This, despite the fact that cochlear implants do not provide hearing, only an electrically coded representation, and hearing aids amplify and compensate for sounds rather than substitute what is missing in the deaf person's audiogram. Given the reification of hearing and the high-flown rhetoric surrounding cochlear implants, a desire for hearing is a culturally enforced and encouraged fetish, but only if the person doing the desiring is already deaf through "natural causes."

Aside from repeated warnings about the irreversibility of hearing loss from the Deaf-Wannabee group's founder, and several heated exchanges online about the potential for taking away British National Health Service (NHS) resources from an "organically" or "naturally" deaf person in order to satisfy desires (or self-inflicted needs) for a hearing aid, there is little discussion of the ethical or sociopolitical ramifications of elective disability. Concerns about "coming out" with these desires could be a masking of the ethical and political difficulties of desiring deafness; as the pretender interviewed on "Ouch!" muses, in response to a question about what her colleagues think about what she does, "You know, I can't even imagine, I don't think I would lose my job, but I know I would lose a lot of respect" (20–21). The interviewer presses her, and she continues, "I can't imagine what that would be like, if somebody were to find out. And it's possible, you know you can't ever keep anything totally secret . . . but I don't even like to think about the possibility" (21).

A few posts from Deaf people on Deaf-Wannabee call upon moral grounds of right and wrong, but none of these arguments are fully articulated because the nature of what is "wrong" with deafening oneself is socially bound in ways that do not easily oppose the ethnicity model of Deaf community membership. If, for example, a person deafens herself, learns ASL, and then becomes a student at Gallaudet University, how is that person superficially different from a late deafened or "oral deaf" person who learns sign language as a young adult at Gallaudet University? Granted, wannabe members tend not to become students at Gallaudet, but the point here is that the distinction between self-deafened and Deaf invites hard-to-quantify descriptions of a "Deaf experience," or a "Deaf tendency," "Deaf internalization" (or "Deaf immersion"), and "Deaf visuality." At its core, the difference seems to rest in experiential and political aspects of living in and through the Deaf World. Yet to state exactly what is "wrong" with self-deafening is to evoke medical models (an evocation many in the Deaf World are understandably reluctant to make).

Aside from the occasional wondering about what a "truly" Deaf person would think about desires to initiate hearing loss ("Why Intrude Here?" Deaf Wannabee, June 2004), there is not much head-on, full-frontal, acknowledgment of "real" Deaf people. One wonders how the discussion would change if there had been more posts from a hearing (and signing) father of a deaf son. This father seems to have joined the group because he does not use his voice when he signs — whenever it is possible — with his son, and so he is often publicly perceived as a Deaf person. He wears ear plugs even on vacation and continues in "hearing but acting deaf" so he can experience the trip the same way his son would: he does this so that when communication deteriorates, for example, at the airport, he can model for his son how a deaf person should be treated. By doing so, he hopes his son will learn how to advocate for himself in his interactions with hearing people when his father is not around ("Hearing Acting Deaf" and "Hearing Acting Deaf II," Deaf Wannabee, August 2004). As a hearing person, he is surprised by how many hearing people do not take the time to help someone communicate his needs, and he implies he is taken aback by what hearing people say about deaf people in their presence ("Hearing Acting Deaf" and "Hearing Acting Deaf II," Deaf Wannabee, August 2004).

Based on his experiences, he concludes that generally, people just don't care ("Hearing Acting Deaf," Deaf Wannabee August 2004). The responses to his e-mails do not address what it means to "care" or to model how a Deaf person — and any deaf or hard-of-hearing person — should be treated with respect and dignity. Instead, in reply to his posting, there are questions about where he found effective ear plugs and also about his use of ASL — for example, how difficult it is for a hearing person to learn sign language ("Hearing Acting Deaf," Deaf Wannabee, August 2004). While this particular respondent does inquire about the logistics of communication between a "hearing" and "non-hearing" person, as well as the "helpfulness" of his son's hearing aid, there is no acknowledgment by members either of the deaf son's individuality or of his father's advocacy for him.

Aside from a heated exchange between Deaf "visitors" and group members on Deaf-Wannabee, there has not been a sustained or productive dialogue between the wannabe online community and the Deaf community. In one angry exchange, Deaf visitors and hearing or deafened members did not fully address the fact that the other group or community existed; instead, the exchange served to register and reinforce the highly emotional content of the discussion surrounding the question, "What's wrong with desiring deafness?"

My intent in this chapter has been to work through a range of theoretical, ethical, and rhetorical issues connected to devotees, pretenders, and wannabes. Given that these sexual subjects remain off the grid of intelligibility in our ableist and audist culture, it is not possible (or perhaps even desirable) to resolve all of these issues. Yet perhaps one contribution to this heated dialogue could be as follows: by highlighting the social underpinnings of "intelligibility" when it comes to ability and disability and desire and pathology, hearing status here is effectively made over into a magical fetish that displaces potency and impotency with ability and disability in an ever circular logic that seamlessly resolves (through disavowal) the challenges of living with difference.

NOTES

1. "Normate" is Rosemarie Garland-Thomson's term for "the social figure through which people can represent themselves as definitive human beings. Normate, then, is the constructed identity of those who, by way of the bodily configurations and cultural capital they assume, can step into a position of authority and wield the power it grants them" (*Extraordinary* 8).

2. The use of the capital letter "D" in "Deaf" references a sociolinguistic and minority community centered around cultural norms and a signed language. In the United States, such usage denotes Deaf people who use American Sign Language, or ASL; some members of western European countries have adopted similar usage to denote their own culturally Deaf communities. The use of lowercase is meant to describe those who are not culturally deaf but who have a similar hearing status.

3. This tendency is in keeping with the findings that fetishists or, to be more precise in terms of psychiatric discourse, people diagnosed with "paraphiliac fixations" tend to be heterosexual men (Aguilera 260; Seligman and Hardenburg 107).

4. Initially, audism was defined as "the notion that one is superior based on one's

ability to hear or behave in the manner of one who hears" (qtd. in Bauman 240). For our purposes here, I point toward the usage of audism to describe "a system of advantage based on hearing ability," whereby "the privilege allotted to hearing people" can be made visible and thus recognized (Bauman 241).

5. "Deaf-Wannabee" is a public Internet discussion group, but I have chosen to identify individual posters not by name but rather by the header title for individual postings and by the date of posting.

6. Quotations in Trudy Suggs's article "Deaf Wanna-bes" are a verbatim recording of the original discussion postings on "Deaf-Wannabee."

7. Alison Kafer expands on Robert McRuer's notion of "compulsory able-bodiedness," writing that able-bodiedness "has been cast as separate from politics, as a universal ideal and a normal way of life, in much the same way as heterosexuality in the 1970s and early 1980s" ("Compulsory Bodies" 79). Perhaps, Kafer suggests, "the most basic manifestation of [compulsory able-bodiedness] is the cultural assumption of able-bodiedness" ("Compulsory Bodies" 80). For those "whose disabilities allow them to pass as nondisabled, the compulsory nature of able-bodiedness throws suspicion on their desire to identify as disabled—under a system of compulsory able-bodiedness, why identify as disabled if you can pass?" (Kafer, "Compulsory Bodies" 80).

Kristen Harmon

....

WORKS CITED

About Schmidt. Directed by Alexander Payne. New Line Cinema, 2002.

Aguilera, Raymond J. "Disability and Delight: Staring Back at the Devotee Community." *Sexuality and Disability* 18.4 (2000): 255–61.

Aguilera, Raymond J. et al. "Admirers: Devotees, Pretenders, Wannabes and . . . Race." *Bent: A Journal of CripGay Voices* (March 2004). ⟨www.bentvoices.org/bentvoices/admirers.htm⟩.

Ahmed, Sara. *Queer Phenomenology: Orientations, Objects, Others*. Durham: Duke University Press, 2006.

Allen, James, Hilton Als, John Lewis, and Leon F. Litwack. *Without Sanctuary: Lynching Photography in America*. Santa Fe: Twin Palms, 2000.

Amato, Toni. "Would I Dare?" Nestle, Howell, and Wilchins, *GenderQueer* 223–27.

American Psychiatric Association. *Diagnostic and Statistical Manual of Mental Disorders, DSM-IV-TR*. 4th ed. Arlington, VA: American Psychiatric Publishing, Inc., 2000.

Americans with Disabilities Act. 1990. ⟨http://www.ada.gov/archive/adastat91.htm⟩.

Amundson, Ron. "Disability, Handicap, and the Environment." *Journal of Social Philosophy* 23.1 (1992): 105–18.

Aston, Maxine. *Aspergers in Love: Couple Relationships and Family Affairs*. Philadelphia: Jessica Kingsley, 2003.

Autism Resource Foundation. "Frequently Asked Questions about ABA." ⟨http://www.autismresourcefoundation.org/info/info.ABA.html⟩.

Bahan, Ben, Robert Hoffmeister, and Harlan Lane. *A Journey Into the DEAF-WORLD*. San Diego: Dawn Sign, 1996.

Barnes, Djuna. *Nightwood*. 1936. New York: New Directions, 1961.

Baron-Cohen, Simon. "Is Asperger's Syndrome/High-Functioning Autism Necessarily a Disability?" 5 January 2000. ⟨http://www.larry-arnold.info/Neurodiversity/Mission/disability.htm⟩.

———. *Mindblindness: An Essay on Autism and Theory of Mind*. Cambridge: MIT Press, 1995.

Barounis, Cynthia. "Cripping Heterosexuality, Queering Able-Bodiedness: *Murderball*, *Brokeback Mountain* and the Contested Masculine Body." *Journal of Visual Culture* 8.1 (2009): 54–75.

Barr, Martin W. "Some Notes on Asexualization; With a Report of Eighteen Cases." *Journal of Nervous and Mental Disease* 51.3 (1920): 231–41.

Bauman, Dirksen. "Audism: Exploring the Metaphysics of Oppression." *Journal of Deaf Studies and Deaf Education* 9.2 (2004): 239–46.

Beatie, Thomas. "Labor of Love: Is Society Ready for This Pregnant Husband?" *Advocate* (April 2008). ⟨http://www.advocate.com/article.aspx?id=22217⟩.

Becker, Gaylene. *Disrupted Lives: How People Create Meaning in a Chaotic World*. Berkeley: University of California Press, 1997.

Bend It Like Beckham. Directed by Gurinder Chadha. Fox Searchlight Pictures, 2002.

Bentley, Toni. *The Surrender: An Erotic Memoir*. New York: Harper Perennial, 2005.

Berlant, Lauren. "Love, A Queer Feeling." *Homosexuality and Psychoanalysis*. Ed. Tim Dean and Christopher Lane. Chicago: University of Chicago Press, 2001. 432–52.

Berlant, Lauren, and Michael Warner. "Sex in Public." *Critical Inquiry* 24.2 (1998): 547–66.

Berrios, G. E., and N. Kennedy. "Erotomania: A Conceptual History." *History of Psychiatry* 13 (2002): 381–400.

Bersani, Leo. *The Freudian Body: Psychoanalysis and Art*. New York: Columbia University Press, 1986.

———. "Fr-oucault and the End of Sex." *Is the Rectum a Grave? And Other Essays*. Chicago: University of Chicago Press, 2010. 133–38.

———. *Homos*. Cambridge: Harvard University Press, 1995.

———. "Is the Rectum a Grave?" 1987. *Is the Rectum a Grave? And Other Essays*. Chicago: University of Chicago Press, 2010. 3–30.

———. "Sociality and Sexuality." 2000. *Is the Rectum a Grave? And Other Essays*. Chicago: University of Chicago Press, 2010. 102–19.

Bérubé, Michael. Foreword. *Claiming Disability*. By Simi Linton. New York: NYU Press, 1998. vii–xi.

Besnier, Niko. "Polynesian Gender Liminality through Time and Space." *Third Sex, Third Gender: Beyond Sexual Dimorphism in Culture and History*. Ed. Gilbert Herdt. New York: Zone, 1996. 285–328.

Bettelheim, Bruno. *The Empty Fortress: Infantile Autism and the Birth of the Self*. New York: The Free Press, 1967.

Bhabha, Homi. *The Location of Culture*. New York: Routledge, 1994.

"Bill to Unsex Morons Gains City's Support." *Chicago Daily Tribune* 4 February 1937: 1–2.

Block, Pamela. "Sexuality, Fertility, and Danger: Twentieth-Century Images of Women with Cognitive Disabilities." *Sexuality and Disability* 18.4 (2000): 239–54.

Bolus, Sonya. "Loving Outside Simple Lines." Nestle, Howell, and Wilchins, *GenderQueer* 113–19.

Boon, Marcus. *The Road of Excess: A History of Writers on Drugs.* Cambridge: Harvard University Press, 2005.

Boone, Joseph. *Libidinal Currents: Sexuality and the Shaping of Modernism.* Chicago: University of Chicago Press, 1998.

Brownworth, Victoria A., and Susan Raffo, eds. *Restricted Access: Lesbians on Disability.* Seattle: Seal, 1999.

Bruno, Richard L. "Devotees, Pretenders, and Wannabes: Two Cases of Factitious Disability Disorder." *Sexuality and Disability* 15.4 (1997): 243–60.

Bullough, Vern L. *Science in the Bedroom: A History of Sex Research.* New York: Basic Books, 1995.

Butler, Judith. *Gender Trouble: Feminism and the Subversion of Identity.* New York: Routledge, 1990.

———. *Undoing Gender.* New York: Routledge, 2004.

Callen, Michael, and Richard Berkowitz. *How to Have Sex in an Epidemic: One Approach.* New York: News from the Front Publications, 1983.

Campbell, Fiona Kumari. *Contours of Ableism: The Production of Disability and Abledness.* New York: Palgrave, 2009.

Campbell, Sue, Letitia Meynell, and Susan Sherwin, eds. *Embodied Agency.* University Park: Penn State University Press, 2009.

Chapelle, P. A., J. Durand, and P. Lacert. "Penile Erection Following Complete Spinal Cord Injury in Man." *British Journal of Urology* 52 (1980): 216–19.

Chase, Cheryl. "Affronting Reason." *Looking Queer: Body Image and Identity in Lesbian, Bisexual, Gay, and Transgender Communities.* Ed. Dawn Atkins. New York: Harrington Park, 1998. 205–19.

———. "Hermaphrodites with Attitude: Mapping the Emergence of Intersex Political Activism." *GLQ: A Journal of Lesbian and Gay Studies* 4.2 (1998): 189–211.

———. "Surgical Process Is Not the Answer to Intersexuality." Dreger, *Intersex in the Age of Ethics* 147–59.

Chen, Mel Y. "Toxic Animacies, Inanimate Affections." *GLQ: A Journal of Lesbian and Gay Studies* 17.2 (2011): 265–86.

Chesser, Eustace. *Love without Fear: How to Achieve Sex Happiness in Marriage.* New York: Signet, 1947.

Child, Margaret, and Richard King. "Overground's Manifesto." *OverGround* 2.2 (1992): 4. 〈http://www.overground.be/policy.php?article=337&lan=en〉.

Childs, Donald J. *Modernism and Eugenics: Woolf, Eliot, Yeats, and the Culture of Degeneration.* Cambridge: Cambridge University Press, 2001.

Childs, J. Rives. *Casanoviana: An Annotated World Bibliography of Jacques Casanova de Seingalt and of Works Concerning Him.* Vienna: Nebehay, 1956.

Chivers, Sally. "Public Properties: The TransCanadian Terry Fox." Unpublished Paper. Delivered at TransCanada Two Conference. Guelph University: 11–14 October 2007.

Clare, Eli. *Exile and Pride: Disability, Queerness, and Liberation*. Cambridge: South End Press, 1999.

———. "Gawking, Gaping, Staring." GLQ: *A Journal of Lesbian and Gay Studies* 9.1–2 (2003): 257–61.

———. "Stolen Bodies, Reclaimed Bodies: Disability and Queerness." *Public Culture* 13.3 (2001): 359–65.

Clifford, James. "Introduction: Partial Truths." *Writing Culture: The Poetics and Politics of Ethnography*. Ed. James Clifford and George E. Marcus. Berkeley: University of California Press, 1986. 1–26.

Colker, Ruth. *Pregnant Men: Practice, Theory, and the Law*. Bloomington: Indiana University Press, 1995.

Colligan, Sumi. "Why the Intersex Shouldn't Be Fixed: Insights from Queer Theory and Disability Studies." Smith and Hutchinson 45–60.

Collins, Patricia Hill. *Black Sexual Politics: African Americans, Gender, and the New Racism*. New York: Routledge, 2004.

Comay, Rebecca. "Perverse History: Fetishism and Dialectic in Walter Benjamin." *Research in Phenomenology* 29 (1999): 51–62.

Cooper, Al, ed. *Sex and the Internet: A Guidebook for Clinicians*. New York: Brunner-Routledge, 2002.

Corbin, Alain. "Charting the Cultural History of the Senses." 2004. *Empire of the Senses: The Sensual Culture Reader*. Ed. David Howe. New York: Berg, 2005. 128–42.

Crimp, Douglas. "How to Have Promiscuity in an Epidemic." AIDS: *Cultural Analysis, Cultural Activism*. Ed. Crimp. Cambridge: MIT Press, 1988. 236–71.

Crow, Liz. "Including All of Our Lives: Renewing the Social Model of Disability." *Exploring the Divide: Illness and Disability*. Ed. Colin Barnes and Geof Mercer. Leeds: Disability Press, 1996. 55–73.

Davidson, Michael. *Concerto for the Left Hand: Disability and the Defamiliar Body*. Ann Arbor: University of Michigan Press, 2008.

Davidson, Robert J. "DSD Debates: Social Movement Organizations' Framing Debates Surrounding the Term 'Disorders of Sexual Development.'" *Liminalis: Journal for Sex/ Gender Emancipation and Resistance* (2009): 60–80.

Davies, Dominic. "Sharing Our Stories, Empowering Our Lives: Don't Dis Me!" *Sexuality and Disability* 18.3 (2000): 179–86.

Davis, Katherine Bement. *Factors in the Sex Life of Twenty-Two Hundred Women*. New York: Harper, 1929.

Davis, Lennard J. *Bending Over Backwards: Disability, Dismodernism, and Other Difficult Positions*. New York: NYU Press, 2002.

———, ed. *The Disability Studies Reader*. New York: Routledge, 1997.

———. *Enforcing Normalcy: Disability, Deafness, and the Body*. New York: Verso, 1995.

———. *Obsession: A History*. Chicago: University of Chicago Press, 2008.

Dawson, Michelle. "Bettelheim's Worst Crime: Autism and the Epidemic of Irresponsibility." 9 September 2003. ⟨http://www.sentex.net/~nexus23/md_01.html⟩.

Deaf-WannaBee Internet Discussion Group. Yahoo Groups. 16 May 2000–present. ⟨http://groups.yahoo.com/group/Deaf-Wannabee/messages⟩.

de Certeau, Michel. *The Practice of Everyday Life*. Trans. Steven Rendall. Berkeley: University of California Press, 1984.

Delany, Samuel R. *Times Square Red, Times Square Blue*. New York: NYU Press, 1999.

de Lauretis, Teresa. "Queer Texts, Bad Habits, and the Issue of a Future." *GLQ: A Journal of Lesbian and Gay Studies* 17.2 (2011): 243–63.

Deleuze, Gilles. *Logique du Sens*. Paris: Éditions de Minuit, 1969.

D'Emilio, John. "Capitalism and Gay Identity." 1983. *The Lesbian and Gay Studies Reader*. Ed. Henry Abelove, Michèle Aina Barale, and David Halperin. New York: Routledge, 1993. 467–76.

D'Emilio, John, and Estelle B. Freedman. *Intimate Matters: A History of Sexuality in America*. New York: Harper and Row, 1988.

Desjardins, Michel. *Le Jardin d'Ombres: La Poétique et la Politique de la Rééducation Sociale*. Sainte-Foy: Presses de l'Université du Québec, 2002.

———. "Tabou Sexuel et Changement Culturel: Le Point de Vue et les Attitudes des Parents." *Revue Francophone de la Déficience Intellectuelle* 16.2 (2005): 49–62.

Dickens, Charles. *A Christmas Carol*. 1843. *The Christmas Books, Volume 1*. Harmondsworth, UK: Penguin, 1985.

Diller, Matthew. "Judicial Backlash, the ADA, and the Civil Rights Model of Disability." Krieger, *Backlash Against the ADA* 62–97.

Dixon, Dwight. "An Erotic Attraction to Devotees." *Sexuality and Disability* 6.1 (1983): 3–19.

Dixon, Melvin. "I'll Be Somewhere Listening For My Name." *Sojourner: Black Gay Voices in the Age of AIDS*. Ed. B. Michael Hunter. New York: Other Countries, 1993. 199–203.

Dorcus, Roy M., and Harry W. Case. "Mental Hygiene Problems in Industry." *Review of Educational Research* 13 5 (1943): 185–89.

Dougherty, Dawn. "A Safe Trip Home." Nestle, Howell, and Wilchins, *GenderQueer* 220–22.

Downing, Lisa. "The Measure of 'Sexual Dysfunction': A Plea for Theoretical Limitlessness." *Transformations: Online Journal of Region, Culture, and Society* 8 (2004): ⟨http://www.transformationsjournal.org/journal/issue_08/article_02.shtml⟩.

Dreger, Alice Domurat. "'Ambiguous Sex'—or Ambivalent Medicine? Ethical Issues in the Treatment of Intersexuality." *Hastings Center Report* 28.3 (1998): 24–36.

———, ed. *Intersex in the Age of Ethics*. Hagerstown, MD: University Publishing Group, 1999.

Dreger, Alice Domurat, and April M. Herndon. "Progress and Politics in the Intersex Rights Movement: Feminist Theory in Action." *GLQ: A Journal of Lesbian and Gay Studies* 15.2 (2009): 199–224.

DuCille, Ann. *The Coupling Convention: Sex, Text, and Tradition in Black Women's Fiction*. New York: Oxford University Press, 1993.

Duggan, Lisa. *Sapphic Slashers: Sex, Violence, and American Modernity*. Durham: Duke University Press, 2000.

———. *The Twilight of Equality: Neoliberalism, Cultural Politics, and the Attack on Democracy*. Boston: Beacon, 2003.

Duke, Lynne, and DeNeen L. Brown. "Tapping into the Secrets of the Stall: Experts Say Anonymous Sex in Public Places Is a Compulsive Behavior." *Washington Post* 30 August 2007. ⟨http://www.washingtonpost.com/wp-dyn/content/article/2007/08/29/AR2007082902435.html⟩.

Duncan, Kath. "The Amorous Adventures of an Amputee Love Goddess." *HQ Magazine* 62 (January-February 1999): 11–69.

Duncan, Kath, and Gerard Goggin. "'Something in Your Belly'—Fantasy, Disability, and Desire in *My One-Legged Dream Lover*." *Disability Studies Quarterly* 22.4 (2002). ⟨http://www.dsq-sds.org/article/view/377/501⟩.

Dupras, André. "La Sexualité des Personnes Handicapées: Interdite ou Permise?" *Élargir les Horizons: Perspectives Scientifiques sur L'Intégration Sociale*. Ed. Anne Hébert, Suzanne Doré, and Ingrid de Lafontaine. Sainte-Foy: Éditions MultiMondes, 1994. 185–90.

———. "La Désexualisation de la Personne Handicapée Mentale ou le Syndrome de *Forrest Gump*." *Revue Européenne du Handicap Mental* 5.18 (1998): 47–52.

———. "La stérilisation de la personne handicapée mentale comme processus de sacralisation." *Psychosomatique et Sexologie* 29 (2001): 908–12.

Durham, Wesley T. "The Rules-based Process of Revealing/Concealing the Family Planning Decision of Voluntary Child-free Couples: A Communication Privacy Management Perspective." *Communication Studies* 59 (2008): 132–47.

Dyer, Isadore. "Discussion." *Southern Medical Journal* 3 (1910): 20–24.

Ebert, Roger. Review of *Murderball*. RogerEbert.com. 22 July 2005. ⟨http://rogerebert.suntimes.com/apps/pbcs.dll/article?AID=/20050721/REVIEWS/50607001⟩.

Eckert, Lena. "'Diagnosticism': Three Cases of Medical Anthropological Research into Intersexuality." Holmes 41–71.

Edelman, Lee. "Ever After." *South Atlantic Quarterly* 106.3 (2007): 470–76.

———. "The Future Is Kid Stuff: Queer Theory, Disidentification, and the Death Drive." *Narrative* 6.1 (January 1998): 18–30.

———. *No Future: Queer Theory and the Death Drive*. Durham: Duke University Press, 2004.

Edgerton, Robert B. *Mental Retardation*. Cambridge: Harvard University Press, 1979.

Eliot, T. S. *The Complete Poems and Plays, 1909–1950*. New York: Harcourt, 1962.

Elliott, Carl. "A New Way to be Mad." *Atlantic Monthly* (December 2000): 72–84.

Elman, R. Amy. "Disability Pornography: The Fetishization of Women's Vulnerabilities." *Violence Against Women* 3.3 (1997): 257–70.

Encyclopedia of Unusual Sex Practices. Advertisement. ⟨www.odd-sex.com/index.htm⟩.

European Charter for Persons with Autism. 9 May 1996. ⟨http://www.autism-help.org/adults-autism-european-charter.htm⟩.

Fahner, Holly. "Is There a Casanova Gene?" *Glamour* (June 2006): 138.

Faulkner, William. *The Sound and the Fury.* 1929. New York: Vintage, 1984.

Feder, Ellen K. "Imperatives of Normality: From 'Intersex' to 'Disorders of Sex Development.'" *GLQ: A Journal of Lesbian and Gay Studies* 15.2 (2009): 225–47.

Ferguson, Roderick A. *Aberrations in Black: Toward a Queer of Color Critique.* Minneapolis: University of Minnesota Press, 2004.

Fernald, Walter. "Possibilities of the Colony." *Proceedings of the National Conference of Charities and Correction at the Thirty-fourth Annual Session Held in the City of Minneapolis, Minn., June 12th to 19th, 1907.* Ed. Alexander Johnson. Indianapolis: Press of Wm. B. Burford, 1907. 411–18.

Fine, Michelle, and Adrienne Asch, eds. *Women with Disabilities: Essays in Psychology, Culture, and Politics.* Philadelphia: Temple University Press, 1988.

Finger, Anne. "Forbidden Fruit." *New Internationalist* 233 (1992): 8–10.

Finkelstein, Naomi. "The Only Thing You Have to Do Is Live." *GLQ: A Journal of Lesbian and Gay Studies* 9.1–2 (2003): 307–19.

Fiol-Matta, Licia. *A Queer Mother for the Nation: The State and Gabriela Mistral.* Minneapolis: University of Minnesota Press, 2002.

Fleche, Anne. "Echoing Autism: Performance, Performativity, and the Writing of Donna Williams." *Tulane Drama Review* 41.3 (1997): 107–21.

Floyd, Kevin. *The Reification of Desire: Toward a Queer Marxism.* Minneapolis: University of Minnesota Press, 2009.

Foucault, Michel. *Fearless Speech.* Ed. Joseph Pearson. Los Angeles: Semiotext(e), 2001.

———. *The History of Sexuality, Volume 1: An Introduction.* Trans. Robert Hurley. New York: Vintage, 1978.

———. *La Volonté de Savoir: Histoire de la Sexualité, Tome 1.* Paris: Gallimard, 1976.

Freud, Sigmund. *Dora: An Analysis of a Case of Hysteria.* New York: Simon and Schuster, 1963.

———. *Studies in Hysteria.* 1895. New York: Basic Books, 2000.

———. *Three Case Histories.* New York: Collier Books, 1963.

Frith, Uta. *Autism: Explaining the Enigma.* Oxford and Cambridge: Basil Blackwell, 1989.

Fromm, Erich. *The Art of Loving.* 1956. New York: Bantam, 1963.

Fuck the Disabled. Directed by Eli Kabillio. Mad Dog Films, Inc., 2001.

Garland-Thomson, Rosemarie. "The Cultural Logic of Euthanasia: 'Sad Fancyings' in Herman Melville's 'Bartleby.'" *American Literature* 76.4 (2004): 777–806.

———. *Extraordinary Bodies: Figuring Physical Disability in American Culture and Literature.* New York: Columbia University Press, 1997.

———. "Integrating Disability, Transforming Feminist Theory." *National Women's Studies Association Journal* 14.3 (2002): 1–32.

———. "The Politics of Staring: Visual Rhetorics of Disability in Popular Photography." Snyder, Brueggemann, and Garland-Thomson 56–75.

———. "Seeing the Disabled: Visual Rhetorics of Disability in Popular Photography." Longmore and Umansky, *The New Disability History* 335–74.

———. "Shape Structures Story: Fresh and Feisty Stories about Disability." *Narrative* 15.1 (2007): 113–23.

Gateaux-Mennecier, Jacqueline. *La Débilité Légère, Une Construction Idéologique*. Paris: Éditions du CNRS, 1990.

Geertz, Clifford. *The Interpretation of Cultures*. New York: Basic Books, 1973.

Giami, Alain. "Stérilisation et sexualité des personnes handicapées mentales." *Les Enjeux de la Stérilisation*. Ed. Alain Giami and Henri Leridon. Paris: Inserm, 2000. 273–86.

Giami, Alain, Chantal Humbert-Viveret, and Dominique Laval. *L'Ange et la Bête: Représentations de la Sexualité des Handicapés Mentaux par les Parents et les Éducateurs*. Paris: Les Publications du CTNERHI, 1983.

Gibbs, C. E. "Sexual Behavior and Secondary Sexual Hair in Female Patients with Manic Depressive Psychoses and the Relation of These Factors to Dementia Praecox." *American Journal of Psychiatry* 4 (1924): 41–56.

Giddens, Anthony. *The Transformation of Intimacy: Sexuality, Love and Eroticism in Modern Societies*. Stanford: Stanford University Press, 1992.

Gilbert, Sandra M., and Susan Gubar. *No Man's Land: The Place of the Woman Writer in the Twentieth Century: Volume 2, Sex Changes*. New Haven: Yale University Press, 1989.

Gilroy, Paul. *The Black Atlantic: Modernity and Double Consciousness*. Cambridge: Harvard University Press, 1993.

Gipps, Richard, ed. *Autism and Intersubjectivity*. Special issue of *Philosophy, Psychiatry, and Psychology* 11.3 (2004).

Goldsby, Jacqueline. *A Spectacular Secret: Lynching in American Life and Literature*. Chicago: University of Chicago Press, 2006.

Goodman, Nelson. *Ways of World Making*. Indianapolis: Hackett, 1978.

Grandin, Temple. *Animals in Translation: Using the Mysteries of Autism to Decode Animal Behavior*. New York: Scribner, 2004.

———. *Emergence: Labeled Autistic*. New York: Warner, 1996.

———. *Thinking in Pictures and Other Reports from My Life with Autism*. New York: Vintage, 1995.

Grealy, Lucy. "In the Realm of the Senses." *Nerve* 25 October 2001. ⟨http://www.nerve.com/dispatches/Grealy/RealmOfTheSenses/⟩.

Gregson, Ian. "The Devotee Issue: Part Two—The Opposing View." *Amputee-Online*. September 2000. ⟨amputee-online.com/amputation/sept00/septoowissues.html⟩.

Grillo, Trina, and Stephanie M. Wildman. "Obscuring the Importance of Race: The Implications of Making Comparisons between Racism and Sexism (or Other Isms)." *Critical White Studies: Looking Behind the Mirror*. Ed. Richard Delgado and Jean Stefancic. Philadelphia: Temple University Press, 1997. 619–26.

Guldin, Anne. "Claiming Sexuality: Mobility-Impaired People and Sexualities in American Culture." Unpublished Master of Arts Paper. Department of Anthropology, University of Iowa, 1999.

———. "Self-Claiming Sexuality: Mobility Impaired People in American Culture." *Sexuality and Disability* 18.4 (2000): 233–38.

Guter, Bob. "How to Find Love with a Fetishist: Bob Guter Interviews Alan Sable." Guter and Killacky 65–81.

Guter, Bob, and John R. Killacky, eds. *Queer Crips: Disabled Gay Men and Their Stories*. New York: Harrington Park, 2004.

Haag, Pamela. "In Search of the 'Real Thing': Ideologies of Love, Modern Romance, and Women's Sexual Subjectivity in the United States, 1920–1940." *American Sexual Politics: Sex, Gender, and Race since the Civil War*. Ed. John C. Fout and Maura Shaw Tantillo. Chicago: University of Chicago Press, 1993. 161–91.

Hagglund, Bette. "The Fascination Attraction—It's Okay." *Fascination*. 1999. ⟨users.erols.com/rvandyke/info.htm⟩.

Hahn, Harlan. "Accommodations and the ADA: Unreasonable Bias or Biased Reasoning?" Krieger, *Backlash Against the ADA* 26–61.

———. "The Social Component of Sexuality and Disability: Some Problems and Proposals." *Sexuality and Disability* 4 (1981): 220–33.

Halberstam, Judith. "F2M: The Making of Female Masculinity." *The Lesbian Postmodern*. Ed. Laura Doan. New York: Columbia University Press, 1994. 210–28.

———. *In a Queer Time and Place*. New York: NYU Press, 2005.

———. "Shame and White Gay Masculinity." *Social Text* 84–85 (2005): 219–33.

Hale, Grace Elizabeth. *Making Whiteness: The Culture of Segregation in the South, 1890–1940*. New York: Pantheon, 1998.

Hall, Kim Q., ed. *Feminist Disability Studies*. Special issue of *National Women's Studies Association Journal* 14.3 (2002).

Hamilton, Toby. "Sexuality in Deaf Blind Persons." *Sexuality and Disability* 2.3 (1979): 238–46.

Harper, Phillip Brian. "The Evidence of Felt Intuition: Minority Experience, Everyday Life, and Critical Speculative Knowledge." *Black Queer Studies: A Critical Anthology*. Ed. E. Patrick Johnson and Mae G. Henderson. Durham: Duke University Press, 2005. 106–23.

Hastrup, Kirsten. "The Ethnographic Present: A Reinvention." *Cultural Anthropology* 5 (1990): 45–61.

Hawlbecker, Hale. "Who Did This to You?" Dreger, *Intersex in the Age of Ethics* 110–13.

Hermaphrodites Speak! Directed by Cheryl Chase. Video. Intersex Society of North America, 1997.

Herndon, April. "More Evidence People Did Well without Surgery!" April Herndon's Blog. 19 October 2005. ⟨http://www.isna.org/node/971⟩.

Herring, Scott. *Queering the Underworld: Slumming, Literature, and the Undoing of Lesbian and Gay History*. Chicago: University of Chicago Press, 2007.

"History of Footwear: Foot Fetishism and Shoe Retifism." Department of Podiatry, Curtin University of Technology, Perth, Western Australia. December 2004. ⟨http://podiatry.curtin.edu.au/fetish.html⟩.

Hockenberry, John. *Moving Violations: War Zones, Wheelchairs, and Declarations of Independence*. New York: Hyperion, 1995.

Holmes, Morgan, ed. *Critical Intersex*. Farnham Surrey, UK: Ashgate, 2009.

Holstein, James, and Jaber Gubrium. "The Active Interview." *Qualitative Research: Theory, Method and Practice*. Ed. David Silverman. Thousand Oaks, CA: Sage, 2004. 140–61.

Hooper, Edward L. "New Insights." *The Ragged Edge: The Disability Experience from the Pages of the First Fifteen Years of* The Disability Rag. Ed. Barrett Shaw. Louisville: Advocado Press, 1994. 78–81.

Hornaday, Ann. "Embodying '69 in the Hair and Now: The Makers of *Taking Woodstock* Ensure Hirsute Historical Accuracy." *Washington Post* 28 August 2009. ⟨http://www.washingtonpost.com/wp-dyn/content/article/2009/08/27/AR2009082704141.html⟩.

Huffer, Lynne. *Mad for Foucault: Rethinking the Foundations of Queer Theory.* New York: Columbia University Press, 2009.

Hunt, William A. "Carney Landis: 1897–1962." *American Journal of Psychology* 75.3 (1962): 506–9.

Hurston, Zora Neale. *Seraph on the Suwanee.* 1948. New York: Harper, 1991.

I Am a Sex Addict. Directed by Caveh Zahedi. IFC Films, 2005.

Ingram, Richard. "Reports from the Psych Wars." *Unfitting Stories: Narrative Approaches to Disease, Disability, and Trauma.* Ed. Valerie Raoul, Connie Canam, Angela Henderson, and Carla Paterson. Waterloo: Wilfrid Laurier University Press, 2007. 237–44.

Intersex Society of North America (ISNA). "What's the History behind the Intersex Rights Movement?" ⟨http://www.isna.org/faq/history⟩.

Irigaray, Luce. *This Sex Which Is Not One.* Trans. Catherine Porter. Ithaca: Cornell University Press, 1985.

J. "Devotees: Are They Necessarily Sexual Harassers?" *OverGround.* 4 February 2001. ⟨http://www.overground.be/features.php?page=THE&article=73&lan=en⟩.

———. "Twins: An Exploration of the Morality of the Feelings of Devotees." *OverGround.* 4 February 2001. ⟨http://www.overground.be/features.php?page=THE&article=81&lan=en⟩.

———. "W. and K.: A Complementary Couple." *OverGround.* 4 February 2001. ⟨http://www.overground.be/features.php?page=PEO&article=55&lan=en⟩.

———. "Why Devotees Sometimes Behave Badly." *OverGround.* 4 February 2001. ⟨http://www.overground.be/features.php?page=THE&article=86&lan=en⟩.

Jackson, Michael. "Introduction: Phenomenology, Radical Empiricism, and Anthropological Critique." *Things as They Are: New Directions in Phenomenological Anthropology.* Ed. Jackson. Bloomington: Indiana University Press, 1996. 1–50.

Jacobs, Barbara. *Loving Mr. Spock: Understanding an Aloof Lover.* New York: Penguin, 2003.

Jain, Sarah. "The Prosthetic Imagination: Enabling and Disabling the Prosthesis Trope." *Science, Technology, and Human Values* 24.1 (1999): 31–54.

Job, Jennifer. "Factors Involved in the Ineffective Dissemination of Sexuality Information to Individuals Who Are Deaf or Hard of Hearing." *American Annals of the Deaf* 149.3 (2004): 264–73.

John. "Sightings." *OverGround.* 4 February 2001. ⟨www.overground.be/features/people/sight.html⟩.

Johnson, Harriet McBryde. "The Disability Gulag." *New York Times Magazine* (23 November 2003): 58–64.

───. *Too Late to Die Young: Nearly True Tales from a Life*. New York: Henry Holt, 2005.

Joyce, James. *Ulysses*. 1922. New York: Random House, 1986.

Junior. Directed by Ivan Reitman. Universal Studios, 1994.

Kafer, Alison. "Amputated Desire, Resistant Desire: Female Amputees in the Devotee Community." *Disability World* 3 (2000). ⟨www.disabilityworld.org/June-July2000/Women/SDS.htm⟩.

───. "Compulsory Bodies: Reflections on Heterosexuality and Able-bodiedness," *Journal of Women's History* 15.3 (2003): 77–89.

───. "Inseparable: Constructing Gender Through Disability in the Amputee-Devotee Community." Smith and Hutchison 107–18.

Kalichman, S. C. et. al. "Sexual sensation seeking: Scale development and predicting AIDS-risk behavior among homosexually active men." *Journal of Personality Assessment* 62 (1994): 385–97.

Katyal, Sonia K. "Sexuality and Sovereignty: The Global Limits and Possibilities of *Lawrence*." *William and Mary Bill of Rights Journal* 14 (2006): 1429–92.

Kaufman, Miriam, Cory Silverberg, and Fran Odette. *The Ultimate Guide to Sex and Disability: For All of Us Who Live with Disabilities, Chronic Pain, and Illness*. San Francisco: Cleis, 2003.

Kempton, Winifred and Emily Kahn. "Sexuality and People with Intellectual Disabilities: A Historical Perspective." *Sexuality and Disability* 9 (1991): 93–111.

Kershaw, Sarah. "For Teenagers, Hello Means 'How about a Hug?'" *New York Times*, 27 May 2009. ⟨http://www.nytimes.com/2009/05/28/style/28hugs.html⟩.

Kessler, Suzanne. *Lessons from the Intersexed*. New Brunswick: Rutgers University Press, 1998.

Kim. "As Is." Dreger, *Intersex in the Age of Ethics* 99–100.

King, Thomas. "Borders." *One Good Story, That One*. Toronto: HarperCollins, 1993.

Kirshenblatt-Gimblett, Barbara. *Destination Culture: Tourism, Museums, and Heritage*. Berkeley: University of California Press, 1998.

Kleege, Georgina. *Blind Rage: Letters to Helen Keller*. Washington, DC: Gallaudet University Press, 2006.

Koyama, Emi, and Lisa Weasel. "From Social Construction to Social Justice: Transforming How We Teach about Intersexuality." *Women's Studies Quarterly* 30.3–4 (2002): 169–78.

Krieger, Linda, ed. *Backlash against the ADA: Reinterpreting Disability Rights*. Ann Arbor: University of Michigan Press, 2003.

───. Introduction. Krieger, *Backlash Against the ADA* 1–25.

Laden, Vicki A., and Gregory Schwartz. "Pyschiatric Disabilities, the Americans with Disabilities Act, and the New Workplace Violence Account." Krieger, *Backlash Against the ADA* 1–25.

Lamm, Nomy. "Private Dancer: Evolution of a Freak." Brownworth and Raffo 152–61.

Landis, Carney, and M. Marjorie Bolles. *The Personality and Sexuality of the Physically Handicapped Woman*. New York: Paul B. Hoeber, 1942.

Langan, Celeste. "Mobility Disability." *Public Culture* 13.3 (2001): 459–84.

Laqueur, Thomas. *Solitary Sex: A Cultural History of Masturbation*. New York: Zone, 2003.

Lawson, Wendy. *Life Behind Glass: A Personal Account of Autism Spectrum Disorder*. Philadelphia: Jessica Kingsley, 2000.

———. *Sex, Sexuality, and the Autism Spectrum*. Philadelphia: Jessica Kingsley, 2005.

Lee, Peter A., et al. "Consensus Statement on Management of Intersex Disorders." *Pediatrics: Official Journal of the American Academy of Pediatrics* 118.2 (2006): 488–500.

Lévi-Strauss, Claude. *La Potière Jalouse*. Paris: Plon, 1985.

Lewis, Bradley. "A Mad Fight: Psychiatry and Disability Activism." Davis, *The Disability Studies Reader* 160–76.

Lingis, Alphonso. "The Physiology of Art." *The Prosthetic Impulse: From a Posthuman Present to a Biocultural Future*. Ed. Marquard Smith and Joanne Morra. Cambridge: MIT Press, 2006. 73–89.

Linton, Simi. *Claiming Disability: Knowledge and Identity*. New York: NYU Press, 1998.

———. *My Body Politic: A Memoir*. Ann Arbor: University of Michigan Press, 2006.

Lock, Margaret, and Nancy Scheper-Hughes. "A Critical-Interpretive Approach in Medical Anthropology: Rituals and Routines of Discipline and Dissent." *Medical Anthropology: Contemporary Theory and Method*. Ed. Thomas Johnson and Carolyn Sargent. New York: Praeger, 1990. 47–72.

Longmore, Paul K. "Conspicuous Contribution and American Cultural Dilemmas: Telethon Rituals of Cleansing and Renewal." Mitchell and Snyder, *The Body and Physical Difference* 134–58.

———. *Why I Burned My Book and Other Essays on Disability*. Philadelphia: Temple University Press, 2003.

Longmore, Paul K., and Lauri Umansky, eds. *The New Disability History: American Perspectives*. New York: NYU Press, 2000.

Lowenstein, L. F. "Fetishes and Their Associated Behavior." *Sexuality and Disability* 20.2 (2002): 135–47.

Luczak, Raymond, ed. *Eyes of Desire: A Deaf Gay and Lesbian Reader*. Boston: Alyson Books, 1993.

Luibhéid, Eithne. *Entry Denied: Controlling Sexuality at the Border*. Minneapolis: University of Minnesota Press, 2003.

Lurie, Samuel. "Loving You Loving Me: Tranny/Crip/Queer Love and Overcoming Shame in Relationship." Guter and Killacky 83–86.

Malet, Lucas. *The History of Sir Richard Calmady*. 1901. Ed. Talia Schaffer. Birmingham: University of Birmingham Press, 2003.

Marcus, George E., and Michael M. J. Fischer. *Anthropology as Cultural Critique: An Experimental Moment in the Human Sciences*. Chicago: University of Chicago Press, 1996.

Marcus, Jane. "Laughing at Leviticus: *Nightwood* as Woman's Circus Epic." *Silence and Power: A Reevaluation of Djuna Barnes*. Ed. Mary Lynn Broe. Carbondale: Southern Illinois University Press, 1991. 221–50.

Marcuse, Herbert. "The Affirmative Character of Culture." *Negations: Essays in Critical Theory*. Ed. Douglas Kellner. Boston: Beacon, 1968. 88–133.

Markovitz, Jonathan. *Legacies of Lynching: Racial Violence and Memory*. Minneapolis: University of Minnesota Press, 2004.

Martin, Emily. *Bipolar Expeditions: Mania and Depression in American Culture*. Princeton: Princeton University Press, 2007.

Masson, Jeffrey Massaieff. *Assault on Truth: Freud's Suppression of the Seduction Theory*. New York: HarperCollins, 1984

Matta, Christina. "Ambiguous Bodies and Deviant Sexualities: Hermaphrodites, Homosexuality, and Surgery in the United States, 1850–1904." *Perspectives in Biology and Medicine* 48.1 (2005): 74–83.

McGeer, Victoria. "Autistic Self-Awareness." *Philosophy, Psychiatry, and Psychology* 11.3 (2004): 235–51.

McRuer, Robert. "As Good As It Gets: Queer Theory and Critical Disability." GLQ: *A Journal of Lesbian and Gay Studies* 9.1–2 (2003): 79–105.

———. *Crip Theory: Cultural Signs of Queerness and Disability*. New York: NYU Press, 2006.

McRuer, Robert, and Abby L. Wilkerson, eds. *Desiring Disability: Queer Theory Meets Disability Studies*. Special issue of GLQ: *A Journal of Lesbian and Gay Studies* 9.1–2 (2003).

Meekosha, Helen, and Russell Shuttleworth. "What's So 'Critical' about Critical Disability Studies?" *Australian Journal of Human Rights* 15.1 (2009): 47–76.

Mellody, Pia. *Facing Love Addiction: Giving Yourself the Power to Change the Way You Love*. New York: HarperCollins, 1992.

Metzl, Jonathan. *Prozac on the Couch: Prescribing Gender in the Era of Wonder Drugs*. Durham: Duke University Press, 2003.

Miller, Heather Lee. "Sexologists Examine Lesbians and Prostitutes in the United States, 1840–1940." *National Women's Studies Association Journal* 12.3 (2000): 67–91.

Miracle. Directed by Gavin O'Connor. Walt Disney Video, 2004.

Mitchell, David T., and Sharon L. Snyder. *Narrative Prosthesis: Disability and the Dependencies of Discourse*. Ann Arbor: University of Michigan Press, 2000.

———, eds. *The Body and Physical Difference: Discourses of Disability*. Ann Arbor: University of Michigan Press, 1997.

Mollow, Anna. "Disability Studies and Identity Politics: A Critique of Recent Theory." *Michigan Quarterly Review* 43.2 (2004): 269–96.

———. "'When *Black* Women Start Going on Prozac': Race, Gender, and Mental Illness in Meri Nana-Ama Danquah's *Willow Weep for Me*." MELUS 31.3 (2006): 67–99.

Money, John. *Love and Love Sickness: The Science of Sex, Gender Difference, and Pair-Bonding*. Baltimore: Johns Hopkins University Press, 1980.

Montgomery, Cal. "Defining Autistic Lives." *Ragged Edge Online*. 30 June 2005. ⟨http://www.ragged-edge-mag.com/reviews/ckmontrubino605.html⟩.

Mulvey, Laura. "Visual Pleasure and Narrative Cinema." 1975. *Feminisms: An Anthology of Literary Theory and Criticism*. Ed. Robyn Warhol and Diane Price Herndl. New Brunswick: Rutgers University Press, 1997. 438–48.

Muñoz, José Esteban. *Cruising Utopia: The Then and There of Queer Futurity*. New York: NYU Press, 2009.

————. "Thinking Beyond Antirelationality and Antiutopianism in Queer Critique." *PMLA* 121.3 (May 2006): 825–26.

Munson, Peggy. "Liminal." Nestle, Howell, and Wilchins, *GenderQueer* 143–46.

Murderball. Directed by Dana Adam Shapiro and Henry-Alex Rubin. ThinkFilm Company, 2005.

Murray, Stephen O. "Self Size and Observable Sex." *Public Sex/Gay Space*. Ed. William L. Leap. New York: Columbia University Press, 1999. 155–86.

Nakken, Craig. *The Addictive Personality: Understanding Compulsion in Our Lives*. New York: Harper and Row, 1988.

Nattress, LeRoy William. "Amelotasis: Men Attracted to Women who are Amputees. A Descriptive Study." Diss. Walden University, 1996.

Nestle, Joan. "My Woman Poppa." Nestle, Howell, and Wilchins, *GenderQueer* 175–78.

Nestle, Joan, Clare Howell, and Riki Wilchins, eds. *GenderQueer: Voices from beyond the Sexual Binary*. Los Angeles: Alyson Books, 2002.

Noll, Steven. *Feeble-Minded in Our Midst: Institutions for the Mentally Retarded in the South, 1900–1940*. Chapel Hill: University of North Carolina Press, 1995.

Norton, Rictor, ed. "The Mollies Club, 1709–10." *Homosexuality in Eighteenth-Century England: A Sourcebook*. 1 December 1999. ⟨http://www.rictornorton.co.uk/eighteen/nedward.htm⟩.

Nuss, Marcel, ed. *Handicaps et Sexualité: Le Livre Blanc*. Paris: Éditions Dunod, 2008.

O'Brien, Mark. "Femininity." Bancroft Library, O'Brien Papers. University of California–Berkeley.

O'Brien, Mark, with Gillian Kendall. *How I Became a Human Being: A Disabled Man's Quest for Independence*. Madison: University of Wisconsin Press, 2003.

Oliver, Mike. *Politics of Disablement: A Sociological Approach*. Basingstoke, UK: Palgrave, 1990.

O'Toole, Corbett Joan. "The View from Below: Developing a Knowledge Base about an Unknown Population." *Sexuality and Disability* 18.3 (2000): 207–24.

"Ouch! Podcast: no. 5." *Ouch! . . . It's a Disability Thing*. August 2006. ⟨http://www.bbc.co.uk/ouch/podcast/podcast5.shtml⟩.

OverGround: A Site for the Disabled and their Admirers, the Devotees and the Wannabes. 2005. ⟨http://www.overground.be⟩.

Pallasmaa, Juhani. *The Eyes of the Skin: Architecture and the Senses*. Hoboken: John Wiley, 2007.

Park, Kristin. "Choosing Childlessness: Weber's Typology of Action and Motives of the Voluntary Childless. *Sociological Inquiry* 75 (2005): 372–402.

Parsons, Deborah. *Djuna Barnes*. Horndon, Devon: Northcote, 2003.

Patton, Cindy. *Sex and Germs*. Boston: South End Press, 1985.

Peele, Stanton, and Archie Brodsky. *Love and Addiction*. 1975. London: Sphere Books, 1977.

Pfister, Joel. "Glamorizing the Psychological: The Politics of the Performances of Modern Psychological Identities." *Inventing the Psychological: Toward a Cultural History of Emotional Life in America*. Ed. Joel Pfister and Nancy Schnog. New Haven: Yale University Press, 1997. 167–213.

Pintner, Rudolph, Jon Eisenson, and Mildred Stanton. *The Psychology of the Physically Handicapped*. New York: F. S. Crofts, 1941.

Plato. *The Collected Dialogues*. Ed. Edith Hamilton and Huntington Cairns. Princeton: Princeton University Press, 1973.

Plumb, Cheryl J. *Djuna Barnes's Nightwood: The Original Version and Related Drafts*. New York: Dalkey Archive Press, 1995.

Plummer, Kenneth. *Intimate Citizenship: Private Decisions and Public Dialogues*. Seattle: University of Washington Press, 2003.

Pound, Ezra. *The Cantos of Ezra Pound*. New York: New Directions, 1973.

Powell, Frederick. *The Politics of Civil Society: Neoliberalism or Social Left?* Bristol: University of Bristol Policy Press, 2007.

Prendergast, Catherine. "The Unexceptional Schizophrenic: A Post-Postmodern Introduction." Davis, *The Disability Studies Reader* 288–97.

Preves, Sharon. *Intersex and Identity: The Contested Self*. New Brunswick: Rutgers University Press, 2003.

Price, Margaret. "'Her Pronouns Wax and Wane': Psychosocial Disability, Autopathography, and Counter-Diagnosis." *Journal of Literary and Cultural Disability Studies* 3.1 (2009): 11–34.

Prince-Hughes, Dawn, ed. *Aquamarine Blue 5: Personal Stories of College Students with Autism*. New York: Swallow Press, 2002.

———. *Songs of the Gorilla Nation: My Journey Through Autism*. New York: Harmony, 2004.

Prosser, Jay. *Second Skins: The Body Narratives of Transsexuality*. New York: Columbia University Press, 1998.

Puar, Jasbir K. *Terrorist Assemblages: Homonationalism in Queer Times*. Durham: Duke University Press, 2007.

Quayson, Ato. *Aesthetic Nervousness: Disability and the Crisis of Representation*. New York: Columbia University Press, 2007.

Reilly, Philip R. *The Surgical Solution; A History of Involuntary Sterilization in the United States*. Baltimore: Johns Hopkins University Press, 1991.

Rembis, Michael A. "'I Ain't Been Reading While on Parole': Experts, Mental Tests, and Eugenic Commitment Law in Illinois, 1890–1940." *History of Psychology* 4.3 (2004): 225–47.

Rice, Anne P., ed. *Witnessing Lynching: American Writers Respond*. New Brunswick: Rutgers University Press, 2003.

Rodier, Alain. *Le Pari de L'Intégration, Témoignage Sur Dix Années de Désin*. Victoriaville: Imprimerie des Bois-Francs, 1988.

Roen, Katrina. "Transgender Theory and Embodiment: The Risk of Racial Marginalization." *Journal of Gender Studies* 10.3 (2001): 253–63.

Rosenbaum, Betty. "Neurotic Tendencies in Crippled Girls." *Journal of Abnormal and Social Psychology* 31 (1937): 423–29.

Rubin, Gayle. "Thinking Sex: Notes for a Radical Theory of the Politics of Sexuality." 1984.

The Lesbian and Gay Studies Reader. Ed. Henry Abelove, Michèle Aina Barale, and David Halperin. New York: Routledge, 1993. 3–44.

Ryan, Joanna, and Frank Thomas. *The Politics of Mental Retardation.* London: Penguin, 1980.

Ryan, Michael. *Secret Life: An Autobiography.* New York: Vintage, 1995.

Samuels, Ellen. "Critical Divides: Judith Butler's Body Theory and the Question of Disability." *National Women's Studies Association Journal* 14.3 (Fall 2002): 58–76.

———. "My Body, My Closet: Invisible Disability and the Limits of Coming-Out Discourse." GLQ: *A Journal of Lesbian and Gay Studies* 9.1–2 (2003): 233–55.

Savage, Dan. *Savage Love Column.* 7 December 2005. ⟨http://www.avclub.com/articles/ december-7-2005,1699/⟩.

Schaffer, Talia. Introduction to *The History of Sir Richard Calmady.* By Lucas Malet. Ed. Schaffer. Birmingham: University of Birmingham Press, 2003. ix–xxxii.

Scheper-Hughes, Nancy, and Margaret Lock. "The Mindful Body: A Prolegomenon to Future Work in Medical Anthropology." *Medical Anthropology Quarterly* 11 (1987): 6–41.

Scholinski, Daphne. *The Last Time I Wore a Dress.* New York: Riverhead, 1997.

Schwartz, Phil. "Identifying, Educating, and Empowering Allies." 2004. ⟨http://www .autistics.org/library/allies.html⟩.

Schweik, Susan M. *The Ugly Laws: Disability in Public.* New York: NYU Press, 2009.

Sedgwick, Eve Kosofsky. *Epistemology of the Closet.* Berkeley: University of California Press, 1992.

———. *Touching Feeling: Affect, Pedagogy, Performativity.* Durham: Duke University Press, 2003.

Sedgwick, Eve Kosofsky, and Adam Frank. "Shame in the Cybernetic Fold: Reading Silvan Tomkins." *Shame and Its Sisters: A Silvan Tomkins Reader.* Ed. Sedgwick and Frank. Durham: Duke University Press, 1995. 1–28.

Seligman, Linda, and Stephanie A. Hardenburg. "Assessment and Treatment of Paraphilias." *Journal of Counseling and Development* 78 (2000): 107–13.

Sex and Love Addicts Anonymous. *Sex and Love Addicts Anonymous Handbook.* Boston: The Augustine Fellowship, 1986.

———. "Frequently Asked Questions." ⟨http://www.slaafws.org/node/146⟩.

Shakespeare, Tom. *Disability Rights and Wrongs.* New York: Routledge, 2006.

———. "Disabled Sexuality: Toward Rights and Recognition." *Sexuality and Disability* 18.3 (2000): 159–66.

———. "The Sexual Politics of Disabled Masculinity." *Sexuality and Disability* 17.1 (1999): 53–64.

Shakespeare, Tom, Kath Gillespie-Sells, and Dominic Davies. *The Sexual Politics of Disability: Untold Desires.* New York: Cassell, 1996.

Shanker, Stuart. "Autism and the Dynamic Developmental Model of Emotions." *Philosophy, Psychiatry, and Psychology* 11.3 (2004): 219–33.

Shildrick, Margrit. *Dangerous Discourses of Disability, Subjectivity and Sexuality.* New York: Palgrave, 2009.

———. "Queering Performativity: Disability after Deleuze." *SCAN: Journal of Media Arts Culture* 1.3 (2004). ⟨http://scan.net.au/scan/journal/display.php?journal%20id=36⟩.

Shuttleworth, Russell P. "Disability and Sexuality: Toward a Constructionist Approach to Access and the Inclusion of Disabled People in the Sexual Rights Movement." *Sexuality Inequalities: Case Studies from the Field.* Ed. Niels Teunis and Gilbert Herdt. Berkeley: University of California Press, 2006. 174–207.

———. "The Pursuit of Sexual Intimacy for Men with Cerebral Palsy." Diss. University of California–San Francisco and Berkeley, 2000.

———. "The Search for Sexual Intimacy for Men with Cerebral Palsy." *Sexuality and Disability* 18.4 (2000): 263–82.

———. "Symbolic Contexts, Embodied Sensitivities, and the Lived Experience of Sexually Relevant, Interpersonal Encounters for a Man with Severe Cerebral Palsy." *Semiotics and Dis/Ability: Interrogating Categories of Difference.* Ed. Linda Rogers and Beth Swadener. Albany: SUNY, 2001. 75–95.

Shuttleworth, Russell P., and Vanessa Gore. "Critical Review of Sexuality and Disability Research since *The Sexual Politics of Disability.*" Unpublished Paper.

Shuttleworth, Russell P., and Linda Mona. "Introduction: Toward a Focus on Sexual Access in Disability and Sexuality Advocacy and Research." *Disability Studies Quarterly* 22.3 (2002): 2–9.

Sicko. Directed by Michael Moore. The Weinstein Company, 2007.

Siebers, Tobin. "Disability in Theory: From Social Constructionism to the New Realism of the Body." Davis, *The Disability Studies Reader* 173–83.

———. *Disability Theory.* Ann Arbor: University of Michigan Press, 2008.

Silvers, Anita. "Formal Justice." *Disability, Difference, Discrimination: Perspectives on Justice in Bioethics and Public Policy.* Lanham, MD: Rowman and Littlefield, 1998. 13–145.

Sins Invalid. "The Dancing Tree." Performance Advertisement. The Brava Theater. San Francisco, 28 April 2006.

Slater-Walker, Christopher, and Gisela Slater-Walker. *An Asperger Marriage.* Philadelphia: Jessica Kingsley, 2002.

Smith, Bonnie G., and Beth Hutchinson, eds. *Gendering Disability.* New Brunswick: Rutgers University Press, 2004.

Smith, Sidonie. "Taking It to a Limit One More Time: Autobiography and Autism." *Getting a Life: Everyday of Autobiography.* Ed. Sidonie Smith and Julia Watson. Minneapolis: University of Minnesota Press, 1996. 226–46.

Snyder, Sharon L., Brenda Jo Brueggemann, and Rosemarie Garland-Thomson, eds. *Disability Studies: Enabling the Humanities.* New York: MLA, 2002.

Solovay, Sondra. *Tipping the Scales of Justice: Fighting Weight-Based Discrimination.* Amherst, NY: Prometheus, 2000.

Somerville, Siobhan B. *Queering the Color Line: Race and the Invention of Homosexuality in American Culture.* Durham: Duke University Press, 2000.

Southern Comfort. Directed by Kate Davis. New Wave Films, 2001.

Spivak, Gayatri Chakravorty. *In Other Worlds: Essays in Cultural Politics.* New York: Routledge, 1988.

St. Clair, Janet. "The Courageous Undertow of Zora Neale Hurston's *Seraph on the Suwanee.*" *Modern Language Quarterly* 50.1 (1989): 38–57.

Stevens, Bethany. *Crip Confessions.* 〈http://www.cripconfessions.com〉.

Stiker, Henri-Jacques. "De Quelques Symbolisations de L'Infirmité." *Contraste* 4 (1996): 33–48.

———. "Franchir les interdits les plus fondamentaux." *Handicaps et Sexualité: Le Livre Blanc.* Ed. Marcel Nuss. Paris: Éditions Dunod, 2008. 234–40.

———. *Pour le Débat Démocratique: La Question du Handicap.* Paris: Éditions du CTNERHI, 2000.

Stone, Deborah A. *The Disabled State.* Philadelphia: Temple University Press, 1984.

Storrs, Bob. "Amputees, Inc.: Amputees Pitching Products—and Themselves—to Devotees of Disability." *New Mobility: Disability Culture and Lifestyle* (June 1997): 26–31.

———. "Caveat Dater: Devotees of Disability." *New Mobility: Disability Culture and Lifestyle* (January 1996): 50–53.

Straker, Gillian. "Race for Cover: Castrated Whiteness, Perverse Consequences." *Psychoanalytic Dialogues* 14.4 (2004): 405–22.

Strakosch, Francis M. *Factors in the Sex Life of Seven Hundred Psychopathic Women.* Utica, NY: State Hospital Press, 1934.

Suggs, Trudy. "Deaf Wanna-Bes." *The Tactile Mind: Quarterly of the Signing Community* (Spring 2003): 43–86.

Tate, Claudia. "Hitting 'A Straight Lick with a Crooked Stick': *Seraph on the Suwanee*, Zora Neale Hurston's Whiteface Novel." *The Psychoanalysis of Race.* Ed. Christopher Lane. New York: Columbia University Press, 1998. 380–94.

Taylor, Sunny. "The Right Not to Work: Power and Disability." *Monthly Review: An Independent Socialist Magazine* 55.10 (March 2005). 〈http://monthlyreview.org/2004/03/01/the-right-not-to-work-power-and-disability〉.

Tolnay, Stewart E., and E. M. Beck. *A Festival of Violence: An Analysis of Southern Lynchings, 1882–1930.* Urbana and Chicago: University of Illinois Press, 1992.

Trachtenberg, Peter. *The Casanova Complex: Compulsive Lovers and Their Women.* London: Eden Books, 1988.

Tremain, Shelley. "On the Subject of Impairment." *Disability/Postmodernity.* Ed. Mairian Corker and Tom Shakespeare. London: Continuum, 2002. 32–47.

Trent, James W., Jr. *Inventing the Feeble Mind: A History of Mental Retardation in the United States.* Berkeley: University of California Press, 1994.

Triea, Kiira. "Power, Orgasm and the Psychohormonal Research Unit." Dreger, *Intersex in the Age of Ethics* 141–44.

Turner, Victor. *From Ritual to Theatre. The Human Seriousness of Play.* New York: PAJ, 1982.

"Urge New Laws as Sole Hope of Curbing Morons." *Chicago Daily Tribune* 20 January 1937: 3.

Vahldieck, Andrew. "Uninhibited." *Nerve.* 19 November 1999. 〈http://www.nerve.com/PersonalEssays/Vahldieck/uninhibited/〉.

Vaid, Urvashi. *Virtual Equality: The Mainstreaming of Gay Liberation.* New York: Anchor, 1995.

Velasco, Sherry M. *Male Delivery: Reproduction, Effeminacy, and Pregnant Men in Early Modern Spain*. Nashville: Vanderbilt University Press, 2006.

Wade, Cheryl Marie. "It Ain't Exactly Sexy." *The Ragged Edge: The Disability Experience from the Pages of the First Fifteen Years of* The Disability Rag. Ed Barrett Shaw. Louisville: Advocado Press, 1994. 88–90.

Waldrep, Christopher, ed. *Lynching in America: A History in Documents*. New York: NYU Press, 2006.

Walker, Alice. Foreword. *Zora Neale Hurston: A Literary Biography*. By Robert Hemenway. Urbana: University of Illinois Press, 1977. xi–xviii.

Walloch, Greg. "Two Performance Pieces." Guter and Killacky 1–5.

Want. Directed by Loree Erickson. DVD. Femmegimp Productions, 2006.

Ward, Amy Paul. "Rape." *Encyclopedia of Disability*. Ed. Gary L. Albrecht. Thousand Oaks, CA: Sage, 2006. 1348–51.

Washington, Mary Helen. "A Woman Half in Shadow." *I Love Myself When I Am Laughing: A Zora Neale Hurston Reader*. Ed. Alice Walker. New York: Feminist Press, 1979. 7–25.

Waxman-Fiduccia, Barbara Faye. "Current Issues in Sexuality and the Disability Movement." *Sexuality and Disability* 18.3 (2000): 167–74.

———. "Sexual Imagery of Physically Disabled Women: Erotic? Perverse? Sexist?" *Sexuality and Disability* 17.3 (1999): 277–82.

Weeks, Jeffrey. "The Sexual Citizen." *Theory, Culture, and Society* 15.3–4 (1998): 35–52.

Weiss, Gail. *Body Images: Embodiment as Intercorporeality*. New York: Routledge, 1998.

———. *Refiguring the Ordinary*. Bloomington: Indiana University Press, 2008.

Wendell, Susan. *The Rejected Body: Feminist Philosophical Reflections on Disability*. New York: Routledge, 1996.

———. "Unhealthy Disabled: Treating Chronic Illnesses as Disabilities." *Hypatia* 16.4 (2001): 17–33.

Westgren, Ninni, and Richard Levi. "Sexuality after Injury: Interviews with Women after Traumatic Spinal Cord Injury." *Sexuality and Disability* 17.4 (1999): 309–19.

White, Patrick. "Sex Education; Or, How the Blind Became Heterosexual." *GLQ: A Journal of Lesbian and Gay Studies* 9.1–2 (2003): 133–47.

Wiegman, Robyn. *American Anatomies: Theorizing Race and Gender*. Durham: Duke University Press, 1995.

Wilchins, Riki. "It's Your Gender, Stupid!" Nestle, Howell, and Wilchins, *GenderQueer* 23–32.

Wilensky, Amy. "The Skin I'm In." *Nerve*. 24 October 2001. ⟨http://www.nerve.com/PersonalEssays/Wilensky/skin/⟩.

Wilkerson, Abby L. *Diagnosis: Difference: The Moral Authority of Medicine*. Ithaca: Cornell University Press, 1998.

———. "Disability, Sex Radicalism, and Political Agency." *National Women's Studies Association Journal* 14.3 (2002): 33–57.

———. "Refusing Diagnosis: Mother-Daughter Agency in Confronting Psychiatric Rhetoric." *Disability and Mothering*. Ed. Cynthia Lewiecki-Wilson and Jen Cellio. Toronto: Demeter, 2010.

Wilkerson, William. "Is There Something You Need to Tell Me? Coming Out and the Ambiguity of Experience." *Reclaiming Identity: Realist Theory and the Predicament of Postmodernism*. Ed. Paula M. L. Moya and Michael R. Hames-García. Berkeley: University of California Press, 2000. 251–78.

Williams, Donna. *Autism: An Inside-out Approach*. Philadelphia: Jessica Kingsley, 1996.

———. *Everyday Heaven: Journeys Beyond the Stereotypes of Autism*. Philadelphia: Jessica Kingsley, 2004.

———. *Nobody Nowhere: The Extraordinary Biography of an Autistic*. New York: Avon, 1992.

———. *Somebody Somewhere: Breaking Free from the World of Autism*. New York: Random House, 1994.

Williams, Raymond. *Marxism and Literature*. Oxford: Oxford University Press, 1977.

Wilson, Anne, and Peter Beresford. "Madness, Distress and Postmodernity: Putting the Record Straight." *Disability/Postmodernity*. Ed. Mairian Corker and Tom Shakespeare. London: Continuum, 2002. 143–58.

Witt, Howard. "$9 Million Award in Beating Case." *Chicago Tribune* 21 April 2007: 3.

———. "Old South Racism Lives in Texas Town." *Chicago Tribune* 5 June 2005: 1, 18.

Worth, Heather. "Bad-Assed Honeys with a Difference: South Auckland *Fa'afafine* Talk About Identity." *Intersections: Gender, History and Culture in the Asian Context* 6 (2001). ⟨http://wwwsshe.murdoch.edu.au/intersections/issue6/worth.html⟩.

Wright, Kai. "Policing Positives." *ColorLines*. 21 November 2005. ⟨http://www.blackaids.org/ShowArticle.aspx?articletype=NEWS&articleid=164&pagenumber=1⟩.

Wyss, Shannon. "'This Was My Hell': The Violence Experienced by Gender Non-Conforming Youth in U.S. High Schools." *Journal of Qualitative Studies in Education* 17.5 (2004): 709–22.

Young, Iris Marion. *Justice and the Politics of Difference*. Princeton: Princeton University Press, 1990.

Žižek, Slavoj. *The Sublime Object of Ideology*. New York: Verso, 1989.

CONTRIBUTORS

CHRIS BELL was a PhD candidate in English at Nottingham Trent University, where his research examined cultural responses to the AIDS crisis. Not long before he passed away, he had begun an appointment as a postdoctoral researcher in the Center on Human Policy, Law, and Disability Studies at Syracuse University. Chris was the Modern Language Association's delegate assembly representative for the Executive Committee of the Division on Disability Studies as well as a past president of the Society for Disability Studies. His essays have appeared in *The Body: Readings in English and American Literature and Culture*; *Blackberries and Redbones: Critical Articulations of Black Hair/Body Politics in Africana Communities*; and *The Disability Studies Reader*. He edited the collection *Blackness and Disability*, which was published by Lit Verlag in 2011.

MICHAEL DAVIDSON is distinguished professor of literature at the University of California, San Diego. He is the author of *The San Francisco Renaissance: Poetics and Community at Mid-Century*; *Ghostlier Demarcations: Modern Poetry and the Material Word*; and *Guys Like Us: Citing Masculinity in Cold War Poetics*. His most recent book is *Concerto for the Left Hand: Disability and the Defamiliar Body*. He is the editor of *The New Collected Poems of George Oppen*. He is the author of five books of poetry, the most recent of which is *The Arcades* (O Books, 1998). With Lyn Hejinian, Barrett Watten, and Ron Silliman, he is the coauthor of *Leningrad*. He has written extensively on disability issues, most recently "Hearing Things: The Scandal of Speech in Deaf Performance," in *Disability Studies: En-*

abling the Humanities; "Phantom Limbs: Film Noir and the Disabled Body," in GLQ; and "Universal Design: The Work of Disability in an Age of Globalization," in *The Disability Studies Reader*. His forthcoming book, *Outskirts of Form: Practicing Cultural Poetics*, will be published in 2011 by Wesleyan University Press.

LENNARD J. DAVIS is distinguished professor of arts and sciences in the English Department in the College of Arts and Sciences at the University of Illinois at Chicago. In addition, he is professor of disability and human development in the College of Applied Health Sciences of the University of Illinois at Chicago, as well as professor of medical education in the College of Medicine. He is also director of Project Biocultures (www.biocultures .org), a think tank devoted to issues around the intersection of culture, medicine, disability, biotechnology, and the biosphere. Davis is the author of *Enforcing Normalcy: Disability, Deafness, and the Body*, which won the Gustavus Myers Center for the Study of Human Rights' annual award in 1996 for the best scholarship on the subject of intolerance in North America, and *The Disability Studies Reader*, now in its third edition. His memoir, *My Sense of Silence*, was chosen as the Editor's Choice Book for the Chicago Tribune, selected for the National Book Award for 2000, and nominated for the Book Critics Circle Award for 2000. He has appeared on National Public Radio's *Fresh Air* to discuss the memoir, which describes his childhood in a Deaf family. Davis has also edited his parents' correspondence *Shall I Say a Kiss: The Courtship Letters of a Deaf Couple, 1936–38*. A collection of Davis's essays entitled *Bending Over Backwards: Disability, Dismodernism, and Other Difficult Positions* was published in 2002. He was awarded a Guggenheim Fellowship in 2002–2003 for his book *Obsession: A History*. His most recent book is *Go Ask Your Father*; it chronicles his search for his biological father using DNA testing. He is currently editing the Routledge Series Integrating Science and Culture. He has written numerous articles in the *Nation*, the *New York Times*, the *Chicago Tribune*, the *Chronicle of Higher Education*, and other print media. Davis has also been a commentator on National Public Radio's *All Things Considered* and appeared on *Morning Edition, This American Life, The Diane Rheim Show, Odyssey, The Leonard Lopate Show*, and other National Public Radio affiliates.

MICHEL DESJARDINS is associate professor of psychology at the University of Saskatchewan. He has done postdoctoral research in both the Université du Québec à Montréal and in the Department of Social Medicine at Harvard Medical School. He has a PhD in anthropology from the Université de Montréal. Desjardins is the author of *Le jardin d'ombres: La poétique et la politique de la rééducation sociale*. His current research explores the social control of sexuality, reproduction, and family life of people labeled intellectually disabled; the paradox of rehabilitation and inclusion strategies within democratic societies; the processes of self and lifeworld reconstruction of people with an acquired brain injury; and the challenges of creating partnerships within the networks of disability services in both Saskatchewan and Quebec.

LEZLIE FRYE is an activist, performance artist, poet, and scholar based in Brooklyn. She was a company member of GIMP, a New York–based interdisciplinary dance project engaging the disabled and abled body as spectacle, and a former member of Sins Invalid, a San Francisco–based artist's collective exploring disabled and abled sexuality. Frye aims to address intersecting forms of oppression and to locate critical resistance in the foxy bodies of cripples everywhere. In conjunction with movement work and performance, she leads workshops and teach-ins around the country. Frye is currently a doctoral student in the American Studies Program, Department of Social and Cultural Analysis, at New York University. Her work explores the regulatory dimensions of U.S. citizenship as shaped through the intersecting projects and processes of race and capacity as well as the counterlogics of crip and queer aesthetics and the alternative politics of life and death they engender.

RACHAEL GRONER is an associate professor of teaching and instruction in English and associate director of the First Year Writing Program at Temple University. She teaches writing and literature (modern and contemporary American literature, women's literature, and graphic novels). She is currently working on an article on emotion in the first-year writing classroom and is revising a book manuscript tentatively titled *Melancholy Subjects: Citizenship, Affect, and Publicity in Contemporary American Culture.*

KRISTEN HARMON is professor of English at Gallaudet University, as well as communications officer and integration of research and education team leader for the National Science Foundation–funded Science of Learning Center at Gallaudet University on Visual Language and Visual Learning (vl²). She received her PhD from the University of Missouri, Columbia, where she specialized in ethnographic studies and creative writing. She was a member of the Modern Language Association's Committee on Disability Issues in the Profession as well as the Executive Committee for the Disability Studies Division and Deaf Studies Discussion Group. Her work has appeared in books and journals in Deaf studies, disability studies, and women's studies. She has also edited a forthcoming collection of contemporary Deaf American creative writing.

MICHELLE JARMAN is assistant professor of disability studies at the University of Wyoming. Her broad research interests include twentieth-century U.S. literature, intersections between feminist theory and disability studies, and cultural representations of disability. Jarman's essays have appeared in journals such as *MELUS*, *Review of Disability Studies*, and several literary and disability studies anthologies.

ALISON KAFER is associate professor and chair of feminist studies at Southwestern University. Her work on gender, disability, and sexuality has appeared in *The Journal of Women's History*, *Gendering Disability*, *That's Revolting! Queer Strategies to Resisting Assimilation*, and *Feminist Interventions in Ethics and Politics.*

RIVA LEHRER is a Chicago-based artist whose work has been featured in both solo and group exhibitions over the past few decades. She is adjunct professor at the School of the Art Institute in Chicago. Her solo exhibition, *Circle Stories*, was featured at the Chicago Cultural Center in 2004 and was the subject of Sharon L. Snyder and David T. Mitchell's documentary *Self-Preservation: The Art of Riva Lehrer*. Riva Lehrer is now represented by Printworks Gallery of Chicago.

NICOLE MARKOTIĆ is associate professor of English at the University of Windsor, where she teaches English literature, creative writing, and disability studies. She is the author of two collections of poetry, *Connect the Dots* and *Minotaurs & Other Alphabets*; a novel about Alexander Graham Bell, *Yellow Pages*; a new novel about Mormonism, disability issues, and daughters and mothers, *Scrapbook of My Years as a Zealot*; and a recently co-edited anthology, *The Problem Body: Projecting Disability on Film*.

ROBERT MCRUER is professor of English and deputy chair of the Department of English at the George Washington University, where he teaches queer studies, disability studies, and critical theory. He is the author of *Crip Theory: Cultural Signs of Queerness and Disability*, which was awarded the Alan Bray Memorial Book Award in 2007 by the Modern Language Association; and *The Queer Renaissance: Contemporary American Literature and the Reinvention of Lesbian and Gay Identities*. With Abby L. Wilkerson, he co-edited "Desiring Disability: Queer Theory Meets Disability Studies," a special issue of *GLQ: A Journal of Lesbian and Gay Studies*. His essays have appeared in a range of locations, including *Genders*, *Journal of Literary and Cultural Disability Studies*, *Journal of Medical Humanities*, *PMLA*, and *Radical History Review*.

ANNA MOLLOW is currently on leave from her studies at the University of California, Berkeley, where she is a PhD candidate in English. Her essays on disability have appeared in *Michigan Quarterly Review*, *MELUS*, *The Disability Studies Reader*, and *WSQ*.

RACHEL O'CONNELL is a postdoctoral research fellow in the English Department at New York University. Her research interests include nineteenth- and early twentieth-century British literature, aestheticism, women's writing, psychoanalytic theory, queer studies, gender studies, and disability studies. Her dissertation, "'A House Not Made with Hands': Modes of Retreat in the Non-Fiction Prose of the British Aesthetic Movement, 1873–1914," explores the politics and ethics of retreat (manifested variously as social withdrawal, ascetic seclusion, and forms of reticence and restraint) in the late nineteenth century.

DAVID SERLIN is associate professor of communication and science studies and chair of the Department of Communication at the University of California, San Diego. He is the author of *Replaceable You: Engineering the Body in Postwar America* (University of Chicago Press, 2004), which was awarded the Alan Bray Memorial Book Award by the Modern Language Association in 2005; the co-editor of two anthologies, *Policing Public Sex: Queer Politics and the Future of AIDS Activism* (South End Press, 1996) and *Artificial Parts, Practical Lives: Modern Histories of Prosthetics* (NYU Press, 2002); and the editor of *Imagining Illness: Public Health and Visual Culture* (University of Minnesota Press, 2010). He is currently completing a book about the relationship between disability and modern architecture since the late nineteenth century.

RUSSELL SHUTTLEWORTH is a medical anthropologist and disability studies researcher. He is currently a lecturer in sexual health at the Faculty of Health Sciences, University of Sydney. His articles on sexuality and disability and disability studies have appeared in many journals, including *Sexuality and Disability*, *Medical Anthropology Quarterly*, *Australian Journal of Human Rights*, and *Disability Studies Quarterly*. His research interests include sexuality and disability, masculinities and disability, sexuality and ageing, impairment disability across cultures, disability ethnography, and the communication issues of people with speech impairments. Shuttleworth worked for many years as a personal assistant for disabled men, and he reflexively incorporates this experience into his research and writing.

TOBIN SIEBERS is V. L. Parrington Collegiate Professor and professor in the Department of English and in the School of Art & Design at the University of Michigan. He has published essays on disability in *American Literary History*, *Cultural Critique*, *Literature and Medicine*, *Michigan Quarterly Review*, PMLA, and contributed to the Modern Language Association's *Disability Studies: Enabling the Humanities*. His most recent books are *Disability Theory* and *Disability Aesthetics*.

ABBY L. WILKERSON is a philosopher whose work focuses on embodied agency and social movements, particularly in the contexts of food, disability, health, and sexuality. Her publications include *The Thin Contract: Social Justice and the Political Rhetoric of Obesity* (forthcoming); *Diagnosis: Difference: The Moral Authority of Medicine*; and articles in anthologies and journals. She co-edited the award-winning "Desiring Disability: Queer Theory Meets Disability Studies," a special issue of GLQ: *A Journal of Lesbian and Gay Studies*, with Robert McRuer. She teaches in the University Writing Program at the George Washington University in Washington, D.C.

INDEX

Note: page numbers in *italics* refer to illustrations; those followed by "n" indicate endnotes.

accommodation model vs. compensation
model, 31

Accord Alliance, 206n11, 207n19

activism. *See* disability rights movement
and activism

ADA (Americans with Disabilities Act),
6–7, 25, 33n3, 314

addiction. *See* sex addiction

"aesthetic nervousness," 138, 144n17

agency, 193–94, 201–2, 303. *See also*
subjectivities

Aguilera, Raymond, 360

Ahmed, Sara, 161–62

AIDS. *See* HIV and AIDS

Alabama v. Garrett, 7

Alcoholics Anonymous (AA), 318–19

Allen, James, 106n6

Amato, Toni, 202–3

American Sign Language (ASL), 367, 368

Americans with Disabilities Act (ADA),
6–7, 25, 33n3, 314

Amox, Christopher, 90

"Amputated Desire, Resistant Desire"
(Kafer), 334

Amputee Coalition of America (ACA),
353n19

amputee devoteeism: ableist unmarked
norm within, 344; access of amputees to networks and photographs
and, 342–44; background of, 331–36;
definition of, 336; desire and ambivalence and, 342–46, 349–50; different
disabilities and devoteeism within,
354n23; exceptionalism and, 335, 336,
341–42; fetishism and, 351n10; as Gordian knot, 344–46; lesbianism and,
351n10; logic of desire and disgust
and, 336–42; models of desire outside of exceptionalism and, 347–49;
power relations and, 344; sexual excess and, 286; "sightings" stories and
harassment and, 339–42; social ac-

ceptance of, 338, 340–41; websites for,
335, 350n4

amputee lived experience. *See* "crip"
experiences

Amputee Times, 339

Amundson, Ron, 33n4

Androgen Insensitivity Syndrome Support Group UK (AISSG), 206n11

animalistic, disability represented as, 102

anonymous sex, 21, 24, 222–23

antirelational thesis, 286, 306–7

anti-Semitism, 133–34

applied behavior analysis (ABA), 278–79

Aquamarine Blue 5 (Prince-Hughes), 274

ASCOTWORLD, 342–43, 351n9, 352n15

ASD. *See* autism and autism spectrum
disorder

asexuality. *See* desexualization and
asexuality

Asperger's syndrome. *See* autism and
autism spectrum disorder (ASD)

Aspies for Freedom, 279–80

Aston, Maxine, 270, 276

Asylum for Idiots and Feebleminded
Youths (Winfield, Kansas), 96–97

athletes. *See* nationalism, crip nationalism, and *Murderball* (film)

audism, 371n4

autism and autism spectrum disorder
(ASD): alternate modes of sexual
and sensual expression and, 273–
78; Bettelheim's theory of the cold
mother and, 278; definition of, 265–
66; description and demographics of,
266–67; emotion and, 276–78; glass
wall metaphor and, 277–78; homosexuality surveillance and disciplining compared to, 20–21; LGBTQ communities and community of, 278–80;
public attention to and false assumptions about, 263–64; queerness,
heteronormativity, and, 265, 270–73,

Bush, George H. W., 25

Bush, George W., 177–78, 187

Butler, Judith: on legitimacy and illegitimacy, 25–26, 31; on new gender politics, 186; on norms and embodiment, 355; Samuels on, 289; on sexuality as mode of being, 362; on transgender and intersex movements, 193; on unintelligibility, 367

Byrd, James, Jr., 90–91, 106n2

Callen, Michael, 3

Campbell, Fiona Kumari, 351n7

"Canto XII" (Pound), 130

capitalism, legitimacy and critiques of, 30–31

care facilities, long-term, 45

Carnegie, Dale, 155

the carnivalesque, in Barnes's *Nightwood*, 136–37, 140

Carriker, Gary Wayne, 211, 216

Cartesianism and autism, 269

Casanova, Giacomo, 322–23

Casanova Complex, 322–23

castration and Barnes's *Nightwood*, 141

castration and lynching. *See* race, disability, and sexual menace narratives

cerebral palsy and touch, 347–49

cerebral palsy study in San Francisco. *See* critical-interpretive ethnography of men with cerebral palsy

Cervantes, Miguel de, 126

Chase, Cheryl, 189–90, 204–5, 207n19

Chen, Mel, 13

Chesser, Eustace, 326

children: applied behavior analysis used on, 279; classroom experiences of, 240–42; clothing choices made for, 236, 240; Edelman on the Child figure, 20, 125–26, 287–93; fear of sexual crimes against, 100; gender identity disorder diagnosis for, harm

from, 194–95; intersex, 189–92; queer, in film *Murderball*, 179–81; sense of self in, 268; as site of dystopic futures in Barnes's *Nightwood*, 134–35; stares of, 234; "You're a freak" encounter in market and, 256–62. *See also* reproduction; sterilization of intellectually disabled people in Quebec

Chivers, Sally, 175, 181n3

choice: abortion and terminology of, 288; addiction and, 321; existentialism vs. sexual culture and, 40; medicalization and, 46; sex addiction and, 321; sexual negotiation and, 317; "voluntary" sterilization and, 80–83

A Christmas Carol (Dickens), 291–93, 295–96

citizenship, sexual: Duggan on gay marriage and reproductive rights and, 53n1; Katyal on sexual sovereignty and, 52n1; new gender and sex identity formations and, 51; places for sex and, 50–51; sexual culture and, 47; Weeks, Plummer, and Wilkerson on, 37–38

Claiming Disability (Linton), 3

Clare, Eli, 199, 205, 347–49

class, 44, 317–18

Clinton, Hillary, 123

clitoris size and clitorectomy, 190, 200–201

clothing, 236, 239–40

codependence, 315, 327

cognitive disability: autism and, 267; in Barnes's *Nightwood*, 140; invisibility and, 280n2; "morons" and, 93, 99–100, 106n4; nation-state and "alien other" and, 175; rethinking models of disability and, 329. *See also* race, disability, and sexual menace narratives; sterilization of intellectually disabled people in Quebec

Colker, Ruth, 6, 140–41

Collins, Patricia Hill, 208

Comay, Rebecca, 358

coming out, 10–12, 350n4, 369

compensation model vs. accommodation model, 31

compulsivity and sex addiction, 325–26

compulsory able-bodiedness, 125, 265, 362, 369, 372n7

compulsory heterosexuality, 161, 265

compulsory reproduction, 125–27, 289

Conrad, Joseph, 25

consciousness, disabled, 300

Corin, Alain, 151

court cases: *Alabama v. Garrett*, 7; Carriker and Cox cases in Georgia, 208–9, 211, 215–16; Johnson and Byrd cases in Texas, 89–91, 105; *Lawrence v. Texas*, 53n1; *Toyota Motor Manufacturing v. Williams*, 6–7

Coventry, Martha, 190

Cox, Gary, 208–9

Craig, Larry, 21

Crimp, Douglas, 3

"crip" as term, 142n1

Crip Confessions blog (Stevens), 2–3

"crip" experiences: with bisexuality and disability, 242–46; clothing and, 236, 239–40; family and childhood homes and, 236–40; home and, 231–32, 246; home of others and, 246–48; lovers and, 248–52; school and, 240–42; the street and sidewalks and, 232–36, 246, 252. *See also* critical-interpretive ethnography of men with cerebral palsy

crip nationalism. *See* nationalism, crip nationalism, and *Murderball* (film)

"cripsploitation," 121n4

crip theory: "crip" as term compared to "queer" and, 142n1; disability theory

vs., 310n4; pregnant man figure and crip identities and, 125–26

Crip Theory (McRuer), 310n4

critical-interpretive ethnography of men with cerebral palsy: cultural transformation and, 65–66; interpretations as collaborative fictions and, 56–59; resistance to asexual status and, 63–65; Scheper-Hughes and Lock's three-body heuristic schema and, 59–60; sexual oppression and normative expectations and, 60–63; theoretical context for, 54–56

Cullen, William, 318

cultural change, 2, 72, 215–16

cultural imperialism, 195, 198–99

culturalism, disability, 167–68, 179

cultural studies, 350n5

Davies, Dominic, 2, 44–45

Davis, Katherine Bement, 150–52

Davis, Lennard, 3, 90–91, 357

deaf wannabes, pretenders, and devotees: audism and, 371n4; cochlear implants and, 369; deaf erotica and, 358–60; Deaf-Wannabee Internet group and, 356–57; Deaf World and, 367–71, 371n2; definitions of, 355–56; dependence element and passive gender roles and, 365–66; *DSM-IV-TR* on "paraphilias" and 360–62; early fascinations and, 364–65; erotic effects of wearing a hearing aid and, 366; fetish theories and, 357–58; hearing aids as supplying deficiency, 363; norms and intelligibility, 355–56; self-deafening, 357, 367–70; semantic reversals and, 367; sexuality and, 362–63; stereotypic representation and displacement and, 364

"death drive," 125, 286–87, 290, 293–302, 305–8. *See also* the "disability drive"

de Certeau, Michel, 85n6

Delany, Samuel R., 30, 218–19, 222, 224

de Lauretis, Teresa, 312n19

de Man, Paul, 293

D'Emilio, John, 224

dependence in deaf fetishism, 365–66

depersonalization, medicalized, 45–46

desexualization and asexuality: autism and, 264; excessive sexuality and, 286, 308; gender, erasure of, 242; humanness and, 308; lived experience of, 58; pride and, 302; resistance to, 63–65, 180; seraphic idiot figure and, 69–71, 85n11; sex as disability and, 304; sexological assumptions and, 152; sexological conclusions about hyposexuality and, 152

desire: amputee devoteeism, desire/ disgust logic in, 336–42; amputee devoteeism as Gordian knot and, 342–47; amputees and touch, beyond devoteeism exceptionalism, 347–49; in Barnes's *Nightwood*, 131–34, 138; Berlant on, 160; defusing the adverse context of, 63–64; flexibility of, 47–48; Freud's case of Dr. Schreber and, 128; knowledge and, 224; in Malet's *The History of Sir Richard Calmady*, 109–11, 114–20; *Murderball* and, 168–71, 178; for offspring, converted into desire for infertility, 79–81; touch and, 146; transgender and, 202; warnings against, 239, 247–48

developmental disability. *See* cognitive disability; race, disability, and sexual menace narratives; sterilization of intellectually disabled people in Quebec

DeVito, Danny, 124

devoteeism. *See* amputee devoteeism; deaf wannabes, pretenders, and devotees

Diagnostic and Statistical Manual of Mental Disorders (DSM-IV-TR), 313, 360–62

Dickens, Charles, 291–93, 295–96

Dionysus, 126

disability, definitions of, 6–7, 25, 33n3

disability activism. *See* disability rights movement and activism

disability and sex as disabling or enabling each other, 23–24

disability culturalism, 167–68, 179

the "disability drive": Bersani's *Homos* and "Fr-oucault" and, 306–7; Bersani's "Is the Rectum the Grave?" and *The Freudian Body* and, 297–302, 309–10; disability as pitiable or disreputable and, 302–5; Edelman on Tiny Tim and *sinthomo*sexuality and, 291–96; Edelman's reproductive futurism and, 287–91; humanity, inhumanity, and O'Brien's *How I Became a Human Being* and, 305–10; rehabilitative futurism and, 287–91; sexual excess and lack connected to disability and, 285–86

disability rights movement and activism: de-institutionalization goal and, 307; disability theory and, 307; intersex and transgender movements and, 183–86; Longmore on, 5–6; rehab and, holistic approaches to, 352n13; sexual access and, 61

disability studies: access and neglect of, 61; disability theory vs., 287; identity emphasis and, 8; legitimacy in, 30–32; major texts and sex coverage and, 3; minoritizing claims in, 22; queering of, 32; sex addiction and, 319–20; sexiness elided in, 29; sexual access and neglect of, 55

disability theory: crip theory vs., 310n4; disability drive and, 27; disability

rights movement and, 307; disability
studies vs., 287; Edelman's *sinthomo-*
sexuality and, 292–94; identity politics and, 310n4; inhumanity and,
305–6; intersex and trans agency and,
184, 188; male pregnancy and, 141; rehabilitative futurism and, 288–89. *See
also* identity and identity politics
disgust and desire in amputee devoteeism, 336–42, 344
"disorders of sexual development" (DSD),
188–89
display. *See* gaze and display; visual
rhetorics
disreputable vs. pitiable disability, 302–5
Dixon, Melvin, 227
Dole, Bob, 206n7
Don Quixote (Cervantes), 126
Dougherty, Dawn, 203, 205
Dragonworks Devotee Community, 360
Dreger, Alice Domurat, 191, 206n10
DuCille, Ann, 107n9
Duggan, Lisa, 53n1, 93, 107n10, 172
Duncan, Kath, 362
Dyer, Isabel, 99

Ebert, Roger, 178–79
Eckert, Lena, 188
Edelman, Lee: antirelational thesis and,
286; on Baudrillard, 293–94; "Ever
After," 308; Huffer and de Lauretis
on, 312n19; on humanity and inhumanity, 305; identity politics and,
289–90; on politics, 291, 308; on queer
family values, 141; on queerness and
sexuality as destructive, 297, 302; on
reproductive futurism and the Child,
20, 125–26, 287–91; on Tiny Tim and
*sinthomo*sexuality, 291–96
EI (environmental illness), 10–13
Eliot, George, 293
Eliot, T. S., 123, 130, 135, 139

Ellis, Havelock, 135
Elman, R. Amy, 339
emotion: autism and, 264, 266, 276–78;
bodily, 57; nationalism and, 181n2
empathy with evaluative gaze, 58–59
Enforcing Normalcy (Davis), 3
environmental illness (EI), 10–13
Erickson, Loree, 353n21
erogenous zones and normative vs. flexible sexuality, 47–48
erotomania, 313–14
erotophobia, 191, 203–4. *See also* desexualization and asexuality
essentialism, genetic vs. surgical, 201
ethnocentrism, 195, 206n14
ethnography. *See* critical-interpretive
ethnography of men with cerebral
palsy
eugenics: degeneration theory and
Barnes's *Nightwood*, 134–37; futurity
and, 127–28; sex addiction and, 316;
tactile exhibits at conferences and,
146–47, *147*. *See also* race, disability,
and sexual menace narratives; sterilization of intellectually disabled
people in Quebec
European Charter for Persons with Autism, 264
"Ever After" (Edelman), 308
ex-gay movement, 279
existential-phenomenological obstruction, 68n9
exploitation: by amputee devotees, 339–
41; as face of oppression, 197–98;
super-exploitive work conditions,
170; transgender, intersex, and, 199
Extraordinary Bodies (Garland-
Thomson), 3, 109, 115
Eyes of Desire (Luczak), 2

fa'afafine Polynesians, 195–96
fascism, 140, 142, 143n5

fatness, 303

Faulkner, William, 97–99

"feebleminded." *See* race, disability, and sexual menace narratives; sterilization of intellectually disabled people in Quebec

Feminine Boy Project (UCLA), 279

"Femininity" (O'Brien), 308–9, 312n21

feminist theory, 8, 43

Ferguson, Roderick A., 13–14

Fernald, Walter, 96, 98

Festival Nights, 126, 143n3

fetishism: amputee devoteeism and, 351n10; Bhabha's "racial fetish," 364; definitions of devotee, pretender, and wannabe, 356; *DSM-IV-TR* on paraphilias, 360–62; foot fetishes, 358; in pornography, 244; theories of, 357–58. *See also* amputee devoteeism; deaf wannabes, pretenders, and devotees

Finger, Anne, 2, 38

Finkelstein, Naomi, 205

Fiol-Matta, Licia, 177

Flanagan, Bob, 17, 121n2

Fleche, Anne, 269

Foucault, Michel: Bersani's "Fr-oucault," 306–7; *Fearless Speech*, 227; on institutions and power, 84; on modernity, 143n12; on regimes of biopower, 329

Frank, Adam, 166

Franklin, Shirley, 209

Fraser, Nancy, 198

"freaks," freak shows, and freakishness: child yelling "You're a freak" in market, 256–62; Garland-Thomson on, 109–10; in Malet's *The History of Sir Richard Calmady*, 109, 111–12, 120; the pregnant male figure and, 124–25; sidewalk experiences of, 246

Freud, Sigmund: Bersani on theoretical collapse in, 300; Bersani's "Fr-oucault," 306–7; Dr. Schreber case

and, 128–29, 141–42; "it's all in your head" skepticism and, 304; theories of primary and secondary gain and, 297

The Freudian Body (Bersani), 299–302

Frith, Uta, 268–69

Fromm, Erich, 326

"Fr-oucault" (Bersani), 306–7

futurism, reproductive, 141, 287–91

futurity, biological. *See* pregnant men and biological futurity

Garland-Thomson, Rosemarie: on accommodation model vs. compensation model, 31; on affluence, 30; *Extraordinary Bodies*, 3, 109, 115; on "extraordinary body," 121n1; on *Murderball*, 166; on the normate, 186, 371n1; "The Politics of Staring," 109; on reframing disability, 357; on Sedgwick's universalizing/minoritizing distinction, 33n5; on visual rhetorics, 109–10, 113–15, 120–21, 121n2

gay and lesbian movement, 30, 32, 278–80. *See also* homosexuality

gaze and display: able-bodied, 109–10; autism and, 274; empathy with evaluative gaze, 58–59; lover's regard and, 236; scopophilia and, 362–63; staring, experience of, 232–34; the street and sidewalks and, 232–36, 246, 252. *See also* visual rhetorics

Geertz, Clifford, 68n6

gender: autism and, 267; binaries of, dominating sex roles, 142; deaf fetishism and passivity and, 365–66; family and, 239; national construction and, 177; new, flexible identity formations and, 51; pregnancy and discrimination of, 140–42; rigid gendering vs. erasure of, 242; sex addiction and, 317–18 gender assignment. *See* intersexuality; transgender and transsexuals

gender identity disorder diagnosis, 194–95

GenderQueer: Voices from Beyond the Sexual Binary (Nestle et al.), 202–3

Genet, Jean, 306, 311n18

Giami, Alain, 82–83

Gibbs, C. E., 150

Giddens, Anthony, 318, 321

Gilbert, Sandra, 129–30

Gillespie-Sells, Kath, 2

Gilroy, Paul, 144n19

glass wall metaphor, 277–78

globalization, 183–84

Goldsby, Jacqueline, 95–96, 107n7

Golem figure, 252

gorillas, autistic experience of, 277–78

Granata, Peter, 100

Grandin, Temple, 264, 269, 274–76

Grealy, Lucy, 37

Grillo, Trina, 289

Gubar, Susan, 129–30

Guggenheim, Peggy, 144n14

Guldin, Anne, 64, 68n7

Guter, Bob, 2

Haag, Pamela, 156–57

Hagglund, Bette, 336–37

Hahn, Harlan, 58

Halberstam, Judith: on Muñoz, 311n6; on "queer subjects," 26–27; on "queer time," 120; on race, 290; on transsexuals, 265, 280; on urban spaces and safety, 222

Hale, Grace Elizabeth, 94

Hall, Stuart, 141, 144n19

harassment by amputee devotees, 339–42

Harper, Phillip Brian, 176

Hastrup, Kirsten, 56–57

Hawking, Stephen, 306

Hawlbecker, Hale, 200–201

health care and borders, 176

health status of both HIV-negative and HIV-positive subjects, 226

hearing aids. *See* deaf wannabes, pretenders, and devotees

Heine, Heinrich, 322–23

Hermaphrodites Speak! (documentary), 200–201

heteronormativity: amputee devoteeism and, 344, 354n24; autism and, 265, 270–73, 275–76, 280; crisis in, 265, 280; definition of, 280n1; Edelman on, 287; *Murderball* and, 172, 179–80, 182n9; sex addiction and, 326; touch as communication and, 160–62

Hicks, James, 90

hiding: amputees and exposure vs., 343; clothing and, 236, 239–40

hierarchy of sexual values, in Rubin, 186, 205n6

"Higher Power" in twelve-step programs, 324, 328

Hinkley, John, Jr., 313

The History of Sir Richard Calmady (Malet): "extraordinary body" in, 108–11, 113, 119–20; mystery and passionate prurience in, 115–21; race, nation, and empire themes in, 121n5; visual rhetorics in, 111–15

HIV and AIDS: anonymous sex and, 222–23; Bersani on phobia of, 298–99; Carriker legal case and, 211, 216; Cox legal case and, 208–9, 215–16; disclosure and transmission laws regarding, 212–13, 215–16, 223, 226; health care and health status for, 223–24, 226; pickup narratives and, 209–17, 219–22, 224–26; responsibility and irresponsibility concerning, 223, 226–27; risk and, 216; sanitization of public urban spaces and, 217–19, 222, 224; sex addiction and, 326; in sexuality studies, 3

Hockenberry, John, 304
Hogsett, Scott, 170–71, 174
home: experiences of, 231–32, 246; of others, 246–48
homoeroticism, 95, 173–74
homophobia: ableism and, 294, 298; Bersani on, 301; Edelman on responses to, 288; minoritizing and universalizing claims and, 22; queerness vs. disability and, 294
Homos (Bersani), 306–7, 311n18
homosexuality: amputee devoteeism and, 351n9, 354n24; autism and, 267; in Barnes's *Nightwood*, 134–35; ex-gay movement and, 279; Festival Nights in eighteenth century and, 126, 143n3; Freud's diagnosis of Dr. Schreber and, 128–29; intersexual surgery to prevent, 192; lesbian murder case and, 93; minoritizing and universalizing conceptions of, 22; in Pound's "Canto XII," 130; race intertwined with, 92; reproductive futurism and legal equality and, 141–42; Shakespeare on gay male subcultures, 29–30; surveillance and disciplining of, compared to autism, 20–21
hospitals and privacy, 44, 50
How I Became a Human Being (O'Brien), 305–9
"How to Have Promiscuity in an Epidemic" (Crimp), 3
How to Have Sex in an Epidemic (Callen and Berkowitz), 3
Huffer, Lynne, 312n19
hugging, 145, 161
humanity and inhumanity, 41, 305–9
Hunt, William A., 148
Hurston, Zora Neale, 101–4
hypersexuality: eugenics and, 96; Mephistophelic idiot figure and,

69–71, 85n1, 85n4; sexual lack and, 286, 308
hyposexuality. *See* desexualization and asexuality

identity and identity politics: as amputee, 336; Edelman and Muñoz on, 289–90; feminist, 8; Ferguson's gestural conception and, 13–14; as historical, 7; invisible disabilities and, 10–12; legitimacy and, 30; model identity, codification of, 12; national identity and disability, 175; new formations of gender and sexed identity, 51; post-identity disability politics, 13–14; problematic of identity claims, 8–10; queer theory's anti-identitarian bent, 8; responses of inclusion, exclusion, or moving away from, 21–22; sex addiction and, 314; sexual culture concept and, 40, 47. *See also* minority model
Igoe, Chris, 173–74
immigrant labor, 168, 170
institutional reflexivity, 321
intellectual disability. *See* cognitive disability; race, disability, and sexual menace narratives; sterilization of intellectually disabled people in Quebec
interdependence, sexual-political, 203–5
Intersex Consensus Group, 188
Intersex Society of North America (ISNA), 204–5, 206n11
intersexuality: definition of, 205n1; erotics and, 200–202; medicalization and surgery and, 188–92; oppression of, 199–200; sexual-political interdependence and, 203–5; transgender compared to, 193
"invalid," 125–26, 129
invisible disabilities: identity politics and, 10–12; material effects of marginaliza-

tion and, 12; Montgomery's argument against distinction and, 280n2; need to differentiate cultural responses to visible disability vs., 303

"Is the Rectum the Grave?" (Bersani), 298–99, 304–5, 309–10

Jacobs, Barbara, 270, 272
Jacobs, Danny, 272, 276
James, Henry, 129
Jay, Peter A., 311n11
Johnson, Billy Ray, 89–90, 105
Johnson, Harriet McBryde, 288
Jong, Erica, 25
jouissance, 293
Joyce, James, 129–30
Junior (film), 123–24
Justice and the Politics of Difference (Young), 196–200

Kafer, Alison, 372n7
Katyal, Sonia K., 52n1
Kessler, Suzanne, 192
Killacky, John R., 2
killing as displacement of fucking, 296
King, John William, 106n2
King, Tom, 174
Kinsey, Alfred, 151, 157
Kinsey Institute, 157
Kipling, Rudyard, 109
Kirshenblatt-Gimblett, Barbara, 146–47
Krafft-Ebing, Richard von, 135
Krieger, Linda Hamilton, 6–7

labor. *See* work
Lacan, Jacques, 293–96
Landis, Carney, 147 48. See also *The Personality and Sexuality of Physically Handicapped Women* (Landis and Bolles)
Langan, Celeste, 170–71
Laplanche, Jean, 300

Law, Cardinal Bernard, 310n5
Lawrence, D. H., 127–28
Lawrence v. Texas, 53n1
Lawson, Wendy, 264, 269–70, 277
Lazarsfeld, Paul, 153
legal cases. *See* court cases
legitimacy, 25–32, 79
lesbian and gay movement, 30, 32, 278– 80. *See also* homosexuality
Lewis, Jerry, 288
liminality: disability as metaphor for, in Barnes's *Nightwood*, 138; Parsons on subculture and, 144n15; Polynesian gender-liminal *fa'afafine*, 195–96
limitation, disability as signifying, 42
Linton, Simi, 3, 314
Lippmann, Walter, 153
lived experience: academic neglect of, 54–55; collaborative interpretation of, 56–59. *See also* "crip" experiences; critical-interpretive ethnography of men with cerebral palsy
lived metaphors, 62–63
Lock, Margaret, 59–60
Longmore, Paul, 5–6, 14, 30–31, 307
Lovaas, O. Ivar, 278–79
love, 276, 326–27
love addiction, 326–27. *See also* sex addiction
Luczak, Raymond, 2
Luibhéid, Eithne, 53n1
Lurie, Samuel, 347–49
lynchings. *See* race, disability, and sexual menace narratives

Malcolm X Park (Washington, D.C.), 18–19, 21, 24
Malet, Lucas, 109. See also *The History of Sir Richard Calmady* (Malet)
Marcus, Jane, 136, 143n5, 143n6
marginalization: as face of oppression, 198; race, disability, and, 103, 290;

marginalization (*continued*)
    sexual, connected to social and political, 290, 349; transgender, intersex, and, 199; unseen illness and, 12
Markovitz, Jonathan, 93
Martin, Greg, 208–9
Martin, Saint, 296
masculinity: *Murderball* and, 166, 170–72; penis size and, 191; sex addiction and, 326
masochism and the disability drive, 302
masturbation: as disease, 330n7; in Landis and Bolles's study, *158*, 158–59; in Malet's *The History of Sir Richard Calmady*, 118–19; *Murderball* and, 174; sex addiction and, 315; sexological studies on, 150
Matta, Christina, 192
McAlmon, Robert, 144n15
McCartney, Paul, 351n11
McGeer, Victoria, 267
McRuer, Robert: on compulsory able-bodiedness, 372n7; *Crip Theory*, 310n4; on crisis in heteronormativity, 265, 280; on Garland-Thomson's visual rhetorics, 121n2
media: amputee devoteeism and, 350n5; lynchings and, 90–91; on "morons," 99–100; TV movie love stories, 242
medical model and medicalization: amputee devoteeism and, 333; applied behavior analysis (ABA) for autism or homosexuality, 278–79; deaf fetishism and, 356, 360–62, 367; depersonalizing effects of, 45–46; eugenic sterilization and castration and, 96–97; Feminine Boy Project (UCLA), 279; gender identity disorder diagnosis and, 194–95; globalization and medical tourism, 183–84; impairment as conferred and, 319; intersexual, 188–92; masturbation

as disease and, 330n7; normate sex and privatization and, 188; photography and, medical, 115; privacy and, eradication of, 43–46; professionalization and, 44–45; "queer subjects" pathologized and, 26–27; sex addiction and, 313–14, 320, 328; transgender and, 193–96; withholding of diagnosis and, 11
medical tourism, 183–84
Mellody, Pia, 324, 327
melodrama, 172
Melville, Herman, 34n9
mental disability. *See* cognitive disability; race, disability, and sexual menace narratives; sterilization of intellectually disabled people in Quebec
mental illness: in Barnes's *Nightwood*, 134, 137–38; as exceptional vs. unexceptional, 34n7
mentoring, 343
Mephistophelic idiot figure, 69–71, 85n1, 85n4
metaphors, lived, 62–63
Metzl, Jonathan, 152
migrant workers, 168, 170
Miller, Heather Lee, 150–51
Million Dollar Baby (film), 126
Mills, Heather, 351n11
minoritizing/universalizing impasse, 22–23, 33n5
minority model: in ADA, and judicial backlash, 6–7; ADA Amendments Act of 2008 and, 33n3; disability drive and, 302–5; rights movement and, 37; sexual minority status, 33n2, 46–51. *See also* sexual culture; sexual minority status
Miracle (film), 165
Missouri HIV disclosure law, 223–24
Mistral, Gabriela, 177
Mitchell, David T., 3

modernity, 143n12, 151

Money, John, 191, 321–22

Montgomery, Cal, 280n2

Moore, Michael, 170

Moreno, Angela, 200

"morons": passing and, 99, 106n4; as sexually aggressive, 93, 99–100

Moroun, Manuel "Matty," 175

Mulvey, Laura, 362–63

Muñoz, José Esteban, 289–90, 311n6

Munson, Peggy, 202–3

Murderball (film). *See* nationalism, crip nationalism, and *Murderball*

Murray, Stephen, 222–23

"My Body, My Closet" (Samuels), 11–12

Nakken, Craig, 327–28

Narrative Prosthesis (Mitchell and Snyder), 3

nationalism, crip nationalism, and *Murderball* (film): classic sports film rivalries and, 165–66; cross-border labor and bodies and, 168–70; disability culturalism and, 167–68; film awards and, 166; Iraq war veterans, rehab, Bush endorsement, and, 177–78; jock body stereotypes and hetero-masculinity and, 170–71; leading with head vs. body or heart and, 173–74; melodramas generating crip national-ism and, 172–74; mobility, health care, national identity, and, 174–77; "queer" subplot of nonathletic son and, 178–80; sex discussion and being "on top" and, 171–72, 180; as subversive or hegemonic, 166–67

Nattress, LeRoy, 338–40, 352n16, 353n19

neoliberalism: crip nationalism and, 167, 171–72, 177; disability studies and, 31; gay male subcultures and, 30; Gid-dens and, 321; marriage and, 32

Nestle, Joan, 202

neurosis, 153–54

New York City, 218–19, 222

Nicholson, Jack, 206n7

Nightwood (Barnes), 123, 127, 131–42

No Future (Edelman). *See* Edelman, Lee

the normate, 186, 371n1

normate sex: disability, intersex, and transgender convergences and, 183–86; globalization and, 183–84; intersex erotics and, 200–202; intersexuality medicalization and, 188–92; non-Western cultures and, 195–96; norms and boundaries of, 186–88; oppres-sion and, 196–200; sexual-political interdependence and, 203–5; trans erotics and, 202–3; transgender medi-calization and, 193–96

normative expectations, social: alterna-tive sexual ethics and, 64–65; Landis and Bolles's narratives and, 159–60; lived experience of, 61–63. *See also* heteronormativity

North by Northwest (film), 293, 296

nymphomania, 317–18

objectification: amputee devoteeism and, 343; exotic dancing and, 277; Garland-Thomson and, 110–11; sex addiction and, 316

O'Brien, Mark, 41, 46, 305–9, 312n21

obstruction, existential-phenomenological, 68n9

Olympics, 34n6

oppression: lived experience of sexual, 60–63; sexual-political interdepen-dence and, 203; of transgender and intersex, 199–200; Young's five faces of, 196–200

Organisation Intersex International (OII), 206n11

orgasms, various kinds of, 49

O'Toole, Corbett Joan, 42, 45–46, 49–51

powerlessness, 198–99, 299

"Prayer of the Golem" (Lehrer), 252–54

"pregnancy of the soul," 307

pregnant men and biological futurity: in Barnes's *Nightwood*, 127, 131–42; eugenics and, 127–28, 134–37; Freud's case of Dr. Schreber and, 128–29, 141–42; gender discrimination and legal equality and, 140–42; in James's *Portraits of a Lady*, 129; in Joyce's *Ulysses*, 129–30; in *Junior* (film), 123–24; in Pound's "Canto XII," 130; queer and crip identities and compulsory reproduction and, 125–27; transgender case of Thomas Beatie and, 124–25

Prendergast, Catherine, 34n7

pressure, autism and, 274–75

pretenders. *See* deaf wannabes, pretenders, and devotees

Preves, Sharon, 201

Price, Margaret, 34n7

pride: autism and, 276–77; desexualization and, 302; disabled sex and, 49–50; in Malet's *The History of Sir Richard Calmady* and, 116; sex addiction and, 314

Prince-Hughes, Dawn, 267, 269–72, 276–78

privacy: on demand, 50; medicalization and, 43–46; property rights and privacy laws, 44; right to places for sex and, 50–51

private/public split: access and, 5; in feminist theory, 43; lynching, eugenic castration, and, 95–96, 104–5; normate sex and privatization, 187

Prohibition, 318

property rights and privacy laws, 44

propriety and the proper, permissible, or punishable, 17–18, 21

Prosser, Jay, 193–94

prostheses, 116, 343, 363

psychiatric survivor movement, 320

Puar, Jasbir K., 181n5, 206n7

puberty, 78, 234, 236, 240

public/private split. *See* private/public split

quad rugby. *See* nationalism, crip nationalism, and *Murderball*

Quayson, Ato, 138, 144n17

Quebec. *See* sterilization of intellectually disabled people in Quebec

queercrip communities, 353n21

Queer Crips (Guter and Killacky), 2

queerness: autism and, 265, 270–73, 275–76, 280; bisexuality, disability, and, 244; death drive and, 297; Edelman on, 287–90, 292–96; Fiol-Matta on flexibility of, 177; *Murderball* and, 166, 171, 177, 179; pregnant man figure and, 125–26, 131; sex addiction and, 325–26; of touch, 146. *See also* "freaks," freak shows, and freakishness

queer theory and queer studies: anti-identitarian bent of, 8; antirelational theory in, 286; disability coverage and, 3; disability studies and, queering of, 32; Edelman on politics and, 291; elision of queerness of disability and, 29; Halberstam on "queer subjects" and, 26–27; heteronormativity crisis and, 265; on legitimacy and illegitimacy, 25–26, 32; performativity, autism, and, 275–76

race: and body in Barnes's *Nightwood*, 132–34; Edelman's *sinthomo*sexual and, 290; fetish, racial, 364; sex addiction and, 317–18

race, disability, and sexual menace narratives: connection between eugenic and lynching narratives, 92–97; in Faulkner's *The Sound and the Fury*,

Snyder, Sharon L., 3
Soares, Bobby, 178–80
Soares, Joe, 167, 172–73, 178–79
social model of disability: Barnes's *Night-wood* and, 137; critiques of, 33n4; impairment vs. disability in, 319; Samuels on visuality and, 12; sex addiction and, 314; Tiny Tim and, 292
Social Security Act, 25
Social Security Disability Insurance (SSDI), 31
Socrates, 126, 142n2, 307
sodomy laws, 216
soldiers, war-injured, 177–78
Somerville, Siobhan, 92
The Sound and the Fury (Faulkner), 97–99
space. *See* place and space
Spivak, Gayatri Chakravorty, 167–68
sports. *See* nationalism, crip nationalism, and *Murderball*
"star groups," 76, 85n4
staring. *See* gaze
Star Trek (TV), 264, 270
St. Clair, Janet, 107n9
sterilization of intellectually disabled people in Quebec: conversion of child into desire for infertility and, 80–81; "extraordinary sexuality" and, construction of, 73–74; future research, 82–83; morality and legitimacy and, parents' evaluation of, 78–79; as rite of passage into full sexuality, 81–82; sample population of, 71–72; scale model world or veiled margin and, 83–84; seraphic idiot and Mephistophelic idiot figures and, 69–71; triple-identity conception and, 75–76; triple-sexuality model and, 76–78. *See also* race, disability, and sexual menace narratives
Stevens, Bethany, 2–3

Stone, Dallas, 90
Stone, Deborah A., 31
Strakosch, Francis M., 150
subjectivities: animal nature and, 137; autism and, 268–69; Bersani on, 299–302; claiming of sexuality and, 64–65; crip nationalism and, 167; Davis study and, 150–52; Lacan's "sinthome" and, 294–95; Landis and Bolles's study and, 158–61; queer theory and, 26–27; touch and, 157–60; transformation of, 66. *See also* desexualization and asexuality
Supplemental Security Insurance (SSI), 31
Symbolic order, 294–95

Tagg, John, 115
Taking Woodstock (film), 206n7
Tate, Claudia, 107n9
telethon, logic of the, 288
temporality, 48–49, 120
Thompson, Raymond, 194
Tillman, Ben, 94
time. *See* temporality
Times Square, New York City, 218–19, 222, 224
Tiny Tim, 291–93, 295–96
"top" and "bottom," 169, 171–72
touch: autism and, 274, 277–78; cerebral palsy and, 347–49; as communication medium, 145–47, 157–62; hugging, 145, 161; queerness of, 146; sexological body studies and hierarchical structures, 151
tourism, medical, 183–84
"Toxic Animacies, Inanimate Affections" (Chen), 13
toxicity and post-identity politics, 13
Toyota Motor Manufacturing v. Williams, 6–7
Trachtenberg, Peter, 322–23
transgender and transsexuals: definition

ROBERT MCRUER is professor of English at the George Washington University.

ANNA MOLLOW is a PhD candidate in English at the University of California, Berkeley.

....

Chapter 1 was previously published as chapter 7, "A Sexual Culture for Disabled People," in *Disability Theory*, by Tobin Siebers (Ann Arbor: University of Michigan Press, 2008), 135–56.

An earlier version of chapter 5 was previously published as "Cripsploitation: Desire, the Gaze, and the Extraordinary Body in *The History of Sir Richard Calmady*," in *Nineteenth Century Gender Studies* 4.2 (Summer 2008).

An earlier version of chapter 6 was previously published as "Pregnant Men: Modernism, Disability, and Biofuturity in Djuna Barnes," in *Novel* 43.2 (2010), 207–26.

Chapter 15 was previously published as chapter 6, "Obsessive Sex and Love," in *Obsession: A History*, by Lennard J. Davis (Chicago: University of Chicago Press, 2008), 161–81.

A quote from the poem "Femininity" by Mark O'Brien in chapter 14 was provided by the Mark O'Brien papers, the Bancroft Library, University of California, Berkeley.

....

Library of Congress Cataloging-in-Publication Data
Sex and disability / Robert McRuer and Anna Mollow, eds.
p. cm.
Includes bibliographical references and index.
ISBN 978-0-8223-5140-5 (cloth : alk. paper)
ISBN 978-0-8223-5154-2 (pbk. : alk. paper)
1. People with disabilities—Sexual behavior. 2. Sociology of disability. 3. Sex (Psychology) 4. Disability studies. I. McRuer, Robert, 1966– II. Mollow, Anna, 1970–
HQ30.5.S46 2012
306.7087—dc23
2011027507